OZ CLARKE
Bordeaux

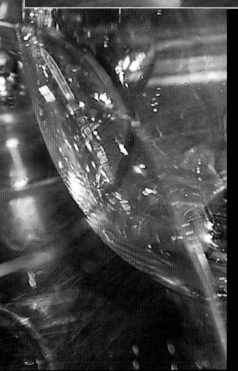

STERLING EPICURE
New York

STERLING EPICURE
New York

An Imprint of Sterling Publishing
387 Park Avenue South
New York, NY 10016

First Sterling Epicure edition 2012. Originally published in the United Kingdom in 2008 by Pavilion Books.

ISBN 978-1-4027-9706-4

Distributed in Canada by Sterling Publishing ᶜ/o Canadian Manda Group, 165 Dufferin Street, Toronto, Ontario, Canada M6K 3H6

For information about custom editions, special sales, and premium and corporate purchases, please contact Sterling Special Sales at 800-805-5489 or specialsales@sterlingpublishing.com.

Editor Fiona Holman
Regional Consultant James Lawther MW

Printed in China

10 9 8 7 6 5 4 3 2 1

www.sterlingpublishing.com

AUTHOR'S ACKNOWLEDGMENTS
I would like to say a particular word of thanks to those of you who have helped me with this book, especially James Lawther in Bordeaux and Bill Evans in London, but above all to my wonderful editor, Fiona Holman. And to all those of you who through the years have opened special bottles and shared them with me – properties, hosts and friends – thank you, too.

READER'S NOTE
Reviews of important châteaux are found in the A–Z section at the end of each regional chapter. Within these pages references to châteaux with their own entries are shown in SMALL CAPITALS. Following the château heading come the appellation and any classification, and the grape varieties planted in descending order of importance.

Page 1: The heart of Bordeaux's Right Bank, the town of St-Émilion. **Pages 2–3:** Remains of a wine tasting in Bordeaux, one of many I have done in researching this book. That's a sample of the famous *garage* wine, Le Dôme. **Page 3 inset:** The spanking new tasting room at Château Latour with views over its vines. **Page 4:** Shopping for wine at Badie, one of Bordeaux city's fabulous wine shops.

Contents

Ah, I love being back in Bordeaux's cellars. Michel Gracia, stonemason and garagiste winemaker looks on while I taste the magnificent Ausone 2005.

Vieux-Château-Certan 1952

What an emotional moment. This is the last bottle of my first ever wine tasting prize – Oxford versus Cambridge (early 1970s, I think). They all said Cambridge would win – as they had the previous dozen years. But they didn't. We did. Winning that Oxford-Cambridge match gave me the confidence to think that perhaps I could do something, be something, in this wine world. The Vieux-Château-Certan was the last wine in the tasting: tremendous weight, lushness almost for such a dry wine, brilliant, my prize (my choice), a whole case of it.

The bottle's open. Just let it be good. I pour and it's dark and viscous, brown gazing back wistfully to red. Old, smoky and slightly burnt on the nose; then, suddenly, from nowhere, sandalwood. Now I can drink it. It's old but it's alive, still strong and rich. Where am I now? Where I began. Bordeaux.

Why Bordeaux matters

What keeps drawing me back? What is it about Bordeaux I can't get out of my system? Why do the names of its wine villages and châteaux play like music in my ears? Why is it the flavour of these wines, more than those of Burgundy, Barolo, Rioja, Barossa or Rhône, that meander teasingly through my taste memory wherever I might be, whatever I might be drinking? Why has this place snuggled its way into my soul, and why can't I cast it out?

I feel like a man explaining to his friends why he clings to a clearly unsatisfactory love affair, telling them that through all the buffets and blows, disappointments and distress, he still loves this wayward, headstrong, selfish mistress, and the very thought of her brings a smile to his lips and warmth to his heart. I've been one of Bordeaux's biggest critics over the last decades. I've railed against the predatory pricing of many of their top wines. I've railed against the poor quality of many of their basic wines that should have been strangled at birth rather than sold to the unsuspecting consumers in exchange for their hard-earned cash. And because of the blithe disregard for so long of so much of the Bordeaux wine trade for the contentment of their customers, more evident in this region of France than any other over the last 20 years, I've led a crusade to persuade the ordinary wine-drinkers to give up trying to work out why they don't like the taste of affordable Bordeaux when old-time wine buffs say they should, and follow me, bedecked with flags, piping wild tunes and dancing crazy steps, to the friendly juicy joys of Australia, of Chile, Argentina and New Zealand, where words like 'ought' and 'should' and 'must' don't exist, but words like 'can' and 'will' and 'want' and 'like' are part of the language and the psyche.

So why am I here? Well, Bordeaux was my first love. We didn't drink wine at home, so I went up to university ignorant but willing, and joined the University Wine Society. My first tasting was of Bordeaux wines. And the final wine was Château Léoville-Barton 1962. I remember to this day every nuance of the wine's flavour. The penetrating blackcurrant flavour was so dry a dragon must have sucked all the sugar from it. A perfume of cedar wood and Havana cigar tobacco that matched the austerity of the fruit but took it to another level of such scented beauty you could begin to wonder whether there wasn't a little sweetness in the wine after all. At my first ever tasting, the gods of wine had thrown me a classic Bordeaux and said, 'Beat that if you can'. And I'd invited a lovely girl as my guest. I forgot to take her to dinner.

So Bordeaux was my first tasting. And my first great wine. And my next. And my next. And my next. Château Montrose '61, Beychevelle '61, Langoa-Barton '53, Haut-Bailly '55, Lynch-Bages '55, all begged or borrowed from richer and older wine lovers than me. Didn't I think of begging for a Burgundy or a Rhône, a Barolo or Barbaresco, a Rioja? Hardly ever. There were a few Burgundies. There may have been some Rhône or Rioja, but the one wine which always guaranteed me another surge of excitement, half from my belly but more from my brain, was Bordeaux. Top Bordeaux, mind you, the type my elders and betters brought out in order to educate me. In an academic environment it seemed natural that the most intellectual of red wines, the most ascetic, the least frivolous, should be the one I chose to dote on. Other wines I've had to learn as I went along – thank goodness they're still appearing from all corners of the globe to keep my enthusiasm for the endless variety of wine undimmed – but Bordeaux has been with me right from the start. And *that* is why I'm here.

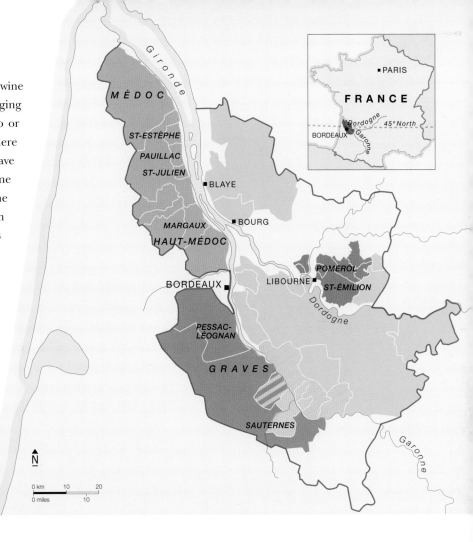

BORDEAUX'S WINE REGIONS

- The Médoc
- Graves & Pessac-Léognan
- The Right Bank
- The Côtes and Between the Rivers
- Sweet White Wines

MARGAUX = major AC wines

— Limit of Bordeaux AC

I was visiting Bordeaux even before I'd left university. Twice in the summer vacations, armed with a couple of letters of introduction, I jumped into my yellow Mini and headed south to Bordeaux. Once I even did the vintage – at Châteaux d'Angludet and Palmer (lunch was better at d'Angludet), at Monbrison, at Malescasse, and I squelched through the mud on the Île de Margaux, floating grim and half-submerged in the Gironde to pick Malbec grapes so sludgy and rotten even the autumn wasps had turned tail. And since then, I've kept going back. I've visited Bordeaux more than any other wine region on earth. And never once have I not been seduced and enthralled by its greatest wines. And rarely have I been anything but disappointed in its basic fare.

Bordeaux calls itself the greatest wine region in the world. Is it? What does that mean? Certainly it has proven over generations, centuries even, that it can produce supreme examples of dry red wines, of white wines and sweet white wines. In the New World you can find single producers who will try to do all three of these things on a single property and with a great variety of grapes – and sometimes they'll succeed, but in Bordeaux whole swathes of thousands of hectares are eminently suited to producing all these styles. So Bordeaux produces world class wine in significant quantities. A top property like Château Lafite-Rothschild has over 100ha (250 acres) under vine and may produce up to 20,000 cases of *grand vin* wine each year, usually of outstanding quality. That means a lot of people round the world can get their hands on it. Many top Burgundies are only produced in quantities of a few hundred cases, sometimes less. Very few people will ever taste them.

This is why the château system has been so influential in creating Bordeaux's reputation worldwide. A château wine, at its most basic, is a wine from a vineyard that has a house on it. This can be tumbledown and shabby or impressively grand. There are hundreds of impressively grand châteaux in Bordeaux, usually with a substantial vineyard attached and therefore a marketable quality of wine under one label. To further promote their supposed superiority in the world of wine, Bordeaux has led the way in classifying its wine. It's been doing this for over 300 years, but the most enduring and influential classification was in 1855. This classification of red and sweet wine, covering 84 different properties in the Médoc and Sauternes (with one Graves, Ch. Haut-Brion) has been followed by classifications of the Graves, St-Émilion and various levels of Cru Bourgeois properties in the Médoc – hundreds of properties boasting some kind of official classification with which to impress customers.

State of the art winemaking at Ch. Haut-Brion in 1924. Well, it might have been state of the art – Haut-Brion has usually been open to innovation – it was the first leading château to buy in stainless steel, for instance. But that was in 1961, not 1924, and a modern winemaker would blanche at so much rough handling being applied to these grapes. But the old-timers say 1924 Haut-Brion was pretty good stuff, so what do we know?

Yet until relatively recently few of these 'classified' wines impressed me. That title of 'world's greatest wine region' was supported on perilously few shoulders. With the rise of fine wine regions in the New World, especially in California and Australia, this title was under threat. I don't think it is now. And the reason is the Bordeaux that I grew up with has changed beyond recognition. The flavour of Bordeaux has changed. The way of growing and vinifying Bordeaux has changed. The way of criticizing and marketing Bordeaux has changed. It has become a harder, more price-conscious place, less friendly, more self-important, but it has become a hotbed of ideas, of experiment and of ambition. The old Bordeaux I knew was conservative and visit after visit I found hardly anything had changed. The new Bordeaux exhausts and excites me as I'm endlessly faced with new people, new places, new flavours. And, although this activity is happening at the upper end of Bordeaux, the qualities of fine wine are increasing every year. Prices of top wines have become absurd – until a château owner says, but the market is prepared to pay:

what's so absurd about that? Point taken. But below the fêted wines of the best Médoc classed growths or the top Pomerols and St-Émilions, more and more exciting wine is appearing. If I looked at my tasting notes for tricky vintages like 1991, '92, '93, '94 and then compared notes with the same châteaux – good but not superstars – for more recent difficult vintages like 2002, '06 and '07, I reckon there's a 500 per cent increase in the number of really attractive wines that I might actually want to buy. Technical ability, and also attitude, have made the difference. In the early 1990s you might still give in when nature got difficult. Now more and more proprietors want to make great wine every year, don't see why nature should stop them, and so bust a gut vintage after vintage to do so. Even so, at the bottom end, there is still a fair amount of poor, thin red wine, but the worst producers are gradually going out of business, and the merchants and co-operatives are becoming more pro-active in the vineyards. Global warming is greatly enhancing the chances of even the most dubious vineyards ripening their crop. And in a competitive world, bad wine doesn't sell. Decent, fairly-priced wine does.

This change has meant that one or two of my favourite flavours of Bordeaux are now not much respected and are difficult to find. The positively austere blackcurrant leaf and cigar tobacco Médoc styles that

Much of making wine is hustle and bustle, frenzy and action and chaos. But maturing wine is different. Here are Ch. Pichon-Longueville's beautifully modern but timeless cellars; silence reigns, as the new wine begins the slow, calm process of marrying all its component parts together during a period in new oak barrels that can last as long as two years. The flavours that will thrill you when you open a bottle of Pichon-Longueville in 10 years, 15 years time were melded here under the quiet gaze of these noble pillars.

It's scenes like this that make me think – oh, wouldn't it be lovely to own a château. The beautiful building on top of the hill, the vines tumbling down the slope beneath the house as I sit blithely on the verandah with a chilled glass of my house white in my hand, watching the sun go down on another perfect day. Well, I bet the people who do own this lovely château – Pardeillan in Blaye-Côtes de Bordeaux – would tell me life is much tougher than that, especially in the lesser known areas of Bordeaux, where you have to make just as much effort to create fine wine as the stars of St-Émilion or the Médoc, and yet you can only charge a fraction of the price. The gentle hills and valleys of places like Blaye, Bourg and Cadillac are some of the loveliest parts of Bordeaux, and some of the toughest to make a living as a wine producer.

needed a dozen years or more just to become drinkable – frankly because they weren't ripe enough in the first place – have largely disappeared, but have been replaced by a flood of wines which do promise blackcurrant and cedar wood, but wrap it up in a ripeness and texture and weight that is entirely modern, and surely better. I used to love the brick-tinged, gentle almost buttery soft styles of St-Émilion. One or two of the lesser vineyards still produce such wines to little acclaim, except from me, but instead, in Pomerol and St-Émilion we have a different selection of styles, scents, textures and flavours – richer, deeper, more powerful, but still based on the disarming succulence of ripe Merlot and Cabernet Franc grapes. And whereas most of the terroirs of the Left Bank Médoc have now been identified and are being exploited, on the Right Bank, from Blaye in the north right round to Castillon in the east, great vineyards are being sought out, bought up and made the best of. More people are beginning to ask the questions – how good could my wine be? Patches of wonderful land, owned by amateurs – doctors and dentists and blacksmiths' widows – are now finding their way into the hands of impassioned professionals, with thrilling results. The Right Bank is more alive because there was so much less snobbery and

For centuries the trade in Bordeaux wines was controlled by merchants called *négociants* based in the city of Bordeaux. These large companies would buy and market the wines from individual properties and also create their own bulk blends to be sold more anonymously. Brokers known as *courtiers* acted as go betweens, matching supplies of wine to the merchants' needs and keeping control of prices in a complex round of annual negotiations with the château owners.

It was these brokers who established the first classification of Bordeaux wines, in 1855, an enduring pecking order that has become another of Bordeaux's great marketing tools and is still the most famous wine classification in the world. This way of trading still operates today, and has given us the spectacle of the annual *en primeur* wine tastings in April, where international merchants and critics pit their palates against the excesses of the Bordeaux hype machine and the prices for the top wines of the vintage gradually emerge in the following months. However, the power of these *négociants* has waned since all the important châteaux now bottle their wine themselves and although they use *négociants* to distribute their wines, the actual promotion – the advertising, the tastings, the wine dinners and the like – is more and more in the hands of the châteaux or little groups of like-minded proprietors who share the burden between them.

THE LIE OF THE LAND

Take a look at the map over the page. Bordeaux has fairly simple natural boundaries which mean that each of the famous sub-regions – Médoc, Graves, the Right Bank and the vast sweep of Entre-Deux-Mers – is quite self-contained. Throughout the whole region, lesser patches of land are devoted to basic Bordeaux.

WHERE THE VINEYARDS ARE

This map shows the greatest fine wine area of the world in all its glory. Although there are vineyards on virtually every segment of the map, with the exception of the great pine forests of the Landes that spread their protective shield along the Bay of Biscay to the west, the best vineyards are those situated close to the rivers Garonne and Dordogne, and the Gironde estuary flowing out to sea.

Bordeaux has fairly simple natural boundaries which means that each sub-region is quite self-contained. The Médoc is the whole tongue of land stretching north of the city of Bordeaux on the Gironde's left bank. Hence the wines from here are colloquially known as Left Bank wines. Its chief section is the southern half, the Haut-Médoc, or Upper Médoc, where the Cabernet Sauvignon grape dominates. As well as being an overall appellation, the Haut-Médoc also contains the greatest wine villages in the region: Margaux, St-Julien, Pauillac and St-Estèphe. The appellation Médoc covers the less well-regarded but nevertheless important northern section.

AC WINE AREAS

1. Médoc
2. Haut-Médoc
3. St-Estèphe
4. Pauillac
5. St-Julien
6. Listrac-Médoc
7. Moulis
8. Margaux
9. Pessac-Léognan
10. Graves
11. Cérons
12. Barsac
13. Sauternes
14. Côtes de Bordeaux-St-Macaire
15. Bordeaux Haut-Benauge or Entre-Deux-Mers Haut-Benauge
16. Ste-Croix-du-Mont
17. Loupiac
18. Cadillac or Premières Côtes de Bordeaux
19. Entre-Deux-Mers
20. Cadillac-Côtes de Bordeaux
21. Graves de Vayres
22. Côtes de Bourg
23. Blaye and Blaye-Côtes de Bordeaux
24. Fronsac
25. Canon-Fronsac
26. Lalande-de-Pomerol
27. Pomerol
28. St-Émilion
29. St-Émilion satellites (Lussac, Montagne, Puisseguin, St-Georges)
30. Castillon-Côtes de Bordeaux
31. Francs-Côtes de Bordeaux
32. Ste-Foy-Bordeaux
33. Bordeaux and Bordeaux Supérieur

N

TOTAL DISTANCE NORTH TO SOUTH
144KM (89½ MILES)

━━━━ Bordeaux and Bordeaux Supérieur AC

───── Other AC boundaries

▓▓▓▓ VINEYARDS

St-Émilion and Pomerol make up the most important areas to the east of Bordeaux, and as a mark of its difference from the Médoc, this region and its style of red wines, based on the juicy Merlot grape, take the name Right Bank, from their location on the right bank of the river Dordogne. Fronsac, the other side of Libourne from Pomerol, and to the east of St-Émilion, Castillon and Francs are their close neighbours, while further north, the vineyards of Blaye and Bourg follow the right bank of the Gironde and were famous as long ago as the Roman times. Cadillac-Côtes de Bordeaux (previously the Premières Côtes de Bordeaux), completing the five 'Côtes' appellations, is on the limestone hills on the right bank of the Garonne. The sweet wine appellations of Sauternes and Barsac clustered along the little river Ciron lie within the Graves region south of the city. For basic Bordeaux the powerhouse of production is in the large wedge of land between the Garonne and Dordogne rivers called the Entre-Deux-Mers or 'Between the Two Seas'.

Some of Bordeaux's châteaux have a fairytale quality that's difficult to beat. Ch. Pichon-Longueville-Lalande not only makes one of the most sublime reds in Pauillac but has a château to match as the evening light catches the golden leaves of autumn in its park.

MONTENDRE

33

L'Isle

Dordogne

24
25

26
27
LIBOURNE
28

29

30

31

20

21

STE-FOY
LA-GRANDE

20

19

32

18

DURAS

15

Dropt

17

16

14

Garonne

LA RÉOLE

11

12

13

LANGON
10

33

MARMANDE

BAZAS

Bordeaux's grapes

Many of the greatest wines of France rely upon a single grape variety for their personality and quality. Hardly any Bordeaux wines do. There can be up to five different varieties used for red wines, and not many good properties use fewer than three. White wines come mainly from three different grapes and almost all properties use at least two of these. But this is a model of simplicity compared to the early 19th century when over 30 red and almost as many white varieties were planted in the region. Each variety not only contributes its own flavour but also complements the flavours of the others to produce the inimitable Bordeaux style.

Cabernet Sauvignon's worldwide fame was originally based on grapes grown on the gravel soils of Bordeaux's Médoc and Graves regions. This pebbly paradise is at Ch. Pichon-Longueville in Pauillac.

RED GRAPES
CABERNET SAUVIGNON

Cabernet Sauvignon is not the most widely planted grape in Bordeaux: that honour goes to Merlot. But Cabernet Sauvignon is the most famous red variety, contributing a powerful colour, a sinewy structure of tannin and a dark, brooding fruit that takes years to open out to blackcurrant, black cherry, cedar and cigars. It doesn't like damp clay and performs best on the deep, well-drained gravel in the Left Bank regions. It is the king of the Haut-Médoc's top vineyards, important in Pessac-Léognan, but much less important in the cooler clays of St-Émilion and Pomerol on the Right Bank.

It is still Bordeaux that is the worldwide benchmark for Cabernet Sauvignon – curiously, perhaps, since it is always blended with other grapes here. The great clarets of the Médoc, Cabernet's heartland, are,

The Bordeaux blend

Cabernet Sauvignon is almost never bottled as a varietal wine in Bordeaux: it usually lacks enough flesh in the middle palate, and needs its somewhat lean profile filled out with the fatter Merlot and the perfumed, fruity Cabernet Franc.

This is the classic blend for red Bordeaux and in general Cabernet Sauvignon will dominate the wines in the Haut-Médoc, while Merlot will make up the lion's share in bottles from the areas on the Right Bank of the Gironde and the Dordogne. Not that there's a standard recipe: each château has its own balance of vines, depending on its soil and climate, and its grand vin may or may not reflect that balance exactly.

With such a fickle climate, including the threats of severe frosts and then heavy rains at vintage time, much depends in Bordeaux on the climatic variations of each particular year. The reason that the region evolved its particular mix of grapes was that not every vine could be relied upon to ripen every year. Each variety buds, flowers and ripens at a different time, so having several varieties in your vineyards means that if, for example, a harvest downpour spoils your late-ripening Cabernet Sauvignon, at least you will have already picked your early-ripening Merlot.

Petit Verdot and Malbec may also be added, though Carmenère, which was once important in

Bordeaux, is now hardly grown here. Malbec is grown patchily – there's some in Fronsac and a bit in St-Émilion. Margaux's lighter soil often produces rather delicate wines, so a small percentage of Petit Verdot may be added for its dark colour and violet perfume.

Further back in history the classic Bordeaux blend included Syrah, which might have been grown either in Bordeaux or in the Rhône Valley. As for the future? Well, with global warming, who knows? Certainly the late-ripening Carmenère may make a comeback. And if Syrah used to flourish here, well, it might do so again – sometime in the future.

however, usually based on at least 60 per cent, and sometimes up to 85 per cent, Cabernet Sauvignon, and it's here that the grape reveals the full majesty of its scents and flavours, producing wines that may be firmly tannic when young, but which mellow with age – perhaps for 20 years or more in the greatest wines – into glorious complex harmonies. Even in its most favoured gravel vineyard sites, Cabernet Sauvignon will not produce sensational wines every year. Traditionally, each ten-year period produced three top-class years, three poor years and four that were somewhere in between. Nowadays, with global warming and improved vineyard management, even if the number of stunning years won't change much, there are very few poor years. Even in difficult vintages like 1999, 2002 and '07, well-run vineyards produced sufficiently ripe Cabernet to make good – definitely not poor – wine. But where there is less gravel – in the northern part of the Médoc, for example – Cabernet can be too austere for fun, never mind for fashion, and needs plenty of Merlot to fatten it up. In St-Émilion it is a minority grape, with Cabernet Franc and, especially, Merlot taking over; and in Pomerol's clay it is hardly found at all. Its style in the Médoc varies: from the mineral austerity of St-Estèphe through violet-scented intensity in Margaux, classic lead pencils and blackcurrant in Pauillac, cedar and cigarboxes in St-Julien, softer and rich in Moulis and somewhat sturdy in Listrac to fragrant and minerally again in Pessac-Léognan. Lesser regions like the southern Graves produce good but leafy blackcurrant flavours, without the intensity of the best sites.

MERLOT

Merlot is the king in St-Émilion and Pomerol, and indeed it is the most planted variety in Bordeaux. It thrives in fertile but cool, damp clay, it gives big yields yet ripens early and produces succulent juicy wines of high alcohol and good colour. In Pessac-Léognan and the Médoc it is planted on less well-drained soils and softens and fattens the austere beauty of Cabernet Sauvignon.

Merlot was always present in Bordeaux, but it was only recently that plantings began to outpace those of Cabernet Sauvignon. Until the 1980s, its fleshy, perfumed style never got as much acclaim as the elegant austerity of Cabernet Sauvignon. Then tastes began to change: suddenly the ability, nay the necessity, to age a wine for a decade or more before drinking it was far less

The grape escape

Two red varieties important in 19th-century Bordeaux but now little grown have found new spiritual homes thousands of miles away in South America.

When Merlot cuttings were exported to Chile, Carmenère hooked along for the ride. It was almost always labelled as Merlot until 1998 and it sometimes still is. When ripe and made with care, it has rich blackberry, plum and spice flavours, with an unexpected but delicious bunch of savoury characters – grilled meat, soy sauce, celery, coffee – thrown in. A true original.

Malbec once played the role of softening the blend that Merlot now takes in many a bottle of Bordeaux, and still features here and there. But in Argentina, Malbec is the most planted French varietal. It has adapted well there, and at an altitude of 1000m (2470ft) in Luján de Cuyo, Mendoza, it produces exceptional wines – deep, damsony and perfumed. Its success there has persuaded growers in Chile, Australia, California and South Africa to take a closer look.

Dr Alain Raynaud's face is a picture of concentration as he helps to sort Merlot grapes at his family estate, Ch. La Croix-de-Gay in Pomerol. Sorting the grapes, or triage, *is now an important task at top estates.*

Petit Verdot ripens very late and doesn't always give a decent crop. But as vineyard conditions warm up, its qualities of deep colour, rich black fruit and violet scent are much appreciated by top properties like Château Pichon-Longueville.

important than the ability to take a wine off the shop shelf and drink it that night. And that's when the Merlot began to prove its value and prices for the very best Merlot-based wines started to match, then outstrip, the Cabernet-based Classed Growths of the Médoc. Producers also realized that Merlot was better adapted than Cabernet to heavy, clay soils, and there is a lot more clay than fabled gravel in Bordeaux. Merlot now constitutes some 64 per cent of plantings overall – but that figure disguises its minority role in the better parts of the Médoc and Graves, where it makes up an average of 25 per cent of the blend, and its dominance in St-Émilion and Pomerol. In the Côtes appellations it is very often the majority grape. In St-Émilion it accounts for over 60 per cent of plantings; in Pomerol about 80 per cent.

Merlot will age, of course. Look at Ch. Pétrus: one of the most expensive reds in the world, made 100 per cent from Merlot, and which has no difficulty in lasting for 20–30 years. And Merlot-dominated Pomerols generally, now in huge demand worldwide, do not exactly fall apart in your glass – in fact, they age more gracefully than many Médocs. Merlot planted in the clay-limestone soils of St-Émilion also produces wines of great 'ageability'. But Merlot does make a rounder, softer wine, which is one reason why it has always been useful in softening the hard

Recommended red wines to try

CLASSIC CABERNET-BASED REDS
- Domaine de Chevalier, Pessac-Léognan
- Ch. Ferrière, Margaux
- Ch. Grand-Puy-Lacoste, Pauillac
- Ch. Kirwan, Margaux
- Ch. Lafon-Rochet, St-Estèphe
- Ch. Lagrange, St-Julien
- Ch. Léoville-Barton, St-Julien
- Ch. Léoville-Poyferré, St-Julien
- Ch. Malescot St-Exupéry, Margaux
- Ch. Montrose, St-Estèphe
- Ch. Pichon-Longueville, Pauillac
- Ch. Pontet-Canet, Pauillac
- Ch. Sociando-Mallet, Haut-Médoc

GOOD-VALUE CABERNET-BASED REDS
- Ch. d'Angludet, Margaux
- Ch. Batailley, Pauillac
- Ch. Cantemerle, Haut-Médoc
- Ch. Chasse-Spleen, Moulis
- Ch. Cos Labory, St-Estèphe
- Ch. Fourcas-Loubaney, Listrac
- Ch. La Gurgue, Margaux
- Ch. Maucaillou, Moulis
- Ch. Monbrison, Margaux
- Ch. Les Ormes-de-Pez, St-Estèphe

- Ch. Patache d'Aux, Médoc
- Ch. Peyrabon, Haut-Médoc
- Ch. Pibran, Pauillac
- Ch. Plagnac, Médoc
- Ch. Potensac, Médoc
- Ch. du Tertre, Margaux

CLASSIC MERLOT-BASED REDS
- Ch. d'Aiguilhe, Castillon-Côtes de Bordeaux
- Ch. Barde-Haut, St-Émilion
- Ch. Beauregard, Pomerol
- Ch. Canon-la-Gaffelière, St-Émilion
- Ch. Destieux, St-Émilion
- Ch. Faugères, St-Émilion
- Ch. Fleur de Boüard, Lalande-de-Pomerol
- Ch. Fonplégade, St-Émilion
- Clos Fourtet, St-Émilion
- Ch. Gazin, Pomerol
- Ch. Grand-Mayne, St-Émilion
- Ch. Latour-à-Pomerol, Pomerol
- Ch. Pavie-Macquin, St-Émilion
- Ch. La Tour Figeac, St-Émilion
- Ch. Vrai Croix de Gay, Pomerol

GOOD-VALUE MERLOT-BASED REDS
- Ch. Annereaux, Lalande-de-Pomerol
- Ch. Bauduc, Bordeaux

- Ch. Bellefont-Belcier, St-Émilion
- Dom. de Cambes, Bordeaux
- Ch. Cap-de-Faugères, Castillon-Côtes de Bordeaux
- Ch. Carteau-Côtes Daugay, St-Émilion
- Ch. La Dauphine, Fronsac
- Ch. Fontenil, Fronsac
- Ch. Girolate, Bordeaux
- Ch. Haut-Bertinerie, Blaye
- Ch. Haut-Carles, Fronsac
- Ch. Haut-Chaigneau, Lalande-de-Pomerol
- Ch. Haut-Colombier, Blaye-Côtes de Bordeaux
- Ch. Joanin-Bécot, Castillon-Côtes de Bordeaux
- Ch. Les Jonqueyres, Blaye-Côtes de Bordeaux
- Ch. Marsau, Francs-Côtes de Bordeaux
- Ch. La Prade, Francs-Côtes de Bordeaux
- Ch. Puygueraud, Francs-Côtes de Bordeaux
- Ch. Les Ricards, Blaye-Côtes de Bordeaux
- Ch. Roc de Cambes, Côtes de Bourg
- Ch. Segonzac, Francs-Côtes de Bordeaux
- Ch. Siaurac, Lalande-de-Pomerol
- Ch. des Tourtes, Blaye-Côtes de Bordeaux
- Ch. Veyry, Castillon-Côtes de Bordeaux
- Ch. de Viaud, Lalande-de-Pomerol
- Vieux Château Pelletan, St-Émilion

edges of Cabernet in the Bordeaux blend. Fruitcake and plum flavours are common. There can be spice, too: cinnamon and cloves and a touch of sandalwood, and truffles, tobacco, licorice and toasted nuts. Now and then there's blackcurrant and mint.

CABERNET FRANC

It's extraordinary how our judgement of grapes and wines is affected by what goes on in the Médoc region. Here, where the Cabernet Sauvignon is king, its cousin the Cabernet Franc isn't even in line for the throne: it's lucky to take up 20 per cent of a vineyard and its soft but leafy flavour does no more than calm the aggression of the Cabernet Sauvignon. Because of this we tend to think of Cabernet Franc as being an unimportant, uninteresting grape variety; yet cross the Gironde into St-Émilion and Pomerol and suddenly it takes a starring role. Many properties here have 30 per cent Cabernet Franc and two of the greatest châteaux, Ausone and Cheval Blanc, use 50 per cent and 60 per cent respectively, blending it with Merlot to add toughness, backbone and deep dark fruit to the luscious, fat Merlot fruit.

PETIT VERDOT

Petit Verdot may be planted only in small quantities in Bordeaux, but it is often highly valued for its colour, structure and lovely violet scent – and it is being regarded with increasing interest in California, Chile and Australia as a useful seasoning for Cabernet Sauvignon, and a wine in its own right. In Bordeaux it is particularly valued in Margaux, where the soils give lighter wines that need the extra tannin and colour that Petit Verdot provides.

I can't forget this view. Years ago I went to a magnificent – and very lively – party here at Ch. Haut-Langoiran perched above a bend in the Garonne river. When the revelry got too hot-blooded, I would sneak out and gaze at the cool glory of this grand river in full flow. The area is known as Cadillac-Côtes de Bordeaux. Once thought of as a producer of mildly sweet whites, these beautiful south and south-west-facing slopes are now producing some of Bordeaux's best affordable red wines.

WHITE GRAPES
SÉMILLON

Sémillon is the most important white variety in Bordeaux, most notably in Graves and Sauternes. On its own the wine can be a bit flat and waxy, but it gains marvellous complexity when fermented in oak barrels, blended with Sauvignon Blanc and aged for a year or two. The two varieties complement each other perfectly: the weighty, smooth, waxy Sémillon needing at least 20 per cent or so of Sauvignon Blanc to liven it up. Ch. Haut-Brion white is 60 per cent or so Sémillon, but many of the other great dry whites of Pessac-Léognan have a greater proportion of Sauvignon Blanc.

Sémillon's susceptibility to rot makes it invaluable in Sauternes. This is one of the few places in the world where rotten grapes are essential – providing that it is the right sort of rot, *Botrytis cinerea*, or noble rot, occurring only at a particular time, once the grapes are ripe. Then the fungus shrivels and dessicates the grapes, sucking the water out and leaving behind it a concentrated, thick, sugary goo, the base material for some of the most complex dessert wines in the world.

What an ugly bunch. But the uglier the better is the general idea in Sauternes where Sémillon grapes are attacked by a fungus called noble rot which massively concentrates the sweetness in the juice. Sémillon is Bordeaux's leading white grape for dry as well as for sweet wines and is almost always blended with Sauvignon Blanc.

SAUVIGNON BLANC

Sauvignon Blanc is a trendy grape, but by itself in Bordeaux it rarely achieves the exciting flavours it can attain in the Loire Valley, especially in Touraine and in Sancerre, or in New Zealand. Indeed, instead of tasting of fresh gooseberries it was in the past liable to taste of old socks. But the spread of clean stainless steel vats and cold fermentation in Bordeaux wineries worked wonders, and the average Bordeaux Blanc Sec, made entirely or mostly from Sauvignon Blanc, is at least likely to be clean and fresh these days, hopefully dry and fruity too. In the northern Graves area of Pessac-Léognan where white wines are made from a majority of Sauvignon Blanc, fermentation and aging in new oak barrels has provided a rich, citrus, tropical fruit and vanilla slant to the variety. Like Sémillon, Sauvignon Blanc is susceptible to noble rot, and the addition of between 10 and 40 per cent Sauvignon Blanc in the blend for Sauternes and Barsac freshens up the wine no end, adding crucial zip. There's also a pink-skinned version of Sauvignon, called Sauvignon Gris, which is less aromatic but can give a nice touch of extra body to a wine.

MUSCADELLE

First things first. Muscadelle is *not* a member of the Muscat family, despite the fact that it too can have a flowery, grapy aroma. But when picked early, Muscadelle has quite an aggressive grapefruity, citrus style that can add tang to a dry Bordeaux. Alternatively, fully ripe examples add a pleasant, honeyed aroma to otherwise neutral Entre-Deux-Mers and Bordeaux Blancs. Many Sauternes properties include small percentages of Muscadelle in their vineyards; they don't need it in the blend most years, but in poor vintages it can be useful for adding some honeyed weight and scent.

OTHER VARIETIES

Colombard adds a crucial green fruity zest to whites, especially in the Bourg and Blaye areas, but Bordeaux's other white grapes are an undistinguished bunch and few will mourn their passing as plantings dwindle to nothing. Ugni Blanc is Cognac's distilling grape and the same as the Trebbiano of Italy. Grown in Bordeaux it produces pretty thin stuff. Merlot Blanc, Mauzac and Ondenc have all almost disappeared.

Recommended dry whites to try

CLASSIC SAUVIGNON-DOMINATED DRY WHITES
- Ch. Talbot, Bordeaux, Caillou Blanc
- Ch. Couhins-Lurton, Pessac-Léognan
- Domaine de Chevalier, Pessac-Léognan
- Ch. La Louvière, Pessac-Léognan
- Ch. Malartic-Lagravière, Pessac-Léognan
- Ch. Pape-Clément, Pessac-Léognan
- Ch. Margaux, Bordeaux, Pavillon Blanc
- Ch. Smith-Haut-Lafitte, Pessac-Léognan

GOOD-VALUE SAUVIGNON-DOMINATED DRY WHITES
- Dourthe 'La Grande Cuvée', Bordeaux
- Dourthe No. 1, Bordeaux
- Ch. La Freynelle, Bordeaux
- Ch. Haut Bertinerie, Blaye
- Cave des Hauts de Gironde, Bordeaux, Quintet Sauvignon
- Ch. Reynon, Bordeaux

CLASSIC SÉMILLON-DOMINATED DRY WHITES
- Ch. Haut-Brion, Pessac-Léognan
- Ch. Laville-Haut-Brion, Pessac-Léognan

GOOD-VALUE SÉMILLON-DOMINATED DRY WHITES
- Ch. Bauduc, Bordeaux, Les Trois Hectares
- Ch. de Chantegrive, Graves, Cuvée Caroline
- Clos Floridène, Graves
- Domaine La Grave, Graves
- Ch. Thieuley, Bordeaux
- Ch. Tour de Mirambeau, Bordeaux, Cuvée Passion

The greenness of these grapes makes me want to sink my teeth into a bunch and get that marvellously nettley, gooseberryish, tangy taste in my mouth. Well, it's unlikely to have quite the tang of a New Zealand example, but in Bordeaux Sauvignon Blanc plays an important role in freshening up the Sémillon in both sweet and dry blends and is sometimes released as a 100 per cent varietal wine.

Bordeaux's wines

The easy thing would be to say Bordeaux's wine styles fall neatly into red, rosé, dry white and sweet white. But it isn't as simple as that, and it never was. Some parts of Bordeaux are perfectly suited to austere, long-lasting reds, some to soft fleshy reds drinkable almost as soon as they are made. Some parts can do either style: some proprietors are traditional and prefer to make conservative wines, some are obsessive, iconoclastic and convinced they can make bigger, denser reds than Bordeaux has ever seen. Dry whites and sweet whites are also made at varying levels of intensity and quality, and even pink wines come in lighter and darker styles. So this chapter lists ten different styles (including fizz), and, frankly, I could divide it up even further because modern Bordeaux is determined to throw off its stylistic straitjacket – and it needs to, as it faces up to the global challenges of the 21st century.

I pulled these two bottles off the shelf when I was out shopping in Bordeaux. The one on the left is a refreshing, earthy red I could have bought with the loose change in my pocket; the other is Pétrus, one of the most expensive and sought after wines in the world. They are poles apart, yet both quintessentially Bordeaux.

THE CLASSICS

Is a classic allowed to change? Can an old classic become a new classic and yet remain fundamentally the same? I think it can. Bordeaux's classic wines are based on grapes grown in special plots of land that are still there, being cultivated, hundreds, and, in some cases, thousands of years after they bore their first vines. But if the location of these plots of land – primarily in the Haut-Médoc, Pessac-Léognan, Sauternes, St-Émilion and Pomerol – hasn't changed, everything else has. The way the land is cultivated, the methods of pruning and trellising, the weather patterns and climate – all of these will bring in grapes flavoured quite differently to those which made the reputation of these plots of land. Once in the winery, the techniques used and the machinery involved is completely different to what went before. So are the attitudes and ambitions of the owners and winemakers involved. And yet, despite wines being riper, richer, denser, cleaner, perhaps more predictable than they were only a generation or so ago, I can still trace the character of great old Bordeaux in the brilliant examples of today. Pauillacs and St-Juliens were a little leaner and more angular in the old days but they sought the thrilling mature perfume of blackcurrant and cedar just as modern examples do. Very few of the dry white wines of Graves were up to much in the old days, but if you taste an old Domaine de Chevalier or Laville-Haut-Brion from the heartland of the Graves that is now called Pessac-Léognan, its fabulous savoury depth is still repeated today, just more regularly and by many more properties. Great Sauternes was always rich, but usually only two or three years in ten. Modern Sauternes has a purity of sweetness rarely achieved in the old days, and nowadays achieved three years in four. And St-Émilion and Pomerol? Well, they were famously soft and juicy in the days when such wines were rare around the world. Now the world makes many such wines, and perhaps here the difference between the old classics and the new classics is most marked.

NEW STYLES AND CULT WINES

The most remarkable changes to have occurred in recent times with Bordeaux involve whites being purer and cleaner and more refreshing than ever before, and reds – well, many of them – discovering a depth, a richness, a hedonistic core of glorious ripe power that would have been unimaginable only 20 years ago. The new wave whites can probably be made pretty well anywhere in Bordeaux – I had several recently from the haughty red wine redoubt of the Haut-Médoc. They simply require a careful attitude to vine cultivation and a positively clinical approach to vinification – either in temperature-controlled stainless steel vats or in clean, constantly monitored oak barrels. When properly done, these dry white styles – oaked or unoaked – are some of France's and, indeed, the world's most refreshing, appetizing and original wines. But no one is

The city of Bordeaux is full of elegant shops showcasing the region's wines. I spent hours here at Badie, rootling around for my favourite bottles.

Bordeaux styles worldwide

Every year, just a few times, I look up happily from tasting a new wine and say 'wow, Bordeaux'. I'm not talking about wines made here in Bordeaux, but wines made in every other corner of the earth; because of all the red wine styles the classic areas of France have produced, it is the reds of Bordeaux, and in particular the Cabernet Sauvignon-dominated reds of the great Médoc villages like Margaux, St-Julien and Pauillac that have obsessed and fascinated winemakers from Spain, Italy and away to Chile, Australia, New Zealand, South Africa and California.

In a way it's a vain quest – so few New World regions are as marginal, as damp, as cool, with

such infertile soil, as the Médoc – but that doesn't stop them trying, and just a few make a pretty good stab at it. With the rise of St-Émilion and Pomerol in Bordeaux's power structure and the global influence of consultant Michel Rolland, we may see rather more Pomerol Merlot lookalikes in coming years. They'll be easier to create. But a Pauillac or a St-Julien will always remain the ultimate prize.

The regions that can claim the closest similarity to Bordeaux conditions are Margaret River in Western Australia, possibly Coonawarra in South Australia, Gimblett Gravels and Waiheke Island in the North Island of New Zealand, and possibly one or two spots in Washington State and South Africa.

Chile may yet turn up somewhere but though it uses Bordeaux varieties, its wines are determinedly Chilean in style.

SOME OF MY FAVOURITE BORDEAUX LOOKALIKES
• Andrew Will Sorella, Washington State, USA
• Cullen Cabernet Sauvignon-Merlot, Margaret River, Australia
• Opus One, Napa Valley, California, USA
• Stonyridge Larose, Waiheke Island, New Zealand
• Vergelegen, Stellenbosch, South Africa
• Villa Maria Reserve Merlot-Cabernet, Gimblett Gravels, New Zealand

Cult wines are seen as a very recent phenomenon, but they've been around for quite a while in Bordeaux. It's just that the actual wines have changed. During the 1980s a group of châteaux just below the First Growths in price and quality began calling themselves the 'Super-Seconds', as they strove to match the First Growths. Ch. Pichon-Lalande (below left) was their leader. More recently, particularly during the 1990s and into the 21st century, the *garagistes* emerged on the Right Bank – tiny properties making dense, super-ripe wines sold for very high prices. Ch. Valandraud (above) was their leader.

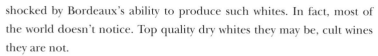

shocked by Bordeaux's ability to produce such whites. In fact, most of the world doesn't notice. Top quality dry whites they may be, cult wines they are not.

For cult wines we need to turn to reds. If one discounts the so-called First Growths – a tiny bunch of properties classified as such in 1855, and able to command a superior price ever since – there have been two major moves towards cult status. The first initially unofficial, but, during the 1980s and '90s, increasingly regarded as semi-official – was the Super-Second movement, almost entirely in the Haut-Médoc, where properties classified as Second Growths in 1855 (or, in the case of Ch. Palmer, Third Growths) set out to ape the styles of the First Growths by restricting yields, improving ripeness, employing new oak barrels for aging, and only selecting the best barrels to be released under the château label. For which they charged considerably more money than their peers although they never quite matched the prices of the First Growths.

The other move is more recent and based on the phenomenal success since the 1980s of the smaller properties in Pomerol and St-Émilion. Aided by a naturally succulent style that found particular favour with the American audience, wine producers began isolating smaller and smaller plots of land – by no means all of them in prime positions – and through obsessive attention to detail and self-confidence in pushing maximum ripeness in their grapes, they created a series of micro-crus, sometimes so small that the wines could be – and indeed sometimes were – made in the proprietor's garage: hence their name, *garage* wines. But it's not just the tiny-production properties that are now following this 'maximalist' route to almost overpowering intensity. Advised by several talented winemaking consultants, led by the jovial and indomitable Michel Rolland, properties big and small all over the Right Bank and even in the Entre-Deux-Mers, and, increasingly, the Médoc are coming up with expressions of richness and fruit intensity inconceivable 20 years ago. From being the perfect 'cult' wines for a new generation of Bordeaux lovers, such wines are now being seen as increasingly mainstream.

RED WINE STYLES
SAVOURY, EARTHY REDS

In a way, this style is the real heart of Bordeaux. Not every red Bordeaux can be magnificent, scented or sumptuous – the soils they grow in aren't always good enough, the investment of money and emotion can't always be present. But every red Bordeaux should be able to achieve the marvellously appetizing mix of earthy, tannic rasp and lean but savoury dry red fruit that makes your palate yearn for food and your mouth water in anticipation. This was always Bordeaux's basic job – to accompany meats and pâtés, sausages, stews and cheese, and today, there are more properties than ever wrapping an attractive cloak of fruit round the earthy core. In general, don't look for these wines in the most famous regions. Médoc is full of them, Haut-Médoc examples are often a little finer. Graves has some, and there are lots of wines of this style in the Côtes de Bourg, the St-Émilion satellites, and the wide swathe of land between the Garonne and the Dordogne.

MELLOW, FRUITY REDS

Winemaking styles and visions of flavour have changed more on the Right Bank than anywhere else in Bordeaux. At the heart of the Right Bank lie Pomerol and St-Émilion, and these regions are also the driving force for the remarkable new wave wines that are creating such a furore in Bordeaux with their super-ripeness and dramatic intensity. The classic Pomerol and St-Émilion wines are altogether mellower, less exuberant, but wonderfully soothing with a relative lack of tannin, gorgeous glyceriny roundness and positively sweet fruit veering between raspberry, plums and blackcurrant. You can also find this style wherever Merlot ripens fully but not excessively and isn't too influenced by the latest fashions for flavour intensification in the winery. There are good examples in Castillon- and Francs-Côtes de Bordeaux. Lalande-de-Pomerol and Fronsac may deliver, though they often have a mineral streak, and Blaye and Blaye-Côtes de Bordeaux have a delightful soothing quality that can be truly Right Bank.

INTENSE, CEDARY REDS

This style encapsulates everything that traditionalists have always loved about Bordeaux. The excitement of their

Meet the neighbours

Looking at the maps you might think the vineyards only stretch to the bright red boundary line. But in fact they keep going to the north and the east, though not to the west. North of Blaye is Charente – mostly involved in producing Cognac brandy, but able to make nice taut white wines. East of St-Émilion are Bergerac, which makes lots of Bordeaux-lookalike red and dry white, and Monbazillac, where they produce some excellent sweet white. East of Entre-Deux-Mers are Côtes de Duras and Côtes du Marmandais, which could be light versions of red and white Bordeaux in anything but name.

SOME OF MY FAVOURITES

- Bergerac: Ch. Tour des Gendres
- Monbazillac: Ch. Tirecul-la-Gravière
- Côtes de Duras: Mouthes le Bihan
- Côtes du Marmandais: Elian Da Ros

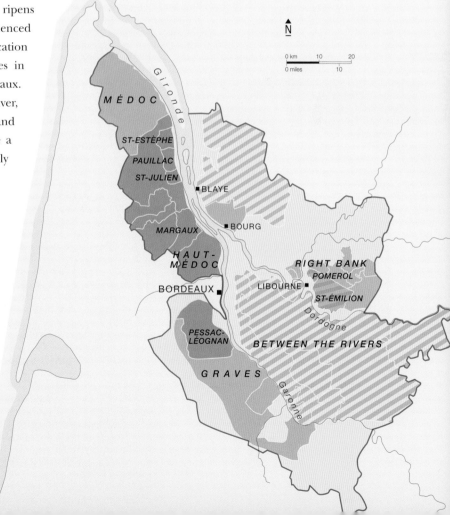

RED WINE STYLES

▨	Savoury, earthy reds
▨	Mellow, fruity reds
▨	Intense, cedary reds
▨	Hedonistic fruit-bombs
▨	Basic red Bordeaux

MARGAUX = major AC wines

—— Limit of Bordeaux AC

flavour is more intellectual than emotional, the aroma and personality take a long time to form in the bottle, and they are often greeted with reverence rather than delight. Well, this is an austere style of wine, but the austerity has an irresistible beauty of ripe but dry blackcurrant and the thoughtful scent of cigarboxes, cedar and lead pencils. And it does take a long time for such flavours to emerge – you'd be lucky to find them in a ten-year-old wine and you might have to wait a generation for these to develop. They're very much the domain of the Haut-Médoc, with muscular Pauillac and marginally more restrained St-Julien leading the way. The best from Margaux and St-Estèphe and a few Moulis and Haut-Médoc wines also get there, as do some Pessac-Léognans and an occasional top St-Émilion.

HEDONISTIC FRUIT-BOMBS

Less than a generation ago, this style of wine would not have been thought of as mainstream, but it is now. The majority of properties don't make it – indeed, many can't make it – but those that do are generally run by passionate, ultra-committed men and women, determined never to be labelled second best. And that's important, because the wines generally come from properties which originally had no great reputation. Most examples are from the Right Bank, in particular Pomerol and St-Émilion, but also lesser known regions like Castillon-Côtes de Bordeaux – even the

Two examples of the stonemason's art, both glorifying the new order in St-Émilion. Ch. Pavie is an ancient property propelled into the stratosphere of dense 'fruit-bomb' brilliance by the obsessive Gérard Perse, while Le Dôme, the archetypal 'garage' wine, is an entirely new creation by Englishman Jonathan Maltus.

Entre-Deux-Mers, where the wines can merely sport a simple Bordeaux or Bordeaux Supérieur appellation that tells you nothing of the ambition of the owner. Often, they will have simple labels and painfully heavy bottles, they will be high in alcohol, rich in super-ripe or over-ripe dark fruit flavours, yet soft in the mouth and awash with the richness of new oak. They don't always work, but when they do, they're magnificent.

CLAIRET AND ROSÉ

There's a boom in demand for pink wine just now, but surprisingly little of it seems to be coming from Bordeaux, which is a pity because Bordeaux makes very good rosé, and the darker version of rosé, called clairet, was the style that gave Bordeaux its famous nickname of claret centuries ago. Since there is a desire in much of the world for darker red wine, one of the easiest ways to achieve this is to drain some of the juice off the skins while the red wine is fermenting. This intensifies the flavour and colour of the remaining red wine, and gives you a decent amount of lighter pink wine from the juice you drained off. The best Bordeaux pinks come from Merlot, and the flavour is leafy, strawberryish, a bit pebbly, and very refreshing. Clairet is a little darker, a little fuller, but light enough to enjoy with or without food. Good rosés come from the following: Ch. Darzac, Bonnet, de Sours, Penin, Thieuley and Belle-Garde; and if you want to try some clairet, look out for Ch. des Chapelains, Darzac, Lestrille Capmartin or Les Vignerons de St-Martin.

WHITE WINE STYLES
FRESH, MOUTHWATERING WHITES

This is almost a forgotten world for Bordeaux. So many white wine vineyards have been ripped up or converted to red that you simply don't see very many examples of bright, breezy dry whites on the shelves anymore. This is such a pity, because Bordeaux is brilliantly suited to white wine, and in its cooler corners, whites consistently outperform reds. It wasn't always like this. A generation ago, the majority of simple

For this book I tasted hundreds of basic Bordeaux reds and whites and was heartened by the ambition and achievement of a new generation of enthusiastic producers.

Quick guide • Basic red Bordeaux

OVERVIEW
The word 'Bordeaux' resonates around the world thanks to the reputation of its finest wines and their influence on winemaking everywhere. But the day-to-day reality of this vast appellation concerns 8,200 growers trying to make a living from the 675 million bottles of wine Bordeaux pumps out each year. Merlot is the main grape variety on the heavy clay soils that make up the majority of the Bordeaux vineyard and is better suited to these simple wines than Cabernet Sauvignon. But the wines, many of them made in bulk by co-operatives and large companies, tend to be unambitious efforts. Nonetheless, red Bordeaux can be an enjoyable, unpretentious drink and a great antidote to overblown, oversweet New World styles.

TASTING NOTE
So what do you get when you open up an anonymous bottle of 'claret' or Bordeaux Rouge? Or one of the growing band of glossier brands? If you are lucky it will be dry, light and quaffable with fresh, grassy fruit and an appetizing, earthy edge – an ideal accompaniment to a homely supper of lamb chops. But, frequently, basic red Bordeaux is still pretty tannic and raw with the grassy fruit diminished to a thin, green lack of ripeness.

WHEN TO DRINK
These are everyday wines. They are ready to drink as soon as they hit the shops and will usually last a year or two at most.

WINES TO TRY
These wines are all Bordeaux or Bordeaux Supérieur AC and show the best face of truly affordable Bordeaux. Most, but by no means all, hail from the Entre-Deux-Mers region.

- Ch. L'Abbaye de Ste-Ferme
- Ch. Bauduc
- Ch. Beauregard-Ducourt
- Beaulieu Comtes des Tastes
- Ch. Bel Orme Martial
- Ch. de Bernadon
- Ch. Buisson-Redon
- Ch. de Camarsac
- Domaine de Cantemerle
- Calvet Réserve
- Ch. Carignan
- Castel Cuvée Réservée
- Ch. Chapelle Maracan
- Ch. Clos Renon
- Ch. La Croix de Queynac
- Dourthe No. 1
- d:vin
- Ch. Fantin
- Ch. Féret-Lambert
- Ch. Freyneau
- Ch. La Freynelle
- Ch. de Gadras
- Girolate
- Ch. Le Grand Verdus

- Ch. Grand Village (Jacques et Sylvie Guinaudeau)
- Ch. les Grangeaux
- Ch. Haut Cruzeau
- Ch. Haut Gay
- Ch. Haut Nadeau
- Ch. Haut Nivelle
- Ch. L'Insolent de Laville
- Ch. St. Jacques de Siran
- Ch. Lacombe Cadiot
- Ch. Larode-Bonvil
- Ch. Lauduc
- Ch. Le Luc-Regula
- Ch. de Lugagnac
- Ch. Malromé
- Ch. Marac
- Ch. Mirambeau Papin
- Ch. de Montval
- Ch. Mont Pérat
- Ch. Moutte Blanc
- Ch. de Parenchère
- Ch. Pascaud
- Ch. Passe Craby
- Ch. Penin Les Cailloux
- Ch. Pey la Tour
- Ch. Peyfaures
- Ch. Pierrail
- Premius
- Ch. La Providence
- Ch. Rebeyrolles
- Ch. Reynier

- Ch. Reynon
- Ch. St-Jacques de Siran
- Ch. Segonzac
- Sirius
- Ch. Tayet
- Ch. Tire Pé
- Ch. Thieuley
- Ch. Turcaud
- Ch. Vieux-Manoir
- Ch. Villepreux
- Ch. Virecourt
- Yvecourt

I saw these bottles of Sauternes glistening in the afternoon sun in a Bordeaux wine shop and couldn't resist getting a photo of them. There was an array of Classed Growths of different vintages, and of different depths and hues of gold, promising totally different flavours, some mature and deep, some bright and fresh, all linked by the thread of gold.

white Bordeaux was muddy and sulphurous, but the greatly reduced volumes mean that most of the stuff that remains is pretty good. Although Sauvignon and Sémillon are the main grapes, neither of these give the same intensity of flavour that they do in places like New Zealand or Australia. But for light, appley, attractively tangy bone dry whites that make brilliant aperitifs or all-purpose drinking, they're hard to beat. They'll usually carry a simple Bordeaux Blanc or Entre-Deux-Mers label, though some Graves are also made like this, and sometimes they'll even announce the grape variety on the label – something which happens all too rarely in Bordeaux. And they won't be expensive.

CREAMY, NUTTY WHITES

These are some of the great unsung heroes of world white wines. Yes, I mean it. Top Bordeaux dry whites are world class, often matching and sometimes outperforming any other dry whites in France. The key to the flavours lies in the method of fermenting the wine in barrel and leaving it in contact with its yeast lees while it matures before bottling. A lean, green dry white is thus transformed into a mouth-filling, sensuous wine, with a core of nectarine and apricot fruit wrapped in a brilliant cocoon of brazil nuts and brioche, *crème fraîche* and custard. And if there's lots of Sauvignon in the blend you'll still taste a delightful tang of blackcurrant leaves and coffee beans. As for aging, they transform after one or two years and will easily shine for ten. Pessac-Léognan is the heartland for these wines, but anywhere that grows decent white grapes can produce

---

Quick guide • Basic white Bordeaux

OVERVIEW
Quality improvements in white Bordeaux have run ahead of the reds and they are often excellent value for money. White grapes occupy just 11% of the vast swathes of the Bordeaux vineyard but if world fashions were to take a swing back towards white wines that figure could happily grow, as many of the sites currently producing red wine would be better suited to white grapes. Sémillon is the most planted variety, with Sauvignon Blanc on the increase. Wines made from 100% Sauvignon are often labelled Bordeaux Sauvignon and are a good bet. Whites produced between the rivers can also use the Entre-Deux-Mers appellation.

TASTING NOTE
You should get a crisp, fresh wine with some light, leafy fruit – dry, refreshing fare for a summer's day – and in better examples this will be fleshed out with flavours of fresh apple, peach and apricot. If the wine is oaked it should add cream and nectarines.

A proportion of Muscadelle grapes in the wine can add some spicy richness.

WHEN TO DRINK
Buy the most recent vintage available and pull the cork as soon as you've chilled the bottle down.

UNOAKED WINES TO TRY
• Ch. des Antonins
• Ch. de Beauregard Ducourt
• Ch. Bel Air Perponcher
• Ch. Belle-Garde
• Ch. Bonnet
• Cave des Hauts de Gironde, Quintet Sauvignon
• Ch. la Commanderie de Queyret
• Dourthe No. 1
• Ch. La Freynelle
• Ch. La Hargue
• Ch. Haut Pougnan
• Ch. Haut Rian
• Ch. Lugagnac, Tricepage
• Premius

• Ch. Rauzan Despagne
• Ch. Reynon
• Ch. Roquefort
• Ch. Thieuley
• Ch. Tour de Mirambeau
• Vieux Ch. Lamothe
• Yvecourt

OAKED WINES TO TRY
• Ch. Bauduc, Les Trois Hectares
• Calvet Réserve
• Ch. Ducla, Experience
• Ch. Haut Bertinerie
• Ch. Lestrille Capmartin
• Ch. de Reignac, Reignac
• Ch. Ste Marie Vieille Vignes
• Sirius
• Ch. Thieuley, Cuvée Francis Courselle
• Ch. Tour de Mirambeau, Cuvée Passion

this style, and you'll find examples from areas as disparate as the Haut-Médoc, Blaye-Côtes de Bordeaux and Entre-Deux-Mers, usually displaying a simple Bordeaux label.

MOUTHFULS OF LUSCIOUS GOLD

These are some of the glories of Bordeaux, yet sadly they are out of fashion as often as they are in. Really sweet wines have never been able to establish a wide enough market of consumers sufficently enthusiastic and well-heeled to buy them and drink them on a regular basis at the high prices they must inevitably command. A bottle of rich Sauternes was once seen as the perfect way to round off a meal but modern high-speed lifestyles, a greater awareness of the dangers of drink-driving, and a keener sense of health and waistline have all conspired to cause the large-scale abandonment of such indulgence. Yet this wine is such precious, irresistible stuff, it's glittering golden colour reflected in the indulgent, exotic flavours of pineapple and peach syrups aging to a brilliant brooding depth of barleysugar and marmalade, the sprinkling of spice dust and bedroom scents, and the creamy cocoon of new oak barrel aging. Sauternes is where most of it is made; Barsac, from the eponymous village at the northern end of the Sauternes appellation, is usually just a little lighter in style.

LIGHTER, LESS LUSH SWEET WHITES

These wines live in the shadow of Sauternes and Barsac, and few manage to reach a really satisfactory level of sweetness. Efforts to position them as an ideal aperitif wines didn't really work either, since they're too sweet to do their job very effectively. Yet there are some satisfyingly full, rather apple-flavoured, relatively syrupy wines made, particularly in the appellations of Loupiac and Ste-Croix-du-Mont, directly across the river Garonne from Barsac, and, to a lesser extent in Cadillac, Cérons and Graves Supérieures. Whether they

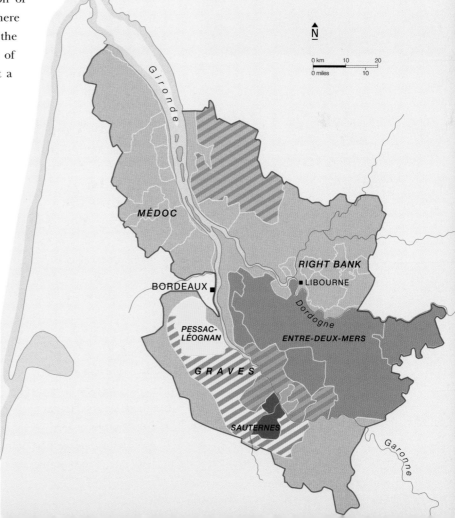

WHITE WINE STYLES

- Fresh, mouthwatering whites
- Creamy, nutty whites
- Mouthfuls of luscious gold
- Lighter, less lush sweet whites
- Basic white Bordeaux

SAUTERNES = major AC wines

— Limit of Bordeaux AC

These are the vines of Ch. du Mont ambling down to the church in Ste-Croix-du-Mont, and the Garonne river. The grapes produce sweet wines but without the misty conditions of Sauternes just across the river, they rely more on the autumn sunshine shrivelling the grapes and concentrating the sugary juice. However, these wines are difficult to sell and an increasing number of properties are making more of these well-sited slopes to produce very tasty everyday dry whites and reds.

are rich or not depends on luck with the vintage and the chance of a rare special piece of land in areas not greatly suited to true sweet wine production. But only rarely will you get the lush, waxy, glyceriny depth of a Sauternes or Barsac – these wines are generally thinner, lighter and less sweet even when they are good.

SPARKLING WINES

Bordeaux fizz doesn't have any great reputation, and I doubt it is much drunk at the region's smartest tables, but there's no reason a Crémant de Bordeaux can't be good. To make good sparkling wine you need a technologically sound winery, and a supply of not quite ripe grapes to provide the acidity that gives fizz its refreshing kick. Bordeaux can provide both, but without the commercial drive of a more demanding clientele, standards are unlikely to rise in the near future from their present levels of pleasant but unmemorable.

EVERYDAY BORDEAUX WINES

Every wine region needs some entry-level wines, some wines for everyday, rather than for high days and holidays. But when you're Bordeaux, arguably the most famous wine region in the world, when 99 per cent of all media coverage that you get is about reds that go from fairly pricy to probably the most expensive in the world, what does everyday mean? Should you make really basic quaffers? Indeed, with a cool maritime climate right next to the tempestuous Bay of Biscay, and a majority of your soils being decidedly damp and clay-clogged, can you make a basic quaffing red of any reasonably attractive style?

EVERYDAY REDS

Well, Bordeaux has been making a great deal of extremely basic red for donkey's years. Long ago, when there wasn't a lot of choice in the wine world, these rough, thin reds still sold, even if they gave little pleasure. But there are now dozens, no, hundreds of places in the world that can and do produce cheap wines more easily than Bordeaux, and it is these riper, softer, easier styles that are now the staple 'everyday' red of much of the wine-drinking race. Yet Bordeaux has clung to the belief it can still operate at the bottom of the market. But at what cost? Bulk prices for Bordeaux halved from 1500 euros to 730 for a 900-litre barrel during the decade to 2004, then really dived as millions of litres of unsold wine were scheduled for distillation after the massive harvest of 2004. Bulk Prices are currently around €6.50. Less than a euro a bottle? You can't survive on that in Bordeaux. Unable to gain an adequate price, much of the bottom end stuff simply doesn't cut the mustard in a modern world, and

3. VINES IN SIGHT OF THE GIRONDE

The Bordelais say that the vines like to see the water, but not get their feet wet. In geographical terms that means they want well-drained sites where they can still benefit from the mild climates that accompany large expanses of water. In the best parts of the Médoc, the choice vineyards in St-Estèphe, Pauillac, St-Julien and Margaux, they should be exquisitely happy: the broad Gironde estuary is just beyond the vineyard and its gravelly soils. This perfectly sited vineyard belongs to First Growth Ch. Latour.

4. POMEROL'S CLAY AND GRAVEL

Pomerol's rich, lush, velvety texture with firm inner core comes down to two factors: a plateau of deep clay and gravel soils planted to a great extent with an early ripening grape variety, Merlot. The clay is a heavy blue, water-retaining clay – you can see how waterlogged it is. I'm crouching down in a puddle in the vineyard of Ch. Pétrus after a shower of no more than ten minutes. This helps provide the deep colour, power and perfume typified by Pétrus. The gravel, by contrast, offers good drainage, favourable ripening conditions and gives the wines a firm tannic structure which allows them to mature and develop complexity.

5. AUTUMN MISTS IN SAUTERNES

This is Ch. d'Yquem on a misty autumn morning, just the sort of weather the Sauternes producers pray for in September and October. Misty nights and early mornings followed by long warm afternoons provide the humidity necessary to provoke the development of noble rot. This fungal spore, also known as *Botrytis cinerea*, perforates the skin of the Sémillon and Sauvignon Blanc grapes and reduces the water content, thereby increasing the concentration of sugar, acidity, flavour and viscosity. It's this special ingredient that produces the luxuriously sweet, unctuous, long-lived wines of Sauternes and Barsac. It's a pure fluke of nature and consequently irregular in its development in any given year and from one year to the next.

Increasingly in the last decade or so cover crops – mainly different grasses – have been planted in Bordeaux's more fertile vineyards, here in the Côtes de Bourg, to provide competition for the vine, reducing its vigour and limiting its yield.

Global warming

If you drink Bordeaux on a regular basis you will have noticed that alcohol levels have steadily crept above the traditional 12 per cent model to as much as 14 per cent. This can partly be put down to global warming and its effect on ripening. Scientists estimate that growing-season temperatures have risen 2°C (3.6° F) over the last 50 years and will continue to increase. You only need to cast your mind back to the super summers of 2003, '05 and '09 to believe their prognostications. There's evidence, too, that rainfall during the period January to September has dropped in recent years. But it's only part of the story. Grapes are also riper because of improvements in vineyard management. With lower yields, leaf-plucking to improve ventilation of the grapes and healthier vines, producers have been able to wait longer for the grapes to achieve phenolic ripeness, so sugar levels have risen as well. Rot and bouts of rain during the harvest are less of a threat with a well-ventilated vine – easy movement of fresh air is called nature's antibiotic.

FAMOUS TERROIRS

The classic division in red Bordeaux is between Left Bank wines – i.e. the Haut-Médoc and Pessac-Léognan – and those from the Right Bank, essentially St-Émilion and Pomerol. Each has its own style and its devotees, but why should there be such a change from one side of a river to the other? The climate is subtly different, yes, but the soils are markedly so, with gravel forming the best sites in the Médoc and limestone and clay being the key to the top wines of St-Émilion and Pomerol. The percentage of Cabernet Sauvignon, Cabernet Franc and Merlot vines planted varies with these factors and so the puzzle begins to fit together. There are infinite small variations and few vineyards in the world have been so throughly picked over in search of the secret of great wine. Nonetheless, the essence of Bordeaux's brilliance in both red wines and sweet whites is its five great terroirs.

CHOICES FOR THE GROWER

It may seem self-evident but you can't make good wine without clean, ripe grapes. The Bordelais have finally grasped this fact and improvements in the wines over the last decade or so have been as much to do with progress in the vineyards as anything else. Talk these days is less of the latest gizmo for the winery and more of pruning and trellising systems, clonal selection and supplementary hours spent leaf plucking and crop thinning. The trouble is most of this work is labour-intensive and costly, meaning only the more prosperous estates can afford the exhaustive vineyard toil necessary. At the other end of the scale machinery can help up to a point but when push comes to shove, and the budget is tight and the market flat, the work needed just isn't done, with a resulting drop in quality.

In 2009 the Bordeaux region had 117,500ha (290,225 acres) of AC vineyards under production. Just about everywhere that can be planted has been and planting rights are now more or less restricted to existing parcels that need replanting. The continuing crisis of overproduction has also led to a gradual reduction in vineyard land. The official view is that Bordeaux needs to lose the equivalent of what it's planted since 1994 – about 10,000ha (24,710 acres) – and it did lose 4000ha (9884 acres) between 2006 and 2009. I'd double that requirement to 20,000ha (49,420 acres) – and then probably add a bit more after I've tasted some of the sad, thin brews that still slouch about under the basic Bordeaux label. It's a thorny subject to which the producers are slowly waking up to. They must. Otherwise the market and the bankruptcy court will do it for them.

One other factor: Bordeaux is now undeniably a red wine region – 89 per cent of the vineyard compared to 50 per cent 30 years ago. But that's because red Bordeaux is fashionable and white Bordeaux isn't. A significant number of the cooler, damper vineyards should be making decent whites rather than feeble reds.

FROST, RAIN AND HAIL

For all the progress Bordeaux has made, two climatic incidences still feared by wine producers are spring frosts during the flowering and summer hail. In spite of all the grower can do, in the chillier parts of Bordeaux it is quite common for the crop to be reduced by spring frost. But apart from localized problems 1991 was the last time Bordeaux was hit by frost in a major way, and old-timers will relate the devastation of 1956. Overall the hazards of frost in the region on a year to year basis are less than say in Chablis so a comprehensive anti-frost system – such as oil-burning stoves (smudge pots), sprinkler systems or wind machines – doesn't warrant the cost in most vineyards. Basically, growers trust to luck, higher trellising systems, and the removal of cover crops between the vines at this period since they can retain humidity.

Rain, essential for the vine's growth, is a major danger when the crop matures. It can bring rot in its wake and ruin a vintage. If it falls during the harvest it can dilute all the juice that the grower has been

The top estates of Bordeaux have always used hand pickers rather than machines at harvest time. Hand pickers can discard all but the best grapes before they are taken off to the winery for a further, more rigorous selection process. These pickers are at Ch. Latour, and this lady is doing one more check for rotten or unripe fruit before it's taken off to a sorting table.

working so hard all year to concentrate. On steep vineyard slopes, too, it can cause erosion of valuable topsoil.

Hail is even more dramatic in its effects. Coming in summer or autumn it will slash through leaves and grapes alike, decimating the crop and even damaging the wood of the vine. Most regions in Bordeaux have suffered hail damage at some point in time. Hail did a fair amount of damage in 2009 in (parts of) Bourg, Blaye, Entre-Deux-Mers, St-Émilion and Castillon. Some growers shoot rockets into the clouds in the hope of making them drop their load elsewhere, but this is expensive and no one will swear it works. Hail insurance is expensive too: most growers trust to luck.

With the onset of cold weather in winter the tidying up begins: cutting away the dead wood and preparing the vineyard for next year's cycle. It's no fun – you can see the frost on the soil as this lady stoically carries a bundle of vine prunings, some of which will be used as firewood for grilling steaks.

Grafting

With a few exceptions, grape vines, like roses, are grafted on to rootstocks rather than allowed to grow on their own. Certainly, this is the case in Bordeaux. But it hasn't always been so: until a minute louse called *Phylloxera vastatrix* devastated the vineyards of Europe at the end of the 19th century, grafting was unknown. Now vines are grafted on to the rootstocks of native North American species, which are immune to phylloxera. Many different rootstocks are available, and the grower can select the right sort for the soil and the vine type.

LUTTE RAISONNÉE, ORGANIC AND BIODYNAMIC VITICULTURE

Most wine would not be made without the aid of chemical sprays and Bordeaux's humid climate and the related problem of disease mitigate against the region embracing organic viticulture on a large scale. However, growers have become more sympathetic to the problems of environment, the overuse of chemicals and the demands of the consumer and an increasing number now follow what is know as the system of *lutte raisonnée*. It means a more reasoned approach and in practice only spraying for disease when necessary (if at all) rather than systematically, and limiting the use of insecticides and weedkillers by employing more environmentally friendly alternatives such as ploughing and the introduction of natural predators. With a climate that poses an endless threat of rot, organic viticulture has a fairly weak hold and those that want to go further down this line are more likely to embrace biodynamics. Anecdotal evidence points to the total absence of some diseases and infections in biodynamic plots, as well as crisper, more characterful flavours in the fruit. A few top estates like Ch. Smith-Haut-Lafitte in Pessac-Léognan have experimented with the idea on small parcels of vines but so far only St-Émilion properties Ch. Fonroque and Ch. La Tour-Figeac and Ch. Pontet-Canet in Pauillac have gone the whole way. Top winemaking consultant Stéphane Derenoncourt also practices biodynamics at his tiny Domaine de l'A property in Castillon-Côtes de Bordeaux.

A year in the vineyard

Work in the vineyard follows a basic pattern the world over, but in Bordeaux as in most European wine regions the timing of each operation is dependent on both the prevailing climate and weather conditions of the year. It's easy for the wine drinkr to forget that vine-growing isn't all the excitement of the harvest. Mundane tasks like ploughing and pruning have to be done in the cold winter months, too.

WINTER

The yearly cycle of the vine begins after the harvest. The leaves fall, the sap descends and the vine becomes dormant. Pruning to remove the previous year's growth and leaving only enough buds to produce a strictly limited yield can be done at any time during the winter and is the most effective way of controlling yields. Pruning starts as soon as the sap has fallen (usually December in Bordeaux), and continues until March. This is a long, chilly task: the warmest part is burning the prunings. Local restaurants and residents often make the most of the surfeit of vine prunings, or *sarments*, by grilling steaks over them.

With lengthening days and rising temperatures the vine awakens. Once the sap begins to rise (the grower may see it dripping from the pruning cuts) the vine is far more vulnerable to cold. A hard spring frost now can kill. Depending on local conditions, weeds may be eradicated or they may be allowed to grow as cover crops then be ploughed in as fertilizer. Treatment for diseases of the wood may need to be applied, too.

SPRING

The first signs of growth appear. From budbreak in late April until early summer the young vine must be protected against frost. The buds are also vulnerable to pests and diseases: sprays help to control these enemies of the vine, though organic and biodynamic growers use other methods. Ploughing and hoeing aerates the soil and clears weeds; fertilizer may be applied. As the ground warms up, new vines can be planted.

Once the vines begin to shoot, the new growth needs to be tied to the wires, otherwise the foliage would shade the fruit and prevent it from ripening; the final trellising takes shape. From the emergence of the leaves many vineyards are regularly sprayed, against diseases such as oidium, mildew and rot, as well as harmful insects, but increasingly in Bordeaux the vineyards are run in a more sustainable fashion with minimal spraying.

SUMMER

Eight weeks after budbreak, in June, the vine flowers for about ten days and then the fruit sets. This period is one of the most nerve-wracking times of the grower's year. Ideally growers would like warm, dry and still weather; and a temperature of 20–25°C (68–77°F). What they like least is cold or rain. That sort of weather can prevent the fruit setting properly (a condition called *coulure* in French); and that means the crop will be reduced.

Different varieties flower at different times – this is an important insurance policy since in some years one variety may fail to flower. Merlot, Bordeaux's most planted variety, is a vigorous, productive vine and buds early, making it susceptible to damage from spring frosts. With its thin skin Merlot is also the most susceptible to rain and disease.Cabernet Sauvignon, on the other hand, is late ripening and therefore needs a thick skin to be able to survive Bordeaux's often heavy autumn rains.

Rain and cold at this stage may yet prevent the young berries from developing evenly (a condition the French call *millerandage*). But really there's not a lot the grower can do at this stage. He must continue to position stray shoots, so that they do not break off in the wind, and remove superfluous ones; he must continue to weed and spray for disease. And he must keep his fingers crossed for a long, warm summer.

Much of the work of growing high-quality grapes is directed towards making the vine do the opposite of what it wants to do. Cutting back the foliage in summer allows more sunlight to reach the fruit and encourages the vine to produce flavoursome grapes, rather than expend its energy on producing more leaves.

In August the grapes begin to change colour (*véraison*). This is the start of the ripening stage: the sugar content of the grapes rises rapidly, and the acid balance changes. At this point a green harvest (*vendange verte*) may be done to reduce the size of the crop. The best bunches change colour first, so you keep those and chop the rest.

Thinning the crop is one of the biggest gambles a grower can take. As the grapes continue to swell they become even more at risk from rain, rot and hail. It only needs one hailstorm later in the summer for the grower to lose the whole crop. So throwing away healthy grapes in the summer means that a grower is determined to produce high-quality wine, whatever the cost.

The non-organic grower must continue to spray whenever rot seems a possibility; growers must also continue to remove excess leaves that may be shading the grapes, or using up the vigour of the plant. But in scorching summers such as 2003, '05 and '09 the opposite is the case; the wilting leaves offer the baking grapes protection from the sun. This is when when the grower starts checking all the fermentation equipment in his winery, in preparation for the busy harvest period. Presses and vats have to be cleaned: everything must be spotless.

AUTUMN

In about the first week of September, sometimes earlier, the grapes for dry white wine are harvested, followed several weeks later by the red grapes. The precise date to ensure top quality is carefully monitored in order to obtain the optimum balance between sugar and acidity and the ripeness of pips and skins (phenolic maturity): underripe grapes lack sugar and flavour, while overripe ones lack aroma and freshness. They must also reach the winery as fast as possible, and undamaged: care now will make the difference between good wine and excellent wine. Some growers like overripeness and wait longer to pick.

Producers of sweet white wine pray for a long Indian summer with misty mornings and warm balmy afternoons to encourage the growth of noble rot on the grapes. For them harvesting necessitates picking over the vineyards several times, often carrying on into late November.

With the harvest over (usually mid to late October apart from the grapes for sweet wines), the leaves change colour and fall, and as the days shorten the sap descends for the winter. The winemaker is busy in the *chai*, watching the fermenting wine and taking hour-by-hour decisions about fermentation temperatures, yeasts and alcohol levels. For the moment the vineyards are empty.

Don't tell me. Health and Safety have decreed that the poor grape pickers might hurt their backs if they had to pick up their baskets. Poor dears. This new style grape-picking (top, at Ch. Mouton-Rothschild and above, at Ch. Belair-Monange) even includes wine wheelies.

PICKING BY HAND OR MACHINE

Top estates will favour pickers rather than machines for their finest wines because pickers can discard all but the best grapes. They can also be moved easily from parcel to parcel for selective picking. The vast majority of the Bordeaux region now uses mechanical harvesting. Mechanical harvesting (done by machines that straddle the rows of vines and strip the grapes from the bunches, leaving the stalks behind) is faster than hand picking, and means that a large area of vineyard can be picked at optimum ripeness – a particularly important consideration if rain is on the way during the harvest. But the use of machines is only feasible on large vineyards and on flat land.

Several important Médoc Classed Growths (particularly in the Margaux appellation) who turned to mechanical harvesting in the 1980s made a succession of mediocre wines and most have now returned to hand picking – with immediate quality improvements. Advances in engineering now enable machines to discriminate between healthy and unhealthy grapes – up to a point, but pickers look better than machines in PR terms.

SELECTION AND CONTROLLING YIELDS

The quality of the final wine can only be as good as the grapes from which it is made. Where yields are too high and the resultant quality poor the producer is usually trying to offset low financial returns by producing a greater volume of wine. Permitted yields are governed by the winemakers' associations but in the end it comes down to the resolve of each estate. Producers looking for quality will prune for lower yields and thin the crop where necessary.

Whatever the basic yield, selection is vital, all through the harvest. The pickers must pick only healthy grapes, discarding any that show signs of rot. Such rigour, inevitably, is expensive; it is one of the reasons why fine wine costs more than bulk-produced wine. All the top estates now use sorting tables to make a further selection when the grapes arrive at the winery.

PRUNING AND TRAINING

The vine is a climbing plant, distantly related to Virginia creeper. Left to itself it will run riot over trees, buildings and anything else in its way. All its energy will go into growth. But when you're growing vines for wine the idea is to coax each plant into producing a relatively small crop of grapes with concentrated flavour; and so the vine must be pruned. The object is then to train it in such a way as to allow the right amount of sunlight on to the grapes, unimpeded by too many leaves. However, the vine must have enough leaves in order to ripen the grapes through photosynthesis.

Higher trellising for better leaf coverage has been a recent feature in Bordeaux. Vine training is now accepted as fundamental to the eventual quality of the wine.

On non-vigorous soils such as the Médoc gravel banks, a simple training system will suffice. Throughout Bordeaux the vine is usually trained to the Guyot system, also known as cane-pruning. The canes, one or two with about six buds to each cane, are tied to a series of horizontal wires stretched along the row of vines. To reduce crop levels the vines can also be closely planted. In Sauternes, however, the Sémillon vines are short-pruned or spur-pruned, resulting in free-standing bushes, each with six or so short spurs, each with two or more buds.

PLANTING DENSITIES

One important decision for the grower is how far apart to plant the rows. This is a choice based on soil and economics. Top estates in the Médoc plant vines 1 metre (3ft) apart, with one metre between the rows. That makes 10,000 vines per hectare. This promotes competition between the vines, the rooting systems being encouraged to descend lower into the deep, gravelly soils for water and nutrients. Soils in St-Émilion are not quite so deep so vines tend to be planted a little further apart, though top properties like Ch. Ausone are now planting at 12,500 vines per hectare in addition to their vines at 10,000 per hectare. Suddenly the permitted crop means something very different. If you produce 50hl/ha from 3000 vines per hectare each vine will produce four times as much fruit as if you've planted 12,000 vines to the hectare. So the juice will be much more diluted.

That's why the top guys are all planting very densely when they have to replace old vines – for better concentration and quality in the grapes. In a basic red Bordeaux vineyard the grower will have richer soils and will be thinking about how to keep costs down. Planting vines even further apart allows space for a standard tractor to pass for spraying and maintenance throughout the year and eventually a machine harvester but it won't help concentrate the flavour in your fruit. Exactly the opposite. In the Entre-Deux-Mers wide spacing on flatter, fertile soils is one of the main reasons why producers there can't produce ripe-flavoured reds.

Just gaze at this photograph and think, gosh, how beautiful, how tranquil. But there is a serious point to it, too. These are the vines of Ch. Troplong-Mondot just outside the town of St-Emilion, and the vines are planted very close together so that they have to compete for nutrients and moisture. This reduces the yield per vine and increases the flavour in what grapes are left.

In the winery

Improvements in the quality of Bordeaux wines since the mid-1990s are more closely associated with the vineyard than the winery. Even at the less prosperous end of Bordeaux growers interested in lifting standards are pruning to curb yields, leaf plucking (perhaps by machine) and harvesting when the grapes are ripe rather than because the neighbour has started or the hunting season is on. But that's not to say that wine-making practices haven't moved on too. Investment in the winery depends on the producer's financial means but the basic necessities across the region are temperature control, cellar hygiene and a destemming machine. At the top end it's a question of ever finer tuning: so you'll see conveyor belts to move the fruit gently rather than pumps, multiple tables for sorting the grapes and a battery of smaller vats, sometimes made of new oak, so that grapes from different plots of vines can be harvested and vinified separately. All this means wines with purer fruit quality and, as a side-effect, higher levels of alcohol.

MAKING RED WINE

Wine is created by fermentation – yeasts turning grape sugar into alcohol. This simple chemical reaction has been refined by hundreds of years of experience, and, more recently, by the application of high technology and microbiological know-how. In Bordeaux the objective has always been to produce red wines that can age, so winemaking methods have been adapted accordingly. Typical features are a relatively lengthy alcoholic fermentation and maceration period for the extraction of colour, fruit and tannins, followed by lengthy barrel ageing for added complexity, to fix the colour and to round out tannins. However, the reality today is that wines are consumed earlier, which has put a greater emphasis on fruit and a supple texture and poses new challenges for Bordeaux's winemakers.

TRIAGE, DESTEMMING AND CRUSHING

The winemaking process begins when the grapes are brought in from the vineyard and are prepared for fermentation. For the finest quality, the grapes must be healthy and at optimum ripeness. Unhealthy grapes are discarded in the vineyard but it's pretty standard now to employ sorting tables at the point of reception for an

Mmm. I bet that tastes good – purple, sweet, half grape juice, half wine. During fermentation, methods for breaking the grapeskin cap include pumping over, or *remontage*, where the juice is taken from the base of the vat and pumped over the top (the method shown here at Ch. Léoville-Barton); punching down, or *pigeage*, where the cap is broken from the top, either mechanically or by hand; and *délestage* where the juice is emptied from the tank, then splashed back over the cap.

additional *tri* and to remove unwanted matter like leaves and insects. Recent innovations include perforated vibrating tables to eliminate tiny, seedless berries that have developed as a result of *millerandage* and placing sorting tables both before and after the destemmer as a catch-all option.

Destemming is now carried out as a matter of course for red grapes to avoid the bitter tannins that the stalks contain. Even machine-harvested grapes are put through the destemmer to get rid of any undesirable green matter. Traditionally, the grapes are then gently crushed between rollers – more a squeeze than a squash – to release the juice before they are pumped to the vat. If there is too much pressure the pips (seeds) will break and release bitter flavours into the juice. 'Gentle handling' is the modern mantra and top estates often now use conveyor belts to move grapes to the vat, where they are crushed as they enter.

FERMENTATION AND MACERATION

The colour of red wine comes from the grape skins: the juice is colourless. To make red wine you ferment the juice with the skins, and then press them afterwards. Yeasts are naturally present on grapes but cultivated yeasts are often used to start fermentation. The addition of sugar (up to a legally defined limit) is permitted to increase potential alcohol when necessary, a process known as chaptalization. Exceptionally, usually in hot years like 2003, acidification may be authorized – but technically never chaptalization.

Vats of varying size and shape and sometimes barrels are used for fermentation according to the whim, and wealth, of the winemaker – who can choose from stainless steel, concrete or oak – sometimes using all three. The alcoholic fermentation usually takes place at a temperature of around 28–30°C (82–86°F) and lasts on average eight to ten days. During the process, the skins, pips and pulp surge upwards, pushed by the stream of carbon dioxide gas released during fermentation. At the top, they form a thick 'cap' which must be mixed back in continually – so that the fermenting wine can extract maximum colour, tannin and flavour. Following the alcoholic fermentation a period of maceration is usually imposed for the added extraction of colour and tannins. The length of time will depend on the quality of the vintage but can last from a few days to several weeks. Some winemakers also employ a cold pre-fermentation maceration to extract fruit aromas and colour.

RUNNING OFF AND PRESSING

When the fermentation and maceration have been completed the fermented juice or 'free run juice' is drained from the vat and the residue of skins is pressed to produce a dark, tannic wine called 'press wine'. A proportion of this may be added to the free run juice to create a

A good château, such as Ch. Margaux shown here, will have lots of different fermentations which they keep separate. In the New Year after the harvest, they're all laid out in their individual bottles and the winemaker tries to produce the best final wine to go out under the château name. This is called the *assemblage*. Those young wines are tough to taste, and a lot end up excluded from the final blend.

Making a garage wine

Garage wines, mainly red and produced in tiny quantities from single plots of land, have a reputation for fruit intensity verging on excess. There's no set formula to making a *garage* wine but the winemaker would be well advised to adhere to some basic principles. The volume needs to be small, 500 to 1000 cases, certainly no more. This inevitably means a small vineyard and low-yielding vines. The grapes need to be picked super-ripe and the wine handcrafted without compromise, using the best equipment money can buy – sorting tables, small new oak vats and 100 per cent new oak *barriques*. The colour should be dark and the wines rich so a cold pre-fermentation maceration and plenty of extraction during the alcoholic fermentation are important. The malolactic fermentation will, of course, be completed in new oak barrels.

Egg whites play an important part in the 'fining' stage of making fine red wine. During the first winter of the second year beaten egg white is added to the wine – up to six eggs per *barrique* – to help remove tiny particles from the wine and to clear it. These are barrels of Ch. Langoa-Barton just about to get the treatment. After which the guy's wife is going to make an awful lot of *crème anglaise*.

Cryo-extraction

This is a process for artificially concentrating grapes by controlled freezing. It's sometimes adopted by sweet wine producers in Bordeaux in wet vintages. The grapes are picked and then stored in a giant freezer where the temperature is dropped to –6°C (21°F). The least ripe grapes or those diluted by rain freeze, leaving the sugar in the richest and ripest in a more extractable state when the grapes are pressed.

deeper, firmer style, or it may be stored apart – it all depends what the winemaker wants. Technically, the wine is now made but it's still in a pretty raw state. To begin with, it has a sharp, green-apple acidity. This is reduced through a second fermentation – the malolactic fermentation – in which a special strain of bacteria converts the tart malic acid to mild lactic acid. If nature were left to take its course this would happen the following spring when the weather gets warmer, but in Bordeaux it is induced after the alcoholic fermentation either by raising the cellar temperature or by injecting the wine with malolactic bacteria. It takes place in vat or, increasingly at top estates, in barrel. This is thought to give a better integration of oak and tannin in the wine's youth – an important factor for making an impression on the wine trade at the spring tastings.

BLENDING AND AGING

Up to this point the individual grape varieties from different plots have been fermented and stored separately. They are now blended together in well-defined proportions according to the judgement of the winemaker. The blending process, known as *assemblage*, is done by tasting and requires great skill. The winemaker must produce the best wine by selecting or rejecting samples from all the different vats, and creating at the highest level a wine that will be at its optimum in several years time. Consultant enologists, like Michel Rolland, lend their experience at this crucial stage. Red wine is aged in vat or preferably oak barrels for anything from nine months to two years in Bordeaux. During this period of *élevage* it clears and matures; and the slow absorption of oxygen helps stabilize colour, soften tannins and increase aromatic complexity. Many winemakers hasten the softening of the wine by introducing tiny amounts of oxygen – a process known as micro-oxygenation.

USE OF OAK

New oak Bordeaux *barriques* of 225 litres (50 gallons) are one of the most fashionable things a winery can have. All oak barrels have an oxidative effect on the wine, but a brand new barrel also guarantees less microbiological spoilage and gives its own flavours to the wine, infusing it with toasty spice, vanilla, mocha and chocolate. But if it is not handled carefully oak can overpower the wine altogether and it is not appropriate for many of the light, savoury reds produced in Bordeaux.

RACKING AND FINING

Traditionally the wine is 'racked' or drawn from barrel or tank to another empty one on a number of occasions (called *soutirage*). This helps clarify and freshen the wine by removing the fine lees or sediment which forms and provides a tiny amount of oxygen to help the aging process. The wine may also be 'fined' (*collage*) using egg white or other materials to settle out particles in suspension which are then removed through further racking.

BOTTLING

This is the moment when the winemaker's work is finally complete. If the wine is bottled too early, it will not reach it's full potential; too late, and it will already have lost its freshness. A light filtration may precede the bottling. Modern bottling lines are fully automated and very fast. They ensure complete hygiene, and breakages are rare.

CLAIRET AND ROSÉ WINES

Rosé wines need just that blush of colour and the expression of fresh red fruit. Hence, red grapes are either pressed directly or the juice allowed a few hours contact with the skins before being run off. Temperature for the alcoholic fermentation is much lower than for reds – 15°C (59°F) – to encourage primary fruit flavours. Carbon dioxide and sulphur provide much-needed protection against oxidation and the wines are bottled early in November or December following the harvest to maintain freshness. Clairet wines are darker in colour, somewhere between red and rosé, and a bit chewier. The period of maceration lasts longer – 24 hours to three days – and the temperature of fermentation is a little higher at 17°C (63°F). The malolactic fermentation may or may not take place (it never does for rosé). Normally, the wine is aged on its lees and bottled in February.

Isn't that colour inviting? Bordeaux makes smashing rosé wine – and ought to make a lot more because many of her lesser vineyards can't fully ripen grapes for red wine, but their slightly underripe green leaf and blackcurrant flavours make excellent rosé. And with the market for rosé being very healthy at the moment, making pink wine could keep some of the producers in business.

MAKING DRY WHITE WINE

The majority of white wine made in Bordeaux today is light and fruity fare for everyday drinking. Hygienic stainless steel vats with refrigeration are the key to making these wines. The style for the rare top whites is altogether different. These are lush, creamy, complex wines for aging and new oak barrels are the most precious tools in their making.

DESTEMMING, CRUSHING AND PRESSING

Grapes for dry whites are usually harvested in late August to early September. When they arrive at the winery they are rapidly pressed to separate the juice from the skins. Alternatively, they may be lightly crushed and destemmed for maceration (see overleaf). Oxidation is the biggest threat as it destroys the fresh fruit flavours, so temperature control is crucial; sulphur dioxide is added at this stage and a blanket of

Micro-oxygenation

Since the mid-1990s a number of winemakers have turned to micro-oxygenation as a substitute for systematic racking. A homeopathic dose of oxygen is bubbled into the wine when it's deemed to need freshening. This technique is often adopted when the wine is held on fine lees in a reductive (i.e. oxygen-free) state to retain aroma and fruit. Micro-oxygenation can also be used at the beginning of the alcoholic fermentation to encourage yeast action and during maceration to soften tannins.

These beautiful new barrels at Ch. Suduiraut in Sauternes are so pristine they could be butter fudge and I want to bite lumps out of them. They may give a basic fudge flavour to the wine because oak contains a lot of vanilla, released and toasted during the manufacturing process. New French oak barrels are in such demand that the minimum price has gone up to about €550–600 (£471/$755–£514/$824) per barrel and some top selections can be €750 (£642/ $1030). At 288 bottles (approximately) per barrel – that's immediately adding 2 to 3 euros to the cost of production of each one.

carbon dioxide is often used in the press, hoses and vats for the same reason. Gentle pneumatic presses are considered the 'must-have' for making white wine.

FERMENTATION AND MACERATION

Some winemakers allow a brief maceration of grapes and juice or 'skin contact' at cold temperatures to extract added flavour elements before pressing. This takes 12–24 hours either in the press or vat. After pressing, the juice is allowed to settle to remove the solid matter or lees and then run off to vat or barrel for fermentation. A suitable yeast culture will normally be added. Stainless steel vats provide a clean, temperature-controlled environment in which to produce a fruitier, fresher style of white. Temperatures are held to 18–20°C (64–68°F), the fermentation lasting up to 15 days. Unlike with reds, the malolactic fermentation is not usually allowed to take place for dry whites in Bordeaux; winemakers prefer to keep the tangy acidity, even for the lusher, oak-rich styles.

RUNNING OFF, BLENDING AND AGING

When the alcoholic fermentation is complete, the wine is run off. The fine lees are sometimes retained and may then be added back at a later date and stirred regularly to enhance flavour. Otherwise the wine is allowed to settle. The ageing process is shorter for whites than for reds – four months for fresh, fruity styles, 9–14 months for fuller whites – and the blending of different grape varieties is done early in the new year.

USE OF OAK

For the fullest white styles, mostly those from Pessac-Léognan, the juice is fermented in oak barrel which imparts a rich, mellow flavour, even to a dry wine, and the temperatures are warmer at 28–30°C (82–86°F). Fermenting white wines in new oak *barriques* gives all the advantages of ageing the wine in new oak – those rich, buttery, toasted flavours – as well as integrating with the flavour better. You really can taste the difference. Barrel-fermented whites are usually aged on their fine lees, which are stirred regularly; a process known as *bâtonnage*. This can now be done by simply rocking the barrels to disturb the sediment. Either way, a richer, creamier, more exciting flavour is the result.

BOTTLING

Crisp, fresh, dry whites like those from Entre-Deux-Mers will be fined, filtered and then bottled in March. The more serious barrel-fermented whites from Pessac-Léognan are usually aged on lees until August then bottled. Some may even go through to December.

MAKING SWEET WHITE WINE

White grapes destined for sweet wines are left on the vine well into the autumn. The best are those attacked by 'noble rot' (*Botrytis cinerea*), the fungus that sucks out the water from already overripe grapes, concentrating the sugar (see also page 277). Noble rot also gives complex flavours, making these grapes far more highly prized than those brought to super-ripeness and concentrated by the sun alone.

PRESSING AND FERMENTATION

Botrytized grapes have to be pressed two or three times to release all their sugar-rich juice. Each pressing contains more sugar than the last. The sticky juice is run off the press into vat to settle overnight – any bits of gunge fall naturally to the bottom. It's then run into barrel or vat for fermentation; the concentration of the juice means this can take anywhere up to a month to complete. Ideally, for the top sweet wines, the grapes are picked with sufficient sugar for a potential alcohol of 21 per cent. Fermentation (sugar converted by yeasts) provides 13.5–14 per cent alcohol, the rest remaining as residual sugar. The process is natural, as yeasts stop working once the alcohol level reaches 15 per cent, but frequently the winemaker will add sulphur dioxide to stop fermentation to achieve the correct balance in the wine.

BLENDING AND AGING

As with red and dry white wines the different grape varieties for sweet white wines are vinified separately then blended in the early months of the year following the harvest. Most of the lesser sweet wines are aged in stainless steel then bottled early to keep the freshness. For the more serious wines aging in barrel can last anything up to three years. The higher alcohol and the sugar content prevents the wine's flavours from drying out, the longer period in barrel providing greater balance and rounding out the wine.

USE OF OAK

Bordeaux's top sweet wines are usually both vinified and aged in new oak *barriques*; some châteaux use as much as 70 to 100 per cent. There's greater microbiological stability when the oak is new and it gives that rich, toasty flavour to complement the sweet, luxurious fruit.

The richness and personality of Ch d'Yquem's famous sweet wine is note solely due to excellent grapes. The heady, syrupy juice is fermented in oak barrels, not stainless steel, and this adds texture, spice and aroma to the fruit flavours. Long maturation in oak barrels intensifies these flavours even further.

Bordeaux as a business

Some wine areas develop because of the perfect suitability of the land and the climate for vines and the evolution of a cuisine that seems to complement the wine flavours perfectly. Food and wine hand in hand. Just as it should be. But Bordeaux as a wine area was created because of business. Almost by chance it has turned out to be wonderfully suited to the production of various styles of red wine, of dry whites and luscious sweet whites, but it was trade that started it all. Bordeaux is a great port, France's greatest port looking out on to the Atlantic and the trade routes to America, Africa and the East. Trade brings money, and money has allowed Bordeaux to become a world leader in quality and style and image, for which we should be thankful – and a world leader in price, which is a more debatable benefit. Yet without the traders' money, and the export markets craving high-quality products they couldn't themselves produce, we'd never have seen the development of Bordeaux into its current position as arguably the world's greatest wine region. And as quality has improved over the centuries, so hierarchies and classifications and methods of controlling and codifying the wine have developed. It makes for a sometimes daunting, but always fascinating landscape, some of it seemingly immutable, some of it remarkably fluid and sensitive to the times.

Above: Ch. de Lamarque in the Haut-Médoc is an impressive fortress surviving from the Middle Ages when the English ruled Aquitaine – and it's also a wine estate; however, not all châteaux in Bordeaux are grand castles.

Top: Ch. d'Angludet in the Margaux appellation makes an excellent and good value red wine but its château is just this modest single-storey house. I'm very fond of it. This is where I spent my first ever night in Bordeaux. Not actually in the house: I slept in a tent out in the long grass, but the owners sent down a jug of lip-staining, purple young wine, so I was in seventh heaven.

THE CHÂTEAU SYSTEM

The word 'château' is a grand-sounding title. Its literal translation is 'castle', and if you have visions of turrets, high fortified walls and portcullis gates guarding the moat – well, that's all right. There are a few châteaux like that in Bordeaux, a very few, and most of them are in the Médoc. The idea of a 'château' coming to represent a particular wine grew up in the 18th century when the wealthy businessmen and parliamentarians of Bordeaux began to hanker for magnificent estates at which to relax and indulge in a bit of showing off. Initially, they would have chosen the Graves region round the city of Bordeaux, but when Dutch engineers drained the marshes of the Médoc, suddenly what had been isolated islands of dry land surrounded by swamps became very desirable gravel outcrops linked to Bordeaux by road. In their hundreds the new élite in Bordeaux seized the opportunity to establish a grand building and plant a seriously good vineyard around it. There are numerous stunning properties right up to the northern tip of the Médoc but understandably many of the most impressive are close to the city.

What also began to happen was the adoption of the title 'château' for an estate's wines, even when there was no imposing building deserving the name. In recent years the use of the word 'château' has spread throughout Bordeaux as a mark of supposed superiority and individuality. A property in a famous area like, say, Pauillac or St-Émilion can still get a good price for its wine even when sold anonymously in bulk. In the lesser appellations, the price for bulk wine is likely to be derisory. Any proprietor determined to improve his wine, and thus his selling price, will find that calling his estate 'Château Something' is the first step in adding value to his wine, however uncastle-like his farmhouse may be.

So a 'château' wine is, basically, the wine of an estate. However, if you look at the historical records, many estates have increased in size over the last century or so, sometimes by ten times or more, so that if the original owner had established a reputation for a wine from the original vineyard, this might now only comprise a tiny part of the total. This would mean that the character of the wine would almost certainly change. But it doesn't mean that the quality would suffer. The better-known properties all nowadays operate a more or less strict selection policy. They select the best parts of the vineyard, then they select the best grapes as

No wonder I'm looking so smug: I've got a bottle each of Bordeaux's First Growths, and I can't decide which one to open first.

The 1855 classification of red wines

This is the current version of the 1855 classification. Many names have changed in the last 150 years and properties have been split up, merged or even disappeared, so there are now 61 châteaux rather than the 58 originally classified. Properties are listed in the order in which they were classified, rather than alphabetically.

FIRST GROWTHS (PREMIERS CRUS)
Lafite-Rothschild (Pauillac); Margaux (Margaux); Latour (Pauillac); Haut-Brion (Pessac-Léognan); Mouton-Rothschild (Pauillac) (since 1973).

SECOND GROWTHS (DEUXIÈMES CRUS)
Rauzan-Ségla (Margaux); Rauzan-Gassies (Margaux); Léoville-Las-Cases (St-Julien); Léoville-Poyferré (St-Julien); Léoville-Barton (St-Julien); Durfort-Vivens (Margaux); Gruaud-Larose (St-Julien);

Lascombes (Margaux); Brane-Cantenac (Margaux); Pichon-Longueville (Pauillac); Pichon-Longueville-Comtesse de Lalande (Pauillac); Ducru-Beaucaillou (St-Julien); Cos d'Estournel (St-Estèphe); Montrose (St-Estèphe).

THIRD GROWTHS (TROISIÈMES CRUS)
Kirwan (Margaux); d'Issan (Margaux); Lagrange (St-Julien); Langoa-Barton (St-Julien); Giscours (Margaux); Malescot-St-Exupéry (Margaux); Boyd-Cantenac (Margaux); Cantenac-Brown (Margaux); Palmer (Margaux); La Lagune (Haut-Médoc); Desmirail (Margaux); Calon-Ségur (St-Estèphe); Ferrière (Margaux); Marquis d'Alesme-Becker (Margaux).

FOURTH GROWTHS (QUATRIÈMES CRUS)
St-Pierre (St-Julien); Talbot (St-Julien); Branaire-Ducru (St-Julien); Duhart-Milon (Pauillac); Pouget (Margaux); La Tour-Carnet (Haut-Médoc); Lafon-Rochet (St-Estèphe); Beychevelle (St-Julien); Prieuré-Lichine (Margaux); Marquis de Terme (Margaux).

FIFTH GROWTHS (CINQUIÈMES CRUS)
Pontet-Canet (Pauillac); Batailley (Pauillac); Haut-Batailley (Pauillac); Grand-Puy-Lacoste (Pauillac); Grand-Puy-Ducasse (Pauillac); Lynch-Bages (Pauillac); Lynch-Moussas (Pauillac); Dauzac (Margaux); d'Armailhac (Pauillac); du Tertre (Margaux); Haut-Bages-Libéral (Pauillac); Pédesclaux (Pauillac); Belgrave (Haut-Médoc); Camensac (Haut-Médoc); Cos Labory (St-Estèphe); Clerc-Milon (Pauillac); Croizet-Bages (Pauillac); Cantemerle (Haut-Médoc).

SUPER-SECONDS

What do you get when you combine ambitious château owners with a classification that was created in 1855 and has hardly changed since? There's no formal list but the notion of Super-Seconds has been adopted in the Bordeaux trade as a way of recognizing that certain Second Growth châteaux are making wine far better than their peers, perhaps even of First Growth standard. Most are charging significantly higher prices than their peers too, sometimes — as in the case or Léoville-Las-Cases — not far off those of a First Growth. This photograph shows my personal selection of Médoc Super-Seconds, plus a longtime favourite, Third Growth Ch. Palmer which is considered a Super-Second too: (from left to right) Pichon-Longueville, Palmer, Montrose, Cos d'Estournel, Ducru-Beaucaillou, Léoville-Las-Cases, Pichon-Longueville-Comtesse de Lalande and Léoville-Barton.

Ch. Pétrus from the 1982 vintage, a milestone for modern Bordeaux. The famous classification of 1855 was based on price, pure and simple. The higher the price you got for your wine on the marketplace, the higher your classification. Easy. Now, it is true that many of the best vineyard sites had been developed for a long time and had been able to build a reputation and thus get top classification. But the red wine classification of 1855 only covered wines from the so-called 'Left Bank'. There were no St-Émilions and Pomerols because nobody then would pay a high price for them.

How things have changed. If we look at the top Bordeaux prices since the 1980s, an increasing number of them are from St-Émilion and Pomerol. If there were a new classification, there would be dozens of wines from these two areas, and Ch. Pétrus would probably be 'First of Firsts'. Average prices for Pétrus for the last ten years have been three times the price asked for a case of Ch Latour. Only Ch. Lafite, the object of Chinese fascination in recent years, has kept up.

they arrive at the winery – at the top properties, literally grape by grape – and then they select the best vats and barrels of wine. These will finally make up what is called the *grand vin* – the 'great wine'. In other words, the wine the owner is proud to put his château name on. A generation ago, even the smart properties would include most of their grapes in the *grand vin*. Not any more.

THE 1855 CLASSIFICATION

It's quite remarkable how the Bordeaux classification of 1855 not only became the most famous wine classification in the world but has remained so for over 150 years. And, with the exception of Cantemerle being pencilled in as a Fifth Growth after the list was finalized, and Mouton-Rothschild being promoted from Second to First Growth status in 1973, it has remained set in stone ever since. Yet it wasn't supposed to be permanent. It was just a ploy to make the display of Bordeaux wines seem a bit more interesting at the Paris Universal Exhibition in 1855. The organizers had asked for a selection of Bordeaux' best wines to be sent to Paris. But which were the best Bordeaux wines? Who would decide, especially since there was less than a month between the request for the wines, and the opening of the exhibition? It could have been a messy disaster, but luckily Bordeaux had 200 years of experience to call upon. Although the hastily compiled list of 58 red wine properties and 21 whites was in effect a snapshot of what was best in Bordeaux at that moment in April 1855, in actual fact the classification had been developing for two centuries, and just because you'd made a star wine in 1854 didn't mean you had a cat in hell's chance of squeezing in to the classification unless your track record went back a considerable way. And what did it matter, the classification would be forgotten within the year.

It wasn't. This almost casual classification of the worth of a Bordeaux property has shown astonishing resilience. Ah, worth. There's the nub of the matter. This list was all about money. It wasn't about tasting – there was no blind tasting held in 1855 to see which wines tasted the best – it was simply about which wines sold for most money. But who decided? And why were there five levels of classifications? Well, let's go back a bit.

The first attempt to classify Bordeaux was in 1647, when the prices achieved by different communes for their wine were recorded. By the end of the 17th century, a handful of superior properties had emerged in the communes of Pessac, Margaux and Pauillac – Haut-Brion, Margaux, Lafite and Latour – and the wine brokers who organized their sales dubbed them 'First Growths'. During the 18th century, especially because of a continued clamour for good quality wines by the British, a further bunch of properties, mostly fairly close to the original First Growths became recognized as serious – and began achieving good prices – though not so good as the original First Growths – and these were marked down by the brokers as 'Second Growths'. As the demand for fine wine continued to expand, more and more properties began to make the effort to improve – and consequently they could gain better prices for their wines, and so a third tier of wines, then a fourth and a fifth, were added by brokers to their records, according to what prices the market would pay for them. By 1855, there had been various classifications, none permanent, and properties had moved up or down, according to how well they were selling. 1855 was simply meant to be yet another temporary classification but those who missed out have had 150 years to rue their luck.

Efforts have been, and continue to be, made to change the 1855 classification, particularly by including other areas of Bordeaux. Why, with the exception of Haut-Brion from the Graves, were Médocs the only reds considered? Simply because the other reds, even the historic properties from the Graves to the south of Bordeaux, didn't command the Médoc prices. And the so-called Right Bank wines, what we'd now call St-Émilion and Pomerol, weren't handled by the brokers in Bordeaux – they had a separate commercial set-up in the port of Libourne which directed most of their wines to the Dutch not the British market, and at the time that market was more concerned with quantity than quality so none of the wines – some of which in Pomerol and St-Émilion now rank among the world's most expensive – were even considered for classification.

If any new classification were to be made – open to every property in Bordeaux – you can be sure that the top Right Bank wines would swamp a number of the leading growths of the 1855 classification. But until that happens the 1855 classification is still revered the world over and, with a few glaring exceptions, has proved a remarkably reassuring indicator of quality and price.

With the astonishing improvement in winemaking during the last part of the 20th century and the beginning of the 21st, I would reckon only four or five properties are not making wine good enough to hold on to their classification. However, which tier they deserve to be in is a different matter. There are fifths that deserve to be seconds and at least one second deserves no more than fifth status. However, they were classified in 1855, and for the foreseeable future, there's nothing anyone can do about it. Only Ch. Mouton-Rothschild has ever managed such a feat, by being promoted to join the First Growths in 1973 after a half-century of vigorous campaigning by the indefatigable genius Baron Philippe de Rothschild.

But if you want to make up your mind about which property is performing and which isn't, well, check out the prices. Go to a website like wine-searcher.com and see what each property's wines will fetch. It's just what the organizers did in 1855.

In the famous classification of 1855 Ch. d'Yquem was classified Superior First Growth above all other Bordeaux wines, and it is still the most famous – and some would say the greatest – sweet wine in the world.

Talk about good business sense – 8 is a lucky number in China. Mouton commissioned a Chinese artist for their label in 2008. So far the wine has increased in value by more than 350%.

I can see why members of a classification want to keep it as exclusive as possible, but there are several properties in Pessac-Léognan of fabulous quality that really must be included in the classification soon. The beautiful Ch. la Louvière, maker of fine reds and outstanding whites, tops this list.

THE 1855 CLASSIFICATION OF BARSAC AND SAUTERNES

After all the hullabaloo about the red wines, it might seem that the 1855 classification of Sauternes and Barsac was a bit of an afterthought, and you shouldn't take all these First and Second Growths too seriously. Twelve First Growths, including Yquem! There were only four red First Growths in 1855. So there were, but this was a classification according to price, and price reflected quality, rarity, and above all, demand. It's clear that demand for the sweet wines of Sauternes was very high in 1855 and that Yquem could reasonably enough regard itself as the top wine of all Bordeaux – it is the only château to boast the classification Premier Cru Supérieur – Superior First Growth. But fashions change. Sauternes went into a long period of decline and unpopularity which wasn't reversed until the 1980s, and red Bordeaux occupied centre-stage. Life is still tough for the Sauternes châteaux, as fashionable interest in sweet white wine ebbs and flows, but the classified growths of Sauternes are once more proving that their classification was not merely a quirk of history.

THE CLASSIFICATION OF THE GRAVES

While the St-Émilion classification is regularly revised, they're still lobbying in the Graves for an expansion that would reflect the fine quality of such non-classified châteaux as La Louvière. But with or without a rejigging, this classification has never caught the imagination like the 1855 classification or the 1954 St-Émilion classification (see below). The first list was drawn up in 1953 and just embraced red wines – all of them from the northern Graves area closer to Bordeaux city now called Pessac-Léognan. Whites were added in 1959, in most cases being the white wine production of châteaux already classified for reds.

Exceptions were Laville Haut-Brion, Couhins and Couhins-Lurton, which were 100 per cent white (Couhins-Lurton is now making red again). There are anomalies – such as Fieuzal and Smith-Haut-Lafitte – whose brilliant whites are not classified – and a new look at the classification is probably overdue.

THE ST-ÉMILION CLASSIFICATION

Although St-Émilion wasn't even considered for classification in 1855 – I'm not sure most of the Bordeaux brokers would even have tasted wine from St-Émilion, from what would have seemed like another world over the Garonne and Dordogne rivers – it nowadays boasts what is probably the most plausible and flexible of the Bordeaux classification systems.

It was started in 1954 and published officially the following year, perhaps to put a spoke in the wheel of the Médocains, who were preparing to celebrate the centenary of their 1855 classification. And whereas the 1855 classification was never meant to be permanent but has become set in stone, the St-Émilion version has flexibility written into its constitution. It is supposed to be reassessed every ten years, and the commitment has largely been honoured. So far there have been reclassifications in 1969 and 1985 (delayed from 1979 by some bureaucratic wrangling over the appellation rules and not published until 1986), then as originally envisaged in 1996. The latest reclassification was in 2006. The changes are rarely seismic, but properties can be promoted and relegated according to their performance and, increasingly, this is precisely what happens, particularly since a number of very obscure properties included in the 1954 list are being whittled away, and a small number of very dynamic properties are due promotion at each reclassification. There was more change than usual in the 2006 edition with two new Premiers Grands Crus Classés B, six Grands Crus Classés and 11 châteaux relegated from the list altogether. The latter caused a right rumpus with legal action from four of the downgraded estates threatening the very existence of the classification.

At the very top are two properties classified as Premier Grand Cru Classé A. Ausone and Cheval Blanc have reigned supreme here since 1954. Below this level there are 13 Premiers Grands Crus Classés B, Pavie-Macquin and Troplong-Mondot the two new members in 2006. The third level is St-Émilion Grand Cru Classé, currently numbering 57 châteaux, down from 55 in 1996, 63 in 1985 and 72 in 1969.

It's worth noting that the classified wines are a special category within the appellation of St-Émilion Grand Cru (*not* Classé). The appellation alone doesn't mean much, as a lot of very basic wines get in as well as the Ausones and Cheval Blancs. In fact, well over half St-Émilion's output qualifies as Grand Cru!

The St-Émilion classification

This is the St-Émilion classification as in 2006. A further update is due in 2012.

PREMIERS GRANDS CRUS CLASSÉS (A)
Ausone, Cheval Blanc

PREMIERS GRANDS CRUS CLASSÉS (B)
Angélus, Beau-Séjour Bécot, Beauséjour (Duffau-Lagarrosse/HDL), Belair-Monange, Canon, Clos Fourtet, Figeac, La Gaffelière, Magdelaine, Pavie, Pavie-Macquin, Troplong-Mondot, Trottevieille.

GRANDS CRUS CLASSÉS
L'Arrosée, Balestard-la-Tonnelle, Bellefont-Belcier, Bellevue, Bergat, Berliquet, Cadet-Bon, Cadet-Piola, Canon-la-Gaffelière, Cap de Mourlin, Chauvin, Clos des Jacobins, Clos de L'Oratoire, Clos St-Martin, La Clotte, Corbin, Corbin-Michotte, La Couspaude, Couvent des Jacobins, Dassault, Destieux, La Dominique, Faurie de Souchard, Fleur-Cardinale, Fonplégade, Fonroque, Franc Mayne, Les Grandes Murailles, Grand Corbin, Grand Corbin Despagne, Grand Mayne, Grand-Pontet, Guadet-St-Julien, Haut Corbin, Haut Sarpe, Laniote, Larcis Ducasse, Larmande, Laroque, Laroze, La Marzelle, Matras, Monbousquet, Moulin du Cadet, Pavie-Decesse, Petit Faurie de Soutard, Le Prieuré, Ripeau, St-Georges (Côte Pavie), La Serre, Soutard, Tertre-Daugay, La Tour Figeac, La Tour du Pin, La Tour du Pin Figeac, Villemaurine, Yon Figeac.

Ch. Ausone and Cheval Blanc have reigned supreme at the top of the St-Émilion tree for decades.

Best of the Bourgeois

SOME OF MY FAVOURITE CRUS BOURGEOIS

Haut-Médoc

Ch. d'Agassac, Ch. d'Arcins, Ch. Balac, Ch. Barryeres, Ch. Beaumont, Ch. Belair, Ch. Bellevue, Ch. Cambon la Pelouse, Ch. Caronne Ste-Gemme, Ch. Charmail, Ch. Cissac, Ch. Citran, Ch. Clément-Pichon, Ch. Hanteillan, Ch. de Lamarque, Ch. Lanessan, Ch. Laniraux, Ch. Larose-Trintaudon, Ch. Lestage Simon, Ch. Magnol, Ch. Malescasse, Ch. Maucamps, Ch. du Moulin Rouge, Ch. Paloumey, Ch. Peyrabon, Ch. Reysson (Réserve), Ch. Sénéjac, Ch. Tour du Haut-Moulin, Ch. de Villambis, Ch. de Villegeorge.

Médoc

Ch. Bournac, Ch. La Branne, Ch. La Cardonne, Ch. d'Escurac, Ch. Fontis, Ch. Les Grands Chênes, Ch. Greysac, Ch. Noaillac, Ch. Les Ormes Sorbet, Ch. Patache d'Aux, Ch. Poitevin, Ch. Preuillac, Ch. Rollan de By, Ch. La Tour de By, Ch. Tour Haut-Caussan, Ch. Vieux Robin. Ch. L'Inclassable, Ch. Ramafort, Ch. Tour Prignac, Ch. Tour St-Bonnet.

Listrac

Ch. Clarke, Ch. Fonréaud, Ch. Fourcas-Dupré, Ch. Fourcas-Loubaney, Ch. Grand Listrac, Ch. Mayne Lalande, Ch. Reverdi, Ch. Saransot-Dupré.

Margaux

Ch. d'Angludet, Ch. Deyrem-Valentine, Ch. Grand Tayac, Ch. La Gurgue, Ch. Labégorce, Ch. Monbrison, Ch. Mongravey, Ch. Paveil de Luze, Ch. Pontac Lynch.

Moulis

Ch. Biston-Brillette, Ch. Branas-Grand-Poujeaux, Ch. Brillette, Ch. Duplessis, Ch Dutruch-Grand-Poujeaux, Ch. Grand-Poujeaux, Ch. Malmaison, Ch. Maucaillou.

Pauillac

Ch. Bellegrave, Ch. La Fleur Peyrabon, Ch. Pibran.

St-Estèphe

Ch. Beau Site, Ch. Le Boscq, Ch. Coutelin-Merville, Ch. Domeyne, Ch. Ladouys, Ch. Lattaye, Ch. Lilian Ladouys, Ch. Meyney, Ch. Plantier Rose, Ch. Tour de Pez.

St-Julien

Ch. du Glana, Ch. les Ormes, Ch. Teynac.

THE CRUS BOURGEOIS OF THE MÉDOC

This classification has undergone major restructuring in recent years but its history and significance is important, so here's the story. I suppose if a bunch of people set themselves up as a self-perpetuating aristocracy of wine like the members of the 1855 classification did, there are going to be those who are mightily aggrieved at not being included in the select group. So what do they do? Form their own group, say 'We're just as good as you' and bang on the door to be let in? Well, sort of. No one has been let in to the 1855 classification since it was formed – not surprising, really; if you've got the Crown Jewels, why should you share? And if you're underperforming you'll be even less willing to change the status quo – the newcomers might kick you out, for goodness sake.

But would you have chosen the title Cru Bourgeois? Doesn't the word 'bourgeois' imply that you're touching your forelock, bending a knee, and admitting your inferiority? Well, that's what the bunch of Médoc and Haut-Médoc châteaux that weren't quite up to snuff in 1855 called themselves. I mean, bourgeois?! Now, it wasn't until 1932 that they banded together and called themselves *bourgeois*, and maybe *bourgeois* meant something different then, but to me it implies something stifling, respectable, conservative and suburban. Not the kind of image I'd want to convey if I were an ambitious château wanting to boast about the quality of my wine.

Well, in 1932 they classified 444 estates supposedly making wine of regular high quality. I'd say that only a few dozen of these were remotely close to the Classed Growths in quality and perhaps a dozen or less could really say, 'We're as good as you'. This question was to some extent addressed in 2003 when there was a new classification of bourgeois properties. This time they had 490 applications for membership from the Médoc and Haut-Médoc and they created three tiers consisting of nine Crus Bourgeois Exceptionnels, 87 Crus Bourgeois Supérieurs and 151 Crus Bourgeois to be re-evaluated every 12 years. So far so good. Those nine 'Exceptionnels' – Ch. Chasse-Spleen (Moulis), Ch. Haut-Marbuzet (St-Estèphe), Ch. Labegorce-Zédé (Margaux), Ch. Les Ormes-de-Pez (St-Estèphe), Ch. de Pez (St-Estèphe), Ch Phelan-Segur (St-Estèphe), Ch. Potensac (Médoc), Ch. Poujeaux (Moulis) and Ch. Siran (Margaux) – have a genuine right to be thought of as equal to Classed Growths, quite a few of the 'Supérieurs' are indeed quite classy and tasty, but the next 151 – what did it mean? Of course, some of these Crus Bourgeois wines are noteworthy and I've picked out the ones that have caught my attention over the years in the list on the left.

It gets worse. In 2005, 77 châteaux that had been removed from the original 1932 list fought a court battle for the right to be re-evaluated as Crus Bourgeois and in 2007 their action managed to get the 2003 classification annulled altogether, the name being banned from labels from the 2007 vintage.

Behind the scenes the producers realised they had shot themselves in the foot and in 2008 plans were put forth for another classification open to all comers in the Médoc appellations which was ratified in 2009. The classification is now decided by independent tasting panels on an annual basis. Châteaux have to adhere to a set of production rules, including a guarantee of 18 months aging in barrel. The 2008 vintage was the first under the new system and saw 243 châteaux granted the label out of 290 candidates. In 2009 246 châteaux out of 304 were classified, covering 26 per cent of the Médoc vineyards or 38 per cent of total production in the Médoc (equivalent to 32 million bottles, for the number crunchers among you). I would expect this figure to diminish rather than increase in future years as the new system beds in. There is still a wide disparity between the best and the worst Crus Bourgeois, though all are at very least a decent drink. The nine 'Exceptionnels' and a number of other high profile châteaux did not apply.

SECOND WINES

Only the finest lots of wine are selected for the *grand vin*, or main château wine – maybe as little as 30 per cent of the crop. Other vats are left out perhaps because they come from younger vines, or from less favoured parts of the vineyard. Younger vines don't give wine with the concentration and staying power demanded of the *grand vin* these days, and most châteaux will exclude wine from vines five to six years old, some from vines as old as ten years. Many major properties have large vineyards, often over 50ha (123 acres), and not all the soils or local climates will be the same. Even in a single vineyard some plots always give better wine, some never do. And a château may own land a significant distance from its core vineyard. Ch. Margaux and Latour, for instance, own vineyards some kilometres away from their heartland of gravel banks overlooking the Gironde. They make excellent wine from these sites, but they go into Le Pavillon de Château Margaux and Les Forts de Latour, not the *grand vin*. These are the names of the second wines, related to, but different from the château name, and almost all of the top châteaux sport a second label identifiably belonging to the property. These wines are normally very good, and in the world of inflated wine

Ch. Latour with its second wine, Les Forts de Latour. Any batches of wine from the core vineyard that don't quite work, for whatever reason, are blended with wine from estate vineyards further inland to create what is still a magnificent cedary second wine, as good as many Classed Growths' first wine. There is also a good third wine just called Pauillac.

The idea of producing a second wine to preserve the quality of your main label isn't new. Ch. Margaux produced the original, 'Le Pavillon–Château Margaux' in 1906. Nowadays every self-respecting château has a second wine.

prices we live in, are often a half to a quarter of the price of the *grand vin* and certainly more than a quarter as good. So they can be excellent buys. You get the general flavour of the château, but in a less concentrated, less ripe mode.

Second wines have been around for years. Ch. Margaux produced its first Pavillon in 1908; Léoville-Las-Cases first labelled its junior wine Clos du Marquis in 1904; and the people at Brane-Cantenac swear they've been producing a second wine since the 18th century! In each case the objective was to concentrate the quality of the *grand vin* while not having to lose money by selling the less good vats off anonymously in bulk. But it was not until the 1980s, the decade when the quality of wine from Bordeaux soared, that second wines proliferated. There were more produced every year – and if having a second wine wasn't enough, some châteaux made a third or even a fourth wine.

During the 1990s things got a bit out of control. More and more properties had a second label, and thus a market to supply, but nature was not sympathetic. In 1991, '92, '93 and '94 the quality of the *grand vin* was pretty erratic, let alone the second wine, and although 1995, '96 and '98 all produced some excellent wines, these were vintages of variable quality. In 1997 and '99 you had to work really hard to get reasonable quality into your top wine, so it follows that whatever you shunted down into the second label was unlikely to be very inspiring. In poor vintages such as these second wines were best treated with caution unless from particularly careful producers or from châteaux that made no *grand vin* at all in that vintage. However, in the 21st century, we've seen a

Top second wines

The second wine phenomenon began in the Médoc but has spread to all Bordeaux. These are the most reliable and offer a chance to experience the style of the *grand vin* at a comparatively affordable price.

MÉDOC
- Alter Ego de Palmer (Ch. Palmer)
- Carruades de Lafite (Ch. Lafite)
- Clos du Marquis and Le Petit Lion (Ch. Léoville-Las-Cases)
- Dame de Montrose (Ch. Montrose)
- Duluc de Branaire Ducru (Ch. Branaire-Ducru)
- Echo de Lynch-Bages (Ch. Lynch-Bages)
- Les Fiefs de Lagrange (Ch. Lagrange)
- Les Forts de Latour (Ch. Latour)
- Hauts de Pontet Canet (Ch. Pontet Canet)
- Ch. Lacoste-Borie (Ch. Grand-Puy-Lacoste)
- Les Pagodes de Cos (Ch. Cos d'Estournel)
- Pavillon Rouge (Ch. Margaux)
- Les Pelerins de Lafon Rochet (Ch. Lafon-Rochet)

- Le Petit Mouton (Ch. Mouton Rothschild)
- Réserve de la Comtesse (Ch. Pichon-Longueville-Comtesse de Lalande)
- Réserve de Léoville-Barton (Ch. Léoville-Barton and Ch. Langoa-Barton)
- Le Sarget de Gruaud-Larose (Ch. Gruaud-Larose)
- Ségla (Ch. Rauzan-Ségla)
- Les Tourelles de Longueville (Ch. Pichon-Longueville)

PESSAC-LÉOGNAN
- La Chapelle de La Mission Haut-Brion (red; Ch. La Mission Haut-Brion)
- Le Clarence de Haut-Brion (from 2007) (red; Ch. Haut-Brion)
- Le Clémentin de Ch. Pape-Clément (red; Ch. Pape-Clément)
- L'Esprit de Chevalier (red and white; Domaine de Chevalier)
- Les Hauts de Smith (red and white; Ch. Smith-Haut-Lafitte)

- La Parde de Haut-Bailly (red; Haut-Bailly)

POMEROL
- Le Benjamin de Beauregard (Ch. Beauregard)
- Blason de L'Evangile (Ch. L'Evangile)
- Pensées de Lafleur (Ch. Lafleur)
- La Petite Église (Ch. L'Église-Clinet)

ST-ÉMILION
- Chapelle d'Ausone (Ch. Ausone)
- Clos Canon (Ch. Canon)
- La Grange Neuve de Figeac (Ch. Figeac)
- Le Petit Cheval (Ch. Cheval Blanc)

SAUTERNES
- Castelnau de Suduiraut (Ch. Suduiraut)
- Les Charmilles de La Tour Blanche (Ch. La Tour Blanche)
- Cyprès de Climens (Ch. Climens)
- Petit Guiraud (Ch. Guiraud)
- Les Remparts de Bastor (Ch. Bastor-Lamontagne)

significant warming in the late summer and autumn, and there's been a resurgence of quality among the second labels. Indeed, you may find some of the recent *grands vins* too intense and concentrated, too super-ripe. A lighter, more appetizing version of the château's style might actually be more immediately attractive. But they'll age too. Jean-Guillaume Prats of Cos d'Estournel reckons that his second wine (Les Pagodes de Cos) is now as good as his *grand vin* was 20 years ago – lovely to drink young, beautifully balanced for ageing, Cos in a pastel hue.

In the less well-known areas like the various Côtes appellations, some owners don't reckon their property name by itself can attract a high enough price. So they do the reverse of the prestigous châteaux and create a *cuvée prestige* – skimming off the cream of the crop and giving it film-star treatment in the cellar. The results are frequently very good, if rather oaky, since it is only the best fruit from the best vineyards that can really cope with loads of new oak. Although the *cuvées prestiges* point up the limitations of many properties – you find yourself saying 'is this the best you can do?' – there are splashes of brilliant soil matched by excellent climatic conditions all over Bordeaux, and this *cuvée prestige* movement is allowing them to shine.

A VIN DE PAYS FOR BORDEAUX

In nearly every French wine region you can find a *vin de pays* (country wine), or IGP as it is called from the 2010 vintage onwards, operating alongside the official *appellations contrôlées*, allowing producers to experiment with different grape varieties and to put the grape names on the label, or soaking up wines from patches of land that didn't receive an appellation. But Bordeaux has never taken to the idea. However, with a current glut of unsellable wines from its lesser regions the pressure to start using a flexible *vin de pays* has become unstoppable and a new Vin de Pays de l'Atlantique, which allows producers to blend in wines from some neighbouring regions outside the Gironde, came into existence with the 2006 vintage for red, white and rosé wines. It allows imaginative producers to make more modern, fruitier, softer wines that they can price competitively, but it hasn't exactly made waves.

The best idea might be to utilize the new 'Vin de France' category so that areas that could do with some lean austere Bordeaux red can blend it into something plumper and chunkier. Bordeaux, which would often benefit at the bottom end from blending with something ripe, should legally be able to do just that. But of course, it won't be called Bordeaux, so will it help the region, or just remove a bit of the anonymous glut?

Best cuvée prestige wines

Some prestige wines are clumsy and over-oaked but these are just right.

- Alios de Ste-Marie (Ch. Ste-Marie, Cadillac-Côtes de Bordeaux)
- Attribut des Tourtes (Ch. des Tourtes, Blaye)
- Ch. Cap St-Martin, Cuvée Prestige, Blaye-Côtes de Bordeaux
- Divinus (Ch. Bonnet, Bordeaux)
- Essence de Dourthe (Dourthe, Bordeaux)
- Fougas Maldoror (Ch. Fougas, Côtes de Bourg)
- Girolate (Ch. Tour de Mirambeau, Bordeaux)
- Ch. du Grand Barrail, Cuvée Prestige (Blaye-Côtes de Bordeaux)
- Les Gruppes (Ch. Charron, Blaye-Côtes de Bordeaux)
- Ch. Les Guyonnets, Cuvée Prestige (Cadillac-Côtes de Bordeaux)
- Ch. Lezongars, Special Cuvée (Cadillac-Côtes de Bordeaux)
- Poupille (Ch. Poupille, Castillon-Côtes de Bordeaux)
- Reignac (Ch. de Reignac, Bordeaux)
- Ch. Roland La Garde, Grand Vin (Blaye-Côtes de Bordeaux)
- Ch. La Rose Bellevue, Cuvée Prestige (Blaye)

Reignac

Ch. de Reignac is a beautiful property in a very unsung part of Bordeaux in the northern Entre-Deux-Mers. But the soil is good and the premium cuvée, Reignac, is outstanding.

I never tire of the thrill of visiting Bordeaux's châteaux and I keenly anticipate the moment the big door swings open, the cool air hits my face and as I gaze into the gloom I can pick out row upon row of barrels, bursting with young wine, slumbering, quietly forming the flavours that will mature in bottle, often for decades. But tasting is damned hard work. Stop laughing! It is. The wine's cold, bitter, acrid, thick and purple and angular. I've got to work out what it'll be like in 10 years' time. And often I'm there in February or March, so I'm frozen anyway. I'm not convincing you, am I?

THE BORDEAUX MARKET

Bordeaux is such a commercial place, it's strange how difficult it actually is to get hold of its best wines. You can't just drive around Pauillac or St-Julien or Pomerol or St-Émilion, stop at a top property and say, 'Hi, can I taste your wines?' You can do this in every other part of France, and only a few very *soignée* producers will refuse to answer the doorbell. In Burgundy or the Rhône, Alsace or the Loire, '*Dégustation – Vente Directe*' signs will be hung outside extremely smart properties and your ready money will be gratefully accepted if you want to buy.

But not in Bordeaux. You can count the number of top properties who might welcome you without a trade introduction on your fingers. Even then, after a tasting, if you said, 'Can I buy some?' they'd refer you back to your trade contact. It's a tightly controlled, mutually dependent mesh of proprietors, go-betweens and merchants called the Place de Bordeaux. All major trade goes through this selling system which makes sure everyone gets their cut and the price of the final product is reassuringly high.

And it is high. The good stuff. Generally higher than equivalent wines from the other parts of France or other parts of the world. And the top wines are not easy to buy. They don't populate the supermarket shelves – though in difficult times a lot will appear in French supermarkets' *foire aux vins* promotions. In the old days respectable merchants would keep stocks of Bordeaux going back 20 vintages. Few do nowadays, although the rise of the internet and of a class of international wine brokers means you can get mature stuff, but the market price will be severe. If you want to make sure of getting top Bordeaux wines, there's only one way to do it. Buy *en primeur* (see right).

There are areas of Bordeaux where it is easier to buy direct, but they are the less successful areas, the ones which can't force the issue on price. Côtes de Bourg, Blaye-Côtes de Bordeaux, Cadillac-Côtes de Bordeaux, Fronsac, Médoc, Graves. You'll find delightful wines in all these regions, and far friendlier properties if you want to visit, taste and buy. You'd expect that the vast tracts of the Entre-Deux-Mers and the thousands of properties who can only claim Bordeaux or Bordeaux Supérieur on their labels would be clamouring to gain your attention. But it's surprising how far you can sometimes drive through Entre-Deux-Mers vineyards without seeing a single château sign. The co-operatives are very strong here, and the prices of bulk wine are so low that many properties – smallholders would be a

better term – have had the stuffing knocked out of them, and their ambition along with it. You can certainly go to the vast industrial co-ops and buy local wine. You might be lucky. You might not be. You might merely be buying the stuff your local discount store is already offering for a rock-bottom price.

THE EN PRIMEUR SYSTEM

I warn you, you can very easily get hooked on buying Bordeaux *en primeur*. It makes you feel as though you're part of an inner circle, a bunch of well-informed – and well-heeled – wise guys who have achieved what we all secretly crave whenever we're in purchasing mode: getting in there before everyone else does. Getting a special price, a deal that lesser mortals aren't offered, and some 'nudge-nudge, wink-wink' advice about what is particularly good this vintage, what's at a particularly keen price. Frankly, once we get caught up in the feeding frenzy of *en primeur* buying for a sexy vintage – and the recent 2009 vintage was about as sexy as a vintage can get – we're fair game for anyone in a pinstripe suit who can get us on the end of a phone.

But I do enjoy it. Even after years in the wine world, even though in the early days a significant number of my *en primeur* purchases either

Nowadays during the *en primeur* week at the beginning of April, the leading châteaux really do don the glad rags to try to impress the leading members of the wine trade and press. If the vintage is good, they're going to make so much profit anyway, I suppose they might as well spend a bit of it schmoozing the merchants and opinion-formers. Ch. d'Yquem was all decked out in pink for the press night in 2006. And a good time was had by all.

Serena Sutcliffe MW has obviously got an enthusiastic buyer on the end of her phone line. She is head of Sotheby's Wine Auctions, and increasingly the top bidders are from the Far East, Russia and the USA.

were never seen or heard of again after my cheque was cashed, or the bottles that I did receive were not quite as thrilling as I'd expected, I really do get a buzz out of choosing and possessing a wine from the very first moments of its life all the way through to the final event when I pull a cork on a bottle that has always been mine and mine only.

Basically, you're buying 'futures' in wine, just as you might in the stock market. Although you are contracting for actual quantities of liquid all finished in bottles with labels and capsules, when you buy the wine it's still sitting around in a barrel. You may have bought it blind. If you're lucky you may have tasted a sample, and the sample may or may not be a reasonable indication of what the wine will taste like. But you won't see your wine until long after your cheque has been cleared. You have to trust a merchant to deliver it to you perhaps a year and a half after you paid for it.

There's a *primeur* season in the spring after each vintage which used to be a relatively gentlemanly affair of merchants, *courtiers* (sort of go-betweens) and château proprietors milling about, chatting, seeing what price the market would bear if you were a proprietor, seeing if you could pressure the price downwards if you were a merchant. Well nowadays, if the vintage is good, it's more like a bun-fight. Merchants and journalists from all over the world descend on Bordeaux to taste and pontificate, mark their star performers, haggle for the allocations they want. And to

Auctions

I used to haunt the sale rooms. Sometimes they would have pre-sale tastings of wines 50 years old or more. And if no one was on the ball, there were some stunning bargains. I once bought four cases of Ch. Pétrus 1964 for £3.75 (€4.96) a bottle. Well, the buyers at auctions are always on the ball these days, and if I wanted those wines now I would have to stump up almost £3000 ($4880/€3500) a bottle. So I don't go to the auction houses so much nowadays, but there are still bargains to be had when the market for a particular vintage is a bit flat and the wine, however good, isn't a sexy label. One advantage of auctions is that the lots are often of mature vintages that are ready to drink. And I still drool over the catalogues for the top sales – wines and vintages that are the stuff of legend.

If you want to buy wine at auction, go prepared and be aware of the pitfalls and hidden costs. First find out all you can about the producer and vintages described in the catalogue. This is important – some merchants take the opportunity to

clear inferior vintages at auction. Also, you have no guarantee that the wine has been well stored, and if it's faulty you have little chance of redress. As prices of the most sought-after wines have soared, so it has become profitable either to forge the bottles and their contents or to try to pass off stock that is clearly out of condition. But for expensive and mature wines, I have to say that the top auction houses nowadays make a considerable effort to check the provenance of the wines. And don't forget that there will usually be a commission, or buyer's premium, to pay, so check out the small print to calculate your bidding power. Online wine auctions are now popular and have similar pros and cons.

RECORD BREAKERS

While you or I might dip a toe in the auction world to pick up some good value wine that is ready to drink, the appearance of really special lots of wine at auction excites the same hysteria among super-rich collectors as an important work by Monet or Van Gogh, and in this heady atmosphere the final sale price can rocket way beyond the auctioneer's

expectations. In December 1985 Christie's, London sold a single bottle of Ch. Lafite from the 1787 vintage for an amazing £105,000 ($204,204/ €138,914). Not only was this bottle approaching its bicentennial but it had allegedly belonged to Thomas Jefferson, third president of the United States, who amassed a fabled cellar during a stint as ambassador to France. In February 2006 the megabucks came out for a bottle of Ch. d'Yquem, once again from the 1787 vintage, which went to a US-based collector for $100,000 (£51,419/ €68,027). In 2007 serious doubt was cast upon the veracity of many of these hoary old bottles. Since then Hong Kong has seen the highest prices paid.

The initials 'Th. J.' – for Thomas Jefferson – etched on this bottle helped it fetch a world-beating price at auction.

try to find out what the price will be. You mean you have to buy without knowing the price? What kind of crazy business is that? Prices do creep out, but no one wants to set their price before the supremo of taste – the American über-guru Robert Parker – and one supremely important magazine, the *Wine Spectator*, publish their scores out of 100 for the wine. Over 95, order the Ferrari. Over 90, confirm the chalet booking at St-Moritz. Less than 90, sack your consultant and enter therapy. Frankly, it's absurd and unhealthy that two arbiters of taste can be so powerful, but that's how it is just now. Things will change, of course. They always do.

In the old days you could be pretty sure that if you bought a good wine en primeur, at what they call the 'opening price', its price would continue to increase and you could then sell half of your stock some years later for twice the purchase price and in effect drink for free. Many universities, colleges, clubs and City of London institutions financed excellent cellars in this way. But the château proprietors are not daft. They've seen the prices of their wines rocket, and other people take the profit. A popular wine now is extremely unlikely to be underpriced at its opening, and its resale value may not budge for a decade, or it may even fall. Just to be sure, a property may release a first *tranche* (or slice) then if that's snapped up, they'll release a second, a third, at prices as high as the market will bear. And you, dear reader, will have to shrug your shoulders and pay up.

So should you buy *en primeur*? If you want the buzz, want to feel you're truly a 'serious' wine fan, and have something of a collectors' state of mind – yes. There are a few wines that no one in the world can replicate. These will cost vast sums even if you can get hold of them, but they will never be cheaper than *en primeur*. However, if you're not a 'label drinker', there are alternatives for most wines, both in Bordeaux and elsewhere, and even in overheated vintages like 2005 and '09, it's only the fashionable properties that can gouge on price. I tasted dozens of 2005s and '09s of no great reputation but superb quality – a good merchant will be offering you these wines. And this is where a big fat golden rule comes in. Only buy from a well-financed, well-established merchant. Fancy Dans always enter the market in 'hot' years. Some may deliver your wine, some will just bank your cash and disappear. As I said, *en primeur* is fun, exciting, but you do want to be sitting gazing at your own beautiful little stash of wine at the end of it all, so only shop with the guys who've done it all before. If you have a personal wine merchant, they'll mail or email you their en primeur offer. Otherwise pick up a copy of a magazine like *Wine Spectator*, *Decanter* or *Wine & Spirits*. From early summer onwards they advertise merchants' offers. But don't just go for the cheapest. Do business with a company you trust.

See that red symbol just above the label? That's the Chinese figure 8 – a lucky number in Chinese culture. Lafite is already the most popular and expensive wine in China – a new vineyard venture there, and the red ∧ on the bottle, will only make it even more popular – and expensive.

Creators of today's Bordeaux

It's no longer correct to see Bordeaux as an unchanging bastion of classical quality. There has never been so much genuine yet fruitful disagreement about what style of wine should be made and how. The possibilities of fine wine, whether in the great châteaux of Pauillac and Pomerol or in unsung but determined properties who believe in the potential quality of their little patch of land, even if no one has yet heard of it, have never been greater. Vineyard and winery technology have advanced so fast in the last 10 years that even the mightiest mover and shaker of them all – Michel Rolland – thinks that the next 10 years might be best employed in consolidation and evaluation. But with so many strong-willed personalities as owners, winemakers and consultants, I wouldn't expect the next decade to be that smooth a ride. And with the emergence of the Far East as a massive new market, complacency shouldn't be a feature. Yet this modern Bordeaux, so full of opportunity, is a relatively recent phenomenon. I am going to begin with four people whose influence has created, and is creating, today's Bordeaux.

I only met Émile Peynaud when he was getting on a bit – I'm not sure he hadn't already taken semi-retirement. But he tasted, he talked, he explained, and if asked, he criticized. I had no doubt I was privileged to know him, however late in his life.

ÉMILE PEYNAUD

If we're looking for the father of modern Bordeaux, I have no doubt that man is the late Professor Émile Peynaud who died in 2004 aged 92. He joined the Bordeaux Institute of Enology in 1946 and, alongside his friend Jean Ribéreau-Gayon, over the next 40 or so years laid the foundations of most of what we now take for granted. He used to say that great Bordeaux wines hadn't been made during the last 200 years, they had occurred. In fine vintages, a number of superb wines could occur because the grapes were ripe and healthy and had sufficient structure and richness not to be ruined by antediluvian practices in the cellar. But in lesser years few decent wines were made, sometimes none at all. Peynaud decided that by teaching, writing and consulting, he could do something about this. Above all he wanted to apply logic and science to the production of wine, thereby eliminating the haphazard – and he had another ambition: to communicate in a simple-to-understand, plausible way so that producers would do what he asked.

He began with the vineyard, lecturing growers on why rotten grapes must be discarded, or how to sample grapes and assess ripening rates of the different varieties and exhorting them to pick only when properly ripe. He also impressed on them the need to separate parcels of grapes with different flavours and ripeness levels from each other rather than ferment them all together. Moving to the winery, he beseeched proprietors to kick out their old wooden vats and barrels since they were full of bacteria and would turn the wines vinegary. Even the best wines before the 1950s usually had a distinct acetic twang to them. And they would also frequently seem to referment in the bottle. This was because no one understood the malolactic, or so-called 'second' – fermentation. Peynaud isolated the bacteria responsible and suddenly the benefits of malolactic fermentation – whereby a wine's raw malic acid is bacterially transformed into softer, creamy lactic acid – could be controlled. All red wines need to undergo malolactic – but in the tank or barrel please, not haphazardly in the bottle.

And during the 1970s, when a certain level of prosperity returned to Bordeaux, he instigated two more practices we now take for granted: the use of new oak barrels to age the wine, imparting a rich, spicy texture and flavour to the wine; and the ruthless selection of the best lots of wine for the top château label, condemning a significant percentage – during the large vintages of the 1980s, it could be as much as 50 per cent – to a second, cheaper label to maximize the concentration and richness of the top wine. This is all everyday stuff in the 21st century. Doesn't every top property do this? Sure they do. Aren't we all grateful? Well, during the 1970s and '80s there was a significant chorus of traditional critics who swore that Peynaud's wines all tasted the same and would never age. I tasted those '70s Peynaud wines as a student. They were thrilling. They didn't all taste the same, and they've aged superbly. One young pupil of Peynaud's was Michel Rolland. He's now as influential as Peynaud was then. And he suffers the same criticisms for his wines – which, by the way, are also thrilling, don't all taste the same and are aging superbly.

MICHEL ROLLAND

Michel Rolland is a delightful, jovial character, a self-confessed epicurean who likes to drink ripe, supple wines for the sheer joy of it, and who has made a very good career out of showing people how to make the kind of wines he enjoys. In fact, he's made such a good career out of it that he's now the most famous and most powerful wine consultant in the world, working on more than 100 different projects in

I think Michel Rolland is a smashing chap. And yet he seems to attract an inordinate amount of criticism. I'm sure jealousy is part of it – he is quite ridiculously successful, on a global scale; I sometimes think I meet him more often in airport lounges than on his home turf of Pomerol. But that home turf is very important. To him. And to our understanding of him. He is proudly unapologetic about making wines that he likes to drink – so, do people criticize him for that? – the answer is yes – and the wines he likes to drink are the lush, sybaritic mouthfuls of Pomerol where he was raised. Now, given that most of his consultancy work is either on the Right Bank, or in parts of the world where such ripeness, such lushness, such richness of fruit as Pomerol is blessed with are easily attainable, doesn't it make sense to keep hold of your roots rather than let them go? The wines Rolland makes around the world don't taste like Pomerol, but every time he enters a winery, he carries a little of the heavy clays of Pomerol with him on his boots.

Every time I see this photograph of Michel Rolland I think of James Bond. Michel Rolland would make a wonderful, plausible but ultra-powerful villain – and he does already rule the world of wine like no other consultant winemaker in history. But he's not evil. He is just very good at what he does – tapping into the desires of so many modern wine lovers, and delivering the style they crave to the highest standard he can achieve. He'd have James Bond reaching for his corkscrew, not his cocktail shaker.

16 different countries. Bordeaux dominates his work, but he's also heavily involved in Italy, California, Argentina, China and Chile, as well as such unlikely spots as Grover Vineyard in India. His influence is vast and he also makes the kind of wines that appeal to the American critic Robert Parker, whose opinion of a wine can make or break a property.

Yet all he is really doing is continuing and evolving the ideas of his own mentor Professor Peynaud, and in particular he is adapting them to suit the Right Bank styles that were less affected by Peynaud's work. He shows properties how important it is to harvest fully ripe grapes – but his view of what's ripe is a bit more extreme than Peynaud's – it can be, because control of disease in the vineyard and changes in climate make it so much easier nowadays to regularly ripen a crop, and his favoured Merlot variety can easily hit 14 per cent alcohol in modern day Bordeaux. He advocates reduced yields, just like Peynaud but more so. He is fanatical about selecting only the best berries for the top wine – and here he uses every device he can, from hand-picking berry by berry if necessary, into tiny plastic trays and then using sorting tables, gravitational carpets, goodness knows what, to make sure that only the best, ripest grapes get into that fermentation vat.

After this he sets up vinification plans for each winery that are concise and detailed about maceration, pump-overs, possible use of micro-oxygenation (actually he doesn't use this tannin-suppressing method as much as he is rumoured to, preferring to ensure he's got ripe tannins in the first place), amounts of new oak, division of the vinification into separate parcels. Well, this, too, is merely an extension of Peynaud's work. It's just that he's taken it further, since Bordeaux is now a much wealthier place, able to push the envelope of quality more and more at whatever cost. What is genuinely new is his espousal of fermentation in small wooden barrels rather than vats. And if I had to say whether he is a winery whizzkid or a vineyard fanatic? I'd say he's a vineyard man, the heavy clays of Pomerol where he was raised clinging to his shoes even today. 'I am a man of the soil' he says, and I believe him. I've spent days trudging the fields of Pomerol and St-Émilion with him and he's never seemed happier, though I have to say it was absolutely fascinating tasting wine with him too. In the late 1980s, Rolland was pioneering the long macerations now commonplace in Bordeaux and it was very clear to me this guy was going to revolutionize the way wine tasted and felt in Bordeaux. But get him into the winery and the tasting room and another side to his talent flicks into place. Organisational skill, a phenomenal memory for flavour and character in the numerous samples of wine he has to taste every day, and a brilliant ability to know which parcel, which barrels will blend best together to create a lush, hedonistic wine, which will garner critical acclaim and leave one more very happy proprietor waving him goodbye as he disappears down the château drive on the way to his next appointment.

DENIS DUBOURDIEU

Denis Dubourdieu is the best sort of professor. You hardly have to ask him the questions you've prepared because he's got so much to say about so many interesting things, and if you come away from meetings with him and realize you only broached half the subjects you intended to – so what? – you've gained a precious insight into numerous other matters that you'd never even considered. And he does have a lot to say about both the good and the bad in Bordeaux, much of which is hard-headed common sense that doesn't sit easily with current fads. He believes that the current wave of over-ripe, over-selected, over-oaked Merlot-based reds – however high the wine critics mark them – are poor wines, harming the typicity of Bordeaux – and, incidentally, that they're exhausting to drink. Micro-oxygenation is a very trendy method of making supple, round red wines. But he casts an academic's eye on it. 'The risk of too much oxygen is greater than the risk of too little.' If you've done your vineyard work properly you shouldn't have to soften the wine's tannins excessively. And if you do, you risk all the wines starting to taste the same – and that would be the death of Bordeaux's unique quality, the ability of thousands of different estates to make wines that taste of their terroir, not of a winemaking textbook.

If this makes Dubourdieu sound reactionary, he isn't at all. He's one of Bordeaux's greatest innovators, but he innovates on the back of hard scientific facts and shrewd commonsense from his work in the vineyards. He is talked of as the father of modern white winemaking in Bordeaux, as the man who persuaded uncertain proprietors of the absolute necessity of cool fermentation temperatures and clean fermentation vessels for their whites; as the man who showed how skin

The fact that I've got my hand flat and Denis Dubourdieu has his in pyramid shape might imply that once again I've missed the point. Ah well, with Denis Dubourdieu there'll be another one along in a minute. Dubourdieu is an influential academic but his work is rooted in his passion for the soil. When I last went to visit him, my objective was to talk about the intricacies of winemaking, but we spent most of the day clambering up and down the vineyards of the Cadillac-Côtes de Bordeaux around Ch. Reynon.

contact, carefully done, could open up a whole array of flavours, especially in Sauvignon Blanc, that Bordeaux had up until then missed; as the man who championed barrel fermentation and did all the science so that the brilliant creamy richness created by lees contact and stirring (*bâtonnage*) was fully understood, and not spoilt by bacterial contamination. He makes fine dry whites and reds at two properties of his own in Cadillac-Côtes de Bordeaux and the Graves, as well as excellent sweet Barsac at two other family estates, and consults for numerous properties and merchant companies both in Bordeaux and abroad in Spain and Italy. But now he has found himself in increasing demand as a red wine consultant – Haut-Bailly and Cheval Blanc are two of his clients – and he is clearly delighted at this challenge, though he won't forego his white wine credentials. Finesse is what he seeks in reds. That used to be a given in Bordeaux's top reds, in the days before the blockbusters that dominate many Bordeaux tastings at present. How encouraging that someone as respected and influential as Dubourdieu has decided that finesse needs to return to centre stage.

Comte Stephan von Neipperg (right) is a good judge of people. He believed in Stéphane Derenoncourt – a totally untried wine consultant – when no one else did. Since their relationship began, the quality of von Neipperg's wines has rocketed and Derenoncourt has become possibly Bordeaux's most influential consultant behind Michel Rolland. Rolland and Derenoncourt both have strong personalities but they don't necessarily agree on how best to maximize the quality in their clients' wines. That's good. The more thinkers and innovators that Bordeaux can produce, the better. Healthy disagreement is good for everyone.

STÉPHANE DERENONCOURT

If Denis Dubourdieu is the consummate academic, albeit one who loves to get his hands and boots dirty, Stéphane Derenoncourt has nothing of the academic about him. The philospher, yes. The thinker, yes. The doer, most certainly. But don't ask him where he trained. He didn't. He's a 'university of life' graduate cum laude who only came to Bordeaux because he was keen on a girl and initially just worked part-time among the vines to pay for his far greater interest in playing the blues. This sense of rebellion wasn't harmed when he got a job in a Fronsac vineyard that happened to be one of the only biodynamic estates in Bordeaux. He also met the man with the most infectious enthusiasm in the world of Bordeaux wine, Michel Rolland, and finally he caught the wine bug and, without a diploma to his name, began to get work as a consultant.

Stephan von Neipperg at Ch. Canon-la-Gaffelière was already one of my favourite people in Bordeaux, but he augmented his place in my affections when I realized that he took on Derenoncourt as a consultant because he liked him and believed in his avant garde ideas regardless of his lack of qualifications. Avant garde? As von Neipperg says, it's allowed him to go back to making wine the way his grandfather would have done it. And this is the genius that Derenoncourt dispenses. It's as though he listens to the soil and what it tells him and his vineyard work is famously concerned with reduction of chemicals and mechanical interventions, and an attitude that coaxes and cajoles the very best out of the land and into the wine's personality. His connection with Burgundy's most passionate advocate of 'green' grape-growing, Claude Bourguignon, only strengthens his reputation as the 'back to the future' expert. His work in the winery is equally impressive and his advocacy of keeping wine on its lees during barrel ageing and employing micro-oxygenation to soften the tannins has endeared him to proprietors who want their wines to show well as soon as the critics arrive in the spring following the vintage. But this is no formulaic wine consultant. Just taste the range of wines he makes with Stephan von Neipperg and you'll see individuality of terroir shining out of every one.

NEW ARISTOCRACY

Is there a new aristocracy in Bordeaux, a new band of château owners lording it over the rest of Bordeaux and over us? To a large extent, yes. But there have been 'new aristocracies' in Bordeaux's wine world for hundreds of years. As society changes, parts of it crumble and fade away, other parts take their place. It's human nature. The new class of parliamentarians and lawyers who began to dominate Bordeaux's commercial and political life in the 17th and 18th centuries didn't find it difficult to buy out most of the old families and install themselves as the grandees. The French Revolution in 1789 put a stop to that with exile and the guillotine, but during the 19th century the whole thing started again as the newly powerful merchants and bankers bought up properties. They were joined by wine brokers and shippers as and when they prospered.

In the 20th century, the ownership of a wine property lost much of its lustre, and châteaux went through decades when they made no money at all. The old families clung on if they could. But one by one they fell. Latour in 1962, Margaux in 1977, and many lesser ones too, often for very little money. A new pattern of ownership began to emerge because from the 1980s onwards it was possible to make a consistent profit from a top Bordeaux property, and by the 21st century you could make a very serious amount of money every good year, as enthusiastic and wealthy markets like the US consolidated and newly wealthy markets like China, India and the Far East piled in. The wealthy took note. And two groups in particular began to circle thirstily. Firstly wealthy individuals, people who had made a fortune in a different business and decided to invest in a smart

Gérard Perse is probably the most controversial character in Bordeaux today. He has a lot of money, he's bought a lot of properties – in particular, the great St-Émilion First Growth, Ch. Pavie and its excellent neighbour, Pavie-Decesse – and he's then proceeded to make wines of a richness, an overripeness, an almost offensive concentration of flavour, that has divided the wine world down the middle as if sliced by a scimitar. Good. Great. Someone doing what they believe in. Many critics of Perse stand on the sidelines carping, but he's the one who's laid his money on the line, he's the one who's said he likes these rich, brash styles, so that's what he'll make, but also he's the one making a difference, offering a new perspective on what Bordeaux might be. We don't have to like it. But we should respect the guy for doing it.

The Médoc doesn't have many public faces – so many of the châteaux are owned by companies rather than people – but Mme May-Eliane de Lencquesaing, of Ch. Pichon-Longueville-Comtesse de Lalande, is one of them; or rather she was, as in 2006 she reluctantly sold Pichon-Lalande to Champagne Roederer. She was the driving force behind the Super-Second movement whereby a small number of predominantly Second Growth châteaux decided to chase the First Growths, both in quality and price, and she has toured the world since the 1980s preaching the gospel. Without doubt the Super-Second châteaux massively improved the quality of their wines and this encouraged many others to make more effort. But they also transformed the pricing levels so that there are now few bargains to be had. Mme de Lencquesaing has now left Pauillac, but she hasn't slowed down. As well as having an apartment in Bordeaux, she is enthusiastically running and promoting her property, Glenelly Estate, in South Africa.

Bordeaux wine château. Partly it was the lifestyle, but also there were big tax advantages. If you sold a business and reinvested in another business which you then ran, you could keep your hands on most of your wealth. That was very attractive to people like the Mentzelopoulos family at Ch. Margaux, the Cathiards at Smith-Haut-Lafitte, Gérard Perse at Ch. Pavie or Bernard Magrez at Ch. Pape-Clément, and not only have they presumably appreciated the exalted social position they have found themselves in, but they have all – and many others like them – put enormous amounts of effort and money into the properties, to the benefit of the whole region.

The second acquisitive group has been the big corporations. Perhaps the most notorious is LVMH (Louis Vuitton-Moët-Hennessy), the luxury goods group that makes more money out of luggage and perfume than wine, and which in 1999 managed to take over Ch. d'Yquem from Comte Alexandre de Lur-Saluces whose family had been in charge at Yquem since 1593. Chanel owns Canon and Rauzan-Ségla, and in 2006 Champagne Roederer bought Pichon-Lalande. AXA is a big insurance group now of enormous importance as owners of top châteaux including Pichon-Baron and Suduiraut. Numerous other insurance companies have leapt in. I'll give you a few initials – SMABPT, GMF, MIAF – OK, don't ask me, but they all own good châteaux. Are these purchases made for prestige alone or can they make money? It's hard to tell. What is clear is that, unlike the transactions of the 1960s and '70s, they have usually paid an exceedingly high price for the properties, and one wonders if they'd always looked closely enough at the books beforehand. But having paid the price, they generally sanction enormous investments – which means the wine prices have to rise – which means people demand even greater quality. But how much more quality can an already excellent wine achieve? More concentration, more weight, more alcohol? Eventually the whole performance becomes a bizarre beauty and brawn contest rather than being related to the production of a highly enjoyable albeit impressive drink.

The châteaux have become vulnerable to takeover partly because of France's Napoleonic inheritance laws, which were designed specifically to prevent the rise of a new all-powerful, immovable aristocracy. There is no primogeniture in France. All children inherit equally, and when this leads to bickering and disagreement, selling the château is often the only way to resolve matters. Of the Bordeaux châteaux classified in 1855, only two – Mouton-Rothschild and Léoville-Barton – are still in the same family hands.

However, the modernizers are aware of the problem. Jean-Michel Cazes of Ch. Lynch-Bages is developing tourist attractions around Pauillac. Ch. d'Arsac in Margaux opened a New World-style visitor centre, La Winery, in 2007. But there's still a long way to go if these parts of Bordeaux are to do more than make their visitors feel like mere underlings gazing from a distance at the domaines of the mighty. Nonetheless, the regional authorities want visitors to come and are making greater efforts to welcome and advise them, to upgrade facilities and to provide a fuller range of attractions. It'll be a long haul, but if you use the official channels and make appointments in advance you should find a welcoming reception. The Office de Tourisme de Bordeaux and regional offices in, for instance, St-Émilion and Pauillac, are useful for information, documentation and planning visits (see addresses on page 230). Find out the dates of the 'Portes Ouvertes' weekends in each appellation when châteaux are open without prior rendezvous. If you're brave, contact the châteaux direct. Some, like Mouton-Rothschild in Pauillac and Giscours in Margaux, have their own wine museums, others such as d'Arche in Sauternes and Loudenne in the Médoc provide comfortable *chambres d'hôtes* accommodation right out in the vineyards.

This rather forbidding scene-setting for what you had hoped would be a relaxing, spontaneous few days visiting and tasting only applies to the world-famous areas. If you are in the areas of less renown – the Graves, the Entre-Deux-Mers, the different Côtes regions on the fringes of St-Émilion and Pomerol – you'll find it much more relaxing and, so long as there's someone at home and not too busy in the fields, you should get a friendly welcome and a chance to visit and taste.

Of course you don't have to make a completely wine-related visit to the area. The city of Bordeaux is one of France's great cities with thrilling civic buildings, street after street of noble architecture and a really atmospheric old town. Newly renovated buildings, a new tram system and a cleaned-up waterfront have transformed the city into one of France's most uplifting urban experiences. And the city has all those things you might have found lacking in the countryside – great shops of every sort, great markets and some fantastic restaurants, from bistro to Michelin-starred. The Atlantic seaboard offers the splendours of the Bay of Arcachon, Cap Ferret and the highest sand dunes in Europe, epitomized by the Dune du Pilat. While for the more sporting-minded there's seriously good golf, some of the best surfing in Europe along the vast sand beach that stretches from the top of the Médoc right down to Spain – even I caught my first wave here – and if you've really been working out, the Marathon du Médoc every September. This is my kind of marathon – there are so many red wine sampling stations en route, you should be past caring by the time you're half-way.

Regional specialities

Foie gras mi-cuit au sel Duck or goose liver cooked in a terrine and served cold in slices with warm toast and, traditionally, a glass of Sauternes.

Assiette de grenier médocain Cooked pork belly, rolled, sliced and served, usually with a garnish of aspic.

Huitres à la bordelaise Fresh oysters from the Bassin d'Arcachon on the Atlantic coast, served with grilled flat, round sausages (known as *crépinettes*) and generously buttered bread or toast.

Cèpes frais persillade Cèpe mushrooms sautéed with garlic and parsley. This can be served as a first course, but there are many recipes for *cèpes* as they are very popular in Bordeaux and are often used to garnish meat and game and in omelettes.

Alose grillée Shad marinated in oil, onions and bayleaf, then grilled.

Lamproie à la bordelaise Lampreys from the Gironde marinated and cooked in red wine with onions, shallots, leeks, garlic, oil, bacon, herbs and Cognac. Ideally, you should drink the same wine as used for the sauce.

Rognons de veau à la bordelaise Lightly fried veal kidneys served in a *bordelaise* sauce made of local red wine, meat stock, marrow and shallots.

Agneau de Pauillac rôti aux gousses d'ail confites Roasted milk-fed lamb accompanied by cloves of garlic cooked in the meat juices.

Entrecôte à la bordelaise Sirloin steak traditionally grilled over *sarments* (vine cuttings) and garnished with diced shallots.

Aiguillettes de canard aux navets Sautéed strips of duck breast served with turnips.

Bécasse au foie gras Woodcock roasted or flambéed with Armagnac served on toast spread with puréed foie gras.

Pintade vigneronne Roasted guinea-fowl cooked with a bacon, shallots, bread and grape stuffing and served with grapes baked alongside.

Poulet bordelais Chicken pieces sautéed with parsley, shallots and crushed garlic.

Pruneaux au vin de Bordeaux Prunes (*pruneaux d'Agen*), marinated for a couple of weeks in Sauternes and Armagnac.

Soupe de cerise au vin de Bordeaux Cherries poached in a sugar and water syrup, then cooked in local red wine. Served slightly chilled.

Fanchonnets Almond millefeuille and meringue pastries.

Cannelés girondins Mini cone-shaped cakes flavoured with rum.

Tucking into cabbage stuffed with foie gras at one of Bordeaux's numerous bistros. The city of Bordeaux is one of France's gastronomic Meccas with an ever-widening range of restaurants, bistros and cafés.

REGIONAL FOOD

Bordeaux doesn't have such a flashy, inventive cuisine as many parts of France, and it's not always easy to get satisfying regional cooking in the villages and smaller towns of the vineyard areas, in particular. The great Médoc wine region could do with more good local restaurants, although things have improved during the last decade. But if you look at some typical regional dishes, you'll see that raw materials are not wanting. Try these for size – large succulent slabs of entrecôte, Pauillac lamb, duck, *cèpes*, foie gras, Arcachon oysters and shad and lampreys from the Gironde. Add to this red or white wine sauces with marrow and shallots (*à la bordelaise*) and a little Spanish and Mediterranean influence, with the liberal use of garlic, onions and herbs, and you've only yourself to blame if you don't eat well.

SEASONAL FARE

The Atlantic Ocean, Gironde estuary and local rivers have long provided a healthy supply of crustaceans, shellfish and sea and river fish. Oysters from the Bassin d'Arcachon, *lamproies* (lampreys) and sturgeon from the Gironde, *alose* (shad) in the spring and *chevrettes* (small shrimps) are just a few of the local specialities. Beef is a staple, most usually found in restaurants as *côte de boeuf*, *entrecôte*, tournedos and veal. Beef from Bazas in the south-east of the Gironde is particularly tasty. Tender Pauillac lamb is milk-fed and raised on the salt-grass pastures of the Médoc; it really is worth tucking into, simply roasted and slightly pink. Poultry (duck, chicken and guinea-fowl) and foie gras are also traditional to Bordeaux, with the source more than likely from within the nearby *départements* of the Dordogne, Gers or Landes.

When the hunting season opens in September game dishes abound, in particular rabbit, hare, wild duck, wood pigeon and the rarer *bécasse* (woodcock). Also available in the autumn is a variety of mushrooms, in particular *cèpes*, big fat meaty mushrooms picked in the forests and sold on roadside stalls. Asparagus from Blaye is another seasonal delicacy. Those with a sweet tooth can indulge in delicious St-Émilion macaroons or the rummy *cannelés* from Bordeaux. A *St-Émilion au chocolat* is a chocolate charlotte made with these macaroons, and exceedingly good it is.

There is a wealth of local food markets selling a variety of regional produce. The Monday market at Castillon-la-Bataille is one of the largest, and in the southern limits of the Entre-Deux-Mers the Saturday market at La Réole on the banks of the Garonne attracts a healthy selection of small, local producers. Picnics are very easy to cater for with local markets and shops providing all the necessary elements. Fillings for freshly baked baguettes – pork, chicken, duck and goose pâtés or *rillettes* – are often produced locally. Cured ham (*jambon de Bayonne*) is also

Where to dine while touring the vineyards

MÉDOC

- **Café Lavinal**
  Place Desquest–Bages, 33250 Pauillac
  Tel 05 57 75 00 09
  hugonaon@bordeauxsaveurs.com
  Café with bistro-style restaurant owned by the Cazes wine dynasty. Great value menu allows you to splash out on wine. Stop in at the bakery opposite, Au Baba d'Andréa, before leaving.

- **Hôtel/Restaurant Château Cordeillan-Bages**
  Route des Châteaux, 33250 Pauillac
  Tel 05 56 59 24 24
  www.cordeillanbages.com
  Less experimental and more classic under chef Jean-Luc Rocha who replaced Thierry Marx in 2010. But still a Michelin 2-star experience. Comprehensive wine list. Top Relais & Châteaux hotel. Also offers wine courses (see the École du Bordeaux, page 91).

- **Restaurant Le Lion d'Or**
  33460 Arcins-en-Médoc
  Tel 05 56 58 96 79
  Country-style seasonal cooking carried out with real flair. Unusually for France, you can bring your own bottle of wine. You'll probably find yourself sitting next to a local winemaker.

- **Restaurant Le St-Julien**
  Place St-Julien, 33250 St-Julien-Beychevelle
  Tel 05 56 59 63 87
  www.le-saint-julien.fr
  This classy restaurant is another regular haunt for local wine growers. My last visit there was with Daniel Llose of Ch. Pichon-Longueville and we had a smashing meal even though, oddly, it was Valentine's night!

GRAVES AND PESSAC-LÉOGNAN

- **Hotel/Restaurant Claude Darroze**
  95 cours Général Leclerc, 33210 Langon
  Tel 05 56 63 00 48 www.darroze.com
  Serious, upscale restaurant, with 16 rooms. Well executed, classic, 1-star Michelin cuisine. Substantial wine list. Alfresco dining in the summer.

- **Le Table de Montesquieu**
  Place St-Jean d'Étampes, 33650 La Brède
  Tel 05 56 78 52 91
  www.latabledemontesquieu.fr
  Creative, Michelin 1-star cuisine. Produce from the owner's farm. Extensive wine list.

- **Les Sources de Caudalie**
  Chemin de Smith-Haut-Lafitte, 33650 Martillac
  Tel 05 57 83 83 83
  www.sources-caudalie.com
  Luxurious hotel-spa complex in the Pessac-Léognan vineyards at Martillac (see page 90). Offers two fine restaurants: the gastronomique La Grand' Vigne and diet-conscious, informal La Table du Lavoir. Extensive wine list at both. Combine a meal with a visit to Ch. Smith-Haut-Lafitte's winery.

RIGHT BANK

- **L'Envers du Décor**
  Rue du Clocher, 33330 St-Émilion
  Tel 05 57 74 48 31
  French equivalent of the gastro pub, at the top end of town. More than competent cuisine. Wide-ranging wine list. Alfresco dining in the summer.

- **L'Essentiel**
  6 Rue Guadet, 33330 St-Émilion
  Tel 05 57 24 39 76
  Seriously cool Deco wine bar and shop owned by Jean-Luc Thunevin of Ch. Valandraud, where bottles are laid out in a dazzling display (see page 194). Top end wines – in high season you'll even find First Growths by the glass.

- **Hostellerie de Plaisance**
  Place du Clocher, 33330 St-Émilion
  Tel 05 57 55 07 55
  www.hostellerie-plaisance.com
  Luxurious Relais & Châteaux hotel-restaurant now owned by Gérard Perse of Ch. Pavie and Monbousquet fame. Inventive cuisine with a strong South-West influence. Extensive list of top St-Émilion wines but few bargains. Great views over the historic town.

- **Logis de la Cadene**
  3 Place du marché au Bois, 33330 St-Émilion
  Tel 05 57 24 71 40 www.logisdelacadene.com
  Family-owned restaurant dating from 1848 in the heart of the old town. Specialises in meats cooked over vine cuttings.

CÔTES AND ENTRE-DEUX-MERS

- **Auberge de L'Ancienne Poste**
  Place Cazeaux-Cazalet, 33410 Rions
  Tel 05 56 27 43 31
  In the charming medieval town of Rions. *Côte de boeuf* grilled over an open fire is a speciality so book a a table in the 'Cheminée' or fireplace room. Alfresco dining in the summer.

- **Comptoir de Genès**
  4 La Croix, 33350 St Genès de Castillon
  Tel 05 57 47 90 03
  Easy-going bistro-style restaurant with a more than comprehensive range of wines from Castillon at unbeatable prices!

- **Restaurant Chez Sylvie**
  33350 Pujols. Tel 05 57 40 50 10
  Simple but delicious country fare and terrific value. Winemakers' hang-out – Monsieur is a *vigneron* providing superior house wine, while Maman does the cooking.

- **Restaurant La Poudette**
  33350 Pujols. Tel 05 57 40 71 52
  Good value fare in a farmhouse setting not far from Castillon-la-Bataille. Well executed dishes. Wine list influenced by winemaking guru Stéphane Derenoncourt.

- **Le St-James**
  3 place Camille Hostein, 33270 Bouliac
  Tel 05 57 97 06 00
  www.saintjames-bouliac.com
  Gourmet restaurant with 2 Michelin stars in the hills overlooking the city of Bordeaux. Contemporary cuisine with regional flavour. Extensive wine list. Also under the same managment are the more casual brasserie Côte Cour, and for hearty meat dishes Le Café de L'Espérance a few steps down the road.

- **Restaurant au Sarment**
  50 rue de La Lande, 33240 St-Gervais
  Tel 05 57 43 44 73
  Just outside Bourg on the road to Bordeaux. Stylish décor with imaginative cooking. Good selection of local wines. Outdoor tables. The Bourg and Blaye wine officials eat here.

SWEET WHITES

- **Restaurant Les Feuilles d'Acanthe**
  5 rue de L'Église, 33490 St-Macaire
  Tel 05 56 62 33 75
  www.feuilles-dacanthe.fr
  Serious, welcoming bistro (and modern rooms) in attractive fortified medieval town just outside Langon.

- **Restaurant Le Saprien**
  14 rue Principle, 33210 Sauternes
  Tel 05 56 76 60 87
  Good selection of Sauternes by the glass. Located in the village overlooking the vineyards.

If you're in Bordeaux you should pop down to the Marché des Capucins market in a slightly rough part of the old town near to the Gare St-Jean. The cheeses, especially, are outstanding.

much in evidence. Marmande tomatoes from neighbouring Lot-et-Garonne arrive in August and September, as do apples, pears and plums grown in the Entre-Deux-Mers.

EATING OUT

The region has a good range of restaurants, although the widest choice is in the city itself. The town of St-Émilion with its ancient streets is also a lively base for the visitor with a huge choice at all levels – however, you need to choose carefully to avoid the tourist traps. Country inns offer simple local dishes or *cuisine ménagère* at reasonable prices and you may find yourself sitting next to a local *vigneron*. Next step up are the restaurants producing regional fare and more elaborate dishes or *cuisine bourgeoise*. Finally, there is the more sophisticated cuisine of the Michelin-starred establishments (there are 14 in the Bordeaux region). All have interesting fixed-price menus, especially at lunchtime.

CLASSIC FOOD AND WINE COMBINATIONS

Bordeaux covers a whole palette of wine styles (dry, fruity or complex whites; sweet whites; rosés; supple or rich, elegant reds; sparkling wines) so whatever the dish, there should be a wine to match. They are in essence food wines. The classic red Bordeaux that has a tannic edge is the perfect foil for the local rich cuisine. If you are having food cooked with wine, you should ideally drink the same style of wine or a superior version with the meal.

Duck or goose liver is traditionally served with a glass of sweet white from Sauternes, Loupiac or Ste-Croix-du-Mont (as is Roquefort cheese) – a combination that may sound unlikely until tried. The local oysters and other shellfish go perfectly with crisp white Graves or Entre-Deux-Mers, as young and fresh as possible. Meat dishes demand more substantial wines and roast lamb and beef will almost certainly be excellent with whatever is the local red: Left Bank, Right Bank, the Côtes, it doesn't matter. But to be more specific, a Pauillac or St-Julien Classed Growth is the classic partner for roast lamb. The choice for beef is open-ended, just make sure you choose a full and rich wine. *Entrecôte à la bordelaise* works very well with a Médoc or red Graves. And try *filet de boeuf* with a Fronsac, but really any Bordeaux red will do. Game cries out for the richer reds of the region, preferably with some bottle age for a dish with a pronounced flavour. This is where St-Émilion, Pomerol and Castillon-Côtes de Bordeaux come into their own.

Fruit-based desserts are delicious with the lighter sweet wines such as Loupiac and Ste-Croix-du-Mont, though anything rich may demand the richer wines of Sauternes or Barsac, or why not just order the Sauternes and forget the dessert.

TOURING THE BORDEAUX REGION

The vines come to life in late April to early May and from then through to the end of the harvest in October is a good time to visit. Be warned, however, that most producers take their holidays in August and do not necessarily welcome visitors during the harvest months of September and October. Accommodation in wine country is limited, with the city of Bordeaux often providing a necessary base from which to make your trips.

Essential to touring in Bordeaux are good road maps and a certain amount of organization. The big Michelin yellow road map of France is one of my favourite books for dipping in and out of all year round whether I'm in France or not – I feel as though I'm half-way there just looking at the maps. It's a bit bulky but it's the best all-purpose map you can get. When I'm on research trips my favourite maps are the small-scale 1:25,000 Série Bleue maps published by the Institut Géographique National. They give every contour, every dip and twist in the hillsides, in the kind of precise detail that that allows you to pinpoint exactly where a vineyard is, however small, and exactly how steep a slope is, how sharp a bend in the road, how flat and reedy a riverbank. The Série Verte is 1:100,000 and also very good. The roads are all well maintained, but distances can be deceptive and signposting vague. I love to get out onto the country roads, but occasionally it may be necessary to cross the town of Libourne or circumnavigate Bordeaux city itself, perhaps using the busy ring road, the Rocade.

The D2 'Route des Châteaux' winds past the major châteaux of the Médoc and is an absolute must for wine-lovers. It starts out pretty drably just north of Bordeaux and you won't be excited by the industrial estates and drear suburbs, but just by Ludon you'll see your first famous château – La Lagune – on the right of the road and from there on you're in for a real treat up through Margaux, St-Julien, Pauillac and St-Estèphe with châteaux and vineyards on both sides of the road. The D2 continues north after St-Estèphe into the Bas Médoc – a calm, broad, marshy backwater of reeds and meadows, wide blue skies and a few vineyards that is an absolute delight to linger in if you need to de-stress. The best road to take if you want to see the Graves, Barsac and Sauternes is the old N113, rather than the autoroute, and make diversions if you want to see Léognan and Sauternes itself. You can even pop over the Garonne to Cadillac if you want and have a look at the vineyards there and get great views back across to Graves, Barsac and Sauternes.

Pomerol is a bit of a non-starter when it comes to scenery, but it's packed with world-famous vines. You won't find a village of Pomerol, so get yourself out of Libourne on the D244 to Catusseau and then, basically, just wander about, but do take the D121 because that'll let you drive past the tiny but stupendous and terribly famous Ch. Pétrus. If you take the D243 from Libourne, that'll take you to the town of St-Émilion through lots of vineyards great and small. You can avoid the town if you

There's more to shopping in St-Émilion than fancy wine shops. This guy sells everything you could possibly want for tending your own vineyard, including an array of lethal-looking hoeing tools. By the way, there's no shop opposite – he just can't bear the idea of you passing by without popping in for a look around.

Ch. d'Arche in the Sauternes region is just one of many lovely places to stay out in the vineyards.

like and keep on the D243 all the way through to St-Genès-de-Castillon, and this will give you a good idea of the plateau vineyards of St-Émilion, as well as taking you past the site of the great *garagiste* Ch. Valandraud just before you get to St-Genès. But what I'd do is drive down the hill through the town of St-Émilion, seeing how tight-packed and small-scale everything seems – especially the beautiful but tiny Ch. Ausone on its limestone escarpment to the right just below the town. Then I'd take a sharp turn left on the D245 – a little road that goes past Ch. Pavie and then hugs the bottom of the famous limestone slopes – the *côtes* – all the the way to St-Étienne-de-Lisse where you can turn left, up the steep *côtes* past the impressive Ch. de Pressac and join the D243 to take you back along the plateau to St-Émilion.

Best châteaux to visit for whole visitor experience

MÉDOC

- **Château Lanessan**
  33460 Cussac-Fort-Médoc. www.bouteiller.com
  Themed visits with a variety of tasting options (vertical of old wines, blending, etc). For horse lovers the Musée du Cheval.

- **Château Lynch-Bages**
  33250 Pauillac. www.lynchbages.com
  Vat to bottling-line visit, former 19th-century cellars kept as a museum piece, contemporary art exhibition, tasting. Dining at nearby Café Lavinal.

- **Château Mouton-Rothschild**
  33250 Pauillac. www.bpdr.com
  Film presentation, wine museum and cellars provide a rounded tour. The tasting is an optional paying extra.

- **Château Pontet-Canet**
  33250 Pauillac. www.pontet-canet.com
  Visit the vineyard in an electric car and compare the 19th-century wooden vat-room to the contemporary version. Tasting as well. All by appointment.

- **Château Prieuré-Lichine**
  33460 Cantenac. Tel 05 57 88 36 28
  Themed visits (by appointment): for example, classic (vinification and tasting), history, taste (food and wine) or terroir. Lunch and dinner can be arranged.

- **La Winery de Philippe Raoux (Château d'Arsac)**
  33460 Arsac. www.lawinery.fr
  New World-style visitor centre opened in 2007 with wine shop and restaurant. Offers tastings, concerts and art exhibitions.

GRAVES AND PESSAC-LÉOGNAN

- **Château Smith-Haut-Lafitte**
  33650 Martillac. www.smith-haut-lafitte.com
  Renovated 14th-century estate with the latest technology, impressive 2000-barrel cellars, own cooperage. Stroll to adjacent Sources de Caudalie spa-hotel complex (see page 85) for *après-visite* refreshment and dining.

- **Château de Chantegrive**
  33720 Podensac. www.chantegrive.com
  Modern cellars. Tasting of red and dry white Graves as well as sweet Cérons.

RIGHT BANK

- **Château La Croix de Gay**
  33500 Pomerol. Tel 05 57 51 19 05
  One of the few Pomerol châteaux open to visitors by appointment. Tasting as well as wines for sale.

- **Château de La Dauphine**
  33126 Fronsac. www.chateau-dauphine.com
  Renovated beautiful 18th-century château with state-of-the-art winery.

- **Château Faugères**
  33330 St-Émilion. Tel 05 57 40 34 99
  www.chateau-faugeres.com
  Cutting-edge winery designed by internationally renowned architect. Consistent St-Émilion Grand Cru. By appointment.

- **Château Figeac**
  33330 St-Émilion. www.chateau-figeac.com
  Cabernet-dominated St-Émilion. Wooden fermentation vats. Still very much a private home. Usually an older vintage to taste.

- **Château Franc Mayne**
  33330 St-Émilion. www.chateau-francmayne.com
  Grand Cru Classé offering luxurious accommodation (8 themed rooms: 'Campagne Française,' 'Black & White,' etc). Quarried limestone cellars; modern, oak-vatted winery.

CÔTES AND ENTRE-DEUX-MERS

- **Château Haut-Bertinerie**
  33620 Cubnezais (Blaye)
  www.chateaubertinerie.com
  Leading estate in Blaye. Investment in cellars and vineyard. Wines to taste and buy.

- **Château Fontenille**
  33670 La Sauve Majeure (Entre-Deux-Mers)
  www.chateau-fontenille.com
  Family property with a chance to meet the owner. Fresh, aromatic Entre-Deux-Mers and good red.

- **Château Penin**
  33420 Génissac (Bordeaux)
  www.chateaupenin.com
  Well-run family property. Meet the owner. Good quality wines to taste and buy.

- **Château Suau**
  33540 Capion (Premières Côtes de Bordeaux)
  www.chateausuau.com
  Family-owned. Modern cellar. Red, dry white and sweet Cadillac to taste and buy.

SWEET WHITES
(See also Ch. de Chantegrive and Suau above)

- **Château d'Arche**
  33210 Sauternes
  www.chateaudarche-sauternes.com
  Good-quality classed growth Sauternes. Some older vintages. Accommodation in attractive 17th-century *chartreuse* surrounded by vineyards (see photograph above).

- **Château La Rame**
  33410 Ste-Croix-du-Mont. Tel 05 56 62 01 50
  One of the best from the Ste-Croix-du-Mont AC. A range of wines and vintages to taste and buy.

- **Château Suduiraut**
  33210 Preignac
  www.suduiraut.com
  Top of the range Sauternes. Complete visit and tasting. See the beautiful gardens designed by Le Nôtre.

WINE REGIONS

Bordeaux is France's largest fine wine region but except for the sweet whites of Sauternes and Barsac, its international reputation is based mainly on its reds. The best wines, or Classed Growths, account for a tiny percentage of the total produced but some of their lustre rubs off on lesser names.

THE MÉDOC PAGE 94

North of the city of Bordeaux and running along the left bank of the Gironde estuary the Médoc peninsula produces a good fistful of the world's most famous red wines from a host of grand châteaux, as well as simpler, juicy, fruity, earthy reds.

THE GRAVES & PESSAC-LÉOGNAN PAGE 164

The northern Graves, now called Pessac-Léognan, is Bordeaux's oldest fine wine region, with some vineyards now located within the city limits. With the introduction of new technology and new ideas the region has improved beyond all recognition in the last decade. In the southern Graves top producers are making a name for fresh, fruity whites.

THE RIGHT BANK PAGE 192

Since the early 1980s the great Merlot-based wines of St-Émilion and Pomerol have caught the imagination of the world. St-Émilion and Pomerol's satellite appellations can produce good fruity reds at less-exalted prices.

THE CÔTES AND BETWEEN THE RIVERS PAGE 250

These less-well known areas of Bordeaux are today producing an enormous range of value-for-money reds and dry whites; and the countryside is some of the most attractive in the whole region.

SWEET WHITE WINES PAGE 274

The most celebrated sweet white wine region in the world is Sauternes and Barsac, west of the town of Langon. Neighbouring areas of Cérons, and, across the Garonne, Cadillac, Loupiac and Ste-Croix-du-Mont produce lighter, less sweet versions but offer excellent value.

What an image of power, control and efficiency. The space age has arrived at Ch. Latour, one of Bordeaux's most historic estates. The computer panel will monitor the temperature of every one of these gleaming vats. Since French billionaire François Pinault took over in 1993 Latour has been completely modernized and upgraded, but the wine's classic flavours are more marked and impressive than ever.

The Médoc

When I dream of stocking my cellar with the red wines I most desire, more of them would come from the Médoc than from any other part of Bordeaux, of France, or of the world. Partly that's because the first great wines I tasted all came from here. Partly it's because I love the long-term commitment you make when you buy a case of young Médoc wine. You know that the wine will be quietly, steadily developing its personality over 15, 20, 30 years and all that time you will possess it and chart its progress in your mind. It is the ultimate collector's wine, and a fine bottle can give you half a lifetime's pleasure before you finally pull the cork. Such red wines with their strong, brooding Cabernet Sauvignon content were probably the first red wines of enough structure and depth to be able to benefit when the rediscovery of the cork and the development of stronger bottles during the 17th and 18th centuries made bottle-aging possible, and since the 18th century these Médoc reds have been the favourites of collectors.

Yet until the 17th century this narrow lip of land running north from the city of Bordeaux between the Gironde estuary and the stormy Bay of Biscay coast was marshland. That was when Dutch engineers were employed to drain the swamps and they liberated the great banks of gravel that now constitute all the best vineyards in the Médoc. These gravel banks provide warm ripening conditions and perfect drainage for the Cabernet Sauvignon grape which dominates the vineyards. All the best wines come from one of the villages with the best gravel banks – Margaux, St-Julien, Pauillac, St-Estèphe, Moulis and Listrac. Further north the land becomes flatter, damper, more pasture than vineyard and the appellation becomes simple 'Médoc' because clay has largely taken the place of gravel, Merlot has displaced Cabernet Sauvignon and a four-square, yeoman, earthy stubbornness has replaced perfume and beauty and magic in the wines.

The vineyards and the winery of Ch. Latour in all their glory. Latour's vineyards are on deep gravel running down to the Gironde estuary. Where the gravel stops, the vines stop, and meadows take their place by the shore. The protective, warming effect of the Gironde on the vines is more marked at Latour than anywhere else in the Médoc.

SPOTLIGHT ON
The Médoc

Without these drainage channels, or *jalles*, that cross the Médoc at right angles to the estuary all the way from the city of Bordeaux in the south to the very tip of the Médoc peninsula in the north the region would still be a flood-prone swamp, with periodic ridges of high ground – but not very high as the peak of the Medoc at Listrac is only 43m (140ft) above sea level. This one is right on the border between Pauillac and St-Julien.

More than any other region of France, I think of the Médoc peninsula north of Bordeaux as my playground. Show me a label of a Margaux, a St-Julien wine, and I can visualize the track leading through the vines to the château gates, the nervous anticipation as I pass through them, the welcome – or rebuff – I last received. Give me a sip of a deep Pauillac red and all the cask samples and barrel tastings I have done crowd into my thoughts. And I feel as though I could take the great Médoc wine road – the D2 – out of Bordeaux blindfold, and I would smell the change in the air as sour industrial estates turn into suburbs, then woodland, then suddenly, beautifully, serenely, into vineyards – the subtle slope of La Lagune at Ludon, the fairytale glade of Cantemerle in Macau and, as the bizarre but lovely half-timbered Deauville casino of Giscours looms to my left, I'm into Margaux and the start of a journey north to St-Estèphe, past château after château whose wine is fabled and precious and rare.

I'm sure this is because when I was learning about wine, all the special bottles whose flavours I can still immediately recall, were wines from the Médoc peninsula. My first ever fine wine – Léoville-Barton 1962 from St-Julien; my first ever 1961s – Montrose from St-Estèphe and Beychevelle from St-Julien; my first ever Pauillac – Lynch-Bages 1955, which I said I preferred to the 1949 St-Émilion superstar Ausone, also proferred; the first time I ever smelt violets in a wine – Malescot 1964 from Margaux. And because of these experiences, I longed to get down to see where these wonderful wines had come from. I did visit St-Émilion and Pomerol, Sauternes and the Graves, but my obsession was with the Médoc and its wines. It still is. I now understand Graves and Pessac-Léognan much better than I did. I can interpret and appreciate the wines from the Right Bank Côtes like Blaye and Bourg and Castillon much more clearly now, and the new wave of producers in St-Émilion and Pomerol are now producing wines of a brilliance that can still leave me breathless and confounded as I try to keep pace with the speed of change both in the people, the mood and the intoxicating flavours of the wines. But if you ask me where my heart and head are, they're in the Médoc.

The Médoc is the geographical term used for the whole of the wine region on the left bank of the Garonne and Gironde. Vines grow for a good 80km (50 miles) of this tongue of land, mostly close to the river and estuary, sometimes venturing towards the centre but never towards the west where the giant sand dunes – Europe's highest – and deep pine forests of the Landes struggle to keep the rough waters of the Atlantic at bay. In wine terms, the Médoc is divided in two. The northern part, much marshier, far less suitable for fine wine, has the appellation Médoc. The southern part, between the city and the hard-working La Maréchale drainage channel north of St-Seurin-de-Cadourne, is the Haut-Médoc and contains all the best vineyards. Six villages have their own appellation – Margaux, Moulis, Listrac, St-Julien, Pauillac and St-Estèphe – and all the patches which aren't included in the communal appellations can use the appellation Haut-Médoc.

Until the 17th century the Médoc was a desolate, dangerous, flood-prone swamp. But a growing merchant and parliamentarian class wanted to show off its success, and having an estate with a grand house close to Bordeaux was a sure way to do it. The Graves region south and south-west of the city was already quite well developed. The Médoc, to the north and equally close, was not. So the Bordelais brought in Dutch engineers – past masters at all things involved with drainage – and they dug the great channels that still exist, and created dry land where only bog existed before. They also liberated the great banks of gravel washed down from the Massif Central and Pyrenees during the Ice Age, and it was these gravel banks that were seized by the local dignitaries as ideal places to create large estates, to build imposing châteaux and develop vineyards to slake the thirst of an export market crazy for wine. Every single great Médoc wine is grown on gravel.

Margaux is quite a busy little town, with a number of its well-known châteaux actually in the town itself.

Quick guide • The Médoc

LOCATION
The Médoc peninsula is a long wedge of land north and west of the city of Bordeaux, dividing the shores of the Gironde estuary from the Bay of Biscay. The vineyards are clustered towards the river and the wines they produce are known collectively as Left Bank wines.

APPELLATIONS
Wines sold as plain Médoc AC are from the northernmost part of the region, where only a few vineyards enjoy ideal conditions. The southern part of the region is known as the Haut-Médoc and this rather variable AC accounts for the vineyards surrounding but outside the world-famous communal appellations of Margaux, St-Estèphe, St-Julien and Pauillac and their less vaunted neighbours of Moulis and Listrac-Médoc. It is within these appellations that most of the classic Médoc gravel soils are found.

GRAPES
This is most definitely red wine country. Cabernet Sauvignon is the main variety, performing brilliantly on the warm gravelly Médoc soils. Complementary varieties are the softer, perfumed Cabernet Franc, Merlot planted on cooler, less well-drained soils, Malbec (in the northern Médoc) and the rarely used Petit Verdot. Plantings of white grapes are few and far between and the white wines from here – even

the sublime Pavillon Blanc of Château Margaux – can only carry the basic Bordeaux AC label.

CLIMATE
The soothing influence of the Gulf Stream sweeping along the Atlantic coast produces long, warm summers and cool, wet winters. The Landes pine forests act as a natural windbreak, sheltering the vineyards. Heavy rains can be a problem at vintage time.

SOIL
The topsoil is mostly free-draining gravel mixed with sand, the subsoil is gravel with sand plus some limestone and clay. The best vineyards are on the gravel outcrops.

ASPECT
Generally low-lying and flat with the main relief provided by gravel ridges and low plateaus, especially in the Haut-Médoc. Most, though not all, of the top vineyards are on very gentle, gravelly rises facing east and south-east towards the Gironde estuary.

VINTAGE VARIATIONS
Weather conditions throughout the year and particularly approaching the harvest have a marked effect on Médoc wines, although the top estates are increasingly adept at handling whatever nature

throws their way. The Médoc thrives in hotter years, when the Cabernet Sauvignon reaches optimum ripeness with pure, intense fruit to balance the firm tannins. The proximity of the ocean and the Gironde estuary reduces the risk of spring frost and rain is not a major issue in well-drained sites, but storms looming in from the Atlantic Ocean occasionally wash out the harvest in even the most promising of years. In poor years lesser estates tend to produce wines with hard tannins and an unripe taste of green pepper and mud.

ORGANIZATION
The Haut-Médoc consists mainly of large estates with an average size of 40ha (100 acres) that produce and bottle their own wine. In the northern part of the region, where wines take the Médoc appellation, vineyards are smaller and co-operatives are important. The top estates were ranked into five categories in the 1855 classification (see page 55).

A FEW FACTS
16,480ha (40, 720 acres) of vines produce 780,000hl of wine, of which 36% comes from communal appellations and 28% from the Haut-Médoc, with the remaining 36% sold as Médoc AC. Only 50ha (123 acres) of white vines are planted in the entire region.

WHERE THE VINEYARDS ARE

This map tells part of the tale of the Médoc immediately. The wide Gironde estuary provides a warming influence to the east, the pine forests to the west protect the region from salt-laden winds coming off the Bay of Biscay and draw off much of the rain from the clouds in wet weather. But the other part of the Médoc's story, the soil, isn't so apparent. All the Médoc's best vineyards are sited on gravelly soil. Where there are concentrations of vineyards, as around the town of Margaux, this is because the banks of warm gravelly soil that are crucial for the ripening of Cabernet Sauvignon dominate the landscape. Where the vineyards are piecemeal, the gravel will have been largely displaced by damp clay. Such vineyards as there are on this type of soil will generally be planted with the earlier-ripening Merlot, but results are rarely thrilling.

Macau and Ludon in the south have good vineyards, but the fireworks only really start at Labarde, one of the five villages in the Margaux AC. The best vineyards are around Cantenac and Margaux itself. North of Soussans, the vineyards become scrappier, as the gravel banks largely disappear until re-emerging at Ch. Beychevelle in the St-Julien AC. West of Arcins are two small but high quality ACs – Moulis and Listrac. There are no Classed Growths here, but there are several good châteaux, especially on the gravel ridge around the village of Grand Poujeaux. The islands in the estuary have vines, but they only qualify for the basic Bordeaux AC.

● CHÂTEAUX FEATURED ON PAGES 116–163

For properties in Margaux see the detailed map on page 103.

1. Ch. Lanessan (Haut-Médoc)
2. Ch. Tour-du-Haut-Moulin (Haut-Médoc)
3. Ch. Malescasse (Haut-Médoc)
4. Ch. Maucaillou (Moulis)
5. Ch. Poujeaux (Moulis)
6. Ch. Chasse-Spleen (Moulis)
7. Ch. Fourcas-Dupré (Listrac-Médoc)
8. Ch. Clarke (Listrac-Médoc)
9. Ch. Mayne-Lalande (Listrac-Médoc)
10. Ch. Citran (Haut-Médoc)
11. Ch. Cambon la Pelouse (Haut-Médoc)
12. Ch. Maucamps (Haut-Médoc)
13. Ch. Cantemerle (Haut-Médoc)
14. Ch. La Lagune (Haut-Médoc)
15. Ch. Sénéjac (Haut-Médoc)

SOUTHERN HAUT-MÉDOC

TOTAL DISTANCE NORTH TO SOUTH 18KM (11 MILES)

 VINEYARDS

0 km   1   2
0 miles   1

outcrop. Yet this gravel is in fact remarkably shallow. You can almost dig with your hands down to a limestone base. Ah, but the vines slope towards the Gironde estuary. That's the secret. Poor, shallow soils and good drainage – a classic combination for scented, elegant wines wherever you are in Bordeaux.

Even so, you only have to continue on the road from this vineyard northwards and the soil rapidly becomes so thick you could be looking at a sugar beet field in Suffolk. It's still in the Margaux appellation, but these heavy clay soils will never produce wines of perfume, although in hot years they may produce rich, beefy wines – good, but not very Margaux in style. The road dips into deep woodland and you think Margaux is over, but it isn't – quite. The village of Soussans is allowed to call itself Margaux and there is some gravel there amongst the clays, though I've yet to come across anything very scented from these heavy acres.

Yet being in the backwoods of Margaux doesn't mean you can't achieve something special, just as being in Margaux village doesn't mean you're certain to shine. If we head south again from Margaux village, we pass the excellent Ch. Palmer and the fragrant d'Issan (significantly on a vineyard that tips quite steeply towards the Gironde), but the road signs

● MARGAUX CHÂTEAUX FEATURED ON PAGES 116–163

1. Ch. Labégorce
2. Ch. Lascombes
3. Ch. La Gurgue
4. Ch. Ferrière
5. Ch. Marquis d'Alesme
6. Ch. Margaux
7. Ch. Malescot St-Exupéry
8. Ch. Durfort-Vivens
9. Ch. Marquis-de-Terme
10. Ch. Palmer
11. Ch. Rauzan-Gassies
12. Ch. Rauzan-Ségla
13. Ch. d'Issan
14. Ch. Cantenac-Brown
15. Ch. Brane-Cantenac
16. Ch. Kirwan
17. Ch. Prieuré-Lichine
18. Ch. Desmirail
19. Ch. Boyd-Cantenac
20. Ch. Pouget
21. Ch. Siran
22. Ch. Dauzac
23. Ch. d'Angludet
24. Ch. Giscours
25. Ch. Monbrison
26. Ch. du Tertre

Vineyards of Ch. Chasse-Spleen at Grand-Poujeaux, Moulis. These vines are on a good gravel ridge and have generally outperformed their neighbours to such an extent that the property is considered unlucky not to have been classified in 1855. That may be so, but there are now a number of equal contenders for any new classification.

to even vaguely well-known châteaux all seem to be pointing inland, and if you want to reach the frontiers of Margaux you'll need to head a few kilometres into the wilds to reach lonely Arsac. On my last trip I drove past the impressive and recently revitalized Ch. Giscours in Labarde, right on the very southern edge of Margaux, but blessed with some good steep gravelly mounds right in front of the château. Then I plunged into woodland and the tracks became more and more overgrown – I could have been a hundred miles from the glitzy world of the Bordeaux Classed Growths – and I was not a little relieved when I finally burst out on to a simply magnificent high gravelly ridge, and then an even better one where the big white pebbles carpeted the ground so thickly you couldn't see the soil at all. This was backwoods Arsac, the knolls of Château Monbrison and, especially, du Tertre, two stunning under-appreciated properties way off the beaten track. There are properties lining the main road in and out of Margaux that can't achieve the beauty and personality of these isolated acres. But then, even if they're jostling Margaux's greatest names, it doesn't mean their soil is so good, or their ambition.

If there's one thing the Margaux appellation has lacked over the last couple of generations, it is a solid core of skilled and ambitious properties determined enough and financially able enough to push the quality limits. Sometimes they have complacently relied on the idea of wine from Margaux being light and elegant – even when their soils were substantially clay rather than the superior fine white gravel – but the true Margaux style is supremely difficult to attain – a balance between finesse and power, scent and structure – otherwise we wouldn't thrill to it so infrequently, and it is never achieved by overcropping the vineyard and casually turning the dilute grapes into wine.

Margaux is still not as reliable an appellation as I would like – perhaps it never will be because of its far-spread boundaries and significant soil differences – but there is a new generation at work here, and for partly emotional reasons and partly hedonistic reasons, I still pine for great Margaux wine almost like no other

MOULIS AND LISTRAC

You can feel prosperity and glamour trail away behind you as you drive north from Margaux. The reason is fundamental. Marshland, *jalles* or drainage channels, heavy-footed water meadows and woodland. In the Médoc you must have the gravel to make the best wine, or at the very least you have to have land that rises above the mud. Just before you come to Lamarque the D5 turns off to the left, to two communes, one with the gravel and one with the height, but neither with the good good conditions to have any of their châteaux make it into the 1855 classification. Five châteaux which only boasted the general Haut-Médoc appellation did get classified status, and one has to presume that the wines of Listrac and Moulis simply weren't thought of as good enough. Since then various voices have been raised saying that in any reclassification of the Haut-Médoc, Moulis at least would be rewarded, but I am not so sure.

There's definitely gravel in one part of Moulis, and it's where the best-known properties are, clustered round the little village of Grand Poujeaux. In fact most of the properties include Poujeaux in their name and are generally good, though none as good as simple Ch. Poujeaux and its neighbour Chasse-Spleen. These last two have produced really exceptional wine now and then, and Chasse-Spleen often exhibits quite impressive depth while Poujeaux's greater strength is mellowness of fruit and smoothness of texture – that's the gravel talking. But this gravel mound isn't consistent, and isn't big – Moulis is the smallest of these Haut-Médoc communal appellations – and it rapidly fades towards the west and the village of Moulis itself where limestone and clays start to reassert themselves. There are some good properties like Duplessis, Brillette and Biston-Brillette, but the soils are cooler and there's a need for a good warm September or even October to produce the typical rich, gentle style of Moulis red.

There's even more need of a warm September in Listrac, just to the north of Moulis. This covers a slightly larger area than Moulis, and the two appellations are usually linked together – they even try to amalgamate now and then but Moulis has so far managed to vote for keeping its independence. And I can see why. Listrac's wines have traditionally been hard work, and when conditions are poor, they still are. But if warm vintages like 2004, '05, '09 and '10 become the norm, Listrac wines will be one of Bordeaux's chief beneficiaries. This is the Médoc's highest vineyard – even if that's only 43m (140ft) – and there's some gravel in the earth, it's mostly cool limestone and clay – and Cabernet Sauvignon in particular will produce rather earthy wines, if the sun doesn't shine. But the sun is shining more and more. The earthiness in such soils is turning to a haughty but attractive minerality, and the best properties are beginning to show a dark ripe fruit they never showed a generation ago. And they *are* good with food. A few years ago I sat in a little Listrac restaurant eating pork kidneys in mustard sauce and drinking the local Ch. Bibian 2000, and the match was excellent. And the evening did throw up a very interesting little oddity – white Listrac. The wine can only be called Bordeaux Blanc, but is very good – round, dry but full of peach and nectarine flavour. Ch. Clarke was the one I drank – loyal to the last, of course – but Fonréaud and Saransot-Dupré also make good ones.

You don't expect to see too much snow in Bordeaux, but the Listrac vineyards are the highest in the Médoc (OK, it's only 43m/140ft) but it does make a difference. Ch. Fonréaud will be grateful for a snowy period to help kill the bugs and keep the vines dormant as long as possible.

0 km   1   2
0 miles   1

1

2

3 4 5   6 ST-CHRISTOLY-MÉDOC

COUQUÈQUES   7

8

ST-YZANS-DE-MÉDOC

9

10

11   12

LESPARRE-MÉDOC

ST-SEURIN-DE-CADOURNE   13   14

ST-ESTÈPHE

VERTHEUIL

15 CISSAC-MÉDOC

ST-SAUVEUR

16

17

18

ST-LAURENT-MÉDOC   19   20

MÉDOC AND NORTHERN HAUT-MÉDOC

TOTAL DISTANCE
NORTH TO SOUTH
25KM (15½ MILES)

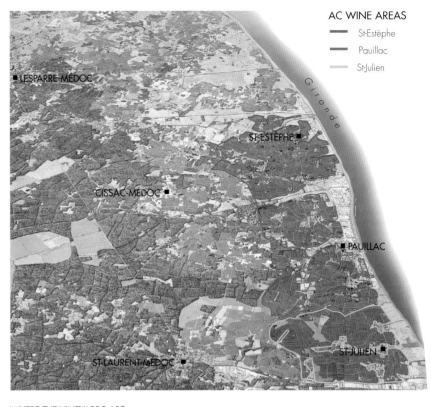

VINEYARDS

N

AC WINE AREAS
— St-Estèphe
— Pauillac
— St-Julien

WHERE THE VINEYARDS ARE

This is the most concentrated area of fine red wine in Bordeaux. Gravel banks begin at Ch. Beychevelle, at the bottom of the map (see detailed map, page 83), and are most impressive close to the waterfront in the St-Julien and Pauillac ACs, where the best properties get the full benefit of the warm estuary and the best drainage. Pauillac ends very abruptly at Ch. Lafite-Rothschild (see detailed map, page 111). A drainage channel and meadow create an interlude, but then there's another low bank covered with vines and we are in the large AC of St-Estèphe. Three of St-Estèphe's five Classed Growths are found here but generally this AC has more clay than gravel, so few of the wines achieve the brilliance of Pauillac. From Blanquefort, on the northern outskirts of Bordeaux, to St-Seurin-de-Cadourne, north of the St-Estèphe AC, wines not covered by the main village ACs are allowed the title Haut-Médoc. The vineyards become patchy as suitable land is more difficult to find. North of St-Seurin-de-Cadourne are the vineyards of the Médoc AC, often good but rarely thrilling.

● CHÂTEAUX FEATURED ON PAGES 116–163

For properties in communal appellations, see the detailed maps on pages 109 (St-Julien), 111 (Pauillac) and 113 (St-Estèphe).

MÉDOC
1. Ch. Escurac
2. Ch. Patache d'Aux
3. Ch. La Tour-de-By
4. Ch. Rollan-de-By
5. Ch. Tour St-Bonnet
6. Ch. Les Grands Chênes
7. Ch. Les Ormes-Sorbet
8. Ch. Bournac
9. Ch. Tour-Haut-Caussan
10. Ch. Ramafort
11. Ch. L'Inclassable
12. Ch. Potensac

HAUT-MÉDOC
13. Ch. Charmail
14. Ch. Sociando-Mallet
15. Ch. Cissac
16. Ch. Peyrabon
17. Ch. Bernadotte
18. Ch. Belgrave
19. Ch. La Tour-Carnet
20. Ch. Camensac

0 km   1   2
0 miles   1

Classic wine styles • St-Julien

OVERVIEW

Here, rather than in the more celebrated vineyards of Pauillac, is where I and many others come to find the essence of red Bordeaux. It's all about balance: a perfect balance between substance and delicacy, opulence and austerity, between the necessary brashness of youth and the lean-limbed genius of maturity. St-Julien is the smallest of the Haut-Médoc communal appellations, but with the greatest concentration of top-class gravelly vineyard land.

TASTING NOTE

A restrained cedarwood perfume and lean but mouthwatering blackcurrant fruit set St-Julien somewhere between the gravitas of Pauillac and the airier charms of Margaux. Some wines are satisfyingly rich and rounded, with perhaps a dose of cherries swirled deep into the fruit, perhaps a scoop of chocolate, hinting at a hedonistic heart beating somewhere behind the Savile Row formality of the tannins.

WHEN TO DRINK

St-Julien's charm is in part due to softer-edged tannins than Pauillac, and most wines are enjoyable from six years of age up to 15 or 20. But wait until at least ten years to experience the full harmony of the blackcurrant and cedar in the best wines, which should stay at their peak for easily another decade.

BEST YEARS

2010, '09, '08, '07, '06, '05, '04, '03, '02, '01, '00, '99, '98, '96, '95, '90, '89, '88, '86.

AFFORDABLE WINES TO TRY

• Ch. du Glana
• Ch. Gloria
• Ch. Lagrange
• Ch. Lalande-Borie
• Ch. Langoa-Barton
• Ch. St-Pierre
• Ch. Talbot
• Ch. Teynac

St-Julien is chiefly a very expensive commune. The neighbouring commune of St-Laurent has three Classed Growths similar in style to the lesser St-Juliens and fairly priced:

• Ch. Belgrave, Haut-Médoc
• Ch. Camensac, Haut-Médoc
• Ch. La Tour-Carnet, Haut-Médoc

For more ideas see page 163

ST-JULIEN

Coming up is one of my favourite moments as I drive the wine road – the D2, the only road for any wine lover to take through the Médoc. I've been passing through what the old-timers called 'the thirsty quarter' – the 13km (8-mile) stretch of road that dips up and down – down through marsh, water meadow and woodland, up, often only five or ten metres up, through broad expanses of vineyard that can seem to spread right into the forests of the west and down to the Gironde estuary in the east. But there are no famous names and, though there is gravel in the soil, it seems a bit blacker and heavier than it did so short a distance back in Margaux. Well, it isn't fair to call this zone 'the thirsty quarter' – there's loads of good wine here. But memorable wine, wine that makes you catch your breath and makes your heart flutter? No. Even so, at Vieux Cussac, and especially Cussac-Fort-Médoc, there are some really stony mounds of soil and you think, a bit of TLC and you could create something really special here. And then the road sinks, slumps back into the marsh, and your spirits with it. But it isn't over. The Médoc's most glorious stretch is just about to start. Your spirits are set to soar.

Whatever speed you're driving, you'll have to slow as you cross one last swollen drainage ditch of thick brown water, because the road sweeps sharply up and left, the vineyards billow confidently into existence once more and you're back in the big time. From now on you'll pass a succession of great properties, mostly with their vines sweeping away from their high gravel ridges down to the Gironde shore. Beychevelle on your right, Branaire and St-Pierre on your left, then Ducru-Beaucaillou, Léoville-Barton, Léoville-Poyferré, Léoville-Las-Cases – and as the road dips across another drainage channel, St-Julien is finished as suddenly as it started, but the brilliance surges on without a pause as neighbouring Pauillac offers you Pichon-Baron, Pichon-Lalande and Latour, on perhaps the proudest gravel bank of them all.

There are other St-Juliens set back from the river in good but heavier soil – Gruaud-Larose, Talbot, Lagrange – and their wine is good to excellent almost every year, but it is those riverfront properties that are at the heart of what has made St-Julien the favourite village of all for many Bordeaux-lovers.

It's not a big appellation – only 920ha (2270 acres) – but of these 79% are owned by the Classed Growths, and amongst them are some of the greatest wines in Bordeaux, but also the most perfect, the most balanced, the ones which best mingle substance and delicacy, opulence and austerity, and offer a necessary youthful brashness that almost guarantees the lean-limbed scented genius of maturity. Whenever I hanker after the unmistakable flavour of fine Bordeaux as it has been known for generations, the quintessence of restrained cedarwood perfume and austere but mouth-watering blackcurrant fruit, I turn without a moment's hesitation to St-Julien.

O km   1   2
O miles   1

O km   1   2
O miles   1

And I find those flavours in the riverfront properties. You must wonder how many more times we're going to talk about gravel and drainage. Quite a few times more, I'm afraid, since it's only because of these great heaps of gravel piled up during ferocious Ice Age floods that we've got any wine to discuss. Bordeaux, especially in its north-west, the Médoc peninsula, is not a warm place to grow grapes, and it's not a dry place. In particular September and October, just when your grapes are finishing ripening, are traditionally prone to heavy rainstorms. Of course I'm not talking about pure gravel – but a soil dominated by gravel yet which does have enough clay, limestone and other material mixed in to the gravel, or present in layers between the gravelly soils, to provide sustenance and water retention for the vine. And the best vineyards have considerable depth between the gravel topsoil and the water table, so the vines delve deep, but have to wrest the nutrients from the earth rather than being able to suck them up at will from the water table. That's why in the Médoc you're always looking out for a rise in the ground – there

Above: The sight of a Ch. Léoville-Barton bottle will gladden the heart of every traditionalist Bordeaux lover. The wine offers the quintessence of cedarwood scent and dry blackcurrant fruit. My first ever fine wine was a Léoville-Barton 1962, and I remember it still.

Left: Ch. Talbot is a beautiful château at the heart of the St-Julien appellation and an important producer of the chunky, soft-centred St-Julien style from vineyards a little away from the Gironde. The wines are very attractive young but can easily last for 20 years.

Classic wine styles • Pauillac

OVERVIEW

The deep gravel banks around the town of Pauillac are the heartland of Cabernet Sauvignon, making these both the most revered and the longest lived of Bordeaux's great wines. For many wine lovers, King Cab's greatest wines are the three Pauillac First Growths (Lafite, Latour and Mouton-Rothschild).

TASTING NOTE

The hallmark flavours of a classic Pauillac are an intense blackcurrant fruit flavour allied to a heady cedarwood and pencil-shaving perfume. Simple to describe yet compelling and infinitely satisfying in the glass. A few properties produce a broader, plummier style but austerity is the watchword for the majority.

WHEN TO DRINK

These wines definitely need cellaring to allow the powerful and forbidding tannins of youth to mellow and the perfume to emerge. A few examples bloom with friendly fruit from an early age, while others retain the froideur of an assiduous school prefect throughout their long lives. Eight to ten years will be enough to bring most wines to a peak and they should drink well for another decade thereafter, two decades for the best wines.

BEST YEARS

2010, '09, '08, '06, '05, '04, '03, '02, '01, '00, '99, '98, '90, '89, '88, '86.

AFFORDABLE WINES TO TRY

- Ch. d'Armailhac
- Ch. Batailley
- Ch. Bellegrave
- Ch. La Fleur Peyrabon
- Ch. Fonbadet
- Ch. Grand-Puy-Ducasse
- Ch. Haut-Bages-Libéral
- Ch. Echo de Lynch-Bages (second wine of Ch. Lynch-Bages)
- Ch. Haut-Batailley
- Ch. Lacoste-Borie (second wine of Ch. Grand-Puy-Lacoste)
- Ch. Lynch-Moussas
- Ch. Pibran

For more ideas see page 163

could be a gravel outcrop, there often is. Yet at river level, you're suddenly squelching through the mud. There are a few vines there, but there shouldn't be as they'll never make a glass of anything you or I would care to drink.

The riverfront at St-Julien, where all the major properties gaze out on the Gironde and piles of pebbles chip and crack the ploughshares as they furrow the soil, this is deep gravel country. A warm soil, protected from extremes of temperature by the estuary, and a free-draining soil, helped by the fact that the water table isn't level here but is slithering downwards towards the river, creating the perfect deep rooting area. All of Bordeaux would love to have these conditions to ripen Cabernet Sauvignon. Perhaps all the world would, because however hard they try in California and Chile, South Africa and Australia, however close they get to creating a good Bordeaux style, that extra brilliance of cigar box and cedarwood scent, austere blackcurrant and a gentle, surprisingly soft texture in maturity, like the fond touch of a favourite grandparent – that's the genius of St-Julien. No one else does it quite the same.

Perhaps potential imitators might have better luck further inland. As you move away from the riverfront, you can see the soil getting heavier and, on the broad plateau of vines between Gruaud-Larose, Talbot and Lagrange, you'll find far less gravel and the vines may take up to a week longer to produce a ripe crop. But look to the south, the vines slip away to the drainage channel you crossed just before Château Beychevelle. If you don't have the gravel for drainage you have to rely on human means. The Dutch built the channels hundreds of years ago. Top properties like Gruaud-Larose and Lagrange gratefully let their vineyards' excess water ooze into these ditches.

PAUILLAC

Usually the boundaries between the Haut-Médoc communes are fairly obvious, but not between St-Julien and Pauillac. There is a little stream but since the vines crowd in on both sides you hardly notice it as you admire the glorious estates of Léoville-Las-Cases and Léoville-Poyferré until the road bounces upwards again and you're in Pauillac outside two of Pauillac's greatest châteaux – Pichon-Baron and Pichon-Lalande – both magnificent and staring slightly uneasily at each other across the road. You've probably missed an even greater one – Latour – over to the right as the gravel bank tumbles steeply downwards to the Gironde. Gravel again? Drainage again? I'm afraid so, but without two such mundane matters we'd never know the full glory of Pauillac.

The gravel banks were deep in St-Julien, they're even deeper in Pauillac. Cabernet Sauvignon was important in St-Julien, and it's even more important in Pauillac. Blackcurrant fruit and cedarwood scent are the marks of a great St-Julien, but in Pauillac the blackcurrant is darker,

more piercing, its power supported by temple columns of tannin that defy anyone to broach a bottle before its twentieth year, and the cedarwood and cigarbox scent swirls and swoons more headily in the glass – how can such a dry scent seem so sweet? Pauillac has 18 Classed Growths and several other good lesser growths, each mingling ripe black fruit with cedar scent, but above all, Pauillac has three of the 1855 classification's five First Growths, and no properties in the world play such a scintillating symphony of cedar, cigarbox and blackcurrant as these three.

And I'm sorry, but it's those gravel banks again. Whereas in Margaux the gravel peaked at 10–15m (35–50ft) above the Gironde, and in St-Julien at 15m (50ft) or a couple more, in Pauillac Lafite-Rothschild and Mouton-Rothschild peak on a broad impressive plateau in the north of the commune at 27m (88ft). Though Latour in the south of Pauillac is on a gravel bank that peaks at 14m (47ft), the Pichon vineyards quickly climb to 20m (66ft) and there are excellent vineyards about a kilometre further inland like Batailley and Haut-Batailley that are over 25m (82ft) high. So Pauillac has the deepest gravel beds in the Médoc, stretched out across two broad plateaux south and north of the town of Pauillac. And there does seem to be some iron in with the gravel and a good deal of iron pan as subsoil. No one's ever proved it, but Pomerol on the Right Bank has lots of iron and makes the deepest, richest wines over there, and a lot of growers reckon Pauillac's iron gives that extra depth to its wine.

Ch. Pichon-Longueville-Comtesse de Lalande led the charge of the Super-Seconds during the 1980s when a breakaway bunch of top properties started making exceptional wine and demanding considerably higher prices than their supposed peers. Lalande was a perfect leader because the wine is positively sumptuous for a Pauillac, almost creamy, spicy rich, yet bursting with a great wave of sweet blackcurrant and black cherry fruit.

Ch. Pontet-Canet's vineyards are directly across the country road from those of Ch. Mouton-Rothschild. Yet Mouton's wines are classified as First Growth and Pontet-Canet's as Fifth. Pontet-Canet partly makes up for this by having the largest production of any Médoc Classed Growth, but more importantly it is now farmed biodynamically. It is one of the Pauillac properties whose wine is most rapidly increasing in value and reputation.

From Latour in the south to Lafite-Rothschild in the north, every signpost bears yet another name dripping with the magic of memorable vintages and no wine lover can drive the D2 from Margaux through to St-Estèphe without getting an incredible thrill – and thirst – from so many famous names. But let's just look at the three great names that are the model for ambitious winemakers the world over when they decide to make as fine a Cabernet Sauvignon as their vineyards will permit. For a start, they're each incredibly different. Latour, in the south, right next to the softer St-Juliens, you could understand being different. Softer, perhaps? Not a chance. Latour, with its intensely gravelly sloping vineyards like a great dome of shingle shoved up above the waterline by rising floodwaters of long ago, is actually the darkest, the most profound, the most challenging but ultimately the most immensely satisfying of the three, its cedar scent as dense as its opaque blackcurrant fruit. If we drive just along the inland edge of the town of Pauillac, across a stream by the railway station, and then swoop up through the village of Le Pouyalet to the very rim of Pauillac's second gravel bank, Mouton-Rothschild guards the southern approach, right by the village, whilst Lafite is Pauillac's last

hurrah at the very northern tip of the AC. Together they form this stone-strewn plateau. Neighbours. But similar? Absolutely not. Great Mouton is a steamy, intoxicating swirl of head-spinning richness, the fruit pure, sweet blackcurrant and the scent cedar and lead pencils and occasionally something as mineral as lead itself. Yet, always, sensuous and sybaritic in its heart. Perhaps Lafite would like to throw off its intellectual aura and academic gown and fling itself into the party time over at Mouton. But that's not Lafite's way, it never has been. Instead, in recent years Lafite has made an art form of a pensive, contemplative but entirely brilliant take on cedar, lead pencils, cigarboxes and, yes, blackcurrant.

Now if you're thinking, 'yes but we're never going to drink these wines', I'm in full sympathy. I don't exactly stumble over boxes of them in my cellar either. Pauillac is never going to be cheap, but if we move inland, as with Margaux and St-Julien, the land gets heavier, the elegance and sophistication melts away, but the fabulous powerful dense blackcurrant and blueberry fruit, streaked through rather than infused with cedar scent, is still there for us at a fraction of the price. If there is such a thing as a bargain in Pauillac, it comes from such properties as Ch. Pibran, Batailley, Haut-Batailley, Echo de Lynch-Bages and Lynch-Moussas. And if you're still wondering is Mouton-Rothschild really as much fun as it sounds, Echo de Lynch-Bages will do you a fair imitation for quite a lot of, but far less, hard-earned cash.

ST-ESTÈPHE

It's less than 500m (1640ft) from the château buildings of the great glitzy First Growth Lafite-Rothschild in Pauillac to the beginning of the vines of Cos d'Estournel in St-Estèphe. But as soon as we step off that Pauillac land we're stepping down a division. In fact if you really want to walk from Lafite to Cos you'll be wading, because you step straight into the eddies of yet another of the Médoc's indispensable drainage channels.

Ch. Cos d'Estournel and Montrose struggle to prove they are the St-Estèphe leaders. Both have made a number of magnificent wines since the 1980s, with those of Cos a little more classical with their blackcurrant and black cherry fruit and dependably cigarbox scent.

Classic wine styles • St-Estèphe

OVERVIEW

St-Estèphe is somewhat burdened by its reputation as the slowest to mature, toughest, and most tannic of all Médoc wines. But the wines are honest, reliable and fair value. Growers are introducing more Merlot in the vineyard to cope with conditions that are a little cooler than in the other more southerly Médoc communes and soils that are decidedly more clogged with clay.

TASTING NOTE

These are the brawniest wines of the Haut-Médoc and the tannins will always give an earthy scratch to the texture, no matter how refined the estate nor how well matured the wine might be. Blackcurrant and cedarwood fruit peek out with age, but never with the brazen beauty of a Pauillac or a St-Julien. Overall the wines are a bit suppler than of yore, muscular where they were once merely rigid, and offer a welcome flutter of alluring fruit to offset all that square-jawed integrity.

WHEN TO DRINK

Generally good St-Estèphe is best enjoyed between ten and 20 years of age, although broader, Merlot-rich wines should open up nicely after six years. Don't expect wine from a leading property to be ready before ten years.

BEST YEARS

2010, '09, '08, '06, '05, '04, '03, '02, '01, '00, '96, '95, '94, '90, '89, '88, '86.

AFFORDABLE WINES TO TRY

- Ch. Andron Blanquet
- Ch. Beau Site
- Ch. Le Boscq
- Ch. Coutelin-Merville
- Ch. Cos Labory
- Ch. Domeyne
- Ch. Haut-Marbuzet
- Ch. Lafon-Rochet
- Ch. Ladouys
- Ch. Lilian Ladouys
- Ch. Meyney
- Ch. Les Ormes-de-Pez
- Ch. de Pez
- Ch. Phélan-Ségur
- Ch. Plantier Rose
- Ch. Tour de Pez

For more ideas see page 163

So take the car, and you'll be immediately impressed by the steep wall of vines that rears up the moment you cross the ditch. This is Cos d'Estournel, arguably St-Estèphe's top property, and in the flat lands of the Médoc where a gradual five or ten metre rise in the land is given a big thumbs up for quality, this is steep. So get out of the car. The soil is also very gravelly, as gravelly as anything you'll find in Pauillac. If this is St-Estèphe, why is everyone so down on it?

Well, this isn't typical St-Estèphe. This is one of a handful of great sites, virtually a last gasp of Pauillac with its deep gravel beds on a base of iron-rich sandstone, and though Cos d'Estournel has the best soils, there are two more good Classed Growths – Cos Labory and Lafon-Rochet – on what is, in effect, an impressive scarp running westwards for all of 2km (1.2 miles) staring out defiantly at Lafite-Rothschild just 500m (1640ft) to the south. But this can't last. And it doesn't. Just past Lafon-Rochet, the plateau sinks away to the west and to meadowland. There are more vines out here, but they're Haut-Médoc, not St-Estèphe, and they'd just love to have the gravel of this mini-Pauillac leavening their clay.

In Pauillac and St-Julien you could basically traverse the entire appellation without coming across any really poor vineyard sites. St-Estèphe isn't like this. That gravel which creates all the great vineyard sites of the Médoc is beginning to peter out. From now on, we will find gravel mounds, and the best of them will have top vineyards planted on them, but the soil is much heavier here and where the gravel disappears you're going to have pretty claggy earth. In Margaux, further south, if you pick up some soil in the less gravelly sites, it's normally fairly light and sandy; you can crumble it easily between your fingers. In St-Estèphe those Ice Age floods have deposited most of their best gravel further upstream, and clay – colder, damper, more fertile – becomes very much the dominant soil type. But there are still gravel mounds, and limestone starts to play a larger part, yet these mounds rarely stretch far and are often only big enough to contain one property. If you drive north from Cos d'Estournel and turn right just after the beautiful tranquil park and château of Le Crock (yes, I'd change the name too), you'll get down to the little road that runs right along the edge of the Gironde. Then turn left, northwards, and you'll see the low hilltop of Montrose – often considered the equal of Cos d'Estournel, but then the land dips into a little brook. Up it rises again for the solid Ch. Meyney – good solid wines too – which probably also has the lowest decent vines in the Médoc: where they roll down to the road they're only 3m (10ft) above sea level, although I doubt these grapes often make the final blend. If you then turn left up towards the village of St-Estèphe, you're on one more gravel and limestone mound – and you're in the vineyards of Ch. Calon-Ségur, the last of St-Estèphe's five Classed Growths, the most northerly Classed Growth, and, really, the end of the glitz and glamour of the Médoc. Stand on the steps of Calon-Ségur and look north and you're gazing out on drainage channels and marsh. There is one more gravel outcrop a couple of kilometres north at St-Seurin-de-Cadourne – and Ch. Sociando-Mallet makes stupendous wines off its warm soils – but that's Haut-Médoc by then. St-Estèphe and the big time end where the marsh sinks deepest, metres short of Sociando-Mallet.

St-Estèphe only has five Classed Growths, partly because the gravel soils that are a virtual necessity for top quality in the Médoc are rare here and, even when you find them, they're likely to have more damp cold clay intermixed. Being further north means the weather's colder here in any case than in Margaux or St-Julien, and the heavier soils will delay ripening even further. You could be picking your grapes two weeks later than in Margaux. All too often the weather breaks and storms pile in from the Bay of Biscay before your harvest is finished. Another reason there are only five Classed Growths is that the area was only being fully developed during the 19th century, so whilst Calon-Ségur is one of the Médoc's oldest properties, Cos d'Estournel only planted its first vines in 1810 and Montrose in 1815. Others didn't have time to develop a reputation before the classification of 1855.

When I started laying down bottles of red Bordeaux, I bought more St-Estèphe than any other, largely because there are a whole fistful of Cru Bourgeois properties, not quite as grand as Cos d'Estournel or Montrose, but a great deal cheaper. And they were serious wines. De Pez, les Ormes-de-Pez, Haut-Marbuzet, Meyney – these were powerful, dense wines I could afford. But they were never beautiful. Even today, the best St-Estèphe's don't have the purity and power of Pauillac, or the scented charm of Margaux. With modern winemaking and an increase in the amount of Merlot vines able to ripen more easily than Cabernet Sauvignon in the heavy soils, the wines do have a sweeter, riper black plum fruit than before, but beneath the surface of all but the best is that cold clay, and when blackcurrant and cedarwood do peek out, it's not with the brazen beauty of a Pauillac or St-Julien, and you greet them with a surprised delight, exposing the fact that you weren't at all sure they would appear.

These vines of Ch. Meyney are on a favoured gravel slope that goes right to the very edge of the Gironde. Those vines at the water's edge are only 3m (10ft) above sea level – the lowest of any leading vineyard in the Haut-Médoc. Meyney benefits from the warming influence of the Gironde and one hopes it doesn't overly benefit from the reactors of the EDF Blayais nuclear power station as well.

Château d'Angludet
Consistent and usually of Classed Growth standard, d'Angludet enjoys one of the best price-quality ratios in the whole of Bordeaux.

Château d'Armailhac
D'Armailhac is part of the Mouton-Rothschild stable – softer than Mouton, the wine still has fine blackcurrant fruit and a whiff of cedar.

Château Batailley
One of the most reliable wines made by the Pauillac Classed Growth estates, Batailley is lovely to drink at only 5 years old.

CHÂTEAU D'ANGLUDET
Margaux AC
❧ Cabernet Sauvignon, Merlot, Petit Verdot, Cabernet Franc

This property has a special place in my heart. It's the first château I ever visited, the first I ever stayed in – well, I was in a tent down by the stream – and the first grapes I ever harvested. I smile every time I see the label. Luckily, the wine has a delicious, approachable burst of blackcurrant-and-blackberry fruit that makes you want to drink it immediately – yet it ages superbly for up to a decade or more.

Recent vintages have started to display more muscle without in any way losing their perfume or luscious fruit, Its price-quality ratio is still one of the best in Bordeaux – if you want to begin buying red wine to lay down I suggest starting with Ch. d'Angludet. It's been owned by the Sichel family, part-owners of Ch. Palmer, since 1961. Second wine: La Ferme d'Angludet. Best years: 2010, '09, '08, '06, '05, '04, '03, '02, '00, '98, '96, '95, '94, '90.

CHÂTEAU D'ARMAILHAC
Pauillac AC, 5ème Cru Classé
❧ Cabernet Sauvignon, Merlot, Cabernet Franc, Petit Verdot

Originally part of the Mouton estate, this property was owned by the d'Armailhacq family until Baron Philippe de Rothschild bought it in 1933. The property was then renamed Ch. Mouton-Baron-Philippe. In 1975 it was renamed again, in honour of the baron's late wife, Ch. Mouton-Baronne-Philippe, but with the 1990 vintage Philippine de Rothschild, his daughter and heir, restored the original name.

There is a similarity between the wines of the famous MOUTON-ROTHSCHILD and its more modest neighbour, though Mouton has the more powerful structure as d'Armailhac's vines are on lighter soils and so produce wines with softer tannins. But the wine does consistently exhibit blackcurrant fruit and a whiff of cedar and provides fine drinking between eight and 15 years, occasionally even longer. Recent vintages are some of the best this property has ever produced. Best years: 2010, '09, '08, '07, '06, '05, '04, '03, '02, '01, '00, '99, '98, '96, '95, '94, '90 '89, '88.

CHÂTEAU BATAILLEY
Pauillac AC, 5ème Cru Classé
❧ Cabernet Sauvignon, Merlot, Cabernet Franc

Owned by *négociant* Émile Castéja of Borie-Manoux, this château is a byword for value-for-money – which, in the rarefied world of Pauillac Classed Growths, is an infrequent accolade indeed.

Made in the plummier, broader Pauillac style, it is be a byword for reliability too, because since the mid-1970s the wine has been very good: marked by a full, obvious blackcurrant fruit (even when very young), not too much tannin, and a luscious overlay of good, creamy, oak-barrel vanilla. As is to be expected from a good Pauillac red, this wine is sturdy enough to age well for at least 15 years, yet it is lovely to drink at only five years. I say 15 years but I recently drank the 1982 and '61 at the château and they were both still memorably good. Best years: 2010, '09, '08, '07, '06, '05, '04, '03, '02, '00, '98, '96, '95, '94, '90, '89.

Château Belgrave

These are chunky solid, impressive wines that in warm vintages will age for up to 20 years.

CHÂTEAU BELGRAVE

Haut-Médoc AC

* Cabernet Sauvignon, Merlot, Cabernet Franc, Petit Verdot

In 1980, the respected Bordeaux firm of Dourthe acquired this large estate with a commitment to improving the quality of the wine. Previously, Belgrave was run-down, with obvious consequences for the standard of the wine. Under the new ownership the vineyards were restructured, and the high proportion of Merlot replaced by more Cabernet Sauvignon. 1998 was the first vintage that really grabbed me with its deep plummy fruit and classy oak, and the wines are now consistently powerful but stylish. As prices are still relatively low, Belgrave is very good value. Drink at between 10 and 15 years. Best years: 2010, '09, '08, '07, '06, '05, '04, '03, '02, '00, '98, '96, '95, '90.

Château Bernadotte

Since the Pichon-Comtesse de Lalande team took over in 1997 the wines have improved enormously and are much more attractive than they used to be.

CHÂTEAU BERNADOTTE

Haut-Médoc AC

* Cabernet Sauvignon, Merlot, Cabernet Franc, Petit Verdot

Ch. Fournas was bought by Mme de Lencquesaing of Ch. PICHON-LONGUEVILLE-LALANDE in 1997 and the name changed to Bernadotte. It's now owned by Roederer (2006). Bernadotte has made rapid progress over the last few years and investment and the winemaking skills of the Pichon team have been important factors. Even so the wines are still a bit on the firm side. They are good for ten years' aging. Best years: 2010, '09, '08, '06, '05, '04, '03, '02, '01, '00, '99, '98.

Château Beychevelle

Beychevelle takes at least a decade to mature into the fragrant cedarwood and blackcurrant flavour for which St-Julien is famous.

CHÂTEAU BEYCHEVELLE

St-Julien AC, 4ème Cru Classé

* Cabernet Sauvignon, Merlot, Cabernet Franc, Petit Verdot

Travelling north from Margaux along the D2 road this beautiful château overlooking the Gironde graciously announces your arrival in St-Julien. Although it is ranked only as a Fourth Growth, its quality is potentially Second. The wine has a beautiful softness even when very young, but takes at least a decade to mature into fragrant cedarwood and blackcurrant flavour. Beychevelle is a sublime wine, and infuriating inconsistency is gradually being replaced by delightful consistency. Second wine: Amiral de Beychevelle. The label with its ship lowering its sail has recently become very popular in China. Best years: 2010, '09, '08, '07, '06, '05, '04, '03, '02, '00, '99, '98, '96, '95, '90, '89.

Château Bournac

The inland Médoc village of Civrac doesn't have many vines but Bournac is one of its leading châteaux.

CHÂTEAU BOURNAC

Médoc AC

* Cabernet Sauvignon, Merlot

Ch. Bournac made steady progress through the 1990s and is now a consistent performer. The wines are supple and finely structured, ready to drink at three to four years. Best years: 2010, '09, '08, '06, '05, '04, '03, '01, '00.

Château Boyd-Cantenac

Since the 2000 vintage, the quality of Boyd-Cantenac has improved, the wine showing more depth and richness.

CHÂTEAU BOYD-CANTENAC

Margaux AC, 3ème Cru Classé

* Cabernet Sauvignon, Merlot, Petit Verdot

For centuries this estate had difficulty maintaining an identity of its own as its vines and wines were merged with others in Margaux. Until 1982 it shared its winery with Ch. Pouget but since then the wines have been vinified separately. A number of fine vintages in the 1970s and earlier testify to the potential of this estate and its soil, but other vintages since then have been disappointing, lacking in fruit and balance, and often tasting positively raisiny. Since 2000, however, the wine has shown more depth and richness thanks to the input of Lucien Guillemet but consistency is still some way off. Drink after five years, though it may improve with 10 or more. Best years: 2010, '09, '08, '07, '06, '05, '04, '03, '00, '98, '96, '90, '89, '86, '85, '83, '82.

Château Branaire-Ducru

Branaire-Ducru is now one of the high fliers in St-Julien, with its soft, chocolaty but deep wines.

CHÂTEAU BRANAIRE-DUCRU
St-Julien AC, 4ème Cru Classé
❊ Cabernet Sauvignon, Cabernet Franc, Merlot, Petit Verdot

Ch. Brainaire-Ducru boasts 50ha (123 acres) of mature vines in several parcels dotted around St-Julien, some of them up to 100 years old. After a long period of mediocrity it chose the difficult 1993 and '94 vintages to signal its renewed ambition. This was long overdue because Branaire gave me a lot of affordable pleasure from its vintages in the 1960s and '70s. Subsequent vintages have confirmed a welcome return to full, structured, but chocolaty form and Branaire is now a very serious yet succulent dark wine. Second wine: Ch. Duluc. Best years: 2010, '09, '08, '07, '06, '05, '04, '03, '02, '01, '00, '99, '98, '96, '95, '94.

Château Brane-Cantenac

One of my favourite châteaux from long, long ago that is now returning to form, and not before time.

CHÂTEAU BRANE-CANTENAC
Margaux AC, 2ème Cru Classé
❊ Cabernet Sauvignon, Merlot, Cabernet Franc

Ch. Brane-Cantenac has been in the hands of the Lurton family since the 1920s and after a long drab period when the wines lacked depth and consistency returned to form in the late 1990s. Henri Lurton, a qualified enologist, took over the estate in 1992 and set about restoring its reputation. Its sprawling 90-ha (210-acre) vineyard is superbly located, principally on the Cantenac plateau, the 65% Cabernet Sauvignon vines being planted on infertile, fine gravelly soils. Second wine: Le Baron de Brane. Best years: 2010, '09, '08, '07, '06, '05, '04, '03, '02, '01, '00, '99, '98, '96, '95, '89.

Château Calon-Ségur

The warm conditions of recent vintages have suited the dark, mineral quality of Calon.

CHÂTEAU CALON-SÉGUR
St-Estèphe AC, 3ème Cru Classé
❊ Cabernet Sauvignon, Merlot, Cabernet Franc, Petit Verdot

This is the most northerly of all the Médoc's Classed Growths and the lowest in altitude, the land averaging less than 10m (30ft) above sea level. What gives Calon-Ségur Classed Growth quality is a spur of chalky, gravelly soil – usually found on higher ground in the Médoc. None of the neighbouring properties – struggling along on heavier clay soils – can produce wine that remotely matches Calon-Ségur. In the mid-1980s Calon-Ségur's problem was that its wine, though quite good, was ever so slightly dull and, at the high prices demanded by Médoc Classed Growths, dullness isn't really on. Reduced yields, more rigorous fruit selection and an increase in the percentage of new oak helped produce notable wines from 1995, with suppler, riper fruit, though the texture can still be fairly dark and forbidding. Second wine: Marquis de Calon. Best years: 2010, '09, '08, '07, '06, '05, '04, '03, '02, '01, '00, '98, '96, '95, '90, '89, '86.

Château Cambon la Pelouse

Light sandy soils in the very south of the Haut-Médoc give a very attractive, almost glyceriny soft wine with just a dash of tannin.

CHÂTEAU CAMBON LA PELOUSE
Haut-Médoc AC
❊ Merlot, Cabernet Sauvignon, Cabernet Franc

Owner Jean-Pierre Marie has astutely provided a consumer-friendly wine since purchasing this property in 1996. Modern winemaking techniques and a high percentage of Merlot (60%) produce a full but supple, fruity, contemporary style of wine at the 65-ha (160-acre) estate located in the southern Haut-Médoc. Best years: 2010, '09, '08, '06, '05, '04, '03, '02, '01, '00, '99.

Château Camensac

Camensac produced an attractive 2003 and the wines will improve even more under the dynamic new owners.

CHÂTEAU CAMENSAC
Haut-Médoc AC, 5ème Cru Classé
❧ *Cabernet Sauvignon, Merlot*

The Forner family invested hugely in this once neglected estate just inland of St-Julien at St-Laurent-Médoc. While there is no pretence here of producing wines of great power, complexity or longevity, Camensac is boldly flavoured, soft and best enjoyed with five to eight years' age. Much improved since 1995, this estate is now justifying its Fifth Growth status. New owners from 2005, the duo Jean Merlaut of Ch. GRUAUD-LAROSE and Céline Villars of Ch. CHASSE-SPLEEN, should result in further advances so watch this wine. Best years: 2010, '09, '08, '06, '05, '03, '02, '01, '00, '99, '98, '96, '95, '90.

Château Cantemerle

Cantemerle's light gravel soil in the southern Haut-Médoc generally gives succulent, quick- maturing but classy reds.

CHÂTEAU CANTEMERLE
Haut-Médoc AC, 5ème Cru Classé
❧ *Cabernet Sauvignon, Merlot, Cabernet Franc, Petit Verdot*

You head out of Bordeaux on the D2, through suburbs, shrubland, damp meadows, and the occasional vineyard, and you begin to wonder if you're on the wrong road for the great wine land of the Médoc. Then the forests fall away and suddenly the land is thick with rows of neatly trained vines. There on the right is Ch. La LAGUNE, then, on the left, Ch. Cantemerle, a jewel set inside its own woodland glade. Drive up the long avenue shrouded with age-old trees and stand in front of the turretted castle. Silence. Stillness. Fairyland. Not far off.

Cantemerle was ranked last in the 1855 Classification of Bordeaux, now the wine is far better than that: rarely a blockbuster – but always soft, easy to drink yet also surprisingly suitable for aging. Second wine: Les Allées de Cantemerle. Best years: 2010, '09, '08, '07, '06, '05, '04, '03, '01, '00, '98, '96, '95.

Château Cantenac-Brown

Cantenac-Brown always has a deep, mineral, stony quality and a dose of tannin, but in recent vintages has wrapped this with sweet black fruit.

CHÂTEAU CANTENAC-BROWN
Margaux AC, 3ème Cru Classé
❧ *Cabernet Sauvignon, Merlot, Cabernet Franc*

Frequent changes of ownership in the 1980s have had an impact on Cantenac-Brown's consistency. Previous vintages are solid enough, but lack distinction and elegance, especially in the 1970s.

Between 1989 and 2006 Cantenac-Brown was owned by AXA-Millésimes, the wine investment arm of the giant French insurance firm AXA, which also owns Pauillac Second Growth Ch. PICHON-LONGUEVILLE, as well as other Bordeaux estates. Vintages in the early 1990s were a disappointment but there has been an upturn in quality since 1995, and while still quite dense, they now have the richness typical of wines from the Cantenac commune. This progress seems to be continuing under the new owner, Simon Halabi. It needs at least five years' aging and top vintages will keep for at least 15 to 20 years. Best years: 2010, '09, '08, '06, '05, '04, '03, '02, '01, '00, '99, '98, '96, '95, '90, '89.

Château Charmail

Charmail is next door to the Haut-Medoc super-star, Ch. Sociando-Mallet, which clearly feeds its ambitions.

CHÂTEAU CHARMAIL
Haut-Médoc AC
❧ *Merlot, Cabernet Sauvignon, Cabernet Franc, Petit Verdot*

This 22-ha (54-acre) estate is located next to Ch. SOCIANDO-MALLET, on the gravelly ridges of St-Seurin-de-Cadourne just across the boundary from St-Estèphe. Owner Roger Sèze uses a system of cold pre-fermentation maceration to give the wine more aroma and suppleness to go with its serious structure. It is matured for a year in oak barrels and neither fined nor filtered before bottling. It is best with at least five to eight years' bottle age. Best years: 2010, '09, '08, '06, '05, '04, '03, '02, '01, '00, '99, '98, '96, '95.

Château Chasse-Spleen

Chasse-Spleen is a Classed Growth in all but name but I feel it has inexplicably lightened up a little in the last few vintages.

CHÂTEAU CHASSE-SPLEEN

Moulis AC

Cabernet Sauvignon, Merlot, Petit Verdot

All owners of lesser Bordeaux properties who gaze wistfully at the Classed Growths and sulk in silent envy at the prices they can charge should look at the example of Chasse-Spleen. I first came across the wine in the 1980s and marvelled at its ripe dark fruit and soothing cocoon of new oak richness – a Classed Growth in all but name. And that was exactly the point. It tasted as good as the top Médocs. So it cost more. And nobody complained. The last few vintages show an unwelcome lightening up and I'd like to see the dark ripe core of fruit return. Best years: 2010, '09, '08, '07, '06, '05, '04, '03, '02, '01, '00, '99, '96, '95.

Château Cissac

These are deeply coloured, high quality, slow-maturing, traditionally made wines for the long haul and you'll normally have quite a wait.

CHÂTEAU CISSAC

Haut-Médoc AC

Cabernet Sauvignon, Merlot, Petit Verdot

Sometimes, tasting Cissac, you feel as if you are in a time warp. The tannin is uncompromising, the fruit dark and stubbornly withheld for many years, the flavour of wood more like the rough, resinous edge of hand-hewn pine than the soothing vanilla creaminess now fashionable. Well, it is something of an anachronism. Although not included in the 1855 Bordeaux Classification, Cissac doggedly refuses to accept the situation, and makes slow-maturing wines by proudly traditional methods: old vines, lots of wood everywhere and meticulous exclusion of below-par wine from the final blend. Tentative introduction of steel vats and other newer technologies from the 2000 vintage have changed things a little bit, but not much. Time – and plenty of it – will tell. Best years: 2010, '09, '08, '06, '05, '04, '03, '02, '00, '98, '96, '95, '94, '90, '89, '88, '86.

Château Citran

The move away from a heavily oaked, chocolaty style of wine under Citran's current owners is very welcome.

CHÂTEAU CITRAN

Haut-Médoc AC

Cabernet Sauvignon, Merlot

Investment from a Japanese group in the late 1980s revived the fortunes of this large estate, tucked in behind the Margaux AC. The property was resold in 1996 to the Taillan group, owners of GRUAUD-LAROSE, CHASSE-SPLEEN and HAUT-BAGES-LIBERAL, so the good work continues. The wine style has changed from powerful and oaky to ripe, round and fleshy, ready for drinking at four to six years. Second wine: Moulins de Citran. Best years: Best years: 2010, '09, '08, '06, '05, '04, '03, '02, '00, '99, '98, '96, '95.

Château Clarke

I open a bottle of 1983 every year on my birthday. I'm down to my last couple, and I am now looking forward to moving on to more modern vintages.

CHÂTEAU CLARKE

Listrac-Médoc AC

Merlot, Cabernet Sauvignon

Sauvignon Blanc, Sémillon, Muscadelle

Thirty-odd years ago Ch. Clarke was just a wistful Anglo-Saxon footnote in the more scholarly books on Bordeaux, and the vineyard looked like a bomb site. Then in 1973 along came the late Baron Edmond de Rothschild. He spent millions on it, totally redoing the vineyards and their drainage, and building imposing new installations – with sparkling new masonry, gleaming steel and reassuring piles of new oak barrels but despite all the efforts the wine never managed to escape from the earthy dryness that typifies Listrac. Things looked up in 1998 when Michel Rolland became a consultant, and, obviously, we Clarkes have to stick together, so here's hoping. Vintages since have been Merlot-dominated (70%) and look good. There's also a tasty, dry white, Le Merle Blanc. Second wine: Les Granges des Domaines Edmond de Rothschild. Best years: 2010, '09, '08, '07, '06, '05, '04, '03, '01, '00, '99, '98.

Cos d'Estournel sits flagrantly, boastfully on the plateau across from Lafite-Rothschild. Yet it isn't a château – Cos hasn't got one – it's just the cellars or cuverie for the vats and barrels. Which is a pity really because this is a truly grand folly, decorated with oriental pagodas, bells and arches; it even boasts a wooden doorway from the Sultan of Zanzibar's harem. An incredible state-of-the-art winery, built within the pagoda building, was inaugurated in 2008.

Château Clerc-Milon
Clerc-Milon is now a fine Pauillac with an exciting blackcurrant fruit and sometimes a whiff of cedar.

CHÂTEAU CLERC-MILON
Pauillac AC, 5ème Cru Classé
❦ *Cabernet Sauvignon, Merlot, Cabernet Franc, Petit Verdot*

In 1970 Baron Philippe de Rothschild bought this 30-ha (74-acre) estate tucked between MOUTON-ROTHSCHILD and LAFITE-ROTHSCHILD on the Gironde side and said to have first-rate soils, the potential of which had never been realized by previous owners. After much replanting, mostly of Cabernet

Sauvignon, the hunch seems to have been proved correct, as Clerc-Milon is clearly enjoying the warmer vintages and producing classy Pauillac. Drinkable young, but the wine will age well for at least 10–20 years. Best years: 2010, '09, '08, '07, '06, '05, '04, '03, '02, '01, '00, '99, '98, '96, '95, '94, '90, '89, '88, '86, '85, '82.

Cos d'Estournel
Cos is often St-Estèphe's top wine and is renowned for its dark, brooding, powerful wines that usually need at least 10 years' aging.

CHÂTEAU COS D'ESTOURNEL
St-Estèphe AC, 2ème Cru Classé
❦ *Cabernet Sauvignon, Merlot, Cabernet Franc, Petit Verdot*

Cos d'Estournel bears more than a passing resemblance to a Chinese temple complete with pagodas and bells. Indeed Monsieur d'Estournel was a horse dealer in the early 19th century who traded extensively with the Far East, bringing back wild horses for breeding on the lush meadows next to the vineyards. He discovered his wine improved enormously if he took it on the journey with him. So he went 'oriental' in a grand manner as a way of promoting his wine.

Cos is now one of Bordeaux's leading châteaux and St-Estèphe's top name. Although St-Estèphe wines are generally less perfumed than those of neighbouring Pauillac, because of the heavier clay soil, Cos has some truly deep gravel banks, but used to make up for the heavier soils by using around 40% Merlot in the blend and through subtle use of new oak barrels. In 1998 and 2000 the château changed hands and it is now owned by businessman, Michel Reybier. Since 2007 Cabernet Sauvignon has been on the increase and is now 65–85% of the blend. Second wine: Les Pagodes de Cos. Best years: 2010, '09, '08, '07, '06, '05, '04, '03, '02, '01, '00, '96, '95, '94, '90, '89, '88, '86.

Château Cos Labory
Cos Labory is enjoying the 21st century and has produced consistently classy wines since 2003.

CHÂTEAU COS LABORY
St-Estèphe AC, 5ème Cru Classé
❧ *Cabernet Sauvignon, Merlot, Cabernet Franc*

A neighbour of the more celebrated Cos d'Estournel, Cos Labory underwent a rapid improvement in quality in the late 1980s. Earlier vintages were soundly made, but lacked structure and density, and did not keep especially well. The 18-ha (44-acre) vineyard has never produced wine with the power of its neighbour, but today it is structured, well-balanced, frequently scented and sensibly priced. It needs six or seven years' bottle age and will age another 10. Second wine: Le Charme Labory. Best years: 2010, '09, '08, '06, '05, '04, '03, '02, '00, '99, '98, '96, '95.

Château Croizet-Bages
Croizet-Bages is outshone by nearly all the other Pauillacs – a pity, because there's nothing wrong with the vineyard site.

CHÂTEAU CROIZET-BAGES
Pauillac AC, 5ème Cru Classé
❧ *Cabernet Sauvignon, Merlot, Cabernet Franc*

The vineyards lie between Ch. Lynch-Bages and Grand-Puy-Lacoste, so expectations of quality should be very high. Unfortunately, this wine, although soundly made and reasonably consistent, has always lacked excitement. Moreover, it matures rapidly and does not have the staying-power of the top Pauillacs. With lower yields, better selection and vinification, however, Croizet-Bages could overcome its shallowness of structure and flavour. Recent vintages have shown more depth but frankly this is still one of the shadowy players here when they could achieve so much more with the vineyards they've got. Drink young. Best years: 2010, '09, '08, '06, '05, '04, '03, '00, '98, '96, '95.

Château Dauzac
Being sited on relatively light, sandy gravel soil, Dauzac prefers the slightly less powerful vintages.

CHÂTEAU DAUZAC
Margaux AC, 5ème Cru Classé
❧ *Cabernet Sauvignon, Merlot, Cabernet Franc*

Although an ancient vineyard site, productive since the early Middle Ages, Dauzac only acquired renown in the mid-19th century, after it became the property of the celebrated Bordeaux merchant Nathaniel Johnston.

At present, it is owned, like so many Médoc properties, by a large insurance company. Since 1992 André Lurton (of La Louvière fame) has controlled viticulture and winemaking and the wines taste richer and riper. The best years since 1995 have the potential to repay 10 years' keeping. Second wine: La Bastide-Dauzac. Best years: 2010, '09, '08, '07, '05, '04, '03, '02, '01, '00, '98, '96, '95.

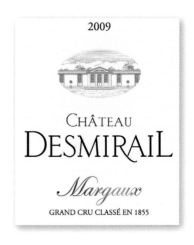

Château Desmirail
Since 2000 there has been a marked improvement here and the wines have gained in density, texture and, above all, bouquet.

CHÂTEAU DESMIRAIL
Margaux AC, 3ème Cru Classé
❧ *Cabernet Sauvignon, Merlot, Cabernet Franc*

This little-known estate was the property of Lucien Lurton, but is now owned by his son Denis. In the 1930s the property was divided up and its wines blended with those of Palmer and Brane-Cantenac. Lucien Lurton slowly reconstituted the estate, acquiring the right to use the name of this Classed Growth from 1980, which is why the first vintage of the reassembled Desmirail was 1981.

The wines tended to be light but had charm and finesse in the mid- to late 1980s. They were disappointing in the '90s, however, except for a smashing '96; but since 2000 there's been marked progress and they are now fun, round, plummy wines typical of southern Margaux. Best vintages will improve for five to ten years. Second wine: Ch. Fontarney. Best years: 2010, '09, '08, '06, '05, '04, '03, '02, '01, '00, '96, '90, '89, '88, '86, '85, '83, '82.

Château Ducru-Beaucaillou

Set on a deep gravel bank directly above the Gironde, Ducru-Beaucaillou produces one of Bordeaux's most elegant reds.

CHÂTEAU DUCRU-BEAUCAILLOU

St-Julien AC, 2ème Cru Classé
❊ *Cabernet Sauvignon, Merlot, Cabernet Franc, Petit Verdot*

You really do get a feeling of quiet confidence as you gaze at this imposing 19th-century château owned by Bruno Borie. If this image also conjures up reliability, then this has been its reputation for many years. Until a disappointing dip in the late 1980s there hadn't been a single bad wine in more than 20 years. Ducru-Beaucaillou was thought of as the best Second Growth – and though the more showy, extrovert Cos d'Estournel, Léoville-las-Cases and Pichon-Longueville-Comtesse de Lalande wines were as good, many people preferred the fragrant cedar perfume, the soft, gently blackcurranty fruit and the satisfying round sensation of Ducru-Beaucaillou.

I am pleased to report that since 1994 (with a further boost from the 2003 vintage) Ducru has been back on form. If you want to seek out the epitome of St-Julien, mixing charm and austerity, fruit and firmness, this is where you'll find it. Second wine: La Croix de Beaucaillou. Best years: 2010, '09, '08, '07, '06, '05, '04, '03, '02, '01, '00, '99, '98, '96, '95.

Château Duhart-Milon

Duhart used to be rather hard and dry but is now showing a bit more of the mellow class of its sibling, Lafite-Rothschild.

CHÂTEAU DUHART-MILON

Pauillac AC, 4ème Cru Classé
❊ *Cabernet Sauvignon, Merlot, Cabernet Franc*

For decades this property was hardly worthy of its classification. Then in 1962 it was acquired by the Rothschilds whose vineyards at Lafite border those of Duhart; the vineyards were replanted and by the 1980s quality had improved dramatically. The growing maturity of the vineyards and new cellars in 2003 have given Duhart a further lift. Recent vintages have shown impressive structure, but rather more rusticity than typical Pauillac style. It used to be understated but prices have risen on the back of the Asian interest in Lafite. Keep for between seven and 15 years and more in top years. Second wine: Moulin de Duhart. Best years: 2010, '09, '08, '07, '06, '05, '04, '03, '02, '01, '00.

Château Durfort-Vivens

Under the same ownerhsip as Brane-Cantenac, Durfort languished for a similar time, but is now making full, soft, juicy Cantenac wines.

CHÂTEAU DURFORT-VIVENS

Margaux AC, 2ème Cru Classé
❊ *Cabernet Sauvignon, Merlot, Cabernet Franc*

Lucien Lurton purchased this property from the Ginestet family in 1961. The wines were sound but, relative to the estate's Second Growth status, disappointing. Since 1992 Lucien Lurton's son, Gonzague, has been at the helm and there's been considerable investment and improvement. Second Growth quality has still to be attained but recent vintages have shown depth and concentration as well as finesse. Can be drunk at five years, or kept for at least a dozen in the best years. Best years: 2010, '09, '08, '06, '05, '04, '03, '02, '01, '00, '98, '96, '95, '90, '89, '86.

Château d'Escurac

It's not easy to ripen Cabernet inland at Civrac, but d'Escurac's black-fruited wine comes from good use of the gravel soils.

CHÂTEAU D'ESCURAC

Médoc AC
❊ *Cabernet Sauvignon, Merlot, Cabernet Franc*

Ch. d'Escurac enjoys a good location at Civrac on one of the Médoc AC's rare gravel crests. The wines used to be vinified at the local co-operative until 1990 but in the 1990s the owning Landereau family invested in a modern winery and cellars. Progress since then has been considerable at the 16-ha (40-acre) estate. These are well-made wines with fruit and structure, best drunk at five to eight years. Second wine: Chapelle d'Escurac. Best years: 2010, '09, '06, '05, '04, '03, '02, '01, '00, '98.

Château Ferrière

Since its purchase by the Merlaut family, Ferrière has become one of the ripest, most perfumed wines in Margaux.

CHÂTEAU FERRIÈRE
Margaux AC, 3ème Cru Classé
Cabernet Sauvignon, Merlot, Petit Verdot

Margaux's smallest Classed Growth, with just 8ha (20 acres) of vines, Ferrière was leased to its larger neighbour Ch. LASCOMBES until 1992, when it was bought by the Merlaut family of Ch. CHASSE-SPLEEN, among others. The improvement has been startling. It is now managed by Claire Villars. Best years: 2010, '09, '08, '07, '06, '05, '04, '03, '02, '01, '00, '99, '98, '96.

Château Fourcas-Dupré

Fourcas-Dupré is benefitting from the warm conditions recently and has made fine wine in hot years like '03, '05 and '09.

CHÂTEAU FOURCAS-DUPRÉ
Listrac-Médoc AC
Cabernet Sauvignon, Merlot, Cabernet Franc, Petit Verdot

The 44-ha (109-acre) vineyard lies on gravel slopes at 42m (138ft) altitude, the highest point in the Médoc. There's been steady investment and the wines, if not brimming with excitement, while remaining consistent and true to the Listrac appellation – firm, fresh and slightly austere – have added flesh and fruit in recent years. They need five or six years' bottle age. Best years: 2010, '09, '08, '06, '05, '04, '03, '02, '01, '00, '98, '95.

Château Giscours

From 2000 the château has been back on track, and the wines are rich, chocolaty, plummy, and, in cooler years, occasionally perfumed.

CHÂTEAU GISCOURS
Margaux AC, 3ème Cru Classé
Cabernet Sauvignon, Merlot, Cabernet Franc, Petit Verdot

Ch. Giscours made a number of lovely wines in the 1960s and '70s. They started off with a rather solid, almost tarry quality but also had a heavenly perfume, just asking for a few years' maturity, and a fruit that was blackberries, blackcurrants and cherries all at once. Things tailed off disappointingly in the 1980s to a rather more typically dilute Margaux style of wine, and infighting among the owners and a scandal in 1998 concerning a vat of Haut-Médoc that found its way into the second wine, La Sirène de Giscours, didn't help. From 2000, though, the château has been back on track. Best years: 2010, '09, '08, '07, '06, '05, '04, '03, '02, '01, '00, '99, '98, '95, '90, '86, '83, '82, '79.

Château Gloria

Traditionally Gloria is ultra-soft St-Julien but the wines now have a bit more stuffing.

CHÂTEAU GLORIA
St-Julien AC
Cabernet Sauvignon, Merlot, Cabernet Franc, Petit Verdot

An interesting property, created out of tiny plots of Classed Growth land scattered all round St-Julien. Generally very soft and sweet-centred, the wine nonetheless ages well. Second wine: Peymartin. Best years: 2010, '09, '08, '07, '06, '05, '04, '03, '01, '00, '99, '98, '95, '90, '89.

Château Grand-Puy-Ducasse

Grand-Puy-Ducasse doesn't always deliver but can often give lovely Pauillac style at a fair price.

CHÂTEAU GRAND-PUY-DUCASSE
Pauillac AC, 5ème Cru Classé
Cabernet Sauvignon, Merlot

After great improvement in the 1980s, form dipped in the early '90s but recovered again in '96. It's been more dependable since 2005. Approachable after five years, the wines can improve for considerably longer. Second wine: Artigues-Arnaud. Best years: 2010, '09, '08, '07, '06, '05, '04, '03, '02, '00, '96, '95, '90, '89.

Some of the Bordeaux châteaux can be very grand. Luckily, in this case the wine matches the architecture. This is Gruaud-Larose, a leading St-Julien Second Growth which makes one of the most powerful yet sumptuous wines in the appellation.

Château Grand-Puy-Lacoste

This is classic Pauillac with plenty of blackcurrant and cigarbox perfume and recent vintages have been splendid.

CHÂTEAU GRAND-PUY-LACOSTE

Pauillac AC, 5ème Cru Classé

❦ *Cabernet Sauvignon, Merlot, Cabernet Franc*

Don't be fooled by this wine only being a Fifth Growth. Because Pauillac dominated the awards of First Growths in the 1855 Classification, one sometimes gets the feeling that several very exciting properties were rather unceremoniously dumped in the Fifth Growths category so as not to upset the other communes.

However, this 55-ha (136-acre) estate, owned by François-Xavier Borie, makes a classic Pauillac. It isn't as weighty and grand as better-known Pauillac wines like Ch. LATOUR and MOUTON-ROTHSCHILD, but the purity of its flavour marks it out as special. Although it begins in a fairly dense way, that's just how a Pauillac should start out; as the years pass the fruit becomes the most piercingly pure blackcurrant and the perfume mingles cedar with lead pencils and the softening sweetness of new oak. Second wine: Lacoste-Borie. Best years: 2010, '09, '08, '07, '06, '05, '04, '03, '01, '00, '99, '98, '96, '95, '94, '90, '89, '88.

Château Les Grands Chênes

Under new ownership these wines have become richer yet they still hold on to a deep, dry Médoc style.

CHÂTEAU LES GRANDS CHÊNES

Médoc AC

❦ *Merlot, Cabernet Sauvignon, Cabernet Franc*

An honest performer in the early 1990s, this 12-ha (30-acre) estate overlooking the Gironde at St-Christoly-du-Médoc has taken on a rich, modern allure since its purchase by Bernard Magrez of Ch. PAPE-CLÉMENT in 1998. The wines are now dark, ripe and unctuous, polished with a coating of fine oak. Drink at five to six years. If you want it

even richer and darker, there's the super-*cuvée* Magrez Tivoli. Best years: 2009, '08, '06, '05, '04, '03, '02, '01, '00, '99, '98.

Château Gruaud-Larose

Recent vintages have been rich, ripe and delicious, combining impressive power and depth with suavity and finesse.

CHÂTEAU GRUAUD-LAROSE

St-Julien AC, 2ème Cru Classé

❦ *Cabernet Sauvignon, Merlot, Cabernet Franc, Petit Verdot*

With 82ha (203 acres) of vines, Gruaud is one of the largest St-Julien estates, now owned by the same family as Ch. CHASSE-SPLEEN, CAMENSAC and HAUT-BAGES-LIBÉRAL. With vineyards set back a little from the Gironde Gruaud traditionally used to exhibit a softer, more honeyed style when young than, say, the trio of Léoville estates whose vineyards slope down to the Gironde. This didn't stop the wine aging superbly and gaining a piercing, dry, blackcurrant and cedarwood aroma over 20 years or so.

The wines of the 1980s and '90s were made darker and deeper, and despite being thick with the flavours of blackberry and plums, sweetened with wood and toughened with tannin, they managed all too often to show a powerful animal scent that usually faded with maturity. Recent vintages have combined power with a little more finesse, despite disappointments in 2002 and '03. Second wine: Sarget de Gruaud-Larose. Best years: 2010, '09, '08, '07, '06, '05, '04, '01, '00, '99, '98, '96, '95, '90, '89, '88.

Château La Gurgue

La Gurgue doesn't produce as many scented wines as it used to, but they are still ripe, dark and finely balanced.

CHÂTEAU LA GURGUE

Margaux AC

※ *Cabernet Sauvignon, Merlot*

The 10-ha (25-acre) vineyard sits in the shadow of Ch. Margaux so you couldn't ask for a better site. Since 1978 the property has been in the hands of the Merlaut family (owners of among others CHASSE-SPLEEN and GRUAUD-LAROSE) and sensible management and investment first by Bernadette Villars and now her daughter Claire (see HAUT-BAGES-LIBÉRAL and FERRIÈRE) has produced supple, sweet-fruited wines which occasionally exhibit heavenly violet scent. For drinking at five to ten years. Best years: 2010, '09, '06, '05, '04, '03, '02, '01, '00, '98.

Château Haut-Bages-Libéral

Haut-Bages-Libéral has loads of unbridled delicious fruit, a positively hedonistic style and, to cap it all, just about reasonable prices.

CHÂTEAU HAUT-BAGES-LIBÉRAL

Pauillac AC, 5ème Cru Classé

※ *Cabernet Sauvignon, Merlot, Petit Verdot*

I accept that Haut-Bages-Libéral is a relatively obscure little property in Pauillac but I don't accept that it is inferior. Although only classified as a Fifth Growth in 1855, it regularly produces deep, dark reds with buckets of delicious plum and blackcurrant fruit. That's not always enough in the rarified world of Pauillac's wine politics, where austerity is often prized more than ebullience. But there's nothing wrong with the location of the Haut-Bages vineyards – they're only separated by a little country lane from those of the great Ch. LATOUR, and since its purchase in 1983 by the Merlaut family there has been an ambitious programme of renovation.

As the replanted vineyards mature, we are seeing that rich blackcurrant fruit being joined by some cigarbox perfume. And now there's no argument about the vineyard's quality. The talented Claire Villars is in charge here, as she is at Ch. FERRIÈRE. Best years: 2010, '09, '08, '06, '05, '04, '03, '02, '01, '00, '99, '98, '96, '95, '90, '89.

Château Haut-Batailley

Haut-Batailley seems to deliver its potential in about one vintage in five, otherwise the wine is generally pleasant but surprisingly light.

CHÂTEAU HAUT-BATAILLEY

Pauillac AC, 5ème Cru Classé

※ *Cabernet Sauvignon, Merlot, Cabernet Franc*

They call this estate the 'St-Julien' of Pauillac. It's a small property of 22ha (54 acres) of vines set back from the melting pot

of brilliant wines close to the Gironde estuary, and is owned by François-Xavier Borie of Ch. GRAND-PUY-LACOSTE.

Ch. Haut-Batailley gets its 'St-Julien' tag because it lacks the concentrated power of a true Classed Growth Pauillac. This doesn't matter if the wines have the perfume and cedary excitement of St-Julien, but until recently they rarely did; they were pleasant, a little spicy, but rarely memorable. Recent vintages have improved, though, with greater depth and structure and, since 2004, a more frequent return to some of the beautiful wines made in the 1970s. The wines can be drunk relatively young. Best years: 2010, '09, '08, '07, '06, '05, '04, '03, '02, '01, '00, '98, '96, '95.

Château Haut-Marbuzet

These are big, ripe, oaky, modern wines but they've been like this for decades. My 1978 is still rich and oaky – and delicious.

CHÂTEAU HAUT-MARBUZET

St-Estèphe AC

※ *Cabernet Sauvignon, Merlot, Cabernet Franc*

Haut-Marbuzet's 61-ha (150-acre) vineyard is sited between its more illustrious neighbours, MONTROSE and COS D'ESTOURNEL. The energetic Monsieur Duboscq treats his wine like a top Classed Growth – right up to using 100 per cent new oak for maturing it – and the great, rich, mouthfilling blast of flavour certainly isn't subtle, but certainly is impressive. The wine also ages extremely well, shaking off its cloak of oak to reveal a complex spectrum of aromas and flavours. Best years: 2009, '08, '07, '06, '05, '04, '03, '02, '01, '00, '99, '98, '96, '95, '94, '90, '89, '88, '86.

Château L'Inclassable

Alcohol levels in the Médoc nowadays reach previously of unheard of levels – but this can add richness to wines from the northern Médoc.

CHÂTEAU L'INCLASSABLE
Médoc AC
❧ *Cabernet Sauvignon, Merlot, Cabernet Franc, Petit Verdot*

A complicated French law suit obliged owner Rémy Fauchey to drop the name Ch. Lafon and rebaptise the 16-ha (40-acre) estate as L'Inclassable from the 2002 vintage. Whatever its name, this is a consistent, well-managed property, producing dark, firmly textured wines for drinking at three to five years. Best years: 2010, '09, '08, '06, '05, '04, '03, '02, '01, '00, '99, '98.

Château d'Issan

Ch. d'Issan's vineyards slope steeply towards the Gironde and can produce one of Margaux's most scented wines.

CHÂTEAU D'ISSAN
Margaux AC, 3ème Cru Classé
❧ *Cabernet Sauvignon, Merlot*

This lovely 17th-century moated property, a classified historical monument, has disappointed me far too often in the past but pulled its socks up in the 1990s. It has been run by Emmanuel Cruse since 1997. Best years: 2010, '09, '08, '07, '06, '05, '04, '03, '02, '01, '00, '99, '98, '96, '95, '90, '89, '85.

Château Kirwan

This Margaux estate has shown considerable improvement since the mid-1990s.

CHÂTEAU KIRWAN
Margaux AC, 3ème Cru Classé
❧ *Cabernet Sauvignon, Merlot, Cabernet Franc, Petit Verdot*

Kirwan frequently used to have a lovely violet scent, but this was marred by angular tannins that never seemed to soften. Now, investment in the cellars, more attention to the vineyards and the advice of consultant Michel Rolland until 2007 has produced wines of greater depth and richness, but the power and the scent are still there. Second wine: Les Charmes de Kirwan. Best years: 2010, '09, 08, '07, '06, '05, '04, '03, '01, '00, '99, '98, '96, '95.

There should be a sleeping princess inside this lovely château, waiting to be kissed back to life. Well, d'Issan's wines have improved so much recently, maybe I'm the prince she's been waiting for.

Château Labégorce

The 2003 was one of the last vintages made by Luc Thienpont before the sale of the château in 2005.

CHÂTEAU LABÉGORCE
Margaux AC
❧ *Cabernet Sauvignon, Merlot, Cabernet Franc, Petit Verdot*

Since 2009 Ch. Labégorce has been returned to its 18th-century form. Industrialist Hubert Perrodo bought Labégorce in 1989, then Labégorce-Zédé in 2005 and a third property l'Abbé Gorce de Gorce, unifying what used to be one estate until the property was split in 1795. The first vintage of the restored 66-ha (163-acre) estate was the 2009. The classed growth Ch. MARQUIS D'ALESME is also under the same ownership. Best years: 2010, '09, '08, '07, '05, '04, '03, '02, '01, '00.

Château Lafite-Rothschild

The trouble with Lafite is it's so damned famous. As a young wine enthusiast keen to experience the best, the chance to talk about Lafite, to read the old-timers' tasting notes, to wonder could it really be that good, occurred all the time. But did we ever get our mitts on a bottle? Almost never. And now the Chinese are buying the lot!

Just about the only First Growth we ever tasted was that other Pauillac great – Ch. Latour – because Latour still made gorgeous wine in feeble vintages which merchants would sell off to us for a quid or two just to clear their shelves. But nobody said that Lafite made delicious wine in poor vintages – rather the opposite, in fact – they said you had to buy the top years – and neither my friends nor I were ever flush enough to do so.

Yet if we had, I suspect we'd have come away mumbling about the Emperor's new clothes, because for an awful long time after the Second World War, while other Bordeaux properties were dusting themselves down and getting back on the quality track, Lafite seemed to be idling. There were excuses. For a start, due to its being owned by the Jewish Rothschild family, Lafite was requisitioned and nationalized during the war, and that took a while to recover from. But when I did at last get a chance to taste Lafite reasonably widely, I was barely more impressed. In a tasting of Latour and Lafite spanning the vintages between 1945 and 1981, Latour romped home every time, excepting 1953 and 1976. Things began improving in the 1980s – strangely the 1984 was rather good, and the '86 was the best wine of the vintage – but it wasn't until the 1990s – 1990 and '96 were star wines – that Lafite began regularly challenging for the top spot in a vintage. And it wasn't until the 21st century, kicking off with superlative wines in 2000 and '01, that Lafite regularly achieved its old position as the best wine in the Médoc, and possibly the best red wine in all Bordeaux.

Best wine is going it a bit, but in the famous 1855 classification of Bordeaux red, Lafite was the top wine – the one getting the best price, creating the most demand. You need more than a great wine to hit the top, you need a bit of luck too, and maybe Lafite had it when the Duc de Richelieu was made governor of Guyenne in Bordeaux in 1755. When he returned to court, Louis XV remarked that he looked 25 years younger, and Richelieu replied that he'd discovered the fountain of youth whilst in Bordeaux, and it was called Lafite. Producing a famous wine in 1811, the year of the comet also helped, and right through the 19th century, whenever the chance came to make a great wine – not so often in those days – Lafite did so. Don't ask me how they tasted; I don't know. But I read the tasting notes and they sure sound good.

Quick guide

CLASSIFICATION
Pauillac AC, Premier Cru Classé

VINEYARD
114ha (282 acres) planted with Cabernet Sauvignon (71%), Merlot (25%), Cabernet Franc (3%), Petit Verdot (1%)

TYPICAL BLEND
80–85% Cabernet Sauvignon, 8–15% Merlot, 1–2% Cabernet Franc, 1–2% Petit Verdot

ANNUAL PRODUCTION OF THE GRAND VIN
240,000 bottles

BEST YEARS
2010, '09, '08, '07, '06, '05, '04, '03, '02, '01, '00, '99, '98, '97, '96, '95, '94, '90, '89, '88, '86, '85, '82, '81

CLASSIC OLDER VINTAGES
1976, '59, '53, '21

SECOND WINE
Carruades de Lafite-Rothschild

Château Lafite-Rothschild
The Lafite of the 21st century is quite unlike the previous incarnation, but is equally exciting and much more consistent.

Above: Just because you are one of the great original estates of the Médoc doesn't mean you can't move with the times. This magnificent, circular underground barrel cellar is one of the Médoc's modern architectural wonders; and I've even had dinner here once.

And talking of luck. What's with the Chinese and Lafite? No one is quite sure why, but in the 21st century, Lafite has become the most sought after wine on Far Eastern tables, with rocketing prices to match.

So what are these modern Lafites like? Don't look for weight, but do look for muscle, beautiful, lithe, willowy muscle. Don't look for a blast of super-ripe fruit, but do look for the beauty of black fruit picked from the vine while the grape skin is still taut and eager and the flavour has the perfect sweetness of blackcurrant, black cherries and plum. And do look for scent. When the wine's young you might still smell new wood, but that won't prevail. Maturity will occasionally bring you the haunting violet scent of Lafite's neighbour Margaux, but always the austere, irresistible perfume of cedar, sometimes so strong you could be rubbing a fresh-cut sliver of golden cedar on your tongue. Of course, elegance is the word most used to describe Lafite. What does it mean? A few mouthfuls of Lafite, and you're a little closer to understanding.

Above: One of the ways grape-growing has improved is to monitor conditions closely in the vineyard – both above and below ground. Behind the computerized weather station, you can see the entrance to the new circular undergound cellar.

Facing page above: A rather more domestic view of Lafite than one is used to, showing how less suitable vine-rowing land is used for market gardening and fruit trees. Only the well-drained gravelly soil you can see rising up to the left of the buildings and at the bottom lefthand corner of the painting is good enough to ripen Cabernet Sauvignon.

Facing page below: Lafite and its estate was purchased by the Rothschild family for the then astronomical sum of five million francs in 1868. The family obviously had a bit of money left over to decorate the interior in the plush Second Empire style of the day. This is the Salon Rouge and these formal rooms are virtually unchanged today. I don't feel quite right there unless I'm wearing black tie.

Below: Renowned taster Michael Broadbent says the 1803 Lafite is 'a sound, fragrant, dry, lean but firm' wine and since he's probably the only person in the world who has a tasting note on it I won't argue.

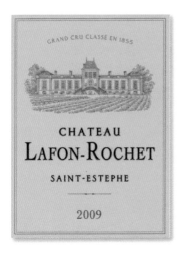

Château Lafon-Rochet

Lafon-Rochet's reputation is for needing a warm summer to ripen, but the mature vineyard is now producing fine wine most years.

CHÂTEAU LAFON-ROCHET

St-Estèphe AC, 4ème Cru Classé

Cabernet Sauvignon, Merlot, Cabernet Franc

Guy Tesseron started the task of improving Ch. Lafon-Rochet in the 1960s and the work has since been continued by his sons, Alfred and now Michel. The effort and investment is now showing in the wines. The vineyard site is a good one: 40ha (99 acres) are planted at the western end of the slopes which are also occupied by COS D'ESTOURNEL, St-Estèphe's leading château, and it looks out across the Jalle du Breuil to Ch. LAFITE-ROTHSCHILD.

The wines used to be considered hard and austere, a problem caused partly by the youthful nature of the vines and also by the high percentage of Cabernet Sauvignon planted on a part of the vineyard that is better suited to Merlot. The vineyard has now matured – the average age of the vines is now more than 30 years – and the percentage of Merlot has been increased, resulting in wines which are more supple than in the past but which still retain a wonderful concentrated dry blackcurrant fruit, often with a tannic edge, and which are not too pricy. Second wine: Les Pélerins de Lafon-Rochet. Best years: 2010, '09, '08, '07, '06, '05, '04, '03, '02, '01, '00, '99, '98, '96, '95, '94, '90, '89.

Château Lagrange

Lagrange now makes wines of tremendous power – always rather tannic but with a marvellously pure fruit.

CHÂTEAU LAGRANGE

St-Julien AC, 3ème Cru Classé

Cabernet Sauvignon, Merlot, Petit Verdot

Sauvignon Blanc, Sémillon, Muscadelle

To many people, this ramshackle, lumbering estate – 109ha (270 acres) of vines at the very western borders of St-Julien beyond Ch. GRUAUD-LAROSE and the largest of the Médoc's Classed Growths – didn't seem a candidate for super-stardom, but it has always had potentially one of the finest vineyards in the whole Médoc. The giant Japanese Suntory company bought Lagrange in 1983, and immediately set about renewing just about everything – the château, *chai* and vineyards. At the time of Suntory's purchase, some of the best parts of the vineyard were even lying fallow. With the aid of huge investment, inspired winemaker Marcel Ducasse (who retired in 2007) transformed the wine style over the next decades.

Lagrange is no longer an amiable, shambling wine, but instead a clear-eyed, single-minded wine of tremendous power and increasing depth and complexity. Since 1983 the wines have aged well but the wines of the '90s and 2000s will be better, if they shed their tannins, showing just how good this vineyard can be. As of 1997 there's a little barrel-fermented white, Les Arums de Lagrange. Second wine: Les Fiefs de Lagrange. Best years: 2010, '09, '08, '06, '05, '04, '03, '02, '01, '00, '98, '96, '95, '90, '89, '88.

Château La Lagune

I owned 102 bottles of La Lagune 1961 once. It was blackcurrant bliss. Modern vintages are more middleweight in style.

CHÂTEAU LA LAGUNE

Haut-Médoc AC, 3ème Cru Classé

Cabernet Sauvignon, Merlot, Cabernet Franc, Petit Verdot

La Lagune is just to the south of the village of Margaux, and is the closest Classed Growth to the city of Bordeaux itself. The 80ha (198 acres) of vineyards have been steadily restructured and retrellised from 1999 when the Frey family bought the property.

You can certainly taste the investment in the charry chestnut sweetness of new oak and the positively mellow texture of most vintages. I felt the 'crowd-pleasing' character was a little overdone (though '04 was a gentle classic). Indeed a new *cuverie* was built in 2004 and the current direction seems to me to make fuller, more structured wine with less evident oak, which I'm all in favour of! Second wine: Moulin de la Lagune. Best years: 2010, '09, '08, '06, '05, '04, '03, '02, '00, '98, '96, '95, '90, '89.

What a beautiful tranquil scene. Whenever I see Ch. Lagrange I wonder if the architect couldn't decide whether he was designing a château or a church. However, this is a hard-working château, with the biggest vineyard in St-Julien, right next to Ch. Gruaud-Larose, and with a reputation for finely crafted, but initially assertive reds needing a few years' maturity to reflect the beauty of the buildings.

Château Lanessan

Lanessan is a little richer now than it used to be but is still restrained and elegant and well worth aging.

Château Langoa-Barton

Langoa-Barton is usually a rich, burly, satisfying mouthful, but can be deep, laden with dark fruit and scented with graphite and cigar.

Château Lascombes

Lascombes is still not achieving much recognisable Margaux finesse but the wines are improving.

CHÂTEAU LANESSAN
Haut-Médoc AC
❊ *Cabernet Sauvignon, Merlot, Cabernet Franc, Petit Verdot*

Lanessan is an attractive but occasionally austere wine from the commune of Cussac-Fort-Médoc that only uses a small percentage of new oak barrels. Yet it often achieves Fifth Growth standard and is rarely overpriced. In fact, Lanessan supposedly missed out on being included in the 1855 Classification because the owner, a certain Monsieur Delbos, forgot to send in the required samples. Lanessan tends to be at its best in top vintages and can easily age for eight to ten years. Second wine: Les Calèches de Lanessan. Best years: 2010, '09, '08, '06, '05, '04, '03, '02, '00, '98, '96, '95, '90, '89.

CHÂTEAU LANGOA-BARTON
St-Julien AC, 3ème Cru Classé
❊ *Cabernet Sauvigon, Merlot, Cabernet Franc*

This 17-ha (42-acre) property has been owned by the Barton family since 1821. The wine isn't necessarily lighter in style than its St-Julien stablemate, Ch. LÉOVILLE-BARTON, but is, in fact, usually richer, jammier, more exuberant, less classic. It's also reasonably priced though no longer cheap and delicious. Drink the wine after seven or eight years, although it will keep for 15 or more. Second wine: Réserve de Léoville-Barton. Best years: 2010, '09, '08, '07, '06, '05, '04, '03, '02, '01, '00, '99, '98, '96, '95, '90, '89, '88.

CHÂTEAU LASCOMBES
Margaux AC, 2ème Cru Classé
❊ *Merlot, Cabernet Sauvignon, Petit Verdot*

Ch. Lascombes is one of the great underachievers in the Margaux appellation, with little wine made in the 1980s and '90s that was worth drinking. The large 84-ha (207-acre) vineyard needs careful management to provide good quality fruit as it is not sited on the best land; in the past it hasn't always had it.

However, American ownership and investment have made some difference – there have been improvements since 2001, but the real spark hasn't yet returned. The wines are richer, riper, full and oaky but still miss the Margaux finesse. Michel Rolland is now the consultant enologist so I hope he re-awakes a flicker of Margaux beauty in the wine. Best years: 2010, '09, '08, '07, '06, '05, '04, '03, '01, '00, '96, '95.

Château Latour

When I was a student and then a touring actor, money was incredibly short and yet, just now and then, I could rustle together enough to buy a First Growth Bordeaux. Château Latour. Not one of the great vintages – I could never have afforded one of them. Not even one of the good vintages.

I bought the bad vintages, the vintages that merchants wanted to clear off their shelves as fast as possible to anyone who offered them a small wodge of ready cash: 1954, '56, '60, '63, '65, '68, '72 – and so it went on. But the thing is, whenever everybody else failed, Latour still came up with delicious wine. And this isn't a recent phenomenon. I even have a tasting note on the 1881, a poor vintage reputed to have produced a small crop of 'mediocre, green, tannic wines'. Except my Latour 1881, which had an austere haughtiness as befitted its great age but also a scent of cedar as though I stood in the depths of a dark cedar forest.

That 1881 is not the only venerable Latour I've tried. I've tasted the 1870, the 1864, and I've actually drunk the 1865, great mouthfuls of it, only a couple of years ago. Old wines can wander down strange pathways, and so it was with the 1865, amazingly deep in colour, peppery, almost fiery, then a deep dry black plum fruit woven through with cedar and brushed with soy sauce savouriness, and after all this, a glittering streak of volatile acidity like country cider that was spellbinding.

So I am deeply grateful to Ch. Latour for making wines that lasted so long and so well. Most old wines I can only read about, but with Ch. Latour I've actually been able to taste back 20, 50, 100, 150 years, to imagine how the world was then, before one world war, before two, to times when kings and emperors ruled, and communism, nuclear power and human flight were distant dreams. That's very precious. Even when I taste a wine of 15 or 20 years' age, I take time to remember what I was doing when it was made, who I was, who I was with. But to be able to drink wines that come from times before I was born, times I could only read about in history books, that experience gives a totally different, humbling yet uplifting dimension to the joys of taste.

And I'm also able to thank Latour for its reliability. With the exception of a period in the 1980s when, for commercial and possibly philosophical reasons, Latour lightened itself up, Latour is brilliant in a reassuringly predictable way – tremendous weight of black fruit, a tannic power that seems to have been wrought from the deep gravel beds of the vineyard itself, and a promise of that greatest, yet simplest of all red Bordeaux pleasures in maturity – pure blackcurrant fruit intertwined with the heavenly scent of cedar.

Quick guide

CLASSIFICATION
Pauillac AC, Premier Cru Classé

VINEYARD
80ha (198 acres) planted with Cabernet Sauvignon (75%), Merlot (20%), Cabernet Franc (4%), Petit Verdot (1%)

TYPICAL BLEND
89% Cabernet Sauvignon, 10% Merlot, 1% Petit Verdot

ANNUAL PRODUCTION OF THE GRAND VIN
132,000 bottles

BEST YEARS
2010, '09, '08, '07, '06, '05, '04, '03, '02, '01, '00, '99, '98, '97, '96, '95, '94, '93, '90, '89, '88, '86, '82

CLASSIC OLDER VINTAGES
1970, '66, '61, '59, '49

SECOND WINE
Les Forts de Latour

Château Latour
Latour loves a challenge – hot vintage, cold vintage, wet or dry – and makes a blockbuster almost every year nowadays.

Above: This isn't the original Latour 'tower', it's just a little Louis XIII dovecote. Nice, though. What's more important is that it sits atop a deep ridge of gravel that sweeps down to the Gironde in the background.

Right: Old vines and gravel. The classic combination for great red wine in Pauillac. This is a 40-year-old Cabernet Sauvignon with roots deep into the gravels of the L'Enclos parcel at the heart of the Latour estate and its grapes will no doubt end up in the *grand vin*.

Below right: This is just one tiny corner of Latour's new first year *chai*. In all, there are over 1000 new barrels stored here each vintage – all new and costing £460 (€600) each. It all adds to the cost of the wine, but Latour has such a deep, intense fruit flavour that oak flavours rarely dominate in the finished wine.

Facing page: These fermentation vats look positively space age, but in fact they copy the shape of the old wooden vats because some experts believe this helps with a gentler yet efficient extraction of colour, tannin and flavour from the skins.

This predictability doesn't mean that Latour isn't modern, doesn't change with the times. Indeed, Latour frequently leads the moves to innovate. But ever since the estate was established, there's been a wonderful sense of continuity. Latour's original brilliance was created by the Ségur family in the 1700s, and they owned it till 1962, when it was sold to a British consortium. In 1993 French tycoon François Pinault bought it. And that's it: three changes of ownership in 300 years. And the vineyard that has created this remarkable, recognizable star is basically the same as that planted by the Ségurs – a billowing ridge of deep gravels overlooking and running down to the Gironde's edge. There's a Médoc saying – you have to be able to see the water to make great wine. Well, no First Growth is closer to the estuary then Latour, so in good years the vineyard soaks up extra heat reflected from the water, yet in years like 1956 and 1991, when frosts devastate the region, Latour is protected by the moderating effect of the wide, warm estuary's embrace, and can calmly get on with creating one of the world's greatest wines.

Château Léoville-Barton
Austere and restrained at first, this excellent traditional St-Julien wine unfolds into a purist's dream of blackcurrant and cedarwood.

CHÂTEAU LÉOVILLE-BARTON

St-Julien AC, 2ème Cru Classé
❋ Cabernet Sauvignon, Merlot, Cabernet Franc

Ah. My first ever great Bordeaux. Léoville-Barton 1962. At my first ever wine tasting. The classical beauty of its dry blackcurrant fruit, mellow texture and haunting cedarwood scent gave me a role model for perfect claret that I shall go on seeking – and occasionally finding – until the last drop passes my lips. Anthony Barton, whose family has run this Second Growth St-Julien since 1826, has resolutely refused to profiteer in spite of considerable pressure to do so, especially in the early to late 1980s, when every Classed Growth Bordeaux vintage was released at a substantially higher price than the last, regardless of actual worth. But he refused to raise the prices of his wines above a level he considered fair. In recent vintages he's finally beginning to charge something closer to the market value – but it's still less than his neighbours.

Yet as he freely declares, he still runs a profitable business. He knows what it costs to make fine wine, he never stints on quality, and he certainly doesn't intend to make a less than satisfactory profit. Top Bordeaux prices since 2005 have gone crazy. Léoville-Barton is still a little island of just affordable sanity.

This 47-ha (116-acre) estate – with 72% Cabernet Sauvignon, 20% Merlot and only 8% Cabernet Franc – makes dark, dry, tannic wines, difficult to taste young and therefore frequently underestimated at the outset, but

over ten to 15 years they achieve a lean yet beautifully proportioned quality, the blackcurrants and cedarwood very dry, but pungent enough to fill the room with their scent. They are a traditionalist's delight. Vintages through the 1990s and 2000s were fantastic and even the off-vintages are good (very good, classic St-Julien). Second wine: Réserve de Léoville-Barton. Best years: 2010, '09, '08, '07, '06, '05, '04, '03, '02, '01, '00, '99, '98, '96, '95, '94, '93, '90, '89, '88.

Château Léoville-Las-Cases
These dark, super-concentrated wines are sometimes hardly recognizable as St-Julien but are powerful expressions of the modern Bordeaux.

CHÂTEAU LÉOVILLE-LAS-CASES

St-Julien AC, 2ème Cru Classé
❋ Cabernet Sauvignon, Merlot, Cabernet Franc, Petit Verdot

The St-Julien AC wasn't accorded a First Growth château in the 1855 Classification. Any re-evaluation might change all that, because Léoville-las-Cases' late owner, Michel Delon, tirelessly maximized the excellent potential of the vineyards. Going to meet Monsieur Delon was rather like having an audience with your headmaster at school, but those challenging tasting sessions with him in his cellars gave one a true understanding of the passion and commitment that is great Bordeaux. His son, Jean-Hubert, is now in charge.

The 97-ha (240-acre) vineyard is the biggest of the three Léoville estates, and a neighbour of the great Ch. LATOUR. There are similarities in the wine because since 1975 Las-Cases has been making wines of dark, deep concentration hardly recognizable as St-Julien. Yet there is also

something sweeter and more enticing right from the start – the fumes of new oak spice linger over the glass even in the wine's most stubborn adolescent sulks, and the tannins, strong though they are, have a habit of dissolving into smiles in your mouth exactly at the moment you've decided that they are just too much. Las-Cases from a good year really needs 15 years to shine. Second wine: Le Petit Lion (from 2007). Clos du Marquis used to be the second wine but is now a separate label. Best years: 2010, '09, '08, '07, '06, '05, '04, '03, '02, '01, '00, '99, '98, '96, '95, '94, '93, '90, '89, '88, '86.

Château Léoville-Poyferré
All the hard work at Poyferré is paying off, plush fruit and spice blending seamlessly with classic St-Julien elegance.

CHÂTEAU LÉOVILLE-POYFERRÉ

St-Julien AC, 2ème Cru Classé
❋ Cabernet Sauvignon, Merlot, Petit Verdot, Cabernet Franc

Until comparatively recently, Poyferré was the least good of the three Léoville properties. The 1980s saw a marked improvement, however, with a string of excellent wines made under the watchful eye of Didier Cuvelier, who has gradually increased the richness of the wine without wavering from its refined style, and has significantly reduced the percentage of Merlot in the vineyard.

The 1990s followed in the same vein, often ranking with the best in St-Julien and achieving the epitome of St-Julien elegance. Recent vintages have been among the best yet. The wines need eight to ten years to blossom but will go on improving for at least twice that length. Second wine: Ch. Moulin-Riche. Best years: 2010, '09, '08, '07, '06, '05, '04, '03, '02, '01, '00, '99, '98, '96, '95, '90, '89, '86.

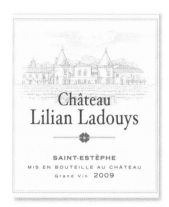

Château Lilian Ladouys

Known for firm, chewy wine, Ladouys has opted for gentler texture and mild, attractive red fruit in recent vintages.

CHÂTEAU LILIAN LADOUYS

St-Estèphe AC

🍇 *Cabernet Sauvignon, Merlot, Cabernet Franc*

This 45-ha (111-acre) property across the road from Lafon-Rochet has had its ups and downs since it was removed from the local co-operative by new owners in 1989 but seems to have got back into stride since the late 1990s. Keep for five to six years. Best years: 2010, '09, '08, '07, '06, '05, '04.

Château Lynch-Bages

Lynch-Bages has made some thrilling wines in the last generation and is now one of the most sought after wines in Pauillac.

CHÂTEAU LYNCH-BAGES

Pauillac AC, 5ème Cru Classé

🍇 *Cabernet Sauvignon, Merlot, Cabernet Franc, Petit Verdot*

🍇 *Sauvignon Blanc, Sémillon, Muscadelle*

Sometimes, tasting this wonderful wine with its almost succulent richness, its gentle texture and its starburst of flavours all butter and blackcurrants and mint, you may wonder why it has a comparatively lowly position as a Fifth Growth Pauillac. It can only be because the chaps who devised the 1855 Bordeaux Classification were basically puritans. They couldn't bear to admit that a wine as open-heartedly lovely as Lynch-

Bages could really be as important as other less generous Growths. Well, it is. Wine is about pleasure. Great wine is about great pleasure and there are few wines which will so regularly give you such great pleasure as Lynch-Bages.

The 97ha (240 acres) of vines are planted in the traditional Pauillac mix, with a lot of Cabernet Sauvignon – 73%. This sounds like a tough wine taking a long time to mature – but that's the magic of Lynch-Bages – rich and ripe and oozing with blackcurrant and damson when young, still heady and succulent but a little more scented at ten years, even more beautiful at 20 years, with the scents of mint leaf and cedarwood coming into their own. Second wine: Echo de Lynch-Bages. A small amount of white wine, Blanc de Lynch-Bages, has been made since 1990. Best years: 2010, '09, '08, '07, '06, '05, '04, '03, '02, '01, '00, '99, '98, '96, '95, '94, '90, '89, '88.

Wow! The space age comes to Pauillac. The château of Lynch-Bages is a friendly, homely 19th-century farmhouse, but maybe the modern paintings on the wall should have prepared me because this eye-popping edifice is the cutting-edge cellar where the Cazes family make their global brand Michel Lynch.

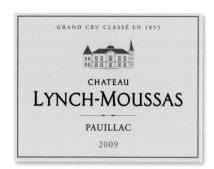

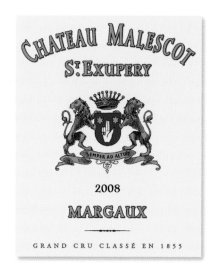

Château Lynch-Moussas

Lynch-Moussas has been improving all through the 2000s, culminating with an excellent 2009.

CHÂTEAU LYNCH-MOUSSAS

Pauillac AC, 5ème Cru Classé

Cabernet Sauvignon, Merlot

Owned, like its neighbour Ch. BATAILLEY, by the famous Bordeaux merchants Borie-Manoux, this fine property was allowed to become run down for much of the 20th century, but underwent a much needed modernization and subsequent revival in the 1970s. In fact, I think I remember a rather good 1970.

The owners had another go during the '90s and the wine is gradually assuming its proper place as a Pauillac classed growth. It's about time, because the soils are good, but replanting meant that the vines have only gradually matured during the 2000s, and each recent vintage is showing more class and depth. At the same time, the price stays reasonable. Recent vintages have shown a little more depth and fruit. Most vintages should be drunk after five or six years' aging. Best years: 2010, '09, '08, '07, '06, '05, '04.

Château Malescasse

Malescasse is an immensely reliable, soft-centred Haut-Médoc, but capable of aging if need be. In short, it is an excellent buy.

CHÂTEAU MALESCASSE

Haut-Médoc AC

Cabernet Sauvignon, Merlot, Cabernet Franc

This 37-ha (91-acre) property with vineyards on excellent gravelly soils near the port of Lamarque has achieved a quiet consistency over the last ten years. I like the way the wines are round and supple and ready for drinking at four to five years but have enough smooth-limbed structure to last for at least twice that time. Best years: 2010, '09, '08, '06, '05, '04, '03, '02, '01, '00.

Château Malescot-St-Exupéry

Drought years like 2003 don't really suit Malescot's perfumed style, but they still made a good, rich wine with more structure than perfume.

CHÂTEAU MALESCOT ST-EXUPÉRY

Margaux AC, 3ème Cru Classé

Cabernet Sauvignon, Merlot, Cabernet Franc, Petit Verdot

This was once one of the most scented, exotic reds in Bordeaux and a model of perfumed Margaux. In the 1980s Malescot lost its reputation as the wine became curiously pale and dilute (excepting a fine, scented 1983). However, since 2000 it has rediscovered that lovely cassis and violet perfume and is back to its winning ways. When it's on song, as in the 1996, '01 or '04 vintages, you'll be hard put to find a more fragrant wine in all of Bordeaux. Best years: 2010, '09, '08, '07, '06, '05, '04, '02, '01, '00, '99, '98, '96, '95.

Château Marbuzet
Marbuzet has a lovely château and good gravelly soils. Until its incorporation into Cos d'Estournel in 2007 the wine was finely balanced with a very attractive sweet core of fruit.

CHÂTEAU MARBUZET
St-Estèphe AC
Cabernet Sauvignon, Merlot, Petit Verdot

The beautiful property with its handsome Louis XVI-style château is owned by Michel Reybier, the owner of St-Estèphe's leading château, COS D'ESTOURNEL. Until the creation of Les Pagodes de Cos by Cos d'Estournel in 1994, Marbuzet was considered as the second wine of Cos even though they are separate estates. Since 2007 Marbuzet has been integrated into Cos d'Estournel. The Marbuzet label is still sometimes used as the second wine for some markets.

Produced from its own 7-ha (17.3-acre) vineyard, the wine is vinified and bottled separately, and now stands on its own merits. It offers a breadth of crunchy fruit on the palate with a finely edged structure. It needs four to five years' bottle aging but will age longer. Best years: 2005, '04, '03, '02, '01, '00, '99, '98, '96, '95, '90, '89.

Gravel becomes less evident in St-Estèphe, and clay starts to dominate, but the best properties are situated on whatever gravel banks do exist. Poised on the top of a gravelly knoll just across the railway line from Cos d'Estournel, Ch. Marbuzet is small and exquisite. Cos is St-Estèphe's most gravelly vineyard and used the label for its second wine until 2007. The Marbuzet vineyard is now a part of Cos d'Estournel.

Château Margaux

I don't think I've been showing Château Margaux enough respect. Margaux is a property whose Palladian portico makes you think you should have turned up for a barrel tasting in black tie, yet I first drank it out of a plastic cup.

Yes, a plastic cup. In the Rhône Valley. In a car park. And it was the legendary 1961, a wine the very mention of which sends shivers of delight down the spine of connoisseurs. And was it any good? Yes, it was fantastic. Without doubt the best wine I've ever drunk out of a plastic cup in a car park. And Margaux 1961 is without doubt the best wine I've ever poured over strawberries and dusted with caster sugar and black pepper. I'm not joking. But I didn't suggest it: my host did. It was his bottle. And it was shockingly good.

Well, those are my only two experiences of 1961. But 1966. Ah, that's something else. The old timers will tell you this wasn't a top Margaux, but I'm here to tell you it was as top as it gets, because this is the one Margaux I've actually owned. And I owned 36 bottles of it. I used to own rather a lot of superb wine from the 1960s and '70s, but, let's put it this way, they are no longer in my possession due to the activities of person or persons unknown. But God bless a doctor friend of mine from university, who rang up one day and said, 'You remember those Château Margaux we bought for three pounds a bottle years ago? Well, I've got three cases of yours under the stairs.' I doubt if he's ever been embraced so fervently.

And I drank those lovely 1966s with food, without food, indoors and out – but always with friends. And quite often watching football (soccer if you're reading this in America). Let me explain. England won the World Cup in 1966. They've won nothing since. So when I watch them play, I drink Bordeaux 1966, trying to will them on to further triumphs. And when it's a really important game, we crack open the Margaux. So far its main job has been to sweeten the bitterness of defeat, but it has done so graciously, sensitively, beautifully. But you do see what I mean about lack of respect? No evening dress and silver service, no flunkies and five-course meals. Just me, my friends and it.

But, if the old Margaux owners were all aristocrats and might have minded, the current powers-that-be at Margaux are extremely modern and might understand. So, what is the precious Margaux like? Well, it was one of the original properties in Bordeaux to begin selling its wine under its own name. Haut-Brion started the practice, but Margaux wasn't far behind and was a sizeable estate by the end of the 17th century. It sits atop the first really grand gravel outcrop that you come to on the road north from Bordeaux, its vineyards shining improbably white in the summer

Quick guide

CLASSIFICATION
Margaux AC, Premier Cru Classé

VINEYARD
82ha (203 acres) planted with Cabernet Sauvignon (75%), Merlot (20%), Petit Verdot (3%), Cabernet Franc (2%); also 12ha (30 acres) for white wine planted 100% with Sauvignon Blanc

TYPICAL BLEND
75–85% Cabernet Sauvignon,
7–18% Merlot, 3–7% Petit Verdot,
0–4% Cabernet Franc

ANNUAL PRODUCTION OF THE GRAND VIN
150,000 bottles

BEST YEARS
2010, '09, '08, '07, '06, '05, '04, '03, '02, '01, '00, '99, '98, '97, '96, '95, '94, '93, '90, '89, '88, '86, '85, '83, '82

CLASSIC OLDER VINTAGES
1979, '78, '66, '61, '53, '28, '00

SECOND WINE
Pavillon Rouge du Ch. Margaux

WHITE WINE
Pavillon Blanc du Ch. Margaux

BEST YEARS
(Whites) 2010, '09, '08, '07, '06, '05, '04, '02, '01, '00, '99, '98

Château Margaux
Margaux 1966. Ah, I know you so well. Only last night I took out my last bottle. I didn't drink it, not quite. But I will. This year. Or next. And it will be beautiful.

This is seriously grand, an unmistakable statement of dignity and power. Built in 1810, Château Margaux is now almost hidden from passers-by on the road by an avenue of tall, stately trees.

Another view of Ch. Margaux's land – but where are the vines? This is the palus, the flat alluvial meadow directly below the gravelly vineyard. Vines are only planted on the gravel slopes, but the meadow still does sterling work, feeding the cows which then provide manure for the vineyard. All very eco-friendly.

sun as the pebbles gleam and virtually obscure the thin earth below. Such soils are perfect for Bordeaux red wines and during the 19th century and much of the 20th century a series of memorable wines were made.

Things went wrong during the 1960s and '70s when the owners – one of Bordeaux's great merchant families, the Ginestets – simply couldn't afford the investment and commitment a supreme property like Margaux requires. Margaux was Bordeaux's most extreme example of the famed French concept of 'terroir' and its precious 'Appelation d'Origine Contrôlée' legal framework failing to ensure that a fabled wine would necessarily taste special. All that 'terroir' means is that the potential for great wine lies in a particular piece of land so long as men and women are prepared to commit their emotions, their muscle and their money to achieving greatness. Without human will a great piece of vineyard land is just a piece of land. Supreme human endeavour is required to unlock that greatness. The Ginestet family were unable to do this. But when the Mentzelopoulos family bought Margaux in 1977 they brought passion, ambition and finance. With the arrival of inspired Wine Director Paul Pontallier in 1983 the stage was set for Margaux to return to the top tier, since when Margaux has regularly produced stunning wine, sometimes the best in all Bordeaux.

Those pale gravel soils are most famous for breeding wines with fabulous perfume, yet Pontallier has added muscle to the beauty. Good vintages of Margaux always lasted surprisingly well given that they seemed frailer than the other First Growths; now, there's no surprise that they age well. What might be surprising is that while the wines have put on bulk, they haven't coarsened. Open a modern Margaux that's aged a few years, and it's still as if some parfumeur had managed to combine a sweet essence of blackcurrants with oil from crushed violets and the haunting scent of cedarwood, then swirled them together with more earthy pleasures like vanilla and roasted nuts and spirited all these into the bottle.

There is also some white wine. The grapes don't come from the precious Margaux vineyards, but from Soussans, outside the best red wine area. There are 12ha (30 acres) of Sauvignon Blanc, which is vinified at the château, but in a separate cellar so that the red wine is not in any way affected. The result is delicious, but Pavillon Blanc must be the most expensive Bordeaux AC by a country mile.

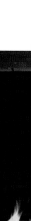

Above: I'm not sure I've ever seen so many barrels stretching away into the gloaming as when I stood here at the top of Margaux's second-year cellar.

Below: Margaux likes to exercise complete control over all aspects of quality and so has its own cooperage which produces three new barrels a day.

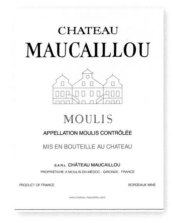

Château Marquis d'Alesme

There are some signs of life at underperforming Marquis d'Alesme as new ownership is rediscovering its ripe, dark-fruited style.

CHÂTEAU MARQUIS D'ALESME

Margaux AC, 3ème Cru Classé
❦ *Merlot, Cabernet Sauvignon, Cabernet Franc, Petit Verdot*

There have been vineyards at this small Margaux estate since the early 17th century. Called Marquis d'Alesme-Becker following its purchase by a Dutchman Mr Becker, in 1809, in 1919 it narrowly escaped being incorporated into Ch. LASCOMBES. The wine used to be old-fashioned and somewhat rustic, sound but unexciting and lacking the verve and finesse that ought to characterize fine Margaux.

In 2006 the estate was acquired by Hubert Perrodo who also owned another Margaux property, Ch. LABÉGORCE. Under the new Perrodo ownership the 'Becker' handle in the name was dropped. There are now signs of improvement. Drink with five years' age. Best years: 2010, '09, '08, '07, '06, '05, '04.

Château Marquis-de-Terme

Since 2000 there has been a discernible improvement and the promise of greater ripeness, complexity and concentration.

CHÂTEAU MARQUIS-DE-TERME

Margaux AC, 4ème Cru Classé
❦ *Cabernet Sauvignon, Merlot, Petit Verdot, Cabernet Franc*

The scattered vineyards of this estate produced until recently a rather four-square and tannic wine that in good vintages needed time to become harmonious and in poor vintages was rarely worth the wait. Great strides were made in the late 1980s but the 1990s were less inspiring. However, since 2000 things have looked up. The wines rarely exhibit much Margaux perfume but increasingly they are showing good, rather chunky dense fruit and structure. Good after five years, the wine can be kept for ten to 15. Best years: 2010, '09, '08, '07, '06, '05, '04, '03, '00, '96, '95, '90, '89, '88, '86, '85, '83.

Château Maucaillou

This isn't the model of Moulis consistency it once was but it can still give a very elegant expression of mild cedar and soft dry fruit.

CHÂTEAU MAUCAILLOU

Moulis AC
❦ *Cabernet Sauvignon, Merlot, Petit Verdot, Cabernet Franc*

Don't be put off by the incongruous look of Ch. Maucaillou just next to the Grand-Poujeaux railway station in the rather backwoods Bordeaux appellation of Moulis. It's been described as extravagant rococo, as 'half Renaissance and half Arcachon villa' – and it does seem out of place in this sleepy village. But the wine in no way reflects the château.

It has been one of the most reliably enjoyable and affordable high-quality reds in Bordeaux: the tannins, the fruit and the careful oak all classically balanced. Latest vintages have been weightier, and I think they seem to have slightly lost sight of that 'classic in miniature' balance that makes the wine so consistently enjoyable – and frequently a godsend in an otherwise dire wine list. If the wine is trying to become more ambitious – I wish it wouldn't. It was doing just right before. Best years: 2010, '09, '08, '06 '05, '04, '03, '02, '00, '98, '96, '95, '90.

GRAND VIN DE BORDEAUX

Château Maucamps

2009

HAUT-MÉDOC

CRU BOURGEOIS

Château Maucamps

Maucamps makes a pleasant darkish, dry wine in cooler years while the warmer years tend to result in attractively soft, juicy flavours.

CHÂTEAU MAUCAMPS

Haut-Médoc AC

✻ *Cabernet Sauvignon, Merlot, Petit Verdot*

Located in the southern part of the Haut-Médoc AC near Ch. CANTEMERLE and Ch. La LAGUNE this 34-ha (84-acre) property produces consistently harmonious wines with generous fruit and a finely honed tannic structure, but it doesn't aim as high as its neighbour, La Lagune. Drink from three to four years. Best years: 2010, '09, '08, '06 '05, '04, '03, '02, '01, '00, '99, '98.

Château Maucaillou is a very grand château for Moulis, an area slightly out of the mainstream. Well, a bit of self-promotion isn't exactly unheard of among the château owners of the Médoc, so I can't blame the Petit-Lalande family, who built this marvel in 1875, for deciding on a 'look at me, look at me' approach to the architecture. In shape, it does have an element of Renaissance grandeur, but the final effect, in two-tone stone and brick, owes more to the French colonial Caribbean flavour of the late 19th century. At least they couldn't complain no one noticed them.

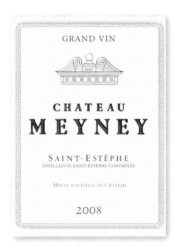

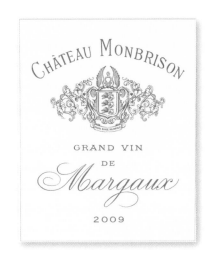

Château Mayne-Lalande

Many Listrac properties do well in warm, dry years like 2003, '05 and '09. Mayne-Lalande makes a full, attractively tannic, polished wine.

Château Meyney

This château has been quietly but determinedly making wines of a regular consistency and quality for a number of years.

Château Monbrison

Monbrison's very stony soils mean that the wines are usually elegant and fragrant, and can be some of the most perfectly balanced in Margaux.

CHÂTEAU MAYNE-LALANDE

Listrac-Médoc AC

❈ *Cabernet Sauvignon, Merlot, Petit Verdot, Cabernet Franc*

Bernard Lartigue has managed to tame the sometimes ungrateful nature of Listrac's soils to produce ripe, generous but powerful wines. A good percentage of Merlot is part of the solution as is picking at optimum ripeness, a draconian process of selection and ageing in quality new oak barrels. The wine needs a minimum of seven to eight years' bottle age and more for the special selection called Alice-Jeanne. Best years: 2010, '09, '08, '06, '05, '04, '03, '02, '01, '00, '99, '98.

CHÂTEAU MEYNEY

St-Estèphe AC

❈ *Cabernet Sauvignon, Merlot, Cabernet Franc, Petit Verdot*

Ch. Meyney's vineyard enjoys a good location – there are 50ha (124 acres) of vines with 67% Cabernet Sauvignon, 25% Merlot, 5% Cabernet Franc and 3% Petit Verdot, overlooking the Gironde on the next plateau to Ch. MONTROSE. But what has made this wine so reliably fine is the uncompromising approach of the management – maximizing the quality and ripeness of the fruit, and ruthlessly selecting only the best vats. The result is big, broad-flavoured wine, generally a little short on nuance but with lovely dark plummy fruit that successfully evolves over 10–15 years, and probably more. Second wine: Prieur de Meyney. Best years: 2010, '09, '08, '06, '05, '04, '03, '02, '01, '00, '99, '98, '96, '95, '94, '90, '89.

CHÂTEAU MONBRISON

Margaux AC

❈ *Cabernet Sauvignon, Merlot, Cabernet Franc, Petit Verdot*

Jean-Luc Vonderheyden put Monbrison on the map in the 1980s and, since his untimely death from leukaemia in 1992, brother Laurent has continued the good work. Situated in the backwoods of Arsac, the vineyards produces yields that are among the lowest in the AC. The wine is wonderfully crafted, complex and balanced and only bettered in the appellation by the likes of Ch. Margaux and Palmer. There was a dip in the 1990s, and vintages in the early 2000s were very erratic in style, but the '04 and '05 showed a magnificent return to form. Keep for five to ten years or more. Best years: 2010, '09, '08, '06, '05, '04.

Château Montrose
In the last few years Montrose has made exceptional wines – lush, not too tannic but bursting with personality and ageability.

CHÂTEAU MONTROSE

St-Estèphe AC, 2ème Cru Classé

Cabernet Sauvignon, Merlot, Cabernet Franc

This leading St-Estèphe property used to be famous for its dark, brooding, Cabernet Sauvignon-dominated style that only slowly revealed its blackcurrant and pencil-shavings scent. Twenty years was regarded as reasonable time to wait before broaching a bottle, and around 30 years to drink it at its prime.

Then vintages of the late 1970s and early '80s underwent a sea change, becoming lighter, softer, less substantial, less interesting frankly, ready to drink at a mere ten years old. Thankfully, this trend was reversed in 1988 and Montrose set about rediscovering its former intensity along with extra richness and ripeness. The 1989 and '90 were stupendous and vintages of the 1990s were equally good until the end of the decade when uncertainty seemed to set in again. Why not just stick to what made you famous in the first place? But the dense black yet sweet 2000 was one of the wines of the vintage and '01 was also exceptional, so it looks as though Montrose is back to its big, beefy self again, but in a richer, more modern idiom. The property of of 68ha (168 acres) was sold in 2006 to the Bouygues family and there has been plenty of investment since. Second wine: La Dame de Montrose. Best years: 2010, '09, '08, '07, '06, '05, '04, '03, '02, '01, '00, '99, '98, '96, '95.

Which signpost do you prefer? Well, it's no contest for me – the old metal post and its sign every time. Montrose used to make one of the most tannic wines in the Médoc, but since the 1980s has produced one of the richest reds, made easier by the spectacular location of its vines on a plateau overlooking the Gironde.

Château Mouton-Rothschild

Baron Philippe wanted to add a sheep's head to
the top of the monument but they discovered it was
too heavy for the obelisk to bear, so he put up a
Star of David instead.

On my first trip to Bordeaux, my newly-discovered wine mentor
granted me a wish. Just tell me what you want to taste, he said, and
we'll arrange it. So I told him that as an enthusiastic but impecunious
student, I'd never tasted wine from a First Growth. No problem, he said.

A couple of days later we sneaked in to his company's office after the last
person had left, clambered up the steep, creaking stairway to his garret
under the eaves, and he proudly placed his bottle in front of me.
Mouton-Rothschild 1959. I couldn't hide my disappointment. 'But, it's
not a First Growth,' I whispered. 'No it's not,' he said, 'but it should be
and it will be.'

So he opened it. He poured it. I smelt it. Ten minutes later, I was
still smelling it. Half an hour later he said he really had to meet his wife
for dinner; I was still smelling it. So he went, and I stayed, mesmerized by
the beauty and the power of this wine. And then I did drink it, cautiously,
reverentially at first, but then in great draughts as if trying to drown the
gales of laughter that I couldn't hold back. Laughter of delight, laughter
of sheer undiluted pleasure, because my wise mentor knew what he was
doing. He wanted my first meeting with great wine to be one that swept
me away, not one that overawed me and confused me. And even now the
merest mention of Mouton 1959 brings back vivid memories of a heady,
hedonistic and ultimately heavenly brew of sweet blackcurrants, scented
with cigar tobacco and cedarwood, invigorated by the cleansing sheen of
shingle, and finally splashed and stirred with an irresistible, unlikely
marriage of menthol and mint, Vicks VapoRub, eucalyptus and lime.

Mouton is a wine for the grand gesture. And modern Mouton was
created by a man for whom risk and adventure, theatricality and
devilment were part and parcel of his enormous appetite for life – Baron
Philippe de Rothschild. When he took over Mouton in 1922 as a callow
21-year-old, it was a run-down, forlorn Second Growth. But he had a
passionate belief that Mouton should be a First Growth along with its
neighbour Lafite-Rothschild, and by a mixture of obsession with quality,
courage, showmanship and political savvy he finally persuaded the
French government to upgrade Mouton to First Growth in 1973. This is
the only change ever made to the fabled 1855 classification.

The first thing he did was to insist on all the estate's wine being
bottled on the estate. Château-bottling we call it, and everyone with any
pretension to quality does it nowadays. But in 1924 most wine, even from
top properties, was carted away from the château in barrels and bottled
anywhere between Bordeaux, Bristol and Bremerhaven. Goodness knows
what the merchants did to most of it but the pure, unadulterated

Left: Lovely, chubby little Bacchus standing guard over the vats. He looks far too young, but you can see he's been on the juice. Maybe he should be replaced by one of the other 500 artefacts held in Mouton's famous wine museum.

Below: This is an impressive sight. A thousand barrels of new red wine, all unusually on a single level because of the imposing size of the Grand Chai, built in 1926 by the same guy who built the Pigalle Theatre in Paris. The Pigalle was also commissioned by Baron Philippe, with the aim of constructing the most modern theatre in the world. Alas it was pulled down in 1958.

Right: I just want to know where the party was. This is the great Baron Philippe at vintage time in 1952. I feel as though he's been up dancing all night and has popped out to share a joke with his pickers en route to breakfast.

Below: They didn't commission an artist for the millennium vintage of 2000, preferring the proud 'mouton' symbol of a ram in gold. 'First I am, Second I was, I Mouton do not change' is their motto. It's a wonderful thing, self-confidence.

product of the property it rarely was. He also revolutionized the fusty world of label design by getting the avant-garde artist Jean Carlu to create a brand new label (see facing page, top right), and since 1945 a new artist has designed the label for each vintage. There has been a Chagall, a Picasso, a Warhol, you name them, with the artist being paid in the wine of the vintage. So some are a good deal luckier than others.

And yet, despite my gratitude to Mouton-Rothschild, it's a wine I approach with some caution because of its damned inconsistency. With its high percentage of Cabernet Sauvignon – almost 80 per cent – and its high percentage of old vines – some are a century old – all planted on one single plateau of arguably the best soil in Pauillac, why the inconsistency? In superb years like 1989, '90, 2000 and '01 why is Mouton easily outclassed by its peers? And then I remember my astonishing baptism of delight with the Mouton '59…

Facing page: A selection of labels commissioned for the *grand vin*. The artists shown are:
Column 1: 1924 Jean Carlu, 1947 Jean Cocteau, 1952 Leonor Fini, 1959 Richard Lippold
Column 2: 1964 Henry Moore, 1970 Marc Chagall, 1971 Wassily Kandinsky
Column 3: 1973 Pablo Picasso, 1975 Andy Warhol, 1980 Hans Hartung
Column 4: 1982 John Huston, 1988 Keith Haring, 2003 was the 150th anniversary of Mouton's purchase by Baron Nathaniel de Rothschild who is depicted on the label along with the deed of sale.

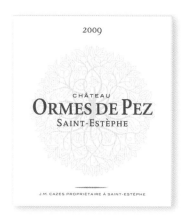

Château Les Ormes de Pez

Les Ormes de Pez is on a roll, making wonderfully juicy, attractive wines. The recent vintages are rich, foursquare and very satisfying.

CHÂTEAU LES ORMES DE PEZ

St-Estèphe AC

❧ *Cabernet Sauvignon, Merlot, Cabernet Franc*

Owned by the Cazes family of LYNCH-BAGES fame, this estate is one of the leading non-classified St-Estèphes. The name derives from some old elm trees (*ormes* in French) that used to exist at the estate which is located in the village of Pez. Wines produced from the 35-ha (86-acre) vineyard are dominated by Cabernet Sauvignon (up to 70%), and are always a delight, the kind of wine that gives you back your faith in reasonably priced, easy to drink but serious and ageworthy Bordeaux. It is rich, full and generous in style. Best with five to six years' bottle age. Best years: 2010, '09, '08, '06, '05, '04, '03, '02, '01, '00, '96, '95, '90, '89, '86.

Château Les Ormes-Sorbet

The high Cabernet Sauvignon content demands a hot year and in the heatwave year of 2003 the wine is rich, dark and satisfying.

CHÂTEAU LES ORMES-SORBET

Médoc AC

❧ *Cabernet Sauvignon, Merlot, Cabernet Franc, Petit Verdot*

Les Ormes-Sorbet is one of the most consistent estates in the Médoc AC. The vineyard is located on a sand, gravel and limestone plateau, assisting the ripening of the Cabernet Sauvignon which can represent up to 75% of the blend. The wine is aged for up to 24 months in oak casks, one-third of which are renewed yearly, and always has an elegant toasted aroma. It is best with at least five years' age. Best years: 2010, '09, '08, '06, '05, '04, '03, '01, '00.

Château Palmer

Palmer includes nearly 50% Merlot, high for a wine from the Haut-Médoc, and the result is classic Margaux perfume married with seductive softness of texture.

CHÂTEAU PALMER

Margaux AC, 3ème Cru Classé

❧ *Cabernet Sauvignon, Merlot, Petit Verdot*

Named after a British major-general who fought in the Napoleonic Wars, Ch. Palmer is a 55-ha (136-acre) site on excellent gravel right next to Ch. MARGAUX.

The wine owes its irresistible plump fruit to the very high proportion of Merlot (47%), with only 47% Cabernet Sauvignon and 6% Petit Verdot. Of all the properties that could justifiably feel underrated by the 1855 Bordeaux classification, Ch. Palmer has traditionally had the best case. Its reputation

Ch. Palmer is elegance personified as it looks out over its vines towards Ch. Margaux, its great rival in the Margaux appellation.

is based, above all, on its perfume. It is as though every black and red fruit in the land has thrown in its ripest scent: blackcurrant, blackberry, plum, loganberry. But Palmer can go further. Sometimes there's a rich, almost fat core to the wine; and curling through the fruit and the ripeness are trails of other fragrances – roses, violets, cedar and cigars, all in abundance. Sometimes.

There was a period in the 1960s and '70s when Palmer held aloft the banner of brilliance for the Margaux AC virtually single-handed. However, as properties like Ch. Margaux itself and various of its neighbours soared to new heights during the 1980s and '90s, Palmer became lighter, less substantial, its fabled perfume now struggling without the original core of sweetness. There were still some notable successes in the 1980s, as in '89, but the 1990 disappointingly failed to find top gear – it was good but unmemorable.

It wasn't until the mid-'90s that Palmer rediscovered its class of former days – the wine was still fragrant, but a little more broad-shouldered than before. There were high hopes for the future following the appointment of Thomas Duroux, formerly with the famous Tuscan estate of Ornellaia, as manager-winemaker in 2004 and they have been triumphantly realized. Palmer is now maximising its succulence and teasing out its heavenly scent more frequently than in living memory – mine, anyway. It's now very expensive, but it's unique, so I can't really complain. Second wine: Alter Ego. Best years: 2010, '09, '08, '07, '06, '05, '04, '03, '02, '01, '00, '99, '98, '96, '95, '90, '89, '88, '86, '85.

Château Patache d'Aux

Patache d'Aux has been a byword for reliability for 30 years or more. The wines are typically dry in style but balanced with full, soft red fruit.

CHÂTEAU PATACHE D'AUX
Médoc AC
❉ *Cabernet Sauvignon, Cabernet Franc, Merlot, Petit Verdot*

A quality orientated 43-ha (106-acre) estate in the north of the Médoc at Bégadan. Fairly soft, dry but juicy wines for drinking at three to four years, but in warm years like 2000, '03 and '05, they'll age much longer than that. Best years: 2010, '09, '08, '06, '05, '04, '03, '02, '01, '00.

Château Pédesclaux

This is one of the lost properties of Pauillac idling along in its own world and quality should be much more impressive.

CHÂTEAU PÉDESCLAUX
Pauillac AC, 5ème Cru Classé
❉ *Cabernet Sauvignon, Merlot, Cabernet Franc, Petit Verdot*

The vineyards of this 20-ha (49-ha) estate, one of the smallest of the Médoc Classed Growths, lie near Ch. PONTET-CANET. The quality should be impressive, but sadly it is

not. Prices are relatively low, which means that fine vintages can offer good value, if less than brilliant quality. Drink with five to ten years' age. A change of ownership and management in 2009 offers hope for the future so keep an eye on this château. Good Pauillac vineyards are too precious to waste on anything not up to scratch. Best years: 2010, '09, '06, '05, '04, '03, '02, '00.

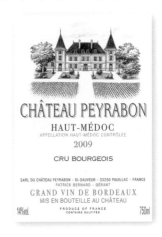

Château Peyrabon

Peyrabon has a definable style: firm, dry fruit, grainy tannin and mellow oak. The 2003 is a good example.

CHÂTEAU PEYRABON
Haut-Médoc AC
❉ *Cabernet Sauvignon, Merlot, Cabernet Franc, Petit Verdot*

This 57-ha (140-acre) estate in the commune of St-Sauveur inland from Pauillac was purchased by *négociant* Patrick Bernard of Millésima, the Bordeaux-based wine retailer, in 1998 and has greatly improved since then. The wines are firm and nicely plummy in the Haut-Médoc style and for drinking at four to five years. Second wine: Ch. Pierbone.

There's also a tiny quantity of Pauillac made from 5ha (12 acres) of vines planted over the communal border. Called Ch. La Fleur Peyrabon, this wine is dryer with a little more depth and persistence. There's been a quiet improvement at Peyrabon for a few years but in 2006 the château seemed to make a real leap forward to producing serious and satisfying wine. Best years: 2010, '09, '08, '06, '05.

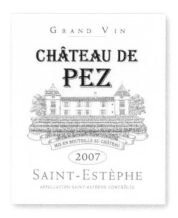

Château de Pez

De Pez is rediscovering its dense, black fruit style but nowadays the fruit is softer and spicier.

CHÂTEAU DE PEZ
St-Estèphe AC

❦ *Merlot, Cabernet Sauvignon, Cabernet Franc, Petit Verdot*

Sturdy fruit, slow to evolve, but mouthfilling and satisfying, with a little hint of cedarwood and a good deal of blackcurrant to ride with its earthy taste – that's St-Estèphe's forte. Ch. de Pez – for long regarded as the appellation's leading non-classified Growth, but now at least equalled by several others, including Ch. MEYNEY, PHÉLAN-SÉGUR, LES ORMES DE PEZ and HAUT-MARBUZET – adds a good leathery, plummy dimension in top vintages.

The 24-ha (59-acre) vineyard, well-placed inland from the Third Growth Ch. CALON-SÉGUR in the far north of St-Estèphe, has 45% Cabernet Sauvignon, 44% Merlot, 8% Cabernet Franc and 3% Petit Verdot. That Petit Verdot helps in warm vintages and the high proportion of Merlot is more important for providing the body and richness that de Pez usually exhibits. Owned since 1995 by the highly regarded Champagne house, Louis Roederer, who also own Ch. PICHON-LONGUEVILLE-COMTESSE DE LALANDE and Ch. BERNADOTTE. Best years: 2010, '09, '08, '07, '06, '05, '04, '03, '02, '01, '00, '99, '98, '96, '95, '90, '89.

Château Phélan-Ségur

Phelan-Segur is relatively soft and approachable for a wine from St-Estèphe but some vintages age well.

CHÂTEAU PHÉLAN-SÉGUR
St-Estèphe AC

❦ *Merlot, Cabernet Sauvignon, Cabernet Franc, Petit Verdot*

As well as an impressive château overlooking the Gironde in its own large park, this large 64-ha (158-acre) estate has one of the best-sited vineyards in St-Estèphe. One part lies next to Ch. MONTROSE and the rest near CALON-SÉGUR. The Gardinier family, which purchased the property in 1985, has spent considerable sums of money on renovating the estate and château and improving the wine and in 2003 it joined the Cru Bourgeois Exceptionnel group, supposedly the best nine non-classified Growths in the Médoc (see page 62). Drinkable at six or seven years, the wine has longer ageing potential. Second wine: Frank-Phélan. Best years: 2010, '09, '08, '07, '06, '05, '04, '03, '02, '01, '00, '99, '98, '96, '95, '90.

Château Pibran

Pibran is a delight – reliably dark, juicy, packed with black fruit, soft enough to drink young yet structured enough to age for 10 years.

CHÂTEAU PIBRAN
Pauillac AC

❦ *Merlot, Cabernet Sauvignon, Petit Verdot*

Good quality Pauillac at a reasonable price is not always easy to find but Pibran fits the bill and is one of my favourite non-classified properties. The 17-ha (42-acre) estate which is located in the north of the appellation betwen the town of Pauillac and Ch. PONTET-CANET was acquired by AXA-Millésimes in 1987 and the wines since vinified at Ch. PICHON-LONGUEVILLE's modern winery.

An important percentage of Merlot (54%) provides luscious generosity of ripe, black fruit but the robust, tannic nature of Pauillac is still refreshingly apparent. Frankly you can drink it straight from the vat due to its gorgeous juicy fruit, but it'll easily age well for ten years. Best years: 2010, '09, '08, '07, '06, '05, '04, '03, '02, '01, '00, '98, '96, '95, '90.

Château Pichon-Longueville

Pichon's gravel soils are not really suited to hot years like 2003, but the wine has triumphed with deep, ripe, black fruit and scented cedarwood.

CHÂTEAU PICHON-LONGUEVILLE
Pauillac AC, 2ème Cru Classé
❦ *Cabernet Sauvignon, Merlot, Cabernet Franc, Petit Verdot*

Somehow Ch. Pichon-Longueville (formerly known as Pichon-Baron) got left behind in the rush. Its Pauillac neighbour, Ch. PICHON-LONGUEVILLE-COMTESSE DE LALANDE, and its St-Julien neighbours, Ch. LÉOVILLE-LAS-CASES and LÉOVILLE-BARTON, leapt at the chance offered by the string of fine vintages from 1978. These châteaux established a leadership at the top of Bordeaux's Second Growths which occasionally challenges the First Growths for sheer quality and equals several of them for consistency.

What about Pichon-Longueville? Its 70ha (173 acres) of vineyards are regarded as superb and its mixture of 60% Cabernet Sauvignon, 35% Merlot, 4% Cabernet Franc and 1% Petit Verdot is ideal for making great Pauillac. Yet it needed the arrival of Jean-Michel Cazes of Ch. LYNCH-BAGES in 1987, supported by his brilliant winemaker, Daniel Llose, and a large investment by the new owners, the giant AXA-Millésimes company, to bring all this to fruition. They immediately stunned the wine world with sublime wines in 1988–1990 and after a period of consolidation, their wines in the 2000s are equal to the best of the Second Growths, with an intensity of dark, sweet fruit and a promise of cedar to come, as well as being structured for a very long life. Cazes has now left but if anything Pichon-Longueville is even better in the last few years, easily up there with the best Super-Seconds. In part this can be explained by the ruthless policy of excluding all but the best grapes but you have to have a vision of flavour in the winery, and they do. The second wine, les Tourelles de Longueville, doesn't suffer and is a fine, classic Pauillac in its own right. Best years: 2010, '09, '08, '07, '06, '05, '04, '03, '02, '01, '00, '99, '98, '96, '95, '91, '90, '89, '88, '86.

Château Pichon-Longueville-Comtesse de Lalande
Lush, scented, otherworldly, sensual – strange adjectives for a Pauillac, but then Pichon-Lalande is no ordinary Pauillac.

CHÂTEAU PICHON-LONGUEVILLE-COMTESSE DE LALANDE
Pauillac AC, 2ème Cru Classé
❦ *Cabernet Sauvignon, Merlot, Cabernet Franc, Petit Verdot*

Of all the top-notch wines in the Haut-Médoc, none in the last generation has been so consistently exciting or beguiling as that of Pichon-Longueville-Comtesse de Lalande, to give it its full name. The 85ha (210 acres) of vineyard are on excellent land on the edge of the Pauillac AC that runs alongside the vines of Ch. LATOUR and LÉOVILLE-LAS-CASES in St-Julien. In fact, some of the vines are actually in St-Julien; this, combined with the highest proportion of Merlot in Pauillac (35% of the blend) and some old, low-yielding Petit Verdot, may account for the sumptuous, fleshy richness of the wine, and its burst of blackcurrant, walnut and vanilla perfume.

But the real cause of Pichon-Lalande's sensual triumph over the usually austere Pauillac community was the inspired, messianic figure of Mme May-Éliane de Lencquesaing. She took over the property in 1978 and for more than a generation led the château upwards in a wave of passion and involvement while the winemaker quietly interpreted her vision with brilliant wine after brilliant wine. This success story has run on through into the new millennium, even though, aged 80, she reluctantly decided to sell the property in 2006. Luckily, she sold it to the Roederer Champagne House who have a worldwide reputation for quality. They have put Sylvie Cazes, one of Bordeaux's brightest female stars in charge – and Mme de Lencquesaing is clearly delighted that a woman is still at the helm of her beloved Lalande. Don't be deceived by the lush caress of the rich fruit – there's lots of tannin and acid lurking, and good examples, though wonderful at six to seven years old, will always last for 20 years or more. The second wine, Réserve de la Comtesse, is of Classed Growth quality, though usually lacking a little of the sheer hedonistic joy of the *grand vin*. Best years: 2010, '09, '08, '07, '06, '05, '04, '03, '02, '01, '00, '99, '98, '96, '95, '91, '90, '89, '88, '86, '85.

Château Pontet-Canet
Pontet-Canet's reputation – and price – have risen rapidly in the 21st century and it is now a classic, powerful, long-lived Pauillac.

CHÂTEAU PONTET-CANET
Pauillac AC, 5ème Cru Classé
❦ *Cabernet Sauvignon, Merlot, Cabernet Franc*

Pontet-Canet was, until the mid-1970s, one of the most popular and widely available of the Haut-Médoc Classed Growths. The 80-ha (198-acre) vineyard next door to Ch. MOUTON-ROTHSCHILD regularly produced the largest amount of wine of any of the Classed Growths, and no wine was château-bottled here until 1972. Since 1975 Pontet-Canet has been owned by the §Tesserons of Ch. LAFON-ROCHET, and we are now seeing a return to the big, chewy, blackcurrant and sweet-oak style that is typical of the great Pauillac wines. Indeed, it has been a rapidly rising star since 2004 and is the only Classed Growth to be run biodynamically – which greatly enhances its reputation. Second wine: Les Hauts de Pontet. Best years: 2010, '09, '08, '07, '06, '05, '04, '03, '02, '01, '00, '99, '98, '96, '95, '90, '89.

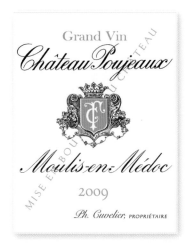

Château Potensac

One of Bordeaux's most consistently satisfying wines, Potensac prefers warm years but even in cool years can make a dark, black-fruited wine for aging.

CHÂTEAU POTENSAC

Médoc AC

❋ *Cabernet Sauvignon, Merlot, Cabernet Franc*

This is no longer a cheap wine, but I can still give it an unreserved thumbs-up for quality, consistency and value. There are two keys to Potensac's success. First, the ridge of gravel here. These are rare in the northern Médoc AC where low-lying, clay-clogged meadows are the order of the day, which in a damp cool area like this means the grapes grown in those conditions have little hope of ripening except in the better years. Gravel is warm, and drains well. And that means you can ripen your grapes and perhaps even make fine wine. Second, the 50-ha (124-acre) estate is owned and run by Jean-Hubert Delon, who runs St-Julien's great Second Growth LÉOVILLE-LAS-CASES and gives Potensac the kind of attention a much more expensive wine would swoon for.

Of all the proprietors in the lowly Médoc AC, Delon is the one who succeeds in drawing out a richness, a concentration and a complexity of blackcurrant, vanilla and spice flavour in his wine which, since the 1980s and '90s, has regularly surpassed many Classed Growths for quality. Potensac can be drunk at four to five years old, but fine vintages will improve for at least ten and last for at least 20. Second wine: Chapelle de Pontensac. Best years: 2010, '09, '08, '07, '06, '05, '04, '03, '02, '01, '00, '99, '98, '96.

Château Pouget

Ch. Pouget does seem to be clawing its way back and has started making deep, dark, quite chewy reds.

CHÂTEAU POUGET

Margaux AC, 4ème Cru Classé

❋ *Cabernet Sauvignon, Merlot, Cabernet Franc*

This little-known, 11-ha (27-acre) Classed Growth is owned by the same family as Ch. BOYD-CANTENAC. The wines have been frankly inadequate but new cellars and efforts from 2000 have raised the level. The wine isn't yet a perfumed Margaux but it has a core of dark, sweet fruit for drinking from five to six years, which, to be honest, I never thought we'd see, but I'm delighted to welcome. Best years: 2010, '09, '08, '07, '06, '05, '04, '03, '02, '00.

Château Poujeaux

Poujeaux has a great ability to make wines of depth and ageability which are, nonetheless, immediately soft and attractive.

CHÂTEAU POUJEAUX

Moulis AC

❋ *Cabernet Sauvignon, Merlot, Cabernet Franc, Petit Verdot*

Poujeaux is one of several properties whose improving winemaking standards in the past 20 years or so have helped to nudge the Moulis AC into the limelight. It's a big property of some 52ha (128 acres) and is beautifully located on the gravel banks around the village of Grand-Poujeaux.

Although its reputation is for dry, long-lived wines, vintages in the 1980s and '90s have been richer, more supple, with a delicious chunky fruit, new-oak sweetness and a slight scent of tobacco. This more accurately reflects the very high percentage of Merlot in the vineyard – 40%, with 50% Cabernet Sauvignon, 5% Cabernet Franc and 5% Petit Verdot. The property was sold to the owners of CLOS FOURTET in St-Émilion in 2007. Best years: 2010, '09, '08, '06, '05, '04, '03, '02, '01, '00, '99, '98, '96, '95, '90, '86.

Château Prieuré-Lichine

Prieuré-Lichine is still trying to recapture its form and perfume is in short supply, but at least an attractive plummy fruit is becoming more common.

CHÂTEAU PRIEURÉ-LICHINE

Margaux AC, 4ème Cru Classé

🌿 *Cabernet Sauvignon, Merlot Petit Verdot, Cabernet Franc*

🍇 *Sauvignon Blanc, Sémillon*

This seriously underachieving 70-ha (173-acre) property was once the pride of Alexis Lichine, an American who did much to promote French wine after World War Two. The property then saw several false dawns before being sold in 1999. Right Bank specialist Stéphane Derenoncourt of PAVIE-MACQUIN and CANON-LA-GAFFELIÈRE fame is now the consultant winemaker, and gradually the wines are taking on greater allure with added fruit and a hint of perfume, but they haven't quite found their way yet. Since 1990 the property has also made a tiny quantity of dry white, Le Blanc de Prieuré-Lichine which isn't bad. Best years: 2010, '09, '08, '07, '06, '05, '04, '03, '01, '00, '99, '98, '96.

Château Ramafort

The Ramafort house style is sound, solid dark fruit, dry but softened with 12 months' aging in 50% new oak.

CHÂTEAU RAMAFORT

Médoc AC

🌿 *Cabernet Sauvignon, Merlot*

This is a solid 20-ha (49-acre) Cru Bourgeois in the commune of Blaignan with a good track record. The vineyard was completely restructured in the 1970s and modern winemaking facilities installed from 1990. The wines are robust and meaty, ready for drinking at three to four years. Best years: 2010, '09, '06, '05, '04, '03, '02, '00.

Château Rauzan-Gassies

Rauzan-Gassies has underperformed for at least a couple of generations, so its recent mellow, scented offerings are a source of relief and anticipation.

CHÂTEAU RAUZAN-GASSIES

Margaux AC, 2ème Cru Classé

🌿 *Cabernet Sauvignon, Merlot, Cabernet Franc*

This 30-ha (74-acre) Margaux Second Growth has excellent vineyards, but had a poor track record until the late 1990s, when improved vineyard and winery practices began to return some personality to the wine. There really is no place in the modern Bordeaux for underperformance from such an outstanding site and clearly the owners have finally realized this.

Quality has improved considerably and in particular Gassies has begun to exhibit a rather attractive sweet blackcurrant fruit, mellow, loose-limbed texture, and a suggestion of Margaux scent. It isn't a particularly complex style and it's still skating way behind the Super-Seconds but I am encouraged. I might even buy some for the first time. Best years: 2010, '09, '08, '07, '06, '05, '04, '03, '02, '01, '00, '98, '96.

Château Rauzan-Ségla

Rauzan-Ségla has a good, rich, oaky style of wine, though I'd prefer it to have a little more fruit focus and perfume.

CHÂTEAU RAUZAN-SÉGLA

Margaux AC, 2ème Cru Classé

🎋 *Cabernet Sauvignon, Merlot, Petit Verdot, Cabernet Franc*

Rauzan-Ségla's much-needed new broom arrived in 1983 with Jacques Théo, who immediately declassified half the crop and produced one of Bordeaux's best 1983s. He continued to excel throughout the 1980s. In 1994 a second new broom arrived when Rauzan-Ségla was bought by French perfume and fashion company Chanel, who implemented a massive programme of investment. I have to say I find the modern wines, good though they are, a bit too dominated by sweet vanilla oak spice; the texture of the fruit is attractive but rather too round and soft for me to believe the haunting Margaux perfume I crave will ever develop. They're good wines but I'd love to see a bit more focus in the fruit. Second wine: Ségla. Best years: 2010, '09, '08, '07, '06, '05, '04, '03, '02, '01, '00, '98, '96, '95, '90, '89, '88.

Château Rollan-de-By

This is a classy property whose blackcurrant fruit and pebbly dryness doesn't always need quite so much new oak.

CHÂTEAU ROLLAN-DE-BY

Médoc AC

🎋 *Merlot, Cabernet Sauvignon, Petit Verdot*

Purchased by Jean Guyon in 1989 and totally renovated, this estate has rarely disappointed since the 1991 vintage. Now expanded to 50ha (125 acres) the vineyard is planted with a majority of Merlot (70%). Producing a second wine allows the possibility of a severe selection for the *grand vin*, improving its concentration.

The wine is full and generously fruity with a slightly overdone toasted oak influence and is best at four to five years. Second wine: La Fleur-de-By. There's also a special *cuvée*, Haut-Condissas, made from a separate parcel of old vines and matured in 100% new oak barrels. Best years: 2010, '09, '08, '07, '06, '05.

Château St-Pierre

St-Pierre wines generally exhibit a round, ripe personality, with deep fruit and glycerine softness supported by tannin.

CHÂTEAU ST-PIERRE

St-Julien AC, 4ème Cru Classé

🎋 *Cabernet Sauvignon, Merlot, Cabernet Franc*

After a century of anonymity, Ch. St-Pierre has stepped forward to claim its place in the sun. It used to be undervalued, and in years like 1982, '85, '89 and '90 you got superb quality at half the price of the better-known St-Juliens. It isn't a big property, only 17ha (42 acres), but the vines, close to Ch. BEYCHEVELLE, are well sited and old.

The wine often lacks the startling beauty of the best St-Julien, but makes up for this with a lush feel and full, almost honeyed flavour – plums and blackberries and soft vanilla backed up by unassertive but effective tannins. It is often ready quite young. Top vintages can easily improve for 20 years. Best years: 2010, '09, '08, '06, '05, '04, '03, '02, '01, '00, '99, '98, '96, '95, '94, '90, '89, '85.

Château Sénéjac

Sénéjac produces a good, dry style of Haut-Médoc and is benefitting from the expertise of new owners.

CHÂTEAU SÉNÉJAC

Haut-Médoc AC

✹ *Cabernet Sauvignon, Merlot, Cabernet Franc, Petit Verdot*

Sénéjac, a large estate in the southern part of the Haut-Médoc with 31ha (77 acres) of vines all in one block, had a pretty good reputation in the 1980s and early '90s under the guidance of New Zealand winemaker, Jenny Dobson. Her homeward departure meant a slight loss of direction until the purchase of the property in 1999 by the owners of the St-Julien Classed Growth, Ch. TALBOT.

Sénéjac is now back to producing full, supple wines with a fine tannic frame for drinking at three to four years but ready to age much longer – I've enjoyed them at 15 years old and more. Biodynamic viniculture has been introduced recently. Best years: 2010, '09, '06, '05, '04, '03, '02, '01, '00, '99, '96, '95, '90.

Château Siran

This is a consistent Margaux property, producing increasingly characterful wine – always full and structured and sometimes even scented.

CHÂTEAU SIRAN

Margaux AC

✹ *Cabernet Sauvignon, Merlot, Petit Verdot, Cabernet Franc*

Owned by the same family since 1859, this estate produces consistently good wine – increasingly characterful, with its black plum and black cherry fruit sometimes coated with chocolate. Approachable young, but with enough structure to last for as long as 20 years. One of the favoured nine properties to join the Cru Exceptionnel group in 2003 (see page 62). Second wine: S de Siran. Best years: 2010, '09, '08, '07, '06, '05, '04, '03, '02, '01, '00, '99, '98, '96, '95, '90, '89.

Château Sociando-Mallet

It took me a while to come round to Sociando-Mallet, but I now think these dense, cedary reds are some of the Médoc's finest.

CHÂTEAU SOCIANDO-MALLET

Haut-Médoc AC

✹ *Cabernet Sauvignon, Merlot, Cabernet Franc, Petit Verdot*

This established star estate holds lonely vigil over the last really decent gravel outcrop of the Haut-Médoc at St-Seurin-de-Cadourne. The château is presided over by the beady-eyed, furiously passionate owner, Monsieur Gautreau, and the results are impressive – dark, brooding, tannic, dry, but with every sign of great, classic red Bordeaux flavours to come if you can hang on for 10–15 years.

So hats off to Monsieur Gautreau for his dedication and for believing so passionately in his wine. He never enters Sociando for any classification or other such palaver, dismissively but correctly saying the wine speaks for itself.

It now easily attains Classed Growth quality – it achieves Classed Growth prices too. Up to 100% of the oak barrels used to mature the wine are new; this is an unusually high percentage and almost unheard of for a non-Classed Growth yet the wine's haughty purity of purpose is never sullied by oaky spice and toast. Second wine: La Demoiselle de Sociando-Mallet. Best years: 2010, '09, '08, '06, '05, '04, '03, '02, '01, '00, '98, '96, '95, '90, '89, '88, '86.

Château Talbot

A well-known label in British and North American markets, Talbot is a consistently satisfying red.

CHÂTEAU TALBOT

St-Julien AC, 4ème Cru Classé

✹ *Cabernet Sauvignon, Merlot, Petit Verdot, Cabernet Franc*

✹ *Sauvignon Blanc, Sémillon*

Talbot is a superb Fourth Growth which regularly makes wine above its ranking. It's a very big estate – 102ha (252 acres) – occupying a single chunk of land bang in the middle of the St-Julien AC.

The wine is big, soft-centred but sturdy, capable of aging extremely well for 10–20 years, going from rather rich, almost sweet beginnings to a maturity of plums, blackcurrants and cigarbox scent. A small amount of very good white Bordeaux, Caillou Blanc de Talbot, is also produced from mainly Sauvignon Blanc. Second wine: Connétable de Talbot. Best years: 2010, '09, '08, '05, '04, '03, '02, '01, '00, '99, '98, '96, '95, '90, '89.

Château du Tertre

Du Tertre is an undervalued château with vines on superb soils that manages to balance weight and richness with perfume.

CHÂTEAU DU TERTRE

Margaux AC, 5ème Cru Classé

Cabernet Sauvignon, Merlot, Cabernet Franc, Petit Verdot

This 50-ha (124-acre) vineyard lies well inland from the Gironde but enjoys a good location atop a knoll (*tertre* means 'knoll') on the highest ground in the AC with some of the purest, deepest white gravel in the Médoc. The mixture of 40% Cabernet Sauvignon, 35% Merlot, 20% Cabernet Franc and 5% Petit Verdot produces wines with wonderful fruit: strawberries, blackcurrants and mulberries are apparent right from the start. There is tannin too, certainly, but also a glyceriny ripeness

coating your mouth, and a marvellous cedar, strawberry and blackcurrant scent building up after a few years of aging. It's usually delicious at five to six years old, but will happily age for 10–15 years.

New ownership in 1997 has led to even greater things. With lower yields, investment in new oak barrels and a spanking new cuverie the wines have taken on more depth, volume and spice and look far better than their Fifth Growth ranking. Best years: 2010, '09, '08, '07, '06, '05, '04, '03, '02, '01, '00, '99, '98, '96, '95.

Château La Tour-de-By

These wines generally have a refreshing leafy acidity to go with delightful savoury fruit.

CHÂTEAU LA TOUR-DE-BY

Médoc AC

Cabernet Sauvignon, Merlot, Petit Verdot

The 74-ha (183-acre) property with a wonderfully gravelly vineyard overlooking

the Gironde at Bégadan really does have a tower that used to be a lighthouse for the hamlet of By. The wines have always exhibited balance and a refreshing style, and have now added a delightful depth of fruit and an aging potential of 10–12 years. Best years: 2010, '09, '08, '06, '05, '04, '03, '02, '00.

Château La Tour-Carnet

Since new ownership in 2000 these wines have become rich, round, ripe and modern, needing at least 10 years to blossom.

CHÂTEAU LA TOUR-CARNET

Haut-Médoc AC, 4ème Cru Classé

Cabernet Sauvignon, Merlot, Cabernet Franc, Petit Verdot

The history of this beautiful, moated, 65-ha (161-acre) property at St-Laurent at the southern end of the Haut-Médoc dates back to the 14th century but the modern era begins in 2000 with its purchase by Bernard Magrez (owner of PAPE-CLÉMENT, FOMBRAUGE and other châteaux).

With a flurry he has restructured the vineyard, modernized and re-equipped the cellars, restored the château and engaged Michel Rolland as consultant enologist. Seemingly overnight, wines that used to be on the rustic side, now have oodles of rich fruit and spicy oak. But, frankly, the oak rather obliterates the fruit when the wine is young. But this is a good terroir and I really hope the estate's true character will shine through as the wines age. Top vintages will

The beauty of the moated castle at Ch. La Tour-Carnet has never been in doubt. Nor has the quality of the vineyard, but until purchased by Bernard Magrez in 2000 the wines underperformed. They're now rich, dense and increasingly 'international' in style.

age successfully for 15–20 years. Best years: 2010, '09, '08, '06, '05, '04, '03, '02, '01, '00, '99, '98, '95, '90, '89.

finesse. Ready with five years' aging but will age for at least ten. Best years: 2010, '09, '06, '05, '04, '03, '02, '00.

and is full-bodied and finely textured with good ageability. Keep for five years or more. Best years: 2006, '05, '04, '03, '02, '01, '00.

Château Tour-Haut-Caussan
A working windmill, originally built in 1734, still stands in the Tour-Haut-Caussan vineyards near the hamlet of Caussan.

Château Tour-du-Haut-Moulin
Goof gravel soils produce a deep but soft-textured style, easy to drink young but serious enough to age.

Château Tour St-Bonnet
Tour-St-Bonnet makes consistently good dry Médoc wines with a fair amount of fruit and an ability to age for a few years.

CHÂTEAU TOUR-HAUT-CAUSSAN
Médoc AC
🌿 *Cabernet Sauvignon, Merlot*

This is one of the top unclassified châteaux in the Médoc AC. Managed by owner Philippe Courrian, the low-yielding vines are still harvested by hand (unusual for the AC) and the wine bottled without filtration. Aging in new oak barriques for 12 months adds an extra note of complexity and

CHÂTEAU TOUR-DU-HAUT-MOULIN
Haut-Médoc AC
🌿 *Cabernet Sauvignon, Merlot, Petit Verdot*

This estate has been in the hands of the Poitou family for many generations. It is consistently one of the best value unclassified properties in the Médoc. The vineyard is situated on good gravel soils at Cussac-Fort-Médoc close to the Gironde and the Fort Médoc. The wine has a deep colour

CHÂTEAU TOUR ST-BONNET
Médoc AC
🌿 *Merlot, Cabernet Sauvignon, Petit Verdot*

The Médoc AC can be a minefield for finding quality wines but Tour St-Bonnet, with its 40ha (99 acres) of vines on gravel banks close to the Gironde at St-Christoly, is pretty consistent. Gravelly soils and good management by the Lafon family who have owned it for over a century are the chief reasons. Best years: 2010, '09, '08, '06, '05, '04, '03, '02, '00.

Quick guide • Best producers

HAUT-MÉDOC AC
Arcins, Agassac, Aurilhac, Balac, Barreyres, Beaumont, Belair, Belgrave, Belle-Vue, Bernadotte, Cambon La Pelouse, Camensac, Cantemerle, Caronne Ste-Gemme, Charmail, Cissac, Citran, Clément-Pichon, Clos du Jaugueyron, Clos La Bohème, Coufran, Hanteillan, La Lagune, Lamarque, Lanessan, Larose-Trintaudon, Lestage Simon, Malescasse, Magnol, Maucamps, Mille Roses, Moulin Rouge, Paloumey, Peyrabon, Reysson, Sénéjac, Sociando-Mallet, La Tour-Carnet, Tour-du-Haut-Moulin, Villambis, Villegeorge.

LISTRAC-MÉDOC AC
Cap Léon Veyrin, Clarke, Clos des Demoiselles, Ducluzeau, Fonréaud, Fourcas-Borie, Fourcas-Dupré, Fourcas-Hosten, Grand Listrac, Mayne-Lalande, Reverdi, Saransot-Dupré.

MARGAUX AC
Angludet, Boyd-Cantenac, Brane-Cantenac, Cantenac-Brown, Dauzac, Desmirail, Durfort-Vivens, Ferrière, Giscours, Grand Tayac, La Gurgue, Issan, Kirwan, Labégorce, Malescot St-Exupéry, Margaux, Marquis-de-Terme, Monbrison, Palmer, Pouget, Rauzan-Gassies, Rauzan-Ségla, Siran, du Tertre.

MÉDOC AC
Bournac, Cardonne, Escurac, Fontis, La Goulée, Les Grands Chênes, Greysac, L'Inclassable, Lacombe-Noaillac, Loudenne, Noaillac, Les Ormes-Sorbet, Patache d'Aux, Poitevin, Potensac, Preuillac, Ramafort, Rollan-de-By, La Tour-de-By, La Tour-Haut-Caussan, Tour St-Bonnet, Vieux Robin.

MOULIS AC
Anthonic, Biston-Brillette, Branas-Grand-Poujeaux, Brillette, Chasse-Spleen, Chemin Royal, Duplessis, Dutruch-Grand-Poujeaux, Gressier-Grand-Poujeaux, Malmaison, Maucaillou, Moulin-à-Vent, Poujeaux.

PAUILLAC AC
Armailhac, Batailley, Clerc-Milon, Duhart-Milon, Fonbadet, Grand-Puy-Ducasse, Grand-Puy-Lacoste, Haut-Bages-Libéral, Haut-Batailley, Lafite-Rothschild, Latour, Lynch-Bages, Lynch Moussas, Mouton-Rothschild, Pibran, Pichon-Longueville, Pichon-Longueville-Comtesse de Lalande, Pontet-Canet.

ST-ESTÈPHE AC
Beau Site, Le Boscq, Calon-Ségur, Clauzet, Le Crock, Cos d'Estournel, Cos Labory, Ch. Coutelin-Merville, Haut-Beauséjour, Haut-Marbuzet, Lafon-Rochet, Lilian Ladouys, Meyney, Montrose, Les Ormes de Pez, Pez, Phélan-Ségur, Sérilhan.

ST-JULIEN AC
Beychevelle, Branaire-Ducru, La Bridane, Ducru-Beaucaillou, Glana, Gloria, Gruaud-Larose, Lagrange, Lalande-Borie, Langoa-Barton, Léoville-Barton, Léoville-Las-Cases, Léoville-Poyferré, St-Pierre, Talbot, Teynac.

The Graves & Pessac-Léognan

The Graves, along with its sub-region of Pessac-Léognan, isn't the best-known part of Bordeaux today, but it was once. Graves is the French word for gravel, and it is on the deep, gravelly land all round what is now the city of Bordeaux that Bordeaux's reputation as a great wine region was formed.

During the period 1154–1453, when Aquitaine in South-West France came under the English crown, the Graves supplied a voracious export market. The first identifiable vineyard estate in Bordeaux was Pape-Clément, given in 1305 to the city of Bordeaux by the archbishop who later became Pope Clement V. Over three centuries later the Graves was in the news again – this time for providing us with the first recorded example of a single-estate wine being exported under its own name – Haut-Brion, or 'Ho Bryan' as Samuel Pepys noted it in his diary in 1663.

In the northern Graves, which boasts the appellation Pessac-Léognan, and where vineyards have to fight with dark forests and ever-encroaching villages and housing estates for use of the deep gravel soil, quality for both red and white wine is probably now higher than it has ever been. In the southern Graves, with only sporadic gravel beds to nurture top quality, whites outshine reds, but both colours struggle to make an impression on the world with their pleasant, dry flavours and reasonable prices.

Graves means gravel in French and the best vineyards on the left bank of the Garonne have loads of it, none more so than at Ch. Smith-Haut-Lafitte, one of the top Pessac-Léognan properties, making a particularly fine white and a fragrant red. They also have a spa on site, Les Sources de Caudalie, that uses numerous red grape extracts to soothe your spirit and invigorate your skin. Then you feel ready to go and eat in their excellent restaurants – and undo all the good work in the most enjoyable way possible.

SPOTLIGHT ON
The Graves & Pessac-Léognan

I think I've visited the smallest vineyard in the Graves. If you arrive at Bordeaux by air, you can't miss it really – it's a sliver of land between the arrivals hall and the bus stop. It's inside the airport buildings at Mérignac. The soil looks beautiful and gravelly, and I should think that being protected on all sides by sheet glass and concrete, and what with the unusually high concentration of global warming carbon dioxide emissions, the wine should be a cracker.

Okay, I haven't tasted it. And it's just a tiny little patch of symbolic vineyard – you could count the number of vines in less than a minute. But Mérignac, where the airport is, was once a very important part of Bordeaux's Graves wine region. A hundred years ago it had 30 different vineyard properties. Now there are just two – not including 'Château Airport'. All the others have disappeared underneath the airport and a ragbag of hotels, industrial parks and tarmac. Beneath all these ugly signs of progress lies to this day wonderful gravelly soil perfect for growing top quality Bordeaux wine. Without knowing it, I bet I've walked over, taken the train over,

The only reason that Ch. La Louvière is not a Graves Classed Growth is that the estate was very run down in the years leading up to the classification in 1959. André Lurton bought La Louvière in 1965 and has since restored both château and estate; the wine, both red and white, is now the star of the unclassified estates.

Quick guide • The Graves and Pessac-Léognan

LOCATION
The Graves region stretches south-east from the outskirts of Bordeaux, roughly following the left bank of the river Garonne for some 60km (35 miles). The towns of Pessac and Léognan, after which the region's premium appellation is named, now form part of Bordeaux's suburban sprawl, with vineyards dotted between houses and industrial estates.

APPELLATIONS
The majority of red and white wines take the Graves appellations. Pessac-Léognan, which was established as an AC in 1987, accounts for those from superior sites in the north of the region. There is also a Graves Supérieures AC for whites, dry or medium-sweet, with a slightly higher minimum alcohol level.

GRAPES
The main red variety is Cabernet Sauvignon backed up by Cabernet Franc, a rather higher percentage of Merlot than in the Médoc further north, and some Petit Verdot. Over a quarter of the region's output is white, for which Sémillon and Sauvignon Blanc dominate the blends with, occasionally, a little Muscadelle.

CLIMATE
These, the most southerly vineyards in Bordeaux are slightly warmer and wetter than the Médoc, leading to earlier ripening for most varieties.

driven over the remains of dozens of Bordeaux's finest original vineyards, now lost beneath relentless urban sprawl – not just west out by the airport, but even more crucially to the south-west and south where the whole great endeavour to make red Bordeaux the world's most famous and most widely exported wine began.

VICTIM OF ITS OWN SUCCESS

This is the Graves region, named after that fabulous gravelly soil – and since the 12th century vineyards have been established right at the very outskirts of the city of Bordeaux. Indeed, Eleanor of Aquitaine's dowry when she married Henry Plantagnet in 1152 included Graves vineyards. This is nothing uncommon: all over the New World, for instance, you find the first vineyards were established on the doorsteps of great cities. But usually people quickly discovered that there were better places to grow grapes further away, and as soon as transport and politics allowed, that's exactly what they did.

Bordeaux, however, was different. The area around the city, particularly to the west, south-west and south, was absolutely brilliant for growing vines. Deep gravel soils – warm, well-drained, more than likely to ripen the crop before the thunderclouds of autumn began to roll in from the nearby Atlantic. Just perfect. So for hundreds of years Bordeaux built a thriving export trade on the produce of these goods so handily and securely

How's this for a real castle? Ch. Olivier in Léognan is a medieval castle and still has its original moat. There has been a sea change in the wine since 2004 and standards have improved dramatically.

SOIL
In the north of the region, nearest Bordeaux, the topsoil is typically gravelly, giving way to sand and clay mixed with limestone further to the south.

ASPECT
Beyond the city's clutches, the landscape is one of low rolling hills, deep forests and numerous small valleys. It is generally higher than the Médoc, providing gentle slopes with good aspect to the sun. This, with the higher overall temperature, aids early ripening of the grapes.

VINTAGE VARIATION
The Graves region is more reliable than the Médoc due to the warmer climate and outstanding drainage provided by the gravelly soils.

ORGANIZATION
Estates are smaller than in the Médoc, averaging 10–15ha (25–37 acres) Many are under 5ha (12 acres) and very few exceed 25ha (62 acres). There are no wine co-operatives. Other than Ch. Haut-Brion, which was included in the 1855 classification of the Médoc, Graves properties were classified in 1959, but it has been proposed that they should be reclassified every 10 years. Not that any date has yet been set for a reclassification.

A FEW FACTS
The Pessac-Leognan AC covers 1600 ha (3400 acres) of vines spread over 10 communes in the northern Graves. Red wine accounts for 80% and dry white the remainder. The Graves AC covers the southern part of the Graves region: 2630ha (6500 acres) for red wines, 750ha (1900 acres) for dry whites and 250ha (620 acres) for Graves Supérieures sweet whites. Pessac-Leognan has 75 châteaux and domaines producing wine whereas there are 300 in the Graves.

WHERE THE VINEYARDS ARE

I'm always surprised when I visit Pessac-Léognan and Graves at how few vineyards there are in such an illustrious pair of wine regions. Lots of suburban villas, lots of pine forests, quite a few meadows and a few orchards, but surprisingly few big chunks of vineyard land. Is it me, I wonder? Am I looking in the wrong places? Well, this map reveals in graphic detail the fact that this famous vineyard area, which was the original source of the Bordeaux wines that were shipped to northern Europe from the 12th century onwards, really doesn't have all that many vineyards. The vines in the whole Graves region cover only 5230ha (13,000 acres), as against more than 10,000ha (24,700 acres) a hundred years ago. Many of the vines that have disappeared since then were in the area at the top left of the map, now covered with the houses of the city of Bordeaux itself. The most important surviving estates in the suburbs of Bordeaux are Ch. Pape-Clément in Pessac and Ch. Haut-Brion and La Mission Haut-Brion in Talence, and these are just tiny sploshes of green surrounded by houses on all sides.

The other highly important vineyard area of Pessac-Léognan is distributed between the small villages of Léognan, Cadaujac and Martillac. South of here the less gravelly, sandier soils spread down the left bank of the Garonne, past the sweet wine enclaves of Cérons, Sauternes and Barsac, finally petering out just south of Langon. The vineyards in the hilly region on the opposite bank of the Garonne are those of the Cadillac-Côtes de Bordeaux, known until recently as the Premières Côtes de Bordeaux.

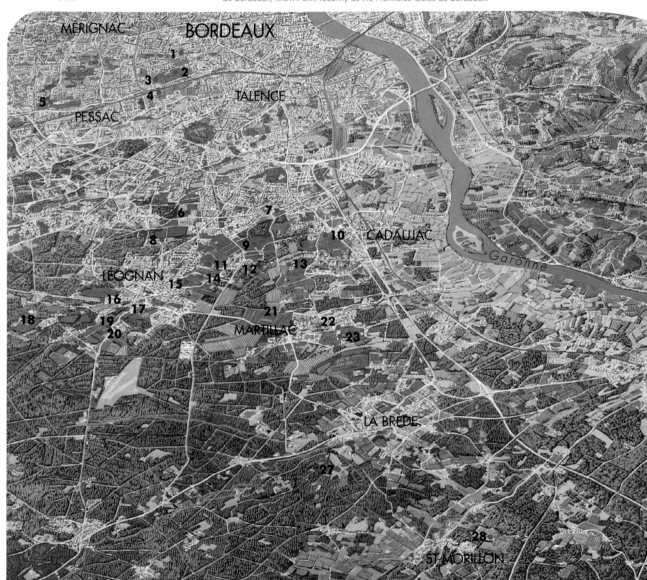

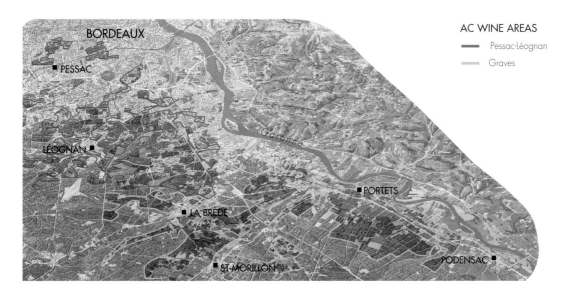

AC WINE AREAS

Pessac-Léognan

Graves

● CHÂTEAUX FEATURED ON PAGES 176-191

PESSAC-LÉOGNAN
1. Ch. Les Carmes Haut-Brion
2. Ch. La Mission Haut-Brion
3. Ch. Haut-Brion
4. Ch. La Mission Haut-Brion Blanc
5. Ch. Pape-Clément
6. Ch. Brown
7. Ch. Couhins-Lurton
8. Ch. Olivier
9. Ch. Carbonnieux
10. Ch. Bouscaut
11. Ch. La Louvière

12. Ch. Le Thil Comte Clary
13. Ch. Smith-Haut-Lafitte
14. Ch. Haut-Bailly
15. Ch. Larrivet-Haut-Brion
16. Ch. Haut-Bergey
17. Ch. Malartic-Lagravière
18. Dom. de Chevalier
19. Ch. de France
20. Ch. de Fieuzal
21. Ch. de Rochemorin
22. Ch. Latour-Martillac
23. Ch. La Garde

GRAVES
24. Vieux Ch. Gaubert
25. Ch. de L'Hospital
26. Ch. Crabitey
27. Ch. Magneau
28. Ch. Villa Bel-Air
29. Ch. de Chantegrive

The following Graves properties lie to the
south-east of the area shown on this map.
Ch. d'Archambeau
Ch. Brondelle
Clos Floridène
Ch. Léhoul
Ch. Respide-Médeville
Ch. St-Robert

NORTHERN GRAVES AND
PESSAC-LÉOGNAN
TOTAL DISTANCE
NORTH TO SOUTH
25KM (15½ MILES)

▦ VINEYARDS

0 km   1   2
0 miles   1

The wine made by the monks who resided at La Mission Haut-Brion already had an excellent reputation by the time of the French Revolution. Since then, there has always been a rivalry between La Mission and Haut-Brion, with Haut-Brion usually winning on grace and elegance, and La Mission getting points for power and depth. Haut-Brion bought La Mission in 1983, and for a few vintages it looked as though they might try to mellow La Mission, but recent vintages show the old character differences are alive and kicking, and both properties are on a roll.

placed all around the city and Bordeaux made itself rich and famous by establishing itself as the main supplier of French wine to northern Europe and north America. So the city gets bigger. So, rip up a few vineyards, admire the gravel soil, then build more houses. The vineyard guys can chop down some forest and plant more vines. And so it went on into the 19th, into the 20th century. Rip out the vines closer to the city, think how wonderfully stable the soil is for drainage and foundations, build houses on it. Ah, progress.

What nobody knew, or I suppose cared about, is that this unique gravelly soil is finite. It was at its purest in the areas closest to the heart of Bordeaux. Every boulevard of suburban villas ate up more perfect vineyard soil, and the further out from the city you went the heavier and more muddled the soil became until, just south of Léognan, the whole gravel structure breaks up into a mishmash of sand and clay and limestone merely streaked here and there with gravel. The last surviving vineyards of this great original gravel bed are in the south-west suburbs at Pessac and Talence, where the world famous Ch. Haut-Brion and La Mission Haut-Brion, facing each other across the main road, and their tiny neighbours Laville Haut-Brion (now renamed La Mission Haut-Brion Blanc) and Les Carmes Haut-Brion, are now hemmed in on all sides by suburban semis. They would never have survived the onslaught of the wrecker's ball had their wines not been sufficiently renowned and in demand to repel efforts to squeeze them out. A hundred years ago there were 138 wine properties in Pessac and Talence. There are just seven now. Old maps show Château Fanning La Fontaine nestling down by the banks of the little river Rau d'Ars. Lovely name. I always wanted to taste that wine. The vineyard is houses now.

A REGION DIVIDED

So far we've been talking about the vines clustered round Bordeaux city. That's because historically they're most significant and, frankly, what's left of them, they're still the best. But though this is the heart of the old

Graves region, the modern appellation is altogether more far flung. Typically for Bordeaux we're now going to spend a minute or so on a touch of geography and a few grubby threads of bureaucracy. So either bear with me or skip the next paragraph.

The Graves is a big region, technically starting north of Bordeaux by the Jalle de Blanquefort at the bottom end of the Médoc region. It then sweeps round and through the city to Langon. That's quite an area, but much more of it is forest than vines, which only cover 5500ha (13,600 acres), and of these 1600ha (3950 acres) now claim a different appellation – Pessac-Léognan. This covers the ten most northerly vineyard communes closest to Bordeaux, and the appellation was granted in 1987 because these communes were dominated by the famous gravel soil and the other communes further south weren't. Frankly, I think the Pessac-Léognan guys were right. There are no properties in the southern Graves that reach the quality of the best Pessac-Léognans. As if to rub the point in, the Graves set up a classification of its red wines in 1953 and its white wines in 1959. There were no southern wines included. They were all from what is now Pessac-Léognan, so you have a situation where the whole region is called the Graves, but the northern bit split off and founded its own appellation Pessac-Léognan, yet the classification title is 'Classed Growth of the Graves' – but on the label they're all using the Pessac-Léognan appellation alongside their Graves classification. I told you to skip this paragraph.

And the producers in the southern Graves – or Graves du Sud as they're sometimes called – do feel left out. This whole region, north and south, has rather lost its reputation. That's why the northern boys fought so hard for the formation of their own appellation. It was like being on a sinking ship with only one lifeboat just big enough for the first class passengers but no room for anyone from steerage. They cut loose to save themselves, and while most Pessac-Léognan wines are considerably less well known – and less expensive – than comparable wines from the ranks of St-Émilion, Pomerol or the Classed Growths in the Médoc, they're still doing a lot better than they were in 1987. From a mere 500ha (1235 acres) of remnant vineyard, Pessac-Léognan has now grown to 1600ha (34000 acres), with a target of 1700ha (4200 acres). And whatever investment there has been available south of Bordeaux city has largely been focused on Pessac-Léognan. To improve your wine and your image and therefore your prices, you need to invest. Invest in replanting and retrellising your vineyards and reducing your yields, invest in your winery – new machinery, new barrels – invest in marketing too. All but a few in

So it's an excess of Pessac-Léognan wine that makes March hares so frisky, is it? This magnificent specimen, captured in bronze by Welsh sculptor, the late Barry Flanagan, is one of several startling modern art pieces at Ch. Smith-Haut-Lafitte.

This is a bunch of wines to make your mouth water. Pessac-Léognan's are some of France's most delicious dry whites, tangy and appetizing, but marvellously married with oak. These five properties are leaders in the region (fom left to right): La Louvière, Smith-Haut-Lafitte, Pape-Clément, La Mission Haut-Brion Blanc (formerly Laville Haut-Brion) and Couhins-Lurton.

the Graves du Sud simply haven't had the funds to do so and since Pessac-Léognan's breakaway haven't even been able to claim reflected glory from being in the same appellation. And even if they did have the money, the results would rarely match those in Pessac-Léognan, because that famous gravel soil largely peters out south of Léognan. Oh, there are patches – you can find them driving south through Portets, Arbanats, Podensac and further inland at Illats and Landiras, but most of the soil simply isn't going to produce thrilling red wine in a very demanding market. It could produce some very nice whites, but the world seems to have decided white Bordeaux is not on the shopping list.

GREAT WHITE HOPE

Yet one of the great selling points of the whole Graves region is its ability to make red and white wines equally well. I say equally well, thinking of the famous red wines like the Haut-Brion and La Mission Haut-Brion which initially created the region's fame, and which today stand on a par with any of Bordeaux's best reds, but if I picked a list of 20 properties in Pessac-Léognan and Graves that made red and white, I'd reckon that in most cases I'd get more excited about the white. Even Haut-Brion and La Mission make whites, and they're rare and stunning. The fact that the authorities felt the need to classify white wines in 1959 after they'd classified the reds in 1953 shows they knew the quality potential, and this double classification makes Graves/Pessac-Léognan the only area in Bordeaux able to honour two wines from the same property. Yet it must have been potential they saw in 1959, because I doubt if many of the

Classic wine styles • Graves & Pessac-Léognan dry white wines

OVERVIEW
White wine of dubious quality was once the mainstay of Graves production. Today whites account for around 25% of the region's wines and the quality revolution of the 1980s and '90s, especially with the winemaking, has set them among France's classics. The wines are generally a blend of Sémillon and Sauvignon Blanc.

TASTING NOTE
There are two main styles. The best estates use new oak barrels to make wines with rich nectarine fruit, soft nutty flavours and creamy vanilla spice – perfumed yet wonderfully dry. But that's not to decry the bone-dry, unoaked style, full of snappy freshness with, once again, the nectarine fruit that sets white Graves apart from most Bordeaux Blanc.

WHEN TO DRINK
Because of the Sémillon component, even the simpler Graves wines can develop interesting flavours over three or four years, though the idea is really to enjoy them when you buy them at one or two years old. More complex barrel-aged wines hit their stride after about four years, with those from top Pessac-Léognan estates improving over ten or even 20 years.

BEST YEARS
2010, '09, '08, '07, '06, '05, '04, '02, '01, '00, '99, '98.

AFFORDABLE PESSAC-LÉOGNAN TO TRY
- Ch. Brown
- Ch. Coucheroy
- Ch. de Cruzeau
- Ch. La Garde
- Ch. Haut-Bergey
- Ch. Larrivet-Haut-Brion
- Ch. Latour-Martillac
- Ch. La Louvière
- Ch. Olivier

- Ch. Rochemorin
- Ch. Le Thil Comte Clary
- Ch. La Tour Léognan

GRAVES WHITES TO TRY
- Ch. d'Archambeau
- Ch. Brondelle
- Ch. Chantegrive
- Clos Floridène
- Ch. Magneau
- Ch. Pont de Brion
- Ch. Rahoul
- Ch. Respide-Médeville
- Ch. Roquetaillade La Grange
- Ch. St-Robert
- Ch. du Seuil
- Ch. Tourteau Chollet
- Ch. Villa Bel-Air

For more ideas see page 191

wines tasted much good then. They'd have been made in cement tanks or ancient vats, sulphured to within an inch of their lives, bottled only when someone came asking, and even then they'd probably want to buy it straight from the tank without a label and cart it off to the city for blending with goodness knows what, because 'Graves' – sticky, sullen, sulphurous, neither dry nor sweet white 'Graves' – was one of the crosses generations brought up before the joys of Liebfraumilch or Muscadet or Mâcon-Villages had to bear (sounds bizarre, doesn't it, but these much-derided wines were in their time a 'great leap forward' in everyday whites). You would see these bottles of clear glass containing a drab, tired fool's gold-coloured liquid the length and breadth of Britain, and they literally did do that all-purpose job that Liebfraumilch took in the 1970s and Australian Chardonnay took over in the 1990s. I've always had this image of a particularly miserable couple sharing a half bottle of Graves for lunch in some stale railway hotel in the foggy Midlands. I'm not sure wine did give much pleasure to most people in those days of the 1950s and '60s, and I'm sure millions of bottles of white Graves were drunk in joyless communion.

Luckily a couple of people knew better. André Lurton, now the owner of Ch. La Louvière in Pessac-Léognan, knew that part of the problem of white Graves' awfulness was uncontrolled fermentation temperatures. He'd seen soldiers during the war wrapping damp cloth around their water bottles to keep them cool. So during the 1950s he wrapped his vats with cloth and poured water down the outsides. It worked. Bingo: cool fermentations! So simple, but at last the brilliant tangy dry fruit of the Sauvignon and Sémillon grapes could be seen. Denis Dubourdieu took it on from there. Unusually in Bordeaux, he was more interested in white wine than red, and as a leading academic and consultant he applied science to Lurton's simple observations. He learned what the Californians and the Australians were doing, and applied the ideas to Bordeaux – properly ripe grapes, clean and healthy, so that you could press the grapes and then steep the skins and juice together before fermentation to draw out all the flavour in the skins that up until then were simply being thrown onto the rubbish heap. In came stainless steel tanks and cold fermentation – rather more precise than Lurton's early efforts. Suddenly, during the 1980s, with a swing towards white wine in the world markets, for the first time Bordeaux, blessed with top grape varieties in Sauvignon and Sémillon – and to a lesser extent Muscadelle – was producing serious quantities of bright, fresh white.

But that wasn't good enough in the top properties of the Graves and Pessac-Léognan. Professor Dubourdieu and others noted that in Burgundy all the top whites were fermented and matured in small oak barrels, not concrete vats or even stainless steel. This was crucial. And it is the development of this idea – which, by the way, had never been let go of by such great properties as Haut-Brion and Domaine de Chevalier –

If you see this capsule staring at you from the wine rack – grab it. The wine is the rare and brilliant white Domaine de Chevalier, in some vintages the most irresistibly scented dry white made in all Bordeaux. The lovely estate is buried in forest on three sides which greatly increases the risk of frost – and makes the delectable white rarer still.

Tradition goes hand in hand with innovation at Ch. Malartic-Lagravière, a property transformed since new ownership in 1997. Amid a sea of shining stainless steel sit these oak vats, used to ferment the best parcels of red grapes. The wheels you see belong to a little mobile tank used to lift grapes to the top of the vats, avoiding them getting bruised by pumping prior to fermentation.

that catapulted white Bordeaux, but more specifically Pessac-Léognan and Graves, into the front rank of world white winemaking. White wine fermented in a barrel – old or new – and then aged on its lees for a while has a totally different, more succulent and mouthfilling texture and character than a stainless steel wine ever has, and if the barrels are new, the fermenting wine interacts with the wood in a quite brilliant way. The yeast action precipitates out the tougher, fibrous wood tannins that would make a white wine seem hefty and thuggish, and yet assimilates the vanilla from the oak to create a thrilling sense of softness and richness combined. This will be further enhanced if you leave the thick, creamy deposits of yeast lees in the bottom of the barrel to interact with the wine. This is how great Burgundies are made, great Chardonnays round the world. But Bordeaux had something else. Two marvellously complementary grapes – the tangy, leafy Sauvignon Blanc and the appley, waxy Sémillon. Blend these wines together after barrel fermentation, and the flavour of nectarine and apricot, lime leaf and custard cream is one of the world's great white experiences. And Pessac-Léognan and the Graves do it better than anyone else, anywhere.

RED WINES

If you think I've gone on a bit long about white wines, it's because a lot of people seem to have forgotten that the Bordeaux region makes whites, and they certainly don't have any idea that Pessac-Léognan is the home of a whole clutch of stellar wines. And while Pessac-Léognan makes a lot of very good reds from Cabernet and Merlot – so does the rest of Bordeaux – and the rest of the world for that matter. Indeed, in the rest of the world it would be perfectly normal for a vineyard to make top reds from Cabernet and Merlot, as well as top whites from Sémillon and Sauvignon. But the leading areas of Bordeaux love to specialize. The Médoc is a red wine area (though some lovely whites are made there which are only allowed the simple Bordeaux AC). Pomerol and St-Émilion are red through and through, while Barsac and Sauternes are sweet white wine fiefdoms. So Graves and Pessac-Légnan are almost, dare I say it, New World in their flexibility, which in the conservative world of Bordeaux seems to have meant not being taken quite seriously enough for either colour.

Well, there's no excuse not to take white Pessac-Léognan and Graves seriously. But it's easier to see what critics mean about the reds, because there is no doubt they are less bumptious, less self-assertive, less immediately recognizable than equivalent reds from the great Médoc villages or the great St-Émilion and Pomerol villages might be. Some wine critics talk about them having a flavour of hot bricks, or terracotta tiles warmed by the sun, or even 'honeyed gravel' – a nice idea. I rather like the idea floated by one of the great old-time Irish wine lovers that many of them are like photographs printed in matt rather than gloss, the sharpness of detail just a little blurred in reproduction. Indeed, I used to describe Pessac-Léognan reds as occupying a useful halfway house between the sternness of the Médoc and the mellow lushness of St-Émilion. However, St-Émilions are much denser and more powerful now than they used to be and in the Médoc, as grapes achieve ever greater ripeness in the vineyards, and new oak barrels clasp even middling wines in their sweet, creamy embrace, the traditional dry, haughty reserve of the great Margaux or Pauillac wines is more and more a rarity.

Red Pessac-Léognans are also now being made in a denser-textured way, yet I still find in them echoes of the Médoc's dry blackcurrant fruit; I still find them satisfyingly dry on the tongue, yet a little looser in texture, which makes them frequently ready to drink at a mere five years old; and I often think I can taste the *terroir* – the great sweeping shingly, shiny gravel beds on which the finest grapes are grown. It's a dry, lean, shiny pebble quality, not at all like the damp clay you can often taste in the lesser St-Émilion wines, although that is there, too. With more clay and sand in the vineyards as you head out of Pessac-Léognan into the southern Graves this minerally streak does indeed become more muddy. And one more thing. If you get the chance to try a mature Pessac-Léognan – ten years old, 20 even – from a top property, you should find a gentle but immensely satisfying flavour of ripe plums and blackcurrants mingled with a heady scent of unsmoked Havana tobacco. That's worth waiting for.

Ch. Pape-Clément is one of the oldest châteaux and vineyards in Bordeaux and one of the first to be talked about in its own right. It's named after Pope Clement V who owned the land in 1299, and is now making powerful reds, with help from Michel Rolland, and graceful whites.

Classic wine styles • Graves & Pessac-Léognan red wines

OVERVIEW
The Graves is the original home of red Bordeaux wine, renowned long before the marshlands to the north of the city had been drained to create the vineyards of the Médoc. Its secret is, as the name suggests, the gravelly vineyards that lie in the northern part of the region, which since 1987 have had their own appellation of Pessac-Léognan.

TASTING NOTE
These wines stand out from their Médoc counterparts from the moment you encounter the rich, earthy scent redolent of tobacco. Within the blackcurrant and plum fruit and creamy layers of flavour you'll find firm mineral nuances and an appealing core of baked earth, a robust reminder that even in its loftiest incarnations wine is a product of soil and sweat. But the Graves is also about juicy, drink-me reds, delivering upfront plummy fruit with a touch of oak spice and a dusting of that appetizing dry earthiness.

WHEN TO DRINK
Even serious wines are approachable fairly young – say from four or five years old – as they tend to be lighter and more supple than Médoc reds, with a significant proportion of Merlot in the blend. The very best wines need a little longer and will keep on going for 10, 20, even 30 years after the vintage.

BEST YEARS
2010, '09, '08, '06, '05, '04, '02, '01, '00, '99, '98, '96, '95

AFFORDABLE PESSAC-LÉOGNAN WINES TO TRY
- Ch. Bouscaut
- Ch. Brown
- Ch. Cantelys
- Dom. de Chevalier
- Ch. de Cruzeau
- Ch. La Garde
- Ch. Haut-Gardère
- Ch. Haut-Lagrange
- Ch. Latour Martillac
- Ch. La Louvière
- Ch. Picque Caillou
- Ch. de Rouillac
- Dom. de La Solitude

GRAVES REDS TO TRY
- Ch. Beauregard-Ducasse
- Ch. Bichon-Cassignols
- Ch. de Castres
- Ch. Crabitey
- Ch. de Chantegrive
- Clos Floridène
- Ch. Gravelière
- Ch. Langlet
- Ch. Peyrat
- Ch. Prieuré-Les-Tours
- Ch. Rahoul
- Ch. de Respide, Cuvée Callipyge
- Ch. Roquetaillade La Grange
- Vieux Ch. Gaubert
- Ch. Villa Bel Air

For more ideas see page 191

Château d'Archambeau

D'Archambeau's smooth, well-balanced red is made from 60% Merlot and is ready for drinking after 3–4 years' aging.

Château Bouscaut

These great old original wines from the Graves took a long time to realize that modernization needn't destroy tradition. The wine's good now.

Château Brondelle

Cuvée Anaïs is the top white from Ch. Brondelle, a rising star in the Graves. A blend of Sauvignon and Sémillon, it is barrel fermented and aged.

CHÂTEAU D'ARCHAMBEAU

Graves AC

❊ Merlot, Cabernet Sauvignon, Cabernet Franc

❊ Sauvignon Blanc, Sémillon

Jean-Philippe Dubourdieu (from the same clan as Denis who owns CLOS FLORIDÈNE) owns and manages this 47-ha (116-acre) estate at Illats. The reds account for two-thirds of the production and regularly show a soft, earthy fruit character. From 2005 the whites have been fermented and aged in oak barrels. The Classed Growth Sauternes, Ch. SUAU, has been under the same ownership since 2002. Best years: (reds) 2010, '09, '08, '06, '05, '04, '03, '02, '01, '00, '98.

CHÂTEAU BOUSCAUT

Pessac-Léognan AC, Cru Classé de Graves

❊ Merlot, Cabernet Sauvignon, Malbec

❊ Sauvignon Blanc, Sémillon

Bought by Lucien Lurton in 1979 and now owned by his daughter Sophie Lurton-Coglombes, Bouscaut used to be in a rut, despite an abundance of old vines. The wine was light, accessible and sensibly priced, but lacked flair. Under the management of Sophie's husband Laurent Coglombes there have been major improvements since 2000, with the 2004 in particular a watershed vintage. A new winery, lower yields and better technical approach have given the wines more flavour, depth and poise, but there's a way to go yet. Drink with five to six years' bottle age. Best years: (reds) 2010, '09,'08, '06, '05, '04, '02, '01, '00, '98; (whites) 2010, '09, '08, '07, '06, '05, '04, '03, '02, '01, '00.

CHÂTEAU BRONDELLE

Graves AC

❊ Cabernet Sauvignon, Merlot, Petit Verdot

❊ Sauvignon Blanc, Sémillon, Muscadelle

Jean-Noël Belloc's grandparents started with 2.5ha (6 acres) of vines in 1925 and would be wide-eyed to see the present 50ha (123 acres) in the southern Graves just south of Langon. The domaine is best known for its whites, in particular the creamy, barrel-fermented Cuvée Anaïs, but the reds have grown in stature, with top of the range Cuvée Damien delivering added fruit and concentration. But I'm not a massive fan of these prestige cuvées. Especially with the whites, I'd stick with the basic stuff. Drink between three and seven years. Best years: (reds) 2010, '09, '08, '06, '05, '04, '03, '02, '01, '00; (whites) 2010, '09, '08, '07, '06, '05, '04, '03, '02, '01, '00.

The beautiful buildings of Ch. Bouscaut have a timeless quality, but they are, in fact, a modern reproduction. The original château was destroyed by fire in 1960. Bouscaut is now owned by the Lurton-Coglombes family, whose patriarch, Lucien Lurton, owned 11 châteaux, one for himself, and one for each of his 10 children. Daughter Sophie runs this greatly improved property, with her husband Laurent.

Château Brown

Brown is an up and coming château and the whites, with their white peach fruit and greengage acidity, are some of the best in Bordeaux.

CHÂTEAU BROWN

Pessac-Léognan AC

- *Cabernet Sauvignon, Merlot, Petit Verdot*
- *Sauvignon Blanc*

Named after a 19th-century Scottish *négociant*, John Lewis-Brown, this 24-ha (59-acre) property has been making quiet progress since the mid-1990s. Owner Bernard Barthe brought investment and change before selling to *négociant* Yvon Mau in 2005. The Cabernet Sauvignon-dominated red is made in a balanced, elegant vein but the barrel-fermented white, with delightful, leafy freshness softened by oak, is still the classiest wine. Best years: (reds) 2010, '09, '08, '06, '05, '04, '03, '00, '99, '98; (whites) 2010, '09, '08, '07, '06, '05, '04, '01, '00, '98.

Château Carbonnieux

Carbonnieux's reds are never intense but are attractively balanced and appetizing and ready to drink at 5–10 years old.

CHÂTEAU CARBONNIEUX

Pessac-Léognan AC, Cru Classé de Graves
- *Cabernet Sauvignon, Merlot, Cabernet Franc, Malbec, Petit Verdot, Carmenère*
- *Sauvignon Blanc, Sémillon, Muscadelle*

The largest of the Graves Classed Growths with 45ha (111 acres) each of red and white varieties, Carbonnieux is a name that has presence on the market. The wines have been slowly improving over the last 10–15 years but there's still a way to go. The whites, clean, crisp and modern in style, are best at three to four years. The firm, dry reds now have lower yields and more new wood. Second wine: (white) Ch. La Tour-Léognan. Best years: (reds) 2010, '09, '08, '07, '06, '05, '04, '02, '01, '00, '99, '98, '96, '95; (whites) 2010, '09, '08, '07, '06, '05, '04, '03, '02, '01, '00, '99, '98.

Château Les Carmes Haut-Brion

The Merlot and Cabernet Franc-dominated red is remarkably consistent and of Classed Growth quality.

CHÂTEAU LES CARMES HAUT-BRION

Pessac-Léognan AC
- *Merlot, Cabernet Franc, Cabernet Sauvignon*

Enclosed by high walls, this tiny 4.7-ha (11.6-acre) vineyard for red wine only is located in the Bordeaux suburb of Pessac opposite Ch. HAUT-BRION. From 1584 until the French Revolution in 1789 it belonged to Carmelite friars. Full, generous and fragrant, the wine is attractive at five to six years but has longer aging potential. Best years: 2010, '09, '08, '07, '06, '05, '04, '03, '02, '01, '00, '99, '98, '96, '95, '90.

Château de Chantegrive

Cuvée Caroline is the top white wine at Ch. de Chantegrive. Fermented and aged in new oak barrels, it is creamy with a nectarine scent.

CHÂTEAU DE CHANTEGRIVE

Graves AC
- *Cabernet Sauvignon, Merlot*
- *Sauvignon Blanc, Sémillon*

Bordeaux *courtier* (broker) Henri Lévêque and his wife Françoise bought their first parcel of 3ha (7 1/2 acres) of vines in 1967. They now have 94ha (232 acres) and the largest estate in the Graves AC, spread over several communes around Podensac, as well as modern winemaking cellars. The regular white Graves is vinified in stainless steel tanks, while the rich, aromatic Cuvée Caroline, produced from equal amounts of Sauvignon Blanc and Sémillon, is barrel-fermented and aged. In exceptional years it can rival the Graves Classed Growths. The red Graves has greatly improved since 1999, with lower yields giving added fruit concentration and some new oak nicely seasoning but not swamping the Graves freshness. Drink at four to five years. Best years: (reds) 2010, '09, '08, '07, '06, '05, '04, '03, '02, '01, '00, '99; (whites) 2010, '09, '08, '07, '06, '05, '04, '03 '02, '01, '00.

Domaine de Chevalier

The brilliant white has been a leader in Pessac-Léognan for decades. In the best vintages it will still be improving at 15–20 years.

DOMAINE DE CHEVALIER

Pessac-Léognan AC, Cru Classé de Graves

🍇 *Cabernet Sauvignon, Merlot, Cabernet Franc*

🍇 *Sauvignon Blanc, Sémillon*

Domaine de Chevalier white is frequently one of the best dry whites in Bordeaux, in fact one of the best dry whites in France. The red used to be similarly thrilling but went through a decade or more when extensive replanting diluted its character and intensity. However, the vintages of this century are beginning to return to the classic Chevalier style, starting out rather dry and reserved, but gaining that piercing, fragrant cedar, tobacco and blackcurrant flavour that leaves you breathless with pleasure over 10–20 years.

Just 15,000 bottles a year of the white are made, as against 90,000 of the red. The white is both fermented and aged in oak barrels. At first a thrilling nectarine scent is very marked, but after three to four years this fades and an increasingly creamy, nutty warmth takes over, building at ten years old to a deep, honeyed, smoky richness, just touched with resin, that is rarely matched in Bordeaux. In the best vintages it will still be improving at 15–20 years. Second wine: (red and white) L'Esprit de Chevalier. The rapidly improving Domaine de La Solitude in nearby Martillac is managed by Olivier Bernard, too. Best years: (reds) 2010, '09, '08, '07, '06, '05, '04, '03, '02, '01, '00, '99, '98, '96, '90, '89, '88; (whites) 2010, '09, '08, '07, '06, '05, '04, '03, '02, '01, '00, '99, '98, '96, '95, '94, '90, '89, '88.

Clos Floridène

From an equal blend of Sauvignon Blanc and Sémillon, this is usually the best white from the southern Graves region.

CLOS FLORIDÈNE

Graves AC

🍇 *Cabernet Sauvignon, Merlot*

🍇 *Sauvignon Blanc, Sémillon*

This estate, owned by Denis Dubourdieu, enologist and professor at Bordeaux' Institute of Enology, produces a beautiful white wine to rival the top Pessac-Léognans and which has frequently been my saviour on dull wine lists. An even mix of Sauvignon Blanc and Sémillon, the wine is barrique-fermented and aged on lees to provide added concentration and complexity. No more than 25% new oak is used.

The much-improved red is made mainly from Cabernet Sauvignon grown on clay-limestone soils, which gives it a fine, fresh, minerally edge but doesn't damage its soft, mellow texture. The red needs three or four years' bottle age, while the white can be drunk young but in the best vintages will age for as much as 15 years. Best years: (reds) 2010, '09, '08, '06, '05, '04, '03, '02, '01, '00, '99, '98; (whites) 2010, '09, '08, '07, '06, '05, '04, '03, '02, '01, '00, '98, '96, '93, '90, '89.

There have been many far reaching changes at Domaine de Chevalier since it changed hands in 1983 but none more dramatic than the magnificent circular cuvier lined inside with stainless steel vats.

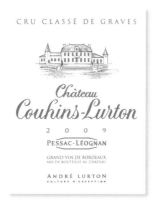

Château Couhins-Lurton

Couhins-Lurton white is a barrel-fermented Sauvignon Blanc which always retains a freshness and zing.

CHÂTEAU COUHINS-LURTON

Pessac-Léognan AC, Cru Classé de Graves (whites only)

🍇 Merlot, Cabernet Sauvignon

🍇 Sauvignon Blanc

André Lurton, Pessac-Léognan's leading owner with La LOUVIÈRE, ROCHEMORIN, BARBE-BLANCHE and others, has appended his name to this estate to distinguish it from the other portion of Ch. Couhins.

The white is delicious young, but becomes really fascinating with bottle age. The red has only been produced since 2002 and appears rich, generous and chocolaty, drinkable at five to six years but it will probably age for much longer. Best years: (reds) 2010, '09, '08, '06, '05, '04, '02; (whites) 2010, '09, '08, '07, '06, '05, '04, '03, '02, '01, '00, '99, '98, '96, '95, '90.

Château Crabitey

The red wine here is labelled Grand Vin de Château Crabitey and has improved enormously in recent years.

CHÂTEAU CRABITEY

Graves AC

🍇 Merlot, Cabernet Sauvignon, Cabernet Franc

🍇 Sauvignon Blanc, Sémillon

It's just possible this wine is made by my first cousin about 20 times removed. I'm a Butler from Kilkenny. So is he. Except his family came to France from Ireland 300 years ago. Ah well, the Irish magic is working because Arnaud de Butler has made huge progress since 2000. The 30-ha (74-acre) vineyard, which was once owned by a religious order, was planted and expanded by his father but under Arnaud's management yields have been reduced and modern viticultural practices adopted.

The reds are consequently richer and riper but still with that fine Graves freshness and structure. They need four to five years' bottle age but offer good craic right from the start. The first vintage of white was made in 2009. Best years: (reds) 2010, '09, '08, '07, '06, '05, '04, '02, '01, '00.

Château de Fieuzal

Less than 10% of the wine at Fieuzal is white but, gorgeous, perfumed and ageworthy, it is the star performer here.

CHÂTEAU DE FIEUZAL

Pessac-Léognan AC, Cru Classé de Graves (reds only)

🍇 Cabernet Sauvignon, Merlot, Cabernet Franc, Petit Verdot

🍇 Sauvignon Blanc, Sémillon

This is a delightful estate, with a reputation for both its red and white wines. Investment during the 1980s in the 48-ha (120-acre) estate, just south of Domaine de CHEVALIER near Léognan, made it one of the most up-to-date properties in the region, and one of my great personal favourites, but a change of ownership in 2001 temporarily put a questionmark over its reputation.

The white wine is fermented and aged in new oak barrels and is rich, opulently fruity and full of nectarines and apricots – and outstandingly good, whether drunk young, or aged. The red used to be equally impressive, succulent, rich and perfumed with damsons. This changed in the late 1990s and early 2000s but vintages from 2006 have started to rediscover their old sensuous nature. Both wines are drinkable almost as soon as they're drawn from the barrel, but both should age for a decade or more. Second wine: (red and white) L'Abeille de Fieuzal. Best years: (reds) 2010, '09, '08, '07, '06, '01, '00, '98, '90, '89, '88; (whites) 2010, '09, '08, '07, '06, '05, '02, '01, '00, '99, '98, '96.

Château de France

Like many others in the region, the wines have improved enormously since the late 1990s. So far, the aromatic, oaky white is better than the red.

CHÂTEAU DE FRANCE

Pessac-Léognan AC
* *Cabernet Sauvignon, Merlot*
* *Sauvignon Blanc, Sémillon*

A close neighbour of Ch. de FIEUZAL, this 38.5-ha (95-acre) property has shifted up a gear since the late 1990s. With Arnaud Thomassin joining his father Bernard at the helm and Michel Rolland as consultant enologist, the wines have taken on a richer, more modern allure. The tiny production of white is aromatic and oaky, if a little formulaic, the red dark and sweet-fruited, ready at five to six years, but not yet consistently impressive. Best years: (reds) 2010, '09, '08, '06, '05, '04, '03, '02, '01, '00, '99, '98; (whites) 2010, '09, '08, '07, '06, '05, '04, '03, '02, '01, '00.

Château La Garde

Ch. La Garde is a sturdy, dark wine with a Graves earthiness and seriousness and ideally meant to be aged for between 5 and 10 years.

CHÂTEAU LA GARDE

Pessac-Léognan AC
* *Merlot, Cabernet Sauvignon, Cabernet Franc, Petit Verdot*
* *Sauvignon Blanc, Sauvignon Gris*

Bordeaux *négociant* CVBG-Dourthe Kressmann bought this 58-ha (143-acre) property in Martillac in 1990 with the aim of making wine of Classed Growth quality. Progress has been steady since then and the reds are now ripe and powerful in style. Production of the enticing, aromatic white, made with 50% Sauvignon Gris, is tiny. Best years: (reds) 2010, '09, '08, '07, '06, '05, '04, '01, '00, '99, '98; (whites) 2010, '09, '08, '07, '06, '05, '04, '02, '01, '00.

Château Haut-Bailly

Recent vintages have shown a greater amount of tannin but I hope the scented succulence of old will find its way back.

CHÂTEAU HAUT-BAILLY

Pessac-Léognan AC, Cru Classé de Graves
* *Cabernet Sauvignon, Merlot, Cabernet Franc*

Haut-Bailly can make the softest and most invitingly charming wines among the Graves Classed Growths. The 31ha (77 acres) of vines are on gravelly soil with rather more sand than usual, just to the east of the village of Léognan, and this contributes to Haut-Bailly becoming agreeably ready to drink very early. However, the wines do age well and what is ready to drink at ten years old often seems magically unchanged at 20 years. New American ownership from 1998 brought a change in direction, which has taken a while to bed down, the wines veering between plummy softness and curiously hard tannins. But recent vintages are showing an exciting return to form – 2009 and '10 are two of the finest in living memory. Second wine: La Parde de Haut-Bailly. Best years: 2010, '09, '08, '07, '06, '05, '04, '03, '02, '01, '00, '99, '98, '96, '95, '90, '89, '88, '86.

Château Haut-Bergey
Vintages since 2000 show real style in the whites and power in the reds that I hope will age gracefully.

CHÂTEAU HAUT-BERGEY

Pessac-Léognan AC

🍇 *Cabernet Sauvignon, Merlot*
🍇 *Sauvignon Blanc, Sémillon*

Purchased in 1991 by Mme Sylviane Garcin-Cathiard, sister of Daniel Cathiard, owner of Ch. SMITH-HAUT-LAFITTE, the property has since been completely renovated and the winery rebuilt. The 26-ha (64-acre) vineyard is sandwiched between Ch. de FIEUZAL, MALARTIC-LAGRAVIÈRE and Dom. de CHEVALIER.

Most of the vintages of the 1990s could be called 'work in progress' but recent vintages have shown marked improvement. Dark, sweet-centred and coated in creamy oak, the red has a modern, New World nuance that is sometimes overdone. The tiny production of Sauvignon-based white wine was light in style but has gained in fruit and flavour since 2000 and is now a good Pessac-Léognan. The recently launched Ch. Branon is also under the same ownership. Second wine: Les Hauts de Bergey. Best years: (reds) 2009, '08, '07, '06, '05, '04, '03, '02, '01, '00, '99, '98; (whites) 2009, '08, '07, '06, '05, '04, '03, '02, '01, '00.

Ch. Haut-Bergey has benefited from massive investment on all sides since new ownership in 1991. The château, an imposing, late 19th-century pile, has always been a beauty, but the wines took more time to come round.

Château Haut-Brion

I've not found Haut-Brion the easiest of the First Growths to appreciate. It's not that the people there aren't nice – I've visited a few times and they were very friendly. But I often used to find myself wondering what kind of flavours, what kind of wine I was actually looking for.

Quick guide

CLASSIFICATION
Pessac-Léognan AC, Premier Cru Classé, Cru Classé de Graves

VINEYARD
48 ha (119 acres) planted to Cabernet Sauvignon (44%), Merlot (42%), Cabernet Franc (13%), Petit Verdot (1%); also 2.9ha
(7 acres) for white wine planted with Sémillon (52%), Sauvignon Blanc (48%)

TYPICAL BLEND
47% Cabernet Sauvignon, 43% Merlot, 10% Cabernet Franc

ANNUAL PRODUCTION OF GRAND VIN
120–168,000 bottles

BEST YEARS
(Reds) 2010, '09, '08, '07, '06, '05, '04, '03, '02, '01, '00, '99, '98, '97, '96, '95, '94, '93, '90, '89, '88

CLASSIC OLDER VINTAGES
1979, '75, '61, '59, '55, '53, '45, '28, '26

SECOND WINE
Le Clarence de Haut-Brion (from 2007); previously Bahans-Haut-Brion

BEST YEARS
(Whites) 2010, '09, '08, '07, '06, '05, '04, '03, '02, '01, '00, '98, '96, '95

2005 was a great vintage of which Haut-Brion took full advantage, producing one of Bordeaux's wines of the vintage.

And then I realized what the problem might be. I've never owned a bottle of Haut-Brion. I've never brought a bottle up from the cellar, brimming with anticipation, and lovingly opened it with a couple of good mates and a whole evening ahead of us to calmly work out exactly how good the wine is. I realized that I nearly always taste it, drink it even, in the company of the Médoc First Growths and probably end up judging it on their terms. That's a mistake. Haut-Brion isn't a Médoc, doesn't taste like a Médoc, and in fact would be perfectly justified in thinking of Margaux, Lafite and the rest as positive parvenus.

Which, I suppose, they are. The great Médoc estates didn't come into being until the Dutch drained the marshes that dominated the landscape north of Bordeaux city in the mid-17th century. Long before then, when the great and good of Bordeaux turned their minds to wine, they headed for the gravelly, sandy soils just to the south and west of the city where one wine in particular shone out for its quality – Haut-Brion. In fact, it's the first Bordeaux wine to have been mentioned by its own name, and Samuel Pepys memorably, if not very grammatically, wrote in his diary of 10 April 1663 about visiting the Royal Oak Tavern in London '…and there I drank a sort of French wine called Ho-Bryan; that hath a good and most particular taste that I have never met with'. King Charles II, a noted toper, also had some in his cellar. And it is a good 50 years before we can find records of any other Bordeaux wines being sold under their own names.

There are several reasons for this early rise to prominence. One was the attitude of the owner Armand de Pontac, who was deeply committed to innovation and improvement. This wasn't just altruism. By the time Pepys was quaffing his fill at the Royal Oak Tavern, Pontac's Haut-Brion was already selling for twice as much as other Bordeaux, presumably because it was better. It has never lost this eminent position and in 1855, when the by now famous and sought-after red wines of the Médoc were classified, Haut-Brion was included as a First Growth, the only non-Médoc red that even got a mention.

But Pontac was growing his grapes in the right place. Nowadays, if you visit Haut-Brion you'll find it hemmed in by the suburban houses of Pessac, a Bordeaux suburb. And quite a few of those homes will be sitting on gravel that used to be Haut-Brion's vineyard, which would explain why

Above: These really are suburbs you see just beyond the vines. If you look on a map of Bordeaux city, Haut-Brion is completely surrounded by housing, and Haut-Brion and its neighbour La Mission Haut-Brion were significantly bigger before the march of Pessac's suburban villas began. Interestingly, recent research showed that pollution is not a problem and the conurbation might actually aid ripening through higher temperatures.

Right: The oldest part of the rather charming, elegant château was built in 1550 and is situated on a piece of land unsuitable for grape-growing. Surrounded by the bustle of Pessac, it's a haven of peace.

The first year *chai* or cellar. Haut-Brion requires 1000 new barrels every year, and they employ their own cooper to produce them. He manages four or five a day.

Haut-Brion is now the smallest of Bordeaux's First Growths at 51ha (126 acres), 48ha (119 acres) of which produce red wine with just under 3ha (7 acres) reserved for a thrilling and rare dry white. But that gravel soil cries out for red grapes. Yet it's not Médoc gravel, and that's why I say I'm being a bit unfair to Haut-Brion in always comparing it to the Médoc. Firstly there's a lot more sand in the gravel here and secondly there's a lot more Merlot in the vineyards – soft, fleshy Merlot constitutes as much as 55 per cent of the final blend. This would explain why Haut-Brion sometimes lacks the sheer power of those Médocs when you taste it young, but don't be fooled. This is a long distance runner, it's just that it gets to a state of sublime drinkability rather quicker than the others and frequently shows a positively creamy roundness at as little as four years old. But hang on. Give Haut-Brion 10, 15, even 20 years, and a gorgeous purity of blackcurrant fruit begins to dominate the flavour, sometimes licked with honey, often furred by a slight earthy undertow, and usually in perfect harmony with a fabulous heady scent of unsmoked Havana tobacco.

Château Olivier

It's now worth keeping an eye on Olivier as the wines, both red and white, have shown a huge improvement in recent vintages.

CHÂTEAU OLIVIER

Pessac-Léognan AC, Cru Classé de Graves
❦ Cabernet Sauvignon, Merlot, Cabernet Franc
❦ Sauvignon Blanc, Sémillon, Muscadelle

Long owned by the de Bethmann family, the vineyards (55ha/136 acres) are grouped round a medieval moated château and it is one of the loveliest estates in the Graves. Despite the ideal location and some old vines the wines used to be generally disappointing, the reds light and lean and the whites lacking depth and character.

Investment in new oak brought some improvement in the 1990s but the big change came in 2002. The new manager, Laurent Lebrun, ushered in a revolution – soil analysis to find the best parcels, a change in vineyard cultivation and a new *cuverie* – and overnight we seem to be looking at different wines. Certainly from the watershed vintage of 2004 the reds have become fine, ripe and balanced, the whites precise, fresh and aromatic. Second wine: Le Dauphin d'Olivier. Best years: (reds) 2010, '09,'08, '06, '05, '04, '02, '01, '00, '99, '98; (whites) 2010, '09, '08, '07, '06, '05, '04, '03, '02.

Château Pape-Clément

Serious investment over the last 20 years has returned Pape-Clément to a leading position in Pessac-Léognan, though I would like less oak and power in the wine.

CHÂTEAU PAPE-CLÉMENT

Pessac-Léognan AC, Cru Classé de Graves (reds only)
❦ Cabernet Sauvignon, Merlot
❦ Sauvignon Blanc, Sémillon, Muscadelle

This famous Graves Classed Growth was languishing in the doldrums until new owners Bernard Magrez and Léo Montagne arrived in the 1980s. With some fine tuning and investment in stainless steel tanks, a system of temperature control and new oak barrels the estate has become one of the established stars of Bordeaux since 1986.

Like Ch. HAUT-BRION down the road, Pape-Clément's 36-ha (89-acre) vineyard is located on Pessac's fine, gravelly soils in the suburbs of Bordeaux, and planted to 60% Cabernet Sauvignon and 40% Merlot. The wines are deep-coloured, rich and powerful. Over-charred oak dominated some of the vintages of the 1990s, but current releases are aromatic though still rich and oaky and should be kept for ten years or more.

In recent years Pape-Clément has also produced a very fine but unclassified white wine from 2.5ha (6 acres) of vines. Barrel-fermented in new oak casks it is rich and full-bodied with the aroma and flavour of citrus fruits, vanilla and just a hint of musk. Second wine: (red) Clémentin. Best years: (reds) 2010, '09, '08, '07, '06, '05, '04, '03, '02, '01, '00, '99, '98, '96, '95, '90, '89, '88; (whites) 2010, '09, '08, '07, '06, '05, '04, '03, '02, '01, '00, '99, '98.

Château Respide-Médeville

From a blend of 60% Cabernet Sauvignon and 40% Merlot, the reds are dark-fruited, full and firm and benefit from 12 months' oak aging.

CHÂTEAU RESPIDE-MÉDEVILLE

Graves AC
❦ Cabernet Sauvignon, Merlot
❦ Sémillon, Sauvignon Blanc, Muscadelle

The 12-ha (30-acre) property at Toulenne just west of Langon is in the same hands as the well known Sauternes châteaux, GILETTE and LES JUSTICES in nearby Preignac and equally well run. The reds are dark-fruited, full and firm, the whites grassy and citrussy, moving to honeyed mellowness with age. Drink from four to five years. Best years: (reds) 2010, '09, '08, '06, '05, '04, '02, '01, '00; (whites) 2010, '09, '08, '07, '06, '05, '04, '03, '02.

Château de Rochemorin

Both the wines here – the supple and lightly oaked red and the delightful, citrus-flavoured, leafy white – are consistently good.

CHÂTEAU DE ROCHEMORIN

Pessac-Léognan AC

✽ *Cabernet Sauvignon, Merlot*

🍃 *Sauvignon Blanc*

Another property belonging to the ubiquitous André Lurton (of Ch. La LOUVIÈRE), and a large one too, with 110ha (272 acres) of which 105ha (260 acres) are planted to red varieties and 18ha (44 acres) to white. Lurton has mastered the art of economies of scale for this size of property and uses machine harvesters and the latest technology, including a new state-of-the-art winery, to produce wines of great appeal and consistent value. Drink the whites young, the reds after three to four years. Best years: (reds) 2010, '09, '08, '06, '05, '04, '02, '01, '00, '99, '98; (whites) 2010, '09, '08, '07, '06, '05, '04, '02, '01.

Château St-Robert

St-Robert has been renowned for whites for a long time but, as elsewhere in the Graves, its vineyards are being replanted in favour of more red varieties.

CHÂTEAU ST-ROBERT

Graves AC

✽ *Merlot, Cabernet Sauvignon, Cabernet Franc*

🍃 *Sauvignon Blanc, Sémillon*

Owned by a bank, the Crédit Foncier de France, for over a century, this 34-ha (84-acre) property has become a consistent performer in the Graves. The regular cuvées are supple and fruity, the Cuvée Poncet Deville (red and white) richer, full-bodied with a dusting of spicy, vanilla oak. Best years: (reds) 2010, '09, '08, '06, '05, '04, '03, '02, '01, '00, '99, '98; (whites) 2010, '09, '08, '07, '06, '05, '04, '03, '02, '01, '00.

Château Smith-Haut-Lafitte

This is one of Bordeaux's best dry whites – a wonderful dry, tangy wine with flavours of nectarine, coffee bean and blackcurrant leaf.

CHÂTEAU SMITH-HAUT-LAFITTE

Pessac-Léognan AC, Cru Classé de Graves (reds only)

✽ *Cabernet Sauvignon, Merlot, Cabernet Franc*

🍃 *Sauvignon Blanc, Sauvignon Gris, Sémillon*

The property at Martillac is one of the region's biggest at 67ha (165 acres), producing about 120,000 bottles of red and 30,000 white a year of the *grand vin*. The vineyard is primarily planted for the reds with 55% Cabernet Sauvignon, 35% Merlot and 10% Cabernet Franc. The soil is good and as gravelly as any in Pessac-Léognan on a swell of ground to the north of Martillac.

The property has undergone a revolution since owners Daniel and Florence Cathiard arrived in 1990. They discovered what they frankly describe as a chemical wilderness when they took over and have turned it into a model of sustainable viticulture. Only the red is classified but until the late 1990s it was rather lean and uninteresting. A reduction in yields, careful tending of the vineyard, severe selection and aging in new oak barrels have resulted in a wine of greater concentration, structure and elegance, but the traditional dryness found in wines from Martillac is only slowly being vanquished. Since the 2000s I rank it among the best in the Pessac-Léognan AC.

The whites have been in the forefront of Bordeaux's white wine revolution. Using barrel fermentation and aging in new oak, today the château stands as a shining example to others in the region of what investment and commitment can do for a wine. So far only 11ha (27 acres) of land are planted with white grapes, which are almost all Sauvignon (there is a little Sémillon and Sauvignon Gris). The white is not classified since there were no white grapes at all when the Graves classification was decided in 1959, but it surely deserves classification today. I'd like them to plant as much white as possible because year by year this is one of the best whites in Bordeaux – tangy, scented with nectarines and coated with savoury cream. Second wine (red and white): Les Hauts de Smith. Best years: (reds) 2010, '09, '08, '07, '06, '05, '04 '03, '02, '01, '00, '99, '98, '96, '95, '94; (whites) 2010, '09, '08, '07, '06, '05, '04, '03, '02, '01, '00, '99, '98.

Vieux Château Gaubert

This is a good, toasty white from an ambitious Graves property keen on achieving the quality level of a Pessac-Léognan.

VIEUX CHÂTEAU GAUBERT
Graves AC
🍇 Merlot, Cabernet Sauvignon
🍇 Sauvignon Blanc, Sémillon

The vineyard in the commune of Portets was planted to a higher density (7000 vines/ha) from 1989 and new oak barrels were introduced at the same time – two reasons why this estate is a leading player in the Graves AC today. The reds are full-bodied and meaty with smoky-vanilla depth and pretty serious structure and need at least four or five years' bottle age. The whites are full and unctuous. Best years: (reds) 2009, '08, '07, '06, '05, '04, '03, '02, '01, '00, '99, '98; (whites) 2009, '08, '07, '06, '05, '04, '03, '02, '01, '00.

Château Le Thil Comte Clary

This is a good, full, savoury white from a blend of Sauvignon and Sémillon and benefits from barrel fermentation and new oak aging.

CHÂTEAU LE THIL COMTE CLARY
Pessac-Léognan AC
🍇 Merlot, Cabernet Sauvignon
🍇 Sauvignon Blanc, Sémillon

Le Thil had all the trappings of grandeur – a distinguished Bordeaux family (the de Laitres), along with a château and park – but until 1989 there were no vines. Now with 17ha (42 acres) it is making a name for its wines. The whites from clay-limestone soils have looked good from the start: elegant and flinty with toasted, waxy, citrus flavours. The Merlot-dominated reds have improved as the vines have aged and are finely structured and fragrant. Drink from four to five years. Best years: (reds) 2009, '08, '06, '05, '04 '02; (whites) 2009, '08, '07, '06, '05, '04, '03, '02, '01, '00, '98.

Château Villa Bel-Air

The soft Graves style of Villa Bel-Air's red shows the influence of the owner, Jean-Michel Cazes of Pauillac's Lynch-Bages.

CHÂTEAU VILLA BEL-AIR
Graves AC
🍇 Cabernet Sauvignon, Merlot, Cabernet Franc
🍇 Sauvignon Blanc, Sémillon, Muscadelle

This 46-ha (114-acre) property at St-Morillon in the northern part of the Graves was put together in the 1980s by Jean-Michel Cazes of Ch. LYNCH-BAGES, which can't be a bad reference. The vines now have an average age of 20 years or so. The barrel-fermented whites are full but fresh and citrussy, coated with creamy oak, the reds attractively fruity and ready to drink at three to four years. Best years: (reds) 2009, '08, '06, '05, '04, '02, '01, '00, '99; (whites) 2009, '08, '07, '06, '05, '04, '03, '02, '01, '00.

Quick guide • Best producers

GRAVES AC
Archambeau, Ardennes, Beauregard-Ducasse, Bichon-Cassignols, Le Bonnat, Brondelle, Castres, Chantegrive, Clos Floridène, Crabitey, Ferrande, Fougères, Grand Enclos du Château de Cérons, Gravelière, Haura, L'Hospital, Léhoul, Magence, Magneau, Perron, Places, Pont de Brion, Rahoul, Respide, Respide-Médeville, Roquetaillade la Grange, St-Jean-des-Graves, St-Robert (Cuvée Poncet Deville), Seuil, Toumilon, Tour Bicheau, Tourteau Chollet, Vieux Château-Gaubert, Vénus, Villa Bel-Air.

PESSAC-LÉOGNAN AC
Bouscaut, Brown, Cantelys, Carbonnieux, Les Carmes Haut-Brion, Dom. de Chevalier, Coucheroy, Couhins-Lurton, Cruzeau, Fieuzal, France, La Garde, Haut-Bailly, Haut-Bergey, Haut-Brion, Haut-Gardère, Haut-Lagrange, Larrivet-Haut-Brion, Latour-Martillac, Laville Haut-Brion (until 2009 vintage), La Louvière, Malartic-Lagravière, La Mission Haut-Brion, Olivier, Pape-Clément, Picque Caillou, Pontac-Monplaisir, Rochemorin, Smith-Haut-Lafitte, Dom de La Solitude, Le Thil Comte Clary, La Tour Haut-Brion (until 2005 vintage).

The Right Bank

The Right Bank produces many of Bordeaux's most sought after red wines at the moment, as well as many of its most controversial. The consultants who increasingly fashion Bordeaux's wines in their own image are largely Right Bank-based, and Bordeaux's buzz is very much in the busy bar-restaurants of St-Émilion rather than in the timid watering holes of the Médoc. Right Bank, Left Bank, there's always been this division in Bordeaux's reds between the austere Cabernet-based styles of the Left Bank Médoc and the lusher Merlot-based styles of St-Émilion and Pomerol which lead the Right Bank charge. But while the Left Bank has dominated the scene for centuries the Right Bank is now at the very least on an equal footing and in many markets – the mighty USA being one of them – may even have gained the upper hand. The Right Bank vineyards are strung along the slopes and plateaux of the northern bank of the Dordogne with the riverside town of Libourne at their centre. Châteaux here are rarely grand, properties are usually small, and in some cases minute, but that hasn't stopped the wines becoming frighteningly fashionable in recent years.

St-Émilion is the biggest area. The thick carpet of vines begins just east of Libourne and fans out up to the plateau above the little Roman hillside town of St-Émilion, and also along the sandy plains down by the river. Pomerol is a featureless plateau on its own that can feel like the back of beyond and yet which makes some of the world's most famous wines, Ch. Pétrus being the star. Fifty years ago the name Pomerol meant next to nothing. Just over the river Isle from Libourne are the wooded hillsides of Canon-Fronsac and Fronsac that were much more renowned a century ago but which are only now beginning to haul themselves back up the quality ladder.

St-Émilion is the liveliest wine town in Bordeaux – and the loveliest, with tiny streets and limestone houses crammed together, and caves and cellars running deep into the rock. Limestone is the key to the region's best wines and it seems fitting that the two churches you can see here are cut into great hunks of it. The vineyards come right up to the town walls: these are the vines of Ch. Pavie.

SPOTLIGHT ON
The Right Bank

If you want to feel the buzz in the wine world in Bordeaux, head to St-Émilion and hang out in its bustling restaurants and wine bars. L'Essentiel wine bar is owned by Jean-Luc Thunevin and the bottles are exhibited in a curling wave of lime green and cherry pink. But they're serious bottles. All the top growths of Bordeaux are here, quite a few of them available by the glass with the added incentive of perhaps having a chat with garagiste extraordinaire Thunevin. I drank a glass of the extremely rare white from one of St-Émilion's hottest properties, Ch. Monbousquet.

I need to make a confession. I used to be a Left Bank snob. By which I mean I valued the austere, intellectual charms of the Médoc more than the lush hedonism of St-Émilion and Pomerol. I preferred to take a 20-year risk on a Cabernet Sauvignon-dominated red that was clasped in a carapace of tannin and uncertain broodiness rather than surrender myself to the sheer, predictable juicy joys of the Merlot grape grown on the right bank of the Dordogne river. I simply didn't accord the Right Bank and its two great regions Pomerol and St-Émilion the same respect, the same attention, the same level of fascinated enquiry that I gave the mighty Médocs and, to a lesser extent, those gravel-influenced reds of Pessac-Léognan just to the south of Bordeaux city.

I stand corrected. If ever anyone in the world of wine writing has consistently proclaimed that unless a wine brightens your eyes, warms your heart, lifts your spirits and makes you glad to be alive, then there's no point to it – I am that writer. And yet in Bordeaux I have denied that firm tenet of my wine-drinking faith for far too long. I've solemnly dissected the flesh and bones of many a fine Médoc in positively intellectual terms when my soul was positively crying out for the exuberant, instantly understandable joys of a St-Émilion or a Pomerol. I peer into my cellar and count row upon row of Pauillacs, St-Juliens, St-Estèphes and Margaux. And just a fleeting Pomerol here, a nervous clutch of St-Émilions there, Fronsacs I can't even find. What a confession.

The thing is, I virtually learnt the whole world of wine at university and thereafter from the bedrock base of Cabernet-dominated red Bordeaux and the white Chardonnay wines of Burgundy. I was a captive

Quick guide • The Right Bank

LOCATION
The vineyards pack the hills and plains around the town of Libourne, on the right bank of the river Dordogne, hence the informal Right Bank designation to distinguish the wines from the Left Bank style of the Médoc.

APPELLATIONS
St-Émilion and Pomerol are the names that slim down fat wallets in double-quick time with wines of hedonistic richness. St-Émilion has a good hand of juicy budget wines too and there are plenty of understudy appellations sometimes offering decent quality at a better price. St-Émilion has four satellites

– Lussac-St-Émilion, Montagne-St-Émilion, Puisseguin-St-Émilion, St-Georges-St-Émilion – and Pomerol's larger neighbour, Lalande-de-Pomerol offers some of the same plummy style. Fronsac and Canon-Fronsac are another pair of fair-value Bordeaux stalwarts, offering a style somewhere between Pomerol and the stonier dryness of the Médoc.

GRAPES
Like the Médoc, the Right Bank is devoted to red wines. But Merlot does best on the cooler, heavier clays of St-Émilion and Pomerol, with greater or lesser amounts of Cabernet Franc on limestone and small plantings of Cabernet Sauvignon on gravel outcrops. There is a minuscule amount of Malbec.

CLIMATE
The maritime influence begins to moderate, producing warmer summers and cooler winters. It is drier than the Médoc with frequent, sometimes severe frosts.

SOIL
A complex pattern shows gravel deposits, sand and clay mixed with limestone. The top vineyards are either on the limestone côtes around the town of St-Émilion or on the gravel outcrops of Pomerol and Ch. Figeac.

of my first wine experiences. And just as they say youth is too precious to be wasted on the young, maybe the unbridled pleasure boats of Pomerol and St-Émilion are too dangerous to be loosed on wine neophytes. If I hadn't had to struggle to comprehend the deep enjoyment wine could give, perhaps I'd never have made the effort to understand the whole glorious but demanding experience the world of wine offers. If I'd begun in the rich pastures of St-Émilion and Pomerol it might have terminally sapped my keen desire to learn, simply because I'd have wondered – can red wine ever be better than this?

I'm older now, wiser perhaps, more prepared to appreciate the remarkable personality of these Right Bank wines, more able to accept that you don't have to suffer to enjoy greatness in wine. Just in time, because the Bordeaux I grew up with has dramatically changed and that change has been led by the Right Bank. Before modern times – let's say the late 1980s at the very earliest – the great guru of wine in Bordeaux was Professor Peynaud. He was a fine teacher, strongly influencing how wine was taught at the enology school in Bordeaux University, and was by far the most important consultant to wine properties. But almost all his work was done on the Left Bank, the Médoc in particular being his stomping ground. From the 1950s to the 1980s he transformed the way Médoc wines were made, especially the great Classed Growths. He taught the importance of limiting the yield, cleaning up the winery and modernizing machinery, using new oak barrels and ruthlessly selecting only the best barrels for your grand vin. But Cabernet Sauvignon was the grape he most admired, especially as grown on the gravel beds of the Médoc, and Cabernet winemaking styles were what he preached and taught.

André Lurton must have been giving himself a 76th birthday present when he bought Ch. de Barbe Blanche in 2000. But it was André's first foray into the Right Bank – his properties hitherto had always been in the Entre-Deux-Mers and Pessac-Léognan. He's already started turning out a good, balanced red from the challenging soils of Lussac-St-Émilion.

ASPECT
Generally flat, especially in Pomerol, the land rises steeply in the côtes south and south-west of St-Émilion. Elsewhere the slopes are at best moderately undulating.

VINTAGE VARIATIONS
Due to the choice of grape varieties Right Bank vineyards harvest earlier than those in the Médoc and so are more likely to beat the onset of autumn rains. But rain is a greater hazard if it does strike due to the heavier soils and greater susceptibility to rot of the Merlot grapes. In the very hottest years (2003 and '09) the Merlot can be broiled to overripeness and lose its structure and acidity, but the Right Bank can cope better than the Médoc in cooler years.

ORGANIZATION
By contrast with the Médoc and Graves, this is a land of small estates, averaging well under 8ha (20 acres), with few grand château buildings and around 15% of the grapes going to the thriving local co-operatives. There are two appellations in St-Émilion: basic St-Émilion AC (which accounts for around 30% of the wines) and St-Émilion Grand Cru (70%). There is also a classification system of Grand Cru Classé and Premier Grand Cru Classé (with 'A' and 'B' subvisions). The classification is revised every 10 years or so, most recently in 2006, and properties do get promoted and demoted. The next classification is due for publication during 2012. Neither Pomerol nor any of the outlying regions has a classification.

A FEW FACTS
12,700ha (31,380 acres) of which 44% are in St-Émilion, producing a total of 560,000hl of wine, all of it red.

ST-ÉMILION, POMEROL AND FRONSAC

TOTAL DISTANCE NORTH
TO SOUTH 20KM (12½ MILES)

VINEYARDS

0 km   1   2
0 miles   1

N

AC WINE AREAS

— Fronsac
— Canon-Fronsac
— Lalande-de-Pomerol
— Pomerol
— St-Émilion
— Montagne-St-Émilion

— St-Georges-St-Émilion
— Lussac-St-Émilion
— Puisseguin-St-Émilion

WHERE THE VINEYARDS ARE

The Libournais covers the area north of the Dordogne
river. Libourne became important as the shipping port for all the wines
produced on the banks of the Dordogne and is still the base for the main
companies shipping St-Émilion, Pomerol and Fronsac. The slopes and hills to the west of
Libourne are those of Fronsac and Canon-Fronsac. This attractive region was an obvious place for
the Libourne business community to build its estates and, until the 19th century, Fronsac wines were seen as
leading lights in the area.

    The area east of the town is now more important. Pomerol and St-Émilion also produce wines of much higher
quality. From the air Pomerol appears as a uniform carpet of vines. But below the surface is an array of soil types
giving different characteristics to its wines, and excellent quality overall. South of St-Émilion, a cleft in the plateau
creates the south and east-facing slopes of the côtes area of St-Émilion, home of many of St-Émilion's finest wines.

● CHÂTEAUX FEATURED ON PAGES 209–249

FRONSAC
1. Ch. Fontenil
2. Ch. Haut-Carles
3. Ch. Villars
4. Ch. Dalem
5. Ch. Moulin Haut-Laroque
6. Ch. La Vieille Cure
7. Ch. Les Trois Croix
8. Ch. de La Rivière
9. Ch. La Rousselle
10. Ch. de La Dauphine

CANON-FRONSAC
11. Ch. Moulin Pey-Labrie
12. Ch. Grand-Renouil
13. Ch. Cassagne Haut-Canon
14. Ch. Barrabaque

LALANDE-DE-POMEROL
15. Ch. Laborderie Mondésir
16. Ch. Perron
17. Ch. Les Cruzelles
18. Ch. Grand Ormeau
19. Ch. Garraud
20. Ch. La Fleur de Boüard
21. Ch. Haut-Chaigneau

POMEROL
22. Ch. Latour-à-Pomerol
23. Ch. Feytit-Clinet
24. Ch. Trotanoy
25. Clos L'Eglise
26. Ch. Clinet
27. Ch. L'Église-Clinet
28. Ch. Le Gay
29. Ch. Hosanna
30. Ch. Lafleur
31. Ch. La Fleur-Pétrus
32. Ch. Pétrus
33. Ch. Gazin
34. Ch. Le Bon Pasteur
35. Ch. L'Évangile
36. Ch. La Conseillante
37. Vieux-Ch.-Certan
38. Ch. Certan-de-May
39. Ch. Petit Village
40. Ch. Le Pin
41. Ch. Nénin
42. Ch. Beauregard
43. Ch. Taillefer

ST-ÉMILION
44. Ch. Quinault l'Enclos
45. Ch. La Tour-Figeac
46. Ch. Cheval Blanc
47. Ch. La Dominique
48. Ch. Figeac
49. Ch. Rol Valentin
50. Clos de L'Oratoire
51. Ch. Soutard
52. Ch. La Gomerie
53. Ch. Grand-Mayne
54. Ch. Angélus
55. Ch. Beauséjour (HDL)
56. Clos St-Martin
57. Ch. Beau-Séjour Bécot
58. Ch. Canon
59. Clos Fourtet
60. Ch. Gracia
61. Ch. Valandraud
62. Ch. Couspaude
63. Ch. Balestard-la-Tonnelle
64. Ch. Trottevieille
65. Ch. Fombrauge
66. Ch. Fleur Cardinale
67. Ch. Faugères
68. Ch. Tertre-Rôteboeuf
69. La Mondotte
70. Ch. Troplong-Mondot
71. Ch. Pavie-Macquin
72. Ch. Pavie-Decesse
73. Ch. Moulin St-Georges
74. Ch. Ausone
75. Ch. Belair-Monange
76. Ch. Magdelaine
77. Ch. Berliquet
78. Ch. L'Arrosée
79. Ch. La Gaffelière
80. Ch. Pavie
81. Ch. Bellefont-Belcier
82. Ch. Canon-la-Gaffelière
83. Ch. Monbousquet
84. Ch. Teyssier

MONTAGNE-ST-ÉMILION
85. Vieux Ch. St-André
86. Ch. Rocher Corbin
87. Ch. Faizeau
88. Ch. Calon
89. Ch. Croix-Beauséjour

ST-GEORGES-ST-ÉMILION
90. Ch. St-Georges

LUSSAC-ST-ÉMILION
91. Ch. de Barbe-Blanche
92. Ch. de Lussac
93. Ch. Lyonnat

PUISSEGUIN-ST-ÉMILION
94. Ch. Durand-Laplagne
95. Ch. La Mauriane

0 km   1   2
0 miles   1

Well, here it is. The lone pine tree that gave its name to Le Pin, arguably the world's most expensive wine. I mean, even the empty wooden box would be worth a full bottle or two of a less exalted wine. There is now a brand new winery on the site including an extensive underground cellar but the the two pine trees nearby have been preserved.

Yet these won't work on the Right Bank. Merlot is the dominant grape here, followed a long way behind by Cabernet Franc and with Cabernet Sauvignon generally an unsuccessful afterthought. The climate is hotter, yet the soils are colder – limestone and limestone clays, sometimes almost pure clays, occasionally leavened with gravel or sand. Not only will Cabernet Sauvignon not ripen here, but if you pick Merlot at the same sugar levels as are acceptable for Cabernet Sauvignon on the Left Bank, the wine will be hard and dry. But give the Merlot time to ripen to an extra degree of potential alcohol and all the fleshy, heady lushness of the grape becomes marvellously apparent. Different grape, different conditions, different techniques.

However, until the 1980s the red wine techniques taught at Bordeaux University were Left Bank Cabernet techniques; all the most important merchants were based in Bordeaux city, as they had been for centuries, and they showed only passing interest in the Right Bank wines; and none of the great wine critics of the time regarded them as the equal – with a few exceptions like Cheval Blanc and Pétrus – of the leading Left Bank wines. It was all about to change.

For a start, one merchant in Libourne realized that the modern world, and particularly the USA, might prefer the rich approachable flavours of Right Bank Merlot to the more daunting delights of Left Bank Cabernet. Jean-Pierre Moueix was the far-sighted wine merchant who identified all the best sites in Pomerol – and many in St-Émilion – and above all gained an exclusivity for Ch. Pétrus. Now he just needed a top vintage, a strong dollar and a new wave critic who thought like him. The 1982 vintage brought all these together – sumptuous wines, a mighty dollar and the emergence of a man who is now the most powerful influence in the world of fine wines: Robert Parker. He caught the mood of America perfectly when in defiance of the early consensus of the more traditional critics he proclaimed 1982 one of the greatest vintages of the century – and especially championed the 1982 wines from St-Émilion and Pomerol. A quarter of a century later his power shows no sign of waning and Pomerol is probably now the most fêted wine region in Bordeaux for red wine obsessives.

But the Right Bank producers still had to be taught how to replicate 1982 – nature wouldn't do it most years. Well just as Peynaud had transformed the Left Bank in the decades after World War Two, a young winemaker called Michel Rolland arrived on the scene to transform the Right Bank. He'd grown up in Pomerol on a wine estate (Ch. Le Bon Pasteur). He's a self-confessed epicurean and pleasure-seeker, and it has been his genius to maximize the hedonism of the wines of Pomerol and St-Émilion – so much so that by the end of the 1990s the ripeness of the Right Bank, with wines now regularly achieving 14–14.5 per cent alcohol, had become the defining style of the new Bordeaux. For centuries the Right Bank players had been rustic country cousins.

Now Rolland and a clutch of similarly-minded consultants and gurus are even crossing the river, spreading their influence into the Médoc and Pessac-Léognan.

The modern Bordeaux is led by Right Bank ideas of ripeness, lushness, density and extraction, regardless of whether the property concerned is really suited to producing such wine. Bordeaux, once the symbol of classicism and studied reserve, is now decked out in glad rags and daubed with rouge. Things will change again of course – in fact there are signs that the pendulum may already have reached the limit of its swing to the hedonistic right. A more restrained style will once more come into fashion some time in the future. New critics will rise to prominence, new winemaking gurus will appear, public taste will alter. But now, for the first time since the Romans left Bordeaux, the Right Bank rules the roost.

The stark beauty of winter. The cold dawn sun silhouettes St-Émilion's spire against the orange sky. Mist lingers among the vines, some already pruned, others still waiting for the numb fingers of the vineyard workers to snip off last year's branches and prepare the wood for the long slow march to harvest next September.

ST-ÉMILION

Nearly all St-Émilion is a tale of limestone, or lack of it, and with the exception of a handful of gravelly hectares to the west on the border with Pomerol, quality and excitement follow the limestone. Almost all of St-Émilion – and all of historic St-Émilion – is either on the limestone plateau, or the tumbled debris of its slopes, or curled around the foot of the slopes, clutching at the last of the limestone before the flat alluvial sandy clays spreading away towards the river try to suck out your chances of making wine with structure, perfume and excitement. St-Émilion is probably the best-known of the regional names in Bordeaux's red wine firmament – along with Sauternes and Graves in the whites. And that's because in the old days every hotel, every restaurant, every grocer's shop – anywhere that sold Bordeaux wine – would be able to offer you Sauternes, Graves and St-Émilion, probably bottled by the local brewer – but the St-Émilion would always taste soft and jammy and amiable, whereas any Médoc on the same lists would have been more likely to taste of iron filings.

Well, the brewers' St-Émilion could have come from anywhere, quite frankly, but the style of wine it was based on – rich, generous, lush and soft – that style, in Bordeaux, could only come from the Merlot grape, and nowhere is it more widely planted than in St-Émilion. It does have a help-mate – Cabernet Franc – which until the late 19th century was frequently more important than the Merlot, but which now generally plays a subsidiary role, adding perfume and freshness to the wine when

Classic wine styles • St-Émilion

OVERVIEW
St-Émilion is a region of smallholdings. The local co-operative, the Union de Producteurs de St-Émilion, is the oldest in the Gironde and of great importance as it vinifies over 20% of the entire crop to a consistently pretty high standard. Merlot is the main grape in the clay-rich soils, with significant plantings of Cabernet Franc on limestone lending support.

TASTING NOTE
What a contrast with the stern, demanding wines of the Médoc! A glass of St-Émilion melts with gorgeous softness, a buttery, toffeeish sweetness and a fruit flavour sticky with the dark chewy richness of raisins and cherries in a fruit cake.

WHEN TO DRINK
Straightforward St-Émilion is enjoyable from the word go and even ambitious wines are bursting with fruity richness from around four years of age. Don't plan to keep too many bottles beyond their tenth birthday, although the best wines, from the limestone slopes around the town of St-Émilion itself, have more structure and longevity.

BEST YEARS
2010, '09, '08, '06, '05, '01, '00, '98, '96, 95.

The classification of St-Emilion is a commendably fluid effort. If you don't perform you get warned, and if you still don't perform, you'll get demoted. On the other hand if you regularly overachieve and keep clamouring at the door demanding promotion in louder and louder tones – well, you can get promoted. The six châteaux on the left – Canon, La Gaffelière, Beauséjour (Duffau-Lagarrosse/HDL), Belair-Monange, Magdelaine and Figeac – are original members of the Premier Grand Cru Classé classification, Angélus after a series of storming performances since the mid-1980s got promoted in 1996. The lovely, silky L'Arrosée has several times been touted for promotion, but I think it will have to wait a little longer. Out of the frame but promoted to Premier Cru Classé in 2006 are Pavie-Macquin and Troplong Mondot.

the hedonistic, self-indulgent Merlot looks in danger of becoming too sweet and overblown for its own good.

St-Émilion wines do generally have a broad beaming smile on their face, but different corners of the appellation give very distinct flavours to the wine. So let's start at the heart of things – up on that limestone plateau by the beautiful ancient town of St-Émilion itself. Crammed into an incredibly small space along the top of the plateau and tumbling over towards the plains below are the majority of St-Émilion's most famous properties. These are called the *côtes* châteaux – the châteaux on the slopes – but their vines are just as likely to be on the top of the plateau, and some vines – but not many – are on the more fertile land at the foot of the slopes.

The generally held view in St-Émilion is that the subsoil gives the character to the wine, and here the subsoil is limestone. Not an incredibly hard limestone – soft enough for it to be quarried and cut into blocks to build the houses that cling together in the steep narrow streets of St-Émilion itself. I've actually stood in the vineyards and crumbled the limestone away with my fingers. But this relative softness – tenderness is how I've heard it described – means that the vines' roots can creep in amongst the rock. On the best sites, the actual topsoil is very shallow, frequently less than a metre and never more than 1.5m (5ft), so the subsoil is of enormous importance. Limestone is cool and moist, so there's not much point in putting a late-ripening grape like Cabernet Sauvignon on these soils – the fruit simply won't ripen. There is some Cabernet Sauvignon, but this was planted on the orders of the appellation bureaucrats: all the locals knew it wouldn't work, and it doesn't. But the cold, damp soil means that early ripeners like Cabernet Franc and Merlot can't ripen as fast as they would in gravel or sand, where they can easily bake and the resulting wine tastes of jam. The limestone keeps the acidity in the grapes higher for longer than warmer soils, and acidity is what keeps flavours gloriously fresh while the sunshine pumps up the sugars in the juice. You can leave your grapes until they are completely ripe, perhaps even verging on the overripe, and the acidity from the limestone stops the whole thing turning to jam. And this is the brilliance of the *côtes* St-Émilions. In the old days they were often picked too early and the wines never lost their hardness. Nowadays they are sumptuous and serious at the same time.

All the most famous *côtes* properties are clustered round the town of St-Émilion at the western end of the plateau – look at the map on pages 196-197, the sheer density is quite striking. But the limestone plateau and its marvellously angled steep slopes continue eastward right into the Côtes de Castillon and beyond. The limestone is a little harder here, and you have to hold off harvesting by perhaps as much as a week to get maximum ripeness, but the results can be stunning and each year more of these 'eastern *côtes*' properties begin to produce glorious wine. It's the same on the plateau itself. Here the depth of the topsoil is of enormous importance. As you head north and north-east from St-Émilion town through a sea of vines, the soil gets deeper, and the roots find it easier to thrive without having to pierce the limestone. The result is large numbers of rich, round, satisfying wines, but few famous ones. Head east, however, through St-Christophe-des-Bardes and on towards Castillon, and the limestone surges towards the surface once more. Right at the eastern edge superb wines are now being made from sites which previously sold their wine in bulk to the co-ops.

If we go back to the town and head north-west, the land very gradually drifts lower. There are vines everywhere, but no famous names. These vineyards are in what are called 'ancient sands' soils. Sandy soils usually produce wines with attractive but loose-knit flavours and that's pretty much what you get here – but we've not finished. Right at the north-western edge, right on the border with Pomerol, there's a little stream and then a series of good ridges towards the north. This is the tiny but brilliant *graves* zone of St-Émilion. There are only about 60ha (150 acres) of this deep gravel soil, but that's enough for two of Bordeaux's finest properties – Figeac and the peerless Cheval Blanc – to benefit from the warm gravel and plant significant amounts of Cabernet Franc and, in Figeac's case, a big chunk of Cabernet Sauvignon as well. Until the recent revival of Ausone, Cheval Blanc had been making St-Émilion's finest wines for generations, and Figeac wasn't far behind.

Not long ago, I would have said that that's all the quality dealt with. The only St-Émilion left is some sandy stuff down by the Dordogne which is pretty forgettable. But that's not fair any more. Admittedly the *sables* (sand) St-Émilions rarely shine but that's because no one has ever thought it worth making the effort with them. The warm sandy soils suffer from what is called 'heat shock' in most summers – the grapes get grilled by the heat and can't finish their ripening successfully. Not surprisingly most of these *sables* grapes end up at the admittedly very good co-operative. But the new wave *garagiste* movement (I'll talk about these guys more over the page) believes that there's no such thing as a rotten piece of land that can't be transformed by passion, commitment and investment and, led by Jonathan Maltus of Château Teyssier – on a famously poor piece of land – and Gérard Perse of Château Monbousquet (promoted to Grand Cru Classé in 2006) – he actually has some gravel amongst the sandy clay – even the *sables* St-Émilions are now starting to turn out fine wine and extract hefty prices from a willing market.

Classic wine styles • St-Émilion

AFFORDABLE WINES TO TRY

- Ch. Balestard-la-Tonnelle (Grand Cru Classé)
- Ch. Barde-Haut
- Ch. Bellevue
- Ch. Bellefont-Belcier (Grand Cru Classé)
- Ch. Bernateau
- Ch. Boutisse
- Ch Cap de Mourlin (Grand Cru Classé)
- Ch. Carteau-Côtes-Daugay
- Clos de la Cure
- Clos de la Madeleine
- Ch. Clos Trimoulet
- Ch. Côte de Baleau
- Ch. Destieux (Grand Cru Classé)
- Ch. Faugères
- Ch. Ferrand Lartigue
- Ch. Fleur Cardinale
- Ch. Fonplégade (Grand Cru Classé)
- Ch. Franc Grâce Dieu
- Ch. Grand Mayne (Grand Cru Classé)
- Ch. Grand-Pontet (Grand Cru Classé)
- Ch. Jean Faure
- Ch. Lapelletrie
- Ch. Laplagnotte Bellevue
- Ch. Lavallade, 'Carpe Diem'
- Ch. Mangot
- Ch. Petit Fombrauge
- Ch. de Pressac
- Ch. Le Prieuré
- Dom. du Rivallon
- Sanctus de la Bienfaisance
- Ch. Tauzinat l'Hermitage
- Ch. Teyssier
- Ch. Tournefeuille
- Ch. du Val d'Or
- Vieux Ch. Pelletan

For more ideas see page 249

La Mondotte is a small vineyard on the plateau of St-Émilion next to Ch. Troplong-Mondot. Stephan von Neipperg, owner of Ch. Canon-la-Gaffelière, wanted to incorporate the Mondotte land into his main property. When the authorities refused permission, he said, 'hell, I'll make it into a separate wine – and I'll make it magnificent'. He's done just that.

Right: I went to the same school as Jonathan Maltus, so I was always going to like his wines. But he clearly gleaned more business sense from the masters than I ever did, because after creating a successful engineering company, he sold it in 1994 and bought Ch. Teyssier in St-Émilion. That was just the beginning. Since then he's been a leader of the garagiste or micro-cru movement, creating a string of limited release, high-octane reds led by Le Carré, Les Astéries and Le Dôme (above). They're all tiny production and they're all truly different, an important point since one criticism of the garagistes is that their wines all taste the same. In 2002 he expanded his garagiste principles into the Barossa Valley in Australia.

LES GARAGISTES

'Why has it taken you 15 years to come and see me?' Jean-Luc Thunevin almost shouted at me across the dining table. He wasn't angry, just bemused because he thought we'd got so much in common. We'd been talking about breaking down the class barriers in Bordeaux, about preaching the meritocratic gospel that everyone should have a right to try and produce something special if they wanted to and were prepared to bust a gut doing so, despite the fact that they might have no money and no fabled ancient plot of vines. And we'd been talking about the pleasure principle. He was mourning the fact that people don't drink his beloved Valandraud, they just taste it then endlessly and aridly dissect it. And finally they mark it out of 100. Why don't they drink it? 'Either you like the wine or you don't like the wine,' he said, 'all the rest is just blah, blah, blah.' (I didn't know the French used this phrase – it sounded wonderfully dismissive in his broad French accent.)

And I had to wonder, why hadn't I come to see this friendly, effusive iconoclast, the creator of the radical, revolutionary wine movement known as Les Garagistes? I decided the reason was that I was rather frightened by the changes they were bringing about in a landscape I loved for its familiarity rather than for its acrid fumes of class warfare. I didn't trust this *garagiste* movement. So I spent quite a bit of

time reading about the men and women and their wines, and hardly ever went out of my way to taste them, let alone buy them and drink them. And the astronomical prices they achieved made me deeply suspicious of the producers' motives.

But Jean-Luc explained that it was imperative to charge a high price to justify the toil and commitment. When you start with nothing, and can only produce a couple of thousand bottles, you have to charge a high price. The trick is to make a wine worth the money. And that's the secret of the true garagiste. The true *garagiste* is someone like Thunevin who started with no money to buy decent vines or smart equipment, no background in vineyards, just a belief that if you sacrifice yourself to whatever vines you have managed to scrape together, reduce their yield by half, care for them one by one, pick the grapes as ripe as possible – almost riper than you dare, and if necessary berry by berry – if you then take them to your shed or shack – and in his case his actual garage squeezed into a backstreet on the lower side of St-Émilion – and you buy the best barrels you can and continue to commit yourself totally to fermenting and maturing the wine, never cutting corners and always ruthlessly removing any portions of wine you think don't reflect your passion – if you do all this, the flame of the *garagiste* is clearly alight in you and you can make a great wine no one has ever heard of before. If you then attract the attention of the merchants and press and demand an exorbitant price, which the market pays, you have proved that the old order can be broken and a new meritocracy can take its place. Just as happens in California or Australia, but up until now had never happened here.

Not all *garagistes* are like Thunevin. Some are; like Michel Gracia, the local stonemason with his impressive Ch. Gracia. Others are like Comte Stephan von Neipperg, owner of Classed Growth Canon-la-Gaffelière, who was refused permission to include a small new plot of excellent land in his Classed Growth property and so built himself a winery and followed all the vigorous demands of the *garagiste* approach to produce his thrilling micro-cru La Mondotte – unclassified but much more expensive than Canon-la-Gaffelière. And there are others like Bernard Magrez who slices off one little amphitheatre of particularly favoured vineyard in his main property and turns it into a dense, powerful micro-cru, as he has done with Magrez-Fombrauge at Ch. Fombrauge.

Maybe these guys aren't imbued with the spirit of the *garage* since they came from a privileged or moneyed background, but they took up the cudgels, albeit in their own interests, after the *garagistes* like Thunevin, or Jonathan Maltus at Ch. Teyssier had led the way. And eventually, as Jean-Luc says, the revolution had to come from the little people, because they had nothing to lose. World famous wines wouldn't put their reputations on the line. And now? 'Well, what we do and what Ch. Latour does is not that different, but they have every possible technical aid. I just have myself and my wife.'

Jean-Luc Thunevin is the revolutionary spirit who sparked the whole garagiste movement which has had such a galvanizing effect on Bordeaux, giving producers all over the region, however faintly regarded, the confidence to say – 'if I want to make great wine and am really prepared to commit myself, then I can'. On recent visits I've tasted outstanding wines from Blaye, Bourg, Castillon and Entre-Deux-Mers which owe their existence to Thunevin. Ch. Valandraud was his first venture – and that's the original vineyard below, 0.6ha (1.5 acres) of St-Émilion land he freely admits was a bit ropey, sitting as it does next to the communal vegetable allotments, but it was all he could afford. Valandraud is much bigger now, with far better land providing most of the grapes. But this cold, drab little patch of vines is where the garagiste revolution was born.

POMEROL

I know all about clay. I grew up in the Kent countryside. My playgrounds were the marshes of the River Stour, the golden woodlands and the clogged potato fields where ploughs turned up ridges of clay as dark as chocolate and so thick they sucked the boots off your feet. You could weigh ten kilos more after struggling through these fields just because of the thick sullen layers of cloddish clay that clamped themselves on to your boots.

So when I say that clay – deep, blue-black, thick and sticky as purgatory – is the reason Pomerol can produce Bordeaux's most famous and most expensive wine, I say so with feeling. Even to this day I don't wear good shoes when I visit the vineyards of Château Pétrus. But hold on. Heavy, cold, wet clay is exactly the kind of soil that winemakers throughout Bordeaux are trying to avoid. So why, in what is called the 'button' of Pétrus, can such a brilliant wine be produced? Well, it really is a button. Pomerol isn't a big area – only 800ha (1980 acres) in toto in a bleak and rather forbidding landscape largely devoid of villages and human activity though dominated by an ever-present church spire. Pomerol begins right next to Cheval Blanc in St-Émilion, and on the high eastern edge (only 35m/115ft high, but that's as high as you get) shares much the same soil. The zone then drifts downwards towards Libourne in the south-west and the Isle river in the west, while the river Barbanne creates an abrupt boundary to the north. And as a generalization, the higher and more easterly your property is, the denser and more powerful your wine will be. Nearly all the world famous properties are crammed into the north-eastern corner round Pétrus. They make wonderful rich, exotic wine – but they don't make Pétrus. The blue-black clay from way down in the earth has only broken through into the topsoil for 20ha (50 acres) of Pomerol, and Pétrus has 11.5 of these hectares (28 acres) planted almost entirely with Merlot.

Merlot is one of the few red grapes to relish cold, heavy clay soils. It's a sensuous grape, an exotic, fleshy grape, and at Pétrus it probes into a realm beyond ordinary wine, producing a liquid richer than any dry red wine should dare to be, creamy and buttery, sprinkled with honeyed spices, peppermint leaves and roasted nuts, all swirled about with sweet blackcurrant and plum and brooding truffles and then this heady brew is speared together by a shaft of mineral power as though someone had wiped the blade of a broadsword across your tongue.

Though Pétrus' vineyards are thick with clay, you'll notice there's also a fair leavening of gravel and, on this high point of Pomerol, the gravel deposited by the river Isle in Ice Age fury is very important, along with ground-up iron crust and sand in the soil, and explains the slightly less lush but exotic yet minerally flavour of the other properties hanging on to Pétrus' coat-tails. The tiny Le Pin is currently the most famous of these, but there are other properties of longer pedigree (and equal quality) – Vieux-Château-Certan, Trotanoy, L'Évangile, La Conseillante, Clinet, Lafleur – and all of these are on the gravelly plateau.

Drive west, however, past Clinet and Trotanoy, and you feel as though you're sliding off a terrace. You are. You've only dropped about 15m (50ft), but the gravels are different, the soils a bit lighter, the wines less startling, less dense, less well known, less expensive. They lose the heart-thumping richness of the greatest Pomerols, yet continue to blow kisses of soft-centred pleasure across the stern brow of Bordeaux. And then you cross the N89, the Libourne to Perigueux road and head towards the railway and the soil becomes lighter, sandier, the vineyard terrain seems broad and bland and empty, and you look up at the plateau behind you to the east and think that perhaps you've been too harsh about its forbidding nature. There were houses, but they were little and dotted about like farm outhouses. You can pass by Pétrus and Clinet, Le Pin and Lafleur without even realizing you've been within a few metres of some of Bordeaux's greatest wineries. That's just the way it is in Pomerol. In places like the Médoc, even in St-Émilion, there are grand châteaux and plenty of signboards telling you so. But here, where the red nectar is most expensive and desired of all, the men and women who own and tend the tiny patches of precious vines prefer to let the wine do the talking.

Some of the aristocrats of Pomerols, yet their nobility is of very recent creation: Certan-de-May, Hosanna, L'Église-Clinet and Trotanoy. None of the properties had any reputation as recently as World War Two, and Ch. Hosanna was only created out of a part of the old Certan-Guiraud vineyard as recently as 1999. Nowadays their lush texture, heady flavours, ready drinkability and limited availability have made them some of the most sought after wines in Bordeaux.

POMEROL AND ST-ÉMILION SATELLITES

The River Barbanne is hardly more than a stream. But it's a symbol of some importance. First, it's an ancient frontier between the lands to the south where people spoke the Langue d'Oc and to the north where they spoke the Langue d'Oil. Oc and Oil were the old words for 'Yes', so it's literally the divide between replying Oc and Oil (or 'Oui' in modern French) when someone asked you if you wanted a coffee. The things you learn on a wine-tasting trip. But this little stream plays a more important role. It's the frontier between the glamour and wealth of the world famous appellations of Pomerol and St-Émilion with their array of wines that thirsty millionaires queue for and what are called their 'satellites', lesser regions clinging to the coat-tails of the great ones and cursing the fact that they weren't born on the other side of the wretched Barbanne.

You could say what rotten luck. But you could also say that these lesser regions don't even deserve the right to tack on the famous name of Pomerol and St-Émilion because they're not as good and not even very similar. Well, their wines don't remotely resemble the top wines of

La Fleur de Boüard has rapidly become a star of the Lalande-de-Pomerol region. Ownership by the proprietors of the St-Émilion front-runner Ch. Angélus clearly helps, but such quality wouldn't be possible without these deep, gravelly soils and old vines on the plateau of Lalande.

their famous neighbours – but as in so many French appellations, the law-makers have been persuaded to push the prestigious boundaries of Pomerol and St-Émilion far wider than quality alone would allow. Pomerols and St-Émilions from the sandy, low-lying environs of Libourne and the Dordogne river, for instance, have as little to do with the world of Pétrus and Cheval Blanc as any pretenders on the northern bank of the Barbanne. And I admit there are a few patches of very good soil to the north, but not many.

The best one is the Pomerol satellite of Lalande-de-Pomerol. This used to be two separate appellations, and if you take the N89 north east out of Libourne, you're pretty much on the boundary between what was Lalande-de-Pomerol to the left and Néac to the right. Néac's not much of a name, so the growers petitioned for the right to call themselves Lalande-de-Pomerol (suddenly it sounds more expensive, doesn't it?) as long ago as 1954. And though the swathes of vineyard spreading away to both sides of the road may look the same, they're not. Much of Lalande's side is low-lying and sandy. Néac's on a plateau. There's a fair amount of gravel breaking up the clay soils which in the best properties are thinly spread over an iron and limestone base. This isn't much different to good Pomerol conditions and there are several fine properties producing rich, plummy, mineral-streaked reds here. And if you take the road south from Néac, what do you come to in barely a kilometre? Château Pétrus, that's what.

The St-Émilion satellites don't have any illustrious neighbours. None of the top St-Émilions are in the north towards the Barbanne, and though the areas of St-Georges and Montagne reaching north to Lussac and east to Puisseguin (these are the four communes which attach themselves to St-Émilion by a hyphen) are charming – rolling vineyards, meadows, delightful country houses and little parks – they haven't been that lucky with their soils. Probably Montagne, with its hilly outcrops of limestone thinly covered with limestone clay and sometimes a little red sandy clay, has the best conditions, and I've certainly found more interesting wines from Montagne-St-Émilion than from the other satellites, but in general the soils are fairly deep and fertile here, the vines get it too easy and so rarely achieve the intense focused flavours that the combination of poor soils and low yields brings.

FRONSAC AND CANON-FRONSAC

As I drove into the Fronsac region near Galgon on my last visit, I passed a welcome sign saying Vignobles de Fronsac. It was old, dilapidated, rusty and spoke of a tired, aimless place with little appetite for marketing and self-promotion so what were my chances of finding exciting wines here?

Well, I've been looking for excitement here ever since I first started paying hard-earned money for my wine and seeking superior flavours for smaller than average outlay. Just occasionally I've been surprised and delighted by the quality, the sweet fruit, the reserved but ripe personality of a Mazeris, a Moulin-Pey-Labrie or a Dalem, but usually I have found the wines heavy, pedestrian, lumber-limbed. I couldn't have agreed more when one of my friends in neighbouring Blaye called Fronsac wines 'Merlot for truckdrivers'. It sort of said it all, I thought.

But then two things happened that made me begin to change my mind. First I came across a bunch of young enthusiastic producers called Expression de Fronsac. Tasting their wines against run-of-the-mill Fronsacs, the flavours were richer, riper, even scented, with none of the musty, metallic rocky dullness of the other wines. And then I tasted a clutch of Fronsacs belonging to the Cercle de Rive Droite, another bunch of determined producers spread all along the Right Bank who had grown tired of having to depend on the whims of the Bordeaux merchant houses for selling their wine and so were setting out to do the promotional work themselves. Again richness, scent, texture, excitement. I didn't know Fronsac could do this stuff. I don't think they could have done without an appreciation as to why Fronsac had failed to deliver for so long. It had worked once.

The Romans – again – were busy here as in St-Émilion. They planted vines here, and in the 18th and 19th centuries Fronsac wines were extremely popular, selling for much more than Pomerols and St-Émilions to the east. But as St-Émilion and then Pomerol at last asserted their brilliance in the second half of the 20th century, Fronsac slipped from view – a lovely steep-sided, wooded region where the Libourne merchants built their weekend villas on the profits they were making from Pomerol and St-Émilion. It's a vicious circle you find all too frequently in Bordeaux – loss of reputation, loss of demand for the wines, inability to charge a decent price, no funds for improvements.

Well, you only have to drive around Fronsac, and its little enclave appellation of Canon-Fronsac, to see the potential. Canon-Fronsac, on steep slopes down towards the Dordogne river, is full of challenging but high-potential vineyard sites. The Fronsac appellation also has steep slopes at La Rivière, looking out towards the Dordogne, and further north around Saillans the hills offer tantalizing views eastward to Pomerol but, more importantly, potentially excellent vineyard conditions. In between these the altitude rises another 30m (100 ft) or so, and in Bordeaux's marginal climate this does retard ripening. None of my favourite châteaux come from this middle section. When I look at my tasting notes all the best wines come from Canon and Saillans with a couple

Fronsac is a most attractive area of Bordeaux but in the past has been inclined to make rather heavy, leaden wines. But Ch. de La Dauphine leapt to the fore when it was bought by the Moueix family of Pomerol fame in 1985. A second change of ownership seems to have revitalized the château in the 21st century and since 2001 the wines have arguably been the best in the appellation.

from La Rivière. It's no coincidence that these are the areas where Expression de Fronsac is most active.

And their modern attitude is crucial. There are wonderful limestone slopes and plateaux here, based on a softish limestone subsoil called the Molasse de Fronsadais. But the topsoils are mostly deep and they contain a fair amount of fertile clay which, if it isn't relentlessly kept in check, will produce large crops of dull, earthy wines. Exactly what Fronsac and Canon-Fronsac were doing until very recently. I know the producers say the improvements have been gathering pace since the late 1980s, but I reckon it's the last few years, the beginning of the 21st century, which have at last seen Fronsac and Canon-Fronsac begin to shine again. Smaller yields, green harvesting, later vintage dates, new oak barrels – all these demand commitment and money. But without them Fronsac can't shine, because these are not soils that are brilliant in themselves – they need a heavy dose of human intervention.

There's also a rusty and dilapidated Vignobles de Fronsac sign as you leave the district to cross the river Isle to Libourne. A lick of paint might be a good start for Fronsac's new image.

Quick guide • The Right Bank understudies

OVERVIEW

The appellations neighbouring St-Émilion and Pomerol are commonly known as the 'satellites'. Together with Fronsac and Canon-Fronsac they make up the Right Bank 'understudies', a group of Merlot-based appellations fitfully capable of measuring up to St-Émilion and Pomerol but valued more for their relative affordability.

TASTING NOTE

Wine from the St-Émilion satellites have some of its chewy sweet fruit, but are a little solid and earthy. Lalande wines are usually full, soft, plummy and even chocolaty. They lack the mineral edge and the concentration of top Pomerols, but are attractive, full, ripe wines. Fronsac and Canon-Fronsac at their best offer finesse, minerality and perfume worthy of a grander reputation.

WHEN TO DRINK

Drink St-Émilion satellites within four years of the vintage. Lalande can be very attractive at only three to four years old, but ages reasonably for up to a decade. Fronsac needs five years to release some perfume and will last up to ten. Canon-Fronsac is more serious. It ages well and, after going through a rather gamy period at a few years old, usually emerges at ten years plus with a lovely, soft, Merlot-dominated flavour and a good mineral tang.

BEST YEARS

2010, '09, '08, '05, '04, '03, '01, '00.

WINES TO TRY

St-Émilion satellites
- Ch de Barbe Blanche Réserve (Lussac)
- Ch. Calon (Montagne)
- Ch. du Courlat, Cuvée Jean-Baptiste (Lussac)
- Ch. La Couronne, Reclos de la Couronne (Montagne)
- Ch. Guibot-'La Fourvieille' (Puisseguin)
- Ch. Haut Bernat (Puisseguin)
- Ch. de Môle (Puisseguin)
- Ch. Roche Corbin (Montagne)
- Ch. La Rose Perrière (Lussac)
- Ch. St-André-Corbin (St-Georges)
- Ch. Vieux Bonneau (Montagne)
- Vieux Ch. St-André (Montagne)

Lalande-de-Pomerol
- Ch. des Annereaux
- Ch. Bertineau St-Vincent
- Ch. La Fleur de Boüard
- Ch. Haut-Chaigneau
- Ch. Haut-Surget
- Ch. Garraud
- Ch. Grand Ormeau
- Ch. Jean de Gué
- Ch. Perron
- Ch Sergant
- Ch. La Sergue
- Ch. Siaurac
- Ch. Tournefeuille

- Ch. de Viaud
- Ch. Les Vieux Ormes

Fronsac
- Ch. Carlamagnus
- Ch. Chadenne
- Ch. Dalem
- Ch. de La Dauphine
- Ch. Fontenil
- Ch. Haut-Carles
- Ch. Moulin Haut Laroque
- Ch. Plain-Point
- Ch. Richelieu
- Ch. de la Rivière
- Ch. Les Trois Croix
- Ch. La Vieille Cure
- Ch. Villars

Canon-Fronsac
- Ch. Barrabaque
- Ch. Canon
- Ch. Cassagne Haut-Canon, La Truffière
- Ch. du Gaby
- Ch. Grand Renouil
- Ch Haut-Mazeris
- Ch. Mazeris
- Ch. Moulin Pey Labrie
- Ch. Vrai Canon Bouché

For more ideas see page 249

Château Angélus
Excellent wines, an energetic owner and talented winemaker brought Angélus well-deserved promotion in the 1996 St-Émilion classification.

CHÂTEAU ANGÉLUS
St-Émilion Grand Cru AC, Premier Grand Cru Classé
❦ *Merlot, Cabernet Franc, Cabernet Sauvignon*

Judging by the price of the wine, you would expect Ch. Angélus to be a leading Premier Grand Cru Classé – and the rich, warm, mouthfilling flavour would confirm this. Yet it was only classified as Premier Grand Cru

Classé in the 1996 revision of the St-Émilion classification and in 2006 (the latest classification) it was being touted for promotion to join CHEVAL BLANC and AUSONE in the top tier. On price alone the lobbyists had a point, and this shows how the influence of an energetic owner, a talented winemaker and investment in the winery can upgrade the quality of a vineyard's wine – just as laziness, incompetence and penny-pinching can dilute it.

Angélus is well placed on the lower part of the *côtes* to the west of the town of St-Émilion, with 23.4ha (58 acres) of vines, but the soil is quite heavy. Until 1979 this resulted in fruity, though slightly bland wine. But in the 1980s lower yields, severe selection and new oak barrel-aging were introduced, adding a sturdy backbone and a richer concentration of fruit. Increasingly gorgeous, perfumed wines were made throughout the 1990s and the early 2000s. Second wine: Le Carillon de L'Angélus. Best years: 2010, '09, '08, '07, '06, '05, '04, '03, '02, '01, '00, '99, '98, '96, '95, '93, '92.

Château L'Arrosée
Sitting right in the middle of St-Émilion's famous limestone côtes, L'Arrosée makes lush, rich wines for aging for at least 10 years.

CHÂTEAU L'ARROSÉE
St-Émilion Grand Cru AC, Grand Cru Classé
❦ *Merlot, Cabernet Sauvignon, Cabernet Franc*

This is one of those unknown properties that swept to international prominence so quickly you had to keep checking your tasting notes to see you hadn't got the name wrong. But this small estate, situated on the western end of the *côtes*, just south-west of the town of St-Émilion, really is exciting: it makes a rich, chewy and wonderfully luscious wine, with a comparatively high proportion (40%) of Cabernet Sauvignon and Cabernet Franc in the blend. This is a real hedonist's wine, especially in the big, broad years of 2009, '05, '95 and '90. A change of ownership and smart new cellars from 2002 has recently given further vigour to the wine. Drink after five years of aging or so but it may also be kept for ten years or longer. Best years: 2010, '09, '08, '07, '06, '05, '04, '03, '02, '00, '98, '96, '95, '90.

This is the charming Hubert de Boüard who has raised the quality of Angélus since the 1980s until it is now one of the best, richest, fleshiest – yet not overdone – wines in St-Émilion. It's also one of the most expensive. The 2005 vintage hit the merchants' lists at £1500 ($2700) a case – that's up to three times as expensive as some of its Premier Grand Cru Classé Brethren. After one promotion in 1996, perhaps Angélus is angling for another one.

Château Ausone

I t's just possible that this is the oldest wine château in Bordeaux. And it's easier to talk about the history of Ausone than to talk about the wine, because this tiny property produces a nectar so rare that you can hardly ever find it on the commercial market.

Quick guide

CLASSIFICATION
St-Émilion Grand Cru AC, Premier Grand Cru Classé

VINEYARD
8ha (20 acres) planted with Cabernet Franc (55%), Merlot (43%), Cabernet Sauvignon (2%)

TYPICAL BLEND
55% Cabernet Franc, 45% Merlot

ANNUAL PRODUCTION OF THE GRAND VIN
17,000 bottles

BEST YEARS
2010, '09, '08, 07, '06, '05, '04, '03, '02, '01, '00, '99, '98, '97, '96, '95, '90, '89, '88

CLASSIC OLDER VINTAGES
1986, '85, '83, '82, '76, '29, '21, '00

SECOND WINE
La Chapelle d'Ausone

2000 was the vintage that finally announced 'Ausone is back'. Alain Vauthier had been making finer and finer wines since 1995, but in 2000 he produced a modern classic. Knowing Vauthier, he'll regard it as the supreme challenge to better it. In 2005 and 2009, he has.

The Roman poet Ausonius had a retirement house in Bordeaux. Was it on the banks of the Garonne? Or was it perched proudly on the very lip of the limestone escarpment that runs around the ancient Roman town of St-Émilion? Hard to say, but if I'd wanted a retirement home with a view, the panorama the modern-day Ch. Ausone commands from the St-Émilion highlands right the way down the slopes, across the flatlands to the Dordogne and beyond would be hard to beat.

Yes, yes, but the wine? Well, in all my years of wine writing I've only done one vertical tasting of Ausone vintages, and even today when I think I've pretty much covered all the top wines of the vintage, I'm still quite likely to say – damn, I haven't tried the Ausone. Yet up to the mid-1990s I might not have been missing that much. Despite a charming and talented young winemaker called Pascal Delbeck being brought on board in 1974, Ausone rarely sang. It seemed to be trying to make a point about its minerality, its leanness, its reserve, and you'd hear cautious whispers round the tasting room from the older and wiser to the effect that you always had to wait generations for Ausone to open up, but when it did, aaah….

Maybe. But despite the arrival of Delbeck bringing great improvements (and we all loved him because he was just about the only Bordeaux winemaker who would tell you 'choose any barrels, you say which ones you want to taste' when we visited his atmospheric but frankly damp cellar cut into the limestone beneath the château) – despite his arrival, Ausone was marking time. This precious little 8-ha (20-acre) sliver of land tumbling down from the top to the bottom of the limestone escarpment, mostly facing south to south-east and cosily protected from the worst of the weather and the chill north wind, needed a visionary to seize it by the collar and haul it unceremoniously up to the exalted level all history said it deserved, yet few living tasters could attest to.

When Alain Vauthier assumed control of the property in 1995, the visionary had arrived. He felt that the previous administration had been too cautious and too unwilling to invest, hoping to creep towards a sort of star quality, rather than grab for it. But during the 1980s and '90s wine styles and the possibilities and visions of flavour, particularly in St-

Above: The limestone is very soft at Ausone. This is great for the vine roots, allowing them to penetrate deep into the stone, but it also means erosion is a serious problem, and this mixture of terracing and retaining walls is necessary to stop the precious vineyard soil washing away.

Right: What, did I drop my pen? These vines are literally growing on the roof of the cellar – somewhere so compact and valuable as Ausone doesn't want to waste valuable vine-growing space – and if you visit the cellar, look upwards and you'll see roots dangling through the ceiling.

Ausone's limestone is not only of value for growing vines. This beautiful arch to the cellars is carved out of limestone bedrock of the vineyard directly above. But the limestone is so soft here, you can scrape it away with your finges – wonderful for vine roots, but I suspect 50 years of wind and rain will do serious damage to the arch's purity of design.

Émilion, had changed far faster than Ausone was prepared to go. Until Vauthier arrived. He knew the vineyard was exceptional, perhaps unique in Bordeaux, and the only one of the so-called First Growths to be on a slope – traditionally thought of as highly desirable for wine quality. He had low-yielding old vines, too – great for quality – with the most ancient section of vines planted in 1906. So he called in St-Émilion's most famous wine guru, Michel Rolland, and between them they changed the harvest dates to get ripe fruit, renovated the historic but musty cellar and created a second label – Chapelle d'Ausone – for any barrels not quite up to scratch. Now, in difficult years like 1999, when Ausone was perhaps the star of the year, 25 per cent of the production may be declassified to Chapelle. Many new quality-enhancing techniques are studied, though only employed if Vauthier is convinced they really do improve the final wine. And in the same way, he's experimenting in the ancient vineyard with a variety of different Cabernet Franc clones and even some Petit Verdot – which could be very interesting – as well taking a good long look at biodynamics. And you can be sure that if he feels the wine could be improved by it, he'll give it a try. But the quality of modern Ausone, sumptuously rich yet robust and challenging in its deep dark heart, is already a triumph. Though trying to get a sample to taste is no easier than ever it was.

Above: These are the ancient cellars cut into the limestone – stonemasons have excavated it over the centuries and used the rock for building homes in adjacent St-Émilion. They're much drier now than they used to be when I first visited, and the wine in the barrels is correspondingly cleaner and purer. Just look at how few barrels there are. That's Ausone.

Right: Don't be fooled by Alain Vauthier's friendly offhand manner; he is a powerhouse in the revival of St-Émilion's reputation and in particular has returned Ausone's wines to a thrilling level of perfume, structure and depth, equalling, possibly surpassing, the very best in Bordeaux.

Château Barrabaque

The well-sited, south-facing vineyards benefit from hot vintage conditions to produce long-lived, full-bodied wines.

Château Balestard-La-Tonnelle

A regular favourite of mine – dark and ripe with some lovely fruit waiting in the wings for maturing in 5–10 years.

Château de Barbe-Blanche

Now in the capable hands of André Lurton, Barbe-Blanche is turning out delicious reds full of summer fruit flavours and a hint of vanilla oak.

CHÂTEAU BALESTARD-LA-TONNELLE

St-Émilion Grand Cru AC, Grand Cru Classé
🎋 *Merlot, Cabernet Franc, Cabernet Sauvignon, Malbec*

I like this château. It never gets massively positive write-ups, critics almost deriding it for its round, plump, come-hither style. Well, what's wrong with that? Plump, juicy flavours are what St-Émilion does so well. Keep at it, Balestard: you've got one major fan here.

The château is located on the limestone plateau east of the town of St-Émilion where the soil is a little deeper and heavier, which may take away some of the finesse, but seems to help create a rich, mouthfilling flavour instead. They've modernized things a bit recently and super-consultant Michel Rolland has been seen in and out of the cellars – the wine now enjoys partial malolactic fermentation in oak and aging takes place in 50% new oak – but the wine is still reasonably priced, wonderfully easy to drink and good to age for 10–20 years. Best years: 2010, '09, '08, '06, '05, '04, '03, '01, '00, '98, '96, '95, '90, '89.

The vineyards of Balestard-La-Tonnelle which, year in year out, makes one of the plumpest, most affable and affordable Crus Classés in St-Émilion. The 15th-century poet Villon described Balestard as 'divin nectar' and you can read all about it on the label. That's pushing things a bit, but for a joyous, juicy glass of red to warm your heart, Balestard's hard to beat.

CHÂTEAU DE BARBE-BLANCHE

Lussac-St-Émilion AC
🎋 *Merlot, Cabernet Franc, Cabernet Sauvignon*

The history of this 28-ha (69-acre) property dates back to at least the 16th century but since 2000 it's been in the capable hands of André Lurton, owner of Ch. La LOUVIÈRE in Pessac-Léognan and others. A prime site on clay-limestone soils, a majority planting of Merlot and proficient winemaking produce a supple, generous wine with the flavour of summer fruits tinted with vanilla oak for drinking at three to eight years. The Réserve has a little more mint and blackcurrant weight. Best years: 2010, '09, '08, '05, '03, '01, '00, '98.

CHÂTEAU BARRABAQUE

Canon-Fronsac AC
🎋 *Merlot, Cabernet Franc, Cabernet Sauvignon*

A leading light in the Fronsac region this tiny property sits on south-facing clay-limestone slopes overlooking the Dordogne river. The Cuvée Prestige is a modern Fronsac, the rougher edges smoothed by ripe fruit and aging in new (40%) oak barrels. Drink after four or five years but can be kept for at least ten. Best years: 2010, '09, '08, '06, '05, '03, '01, '00, '99, '98.

Château Beauregard

Beauregard is in the south of Pomerol, but still on good soils and produces a rich, black fruit and savoury butter style of wine.

CHÂTEAU BEAUREGARD

Pomerol AC

Merlot, Cabernet Franc

This property on the southern edge of the Pomerol plateau is one of the rare ones in the appellation to possess a proper château and also to have its 17.5-ha (43-acre) vineyard in practically one holding. The wine showed a steady improvement through the 1980s but since being acquired by a French banking group in 1991 progress has been greater still. It now has ripe black fruit richness and lush texture in warm years, though it struggles a bit in lesser years (a very good '93 is an exception). It's not cheap, but, for a Pomerol, is still pretty good value. Drink from six or seven years but it can keep longer. Second wine: Benjamin de Beauregard. Best years: 2010, '09, '08, '06, '05, '04, '01, '00, '98, '96, '95.

Château Beauséjour

Lush, ripe but structured wine from well-placed vineyards just west of the town of St-Émilion that will benefit from 10–15 years' aging.

CHÂTEAU BEAUSÉJOUR (HDL)

St-Émilion Grand Cru AC, Premier Grand Cru Classé

Merlot, Cabernet Franc, Cabernet Sauvignon

This small 7-ha (17-acre) estate, owned by the Duffau-Lagarrosse family, is located just to the west of the town of St-Émilion. The wine used to be rather light and insipid, but since 1985 it has acquired more stuffing. Beauséjour has probably been underrated in the past, overshadowed by its illustrious neighbours such as Ch. CANON.

In 2000 and 2005 and the best years since, the property made luscious wine with tremendous fruit and depth of flavour, fully justifying its Premier Grand Cru Classé ranking within St-Émilion. Consultant Stéphane Derenoncourt has been fine tuning the wine since 2009. Drink after five years or keep for ten or more. Best years: 2010, '09, '08, '06, '05, '04, '03, '02, '01, '00, '99, '98, '96, '95, '94, '93, '90, '89.

Château Beau-Séjour Bécot

A true example of the deep, dry but deliciously ripe wines for long aging that come from the St-Émilion côtes.

CHÂTEAU BEAU-SÉJOUR BÉCOT

St-Émilion Grand Cru AC, Premier Grand Cru Classé

Merlot, Cabernet Franc, Cabernet Sauvignon

There was a hue and cry when Beau-Séjour Bécot was demoted from the ranks of St-Émilion's Premiers Grands Crus Classés in 1985, following a misunderstanding about expanding their vineyards. Luckily, brothers Gérard and Dominique Bécot wasted little time dwelling on the problem and the estate was reinstated in 1996, the vineyard much improved and the wine back to its very best.

Beau-Séjour Bécot's 16.6-ha (41-acre) vineyard is on St-Émilion's limestone plateau and *côtes* and planted with 70% Merlot, 24% Cabernet Franc and 6% Cabernet Sauvignon. The wines are pretty powerful but rich and ripe virtually every year with a fine tannic structure and significant oakiness. Beau-Séjour Bécot is one of the best St-Émilion properties at balancing the old and new styles, and the wines improve with at least eight to ten years' aging. Best years: 2010, '09, '08, '07, '06, '05, '04, '03, '02, '01, '00, '99, '98, '96, '95, '90, '89.

Château Belair-Monange

Belair-Monange traditionally produces a mellow, gentle style of St-Emilion. Until 2008 the wine was known as simple Belair.

CHÂTEAU BELAIR-MONANGE

St-Émilion Grand Cru AC, Premier Grand Cru Classé

Merlot, Cabernet Franc

Belair is Ch. AUSONE's neighbour on the steep, south- and south-east-facing clay limestone slopes or *côtes* just below the town of St-Émilion. The fortunes of the estate were revived in the late 1970s with the arrival of winemaker Pascal Delbeck, until 1996 also responsible for the winemaking at Ausone. Delbeck was owner of Belair until 2008 when the Moueix family acquired full ownership, adding the name Monange in honour of a family matriarch.

Delbeck was an early convert to the challenges of biodynamic vineyard management and he greatly improved the wine during the 1990s without fundamentally changing their delicate style. Even then I often used to feel Belair was a bit too frail. Given its fabulous vineyard, I wanted more. The new Moueix ownership and their abandonment of Delbeck's biodynamic methods is bound to have an effect on the wine's character. Since 1995 I've tasted a succession of delightful, succulent, full-flavoured yet delicate, almost buttery soft Belairs that in the modern, turbo-charged St-Émilion world are pure delight. Best years: 2010, '09, '08, '06, '05, '04, '03, '02, '01, '00, '99, '98, '95, '90, '89, '88, '86, '85.

Château Belair-Monange is a beautiful property and one of the oldest wine estates in the Libourne region. Its situation on both the plateau next to Ch. Canon and on the slopes right next to Ausone means its vineyards are potentially some of the best in St-Émilion. New owners, Moueix of Petrus fame, will set out to maximize this potential.

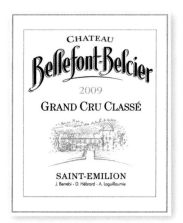

Château Bellefont-Belcier

One of the most improved St-Émilion properties, now making classic, ripe but balanced and long-lasting wines.

Château Berliquet

Berliquet is now very good and really beginning to hit form – the wine is rich and oaky, but with a good reassuring ripe tannic structure.

Château Le Bon Pasteur

Le Bon Pasteur can be mellow and gentle right from the start, but in serious classic vintages the wine is powerful, demanding 10 years' aging.

CHÂTEAU BELLEFONT-BELCIER

St-Émilion Grand Cru AC, Grand Cru Classé AC

Merlot, Cabernet Franc, Cabernet Sauvignon

The 13-ha (32-acre) vineyard of this estate is ideally situated on St-Émilion's southern *côtes* alongside that of neighbouring Ch. Larcis Ducasse. In fact, it starts on the plateau above, rolls down the hill and finishes on the *pied de côtes* below. Until the present ownership (a partnership of two French business men and *négociant* Dominique Hébrard) bought the property in 1994 Bellefont-Belcier had been making fairly uninspiring wines despite the potential of its limestone-clay soils.

A makeover in the vineyard, investment in the cellars and a little more technical expertise and all this changed. The result was classification as Grand Cru Classé in 2006. The wines are full-bodied and long aging but used to be a little too oaky. This has been toned down and there's been more finesse since 2005. Best years: 2010, '09, '08, '07, '06, '05, '04, '03, '02, '01, '00, '98, '96, '95, '90, '89.

CHÂTEAU BERLIQUET

St-Émilion Grand Cru AC, Grand Cru Classé

Merlot, Cabernet Franc, Cabernet Sauvignon

I used to visit the local wine co-operative and after tasting all their various blends, they'd proudly open up a bottle of Berliquet and point out of the windows to this perfect, south-facing slope adjoining Ch. MAGDELAINE and CANON – and say 'that's Berliquet'. But with a slope like that it should have been a Premier Grand Cru Classé. Yes, but if the owners aren't bothered and let the co-operative deal with the grapes – and by the way, make quite a nice wine out of it – you're never going to get due recognition for your wine, however good the vineyard.

The turnaround came in 1997 when the owners, the de Lesquen family called in Patrick Valette, formerly of Ch. PAVIE, as consultant and there was a change in winemaking philosophy. The vineyard was restructured, yields lowered, the *cuverie* modernized and new barrels purchased. Since then Stéphane Derenoncourt has replaced Valette and Berliquet has leapt ahead. The wines are now rich in fruit, smoothly textured and intense. Best years: 2010, '09, '08, '06, '05, '04, '03, '01, '00, '99, '98, '95, '90, '89.

CHÂTEAU LE BON PASTEUR

Pomerol AC

Merlot, Cabernet Franc

When the great flying winemaker Michel Rolland needs to reconnect with his roots this is where he comes, to this small château right on the north-east tip of Pomerol on the border with St-Émilion. It's his family château where he first muddied his boots and trudged through the vines with some pruning scissors in his hand.

And despite the fact that he is now the world's most famous winemaker, he and his wife Dany still lavish personal care on this 7-ha (17-acre) vineyard with its reasonable but not fantastic terroir. The wines are gentle, warm, flushed with blackcurrant and black cherry fruit – and quite different from any other wines he makes in Bordeaux. I always think they have a very welcoming, homely quality while many of the wines he makes as a consultant are set up to be impressive, to stand out in the crowd. Quite right too. After all, this is what he'll be drinking with his Sunday lunch. Best years: 2010, '09, '08, '06, '05, '04, '03, '01, '00, '99, '98, '96, '95, '94, '90, '89, '88.

Château Calon
The Calon vineyards are on the highest point of the St-Émilion vineyards and the windmills depicted on the label have been restored.

CHÂTEAU CALON
Montagne-St-Émilion AC

🌿 *Merlot, Cabernet Franc, Cabernet Sauvignon, Malbec*

Owned by Jean-Noël Boidron, a former professor at Bordeaux University's Institute of Enology, Calon has been one of the sure-fire value-for-money wines in the St-Émilion 'satellites' for a number of years. The wines have lively fruit and freshness and are ready to drink at three to four years. The vineyards are sizeable, covering 50ha (124 acres) on some of St-Émilion's highest land with wonderful views all around; part of the domaine falls into the neighbouring St-Georges-St-Émilion AC from which a more full-bodied wine is produced.

Monsieur Boidron also owns the reliable St-Émilion Grand Cru Classé, Ch. Corbin-Michotte in the north-west corner of St-Émilion near CHEVAL BLANC. Best years: 2010, '09, '08, '05, '04, '03, '02, '01, '00, '99, '98.

Château Canon
An old-fashioned label that has changed little since the first bottle I ever came across – the 1958 – which was rather good.

CHÂTEAU CANON
St-Émilion Grand Cru AC, Premier Grand Cru Classé

🌿 *Merlot, Cabernet Franc*

Canon used to make some of the most perfect, most recognizable, most reliably rich St-Émilion – reeking of that toffee-butter-and-raisins, mellow ripeness which only Merlot can impart. The wine was deep, with a rich plummy fruit, and in good vintages was impressively tannic at the outset. But at the end of the 1980s, after shining through most of Bordeaux's golden decade, it went into one of those inexplicable declines, begun by faults in the winery and compounded by vineyard disease, loss of will and underinvestment. It wasn't until 1996 that the decline was reversed when the Fournier family sold Canon to the French fashion and perfume company Chanel, owners also of Ch. RAUZAN-SÉGLA in Margaux. The new owners have pulled out all the stops to get things right and by 1998 it was clear that Canon was returning to form and recent vintages have consistently confirmed Canon's quality.

The vineyard is just west of the town of St-Émilion, surrounded by other First Growths such as Ch. BEAUSÉJOUR. In 2000 the 3.9-ha (9.7-acre) vineyard of Grand Cru Classé Ch. Curé-Bon was bought and incorporated into the estate. In good vintages the wine is tannic and rich at first but is well worth aging for 10–15 years to achieve that gorgeous, old-style St-Émilion mellow maturity. Second wine: Clos Canon. Best years: 2010, '09, '08, '07, '06, '05, '04, '03, '02, '01, '00, "98, '89, '88.

I've got very fond memories of Ch. Canon's courtyard. I dined there one balmy summer night with tables and chairs strewn across the cobblestones, and we feasted on vintages all the way back to a glorious 1961. Or was it the 1947? Oh dear. Great wine alfresco plays awful tricks with my memory.

Château Canon-La-Gaffelière

Canon-la-Gaffeliere used to be regarded as slightly second division St-Émilion – but not any more – it's now dark, lush and much sought after.

CHÂTEAU CANON-LA-GAFFELIÈRE

St-Émilion Grand Cru AC, Grand Cru Classé

❄ *Merlot, Cabernet Franc, Cabernet Sauvignon*

I used to drink a lot of this – mellow, orange-red in colour, tasting of butterscotch and cream – and cheap. Ah, but that was the old Canon-la-Gaffelière, before Stephan von Neipperg took over in 1983 and set about producing a wine as good as St-Émilion's best, even though his terroir was mostly fairly ordinary, on sandy soil at the foot of the slopes rather than on the slopes themselves. It shows what passion can achieve.

In both vineyard and cellar he has single-mindedly pursued quality. By the late '90s Canon-la-Gaffelière's rich, dark, scented wine was without doubt one of the top St-Émilions. Von Neipperg also owns CLOS DE L'ORATOIRE and the remarkable micro-cru La MONDOTTE, both in St-Émilion, and the Castillon-Côtes de Bordeaux property Ch. d'AIGUILHE. Best years: 2010, '09, '08, '07, '06, '05, '04, '03, '02, '01, '00, '99, '98, '96.

Château Cassagne Haut-Canon

The name 'La Truffière' implies a savoury element in the wine and this does have a savoury scent overlaying the deep black fruit.

CHÂTEAU CASSAGNE HAUT-CANON

Canon-Fronsac AC

❄ *Merlot, Cabernet Franc, Cabernet Sauvignon*

The vineyard here on steep, terraced slopes, overlooking the river Dordogne is planted with a high proportion of Cabernet Franc and Cabernet Sauvignon (20% each), as well as the usual Merlot.

'La Truffière,' named after the truffle oaks planted on the vineyard's limestone slopes, is the most interesting wine here – it has good, focussed, black plum fruit, savoury spice and for once the Fronsac metal streak cuts an attractive swathe through the fruit, rather than providing a stubborn core, as it so often does in wines from this appellation. Best years: 2010, '09, '08, '06, '05, '03, '01, '00, '98.

Château Certan-de-May

From the vineyard's location you would expect a blockbuster wine but in fact even in the warmest years the wine is attractively ripe and gentle.

CHÂTEAU CERTAN-DE-MAY

Pomerol AC

❄ *Merlot, Cabernet Franc, Cabernet Sauvignon*

The tiny 5-ha (12-acre) vineyard of Certan-de-May is situated on the Pomerol plateau between VIEUX-CHÂTEAU-CERTAN and PÉTRUS. The wine, from vines with an average age of 40 years, is the epitome of suave, unctuous, succulent Pomerol with a power and structure for long aging. The relatively high proportion of Cabernet Franc and Cabernet Sauvignon, together making up one-third of the blend, contributes to the wine's longevity and quite austere, youthful tannin. Always beautifully balanced, the wine takes some time to settle down and is at its best with eight years' aging or more. Best years: 2010, '09, '08, '06, '05, '04, '01, '00, '98, '95, '90, '89, '88.

Master of all he surveys, Comte Stephan von Neipperg only arrived in St-Émilion in 1983 from his estates in Württemberg to take over Canon-la-Gaffelière from his father but since then he has become a leader of opinion and quality – and dress sense – in this lively appellation.

Château Cheval Blanc

I feel a bit silly for saying this, but I used to undervalue Cheval Blanc because it was so absolutely delicious. Pathetic, isn't it? What's wine supposed to be about? Pleasure. What's great wine supposed to be about? Extreme pleasure.

Quick guide

CLASSIFICATION
St-Émilion Grand Cru AC, Premier Grand Cru Classé

VINEYARD
37ha (91 acres) planted with Cabernet Franc (58%), Merlot (42%)

TYPICAL BLEND
The Cabernet Franc component can vary from 40–70%, depending on the year

BEST YEARS
2010, '09, '08, '07, '06, '05, '04, '03, '02, '01, '00, '99, '98, '96, '95, '90, '89, '88, '86, '85

CLASSIC OLDER VINTAGES
1982, '64, '61, '59, '53, '49, '48, '47, '21

SECOND WINE
Le Petit Cheval

Renowned taster Michael Broadbent says the 1947 Cheval Blanc is 'unquestionably one of the greatest wines of all time'; and since he's probably tasted all the others I'm bound to agree.

And yet when something as oozing with joy and delight as Cheval Blanc comes along in a tasting, some withered old ghost from my distant puritan past rears up and rails against the wine because it is so utterly, sinfully delicious. Well, so it is. I think it was the blinding purity of its blackcurrant fruit, perfumed with peppermint, frequently swaddled in a cocoon of fresh farm-gate cream and chocolate sauce that caused me to rear back at the very same time as my heart and my palate gasped for another shot of this gorgeous nectar. And this experience might be from a one-year-old, a five-year-old or a ten-year-old Cheval Blanc. When Cheval Blanc gets it right – and it usually does – it is an irresistible wine.

So, what is it? Well, it's the most famous wine in St-Émilion by a country mile. It shares the top classification with Ausone but until the last decade is used to outshine Ausone without breaking sweat. These two now slug it out for top honours each vintage – although some of the 'new wave' producers from supposedly less favoured vineyard sites would suggest that they too deserve consideration – but there is a significant difference in style and flavour. Where there is still a certain sternness at the heart of Ausone, Cheval Blanc lets rip a triumphant peal of delight. Some of the most famous wines in the history of Bordeaux have been super-ripe versions of Cheval Blanc, so memorably rich that even the driest of old-time Bordeaux connoisseurs had to drop their guard and admit to its thrill. 1921 Cheval Blanc, from a broiler of a year – I haven't tasted it, but I know a man who has – was unctuous beyond belief. People who are old enough or lucky enough are still arguing about whether the 1947 or the '49 was the ultimate hedonist's red. And the 1982 and '90 – well, I have tasted these several times. No, I've drunk these several times. I don't remember being able to bring myself to spit them out. If you crave being swept off your feet by a wine, swooning in the arms of a great rich red, these – and I suspect, the 2005 and 2009 – will leave you sated.

Paradoxically, Cheval Blanc manages to be St-Émilion's best wine by not being typical. For a start, there's the vineyard – the soil, the terroir. Cheval Blanc is right on the north-western edge of St-Émilion, its vines bang next to those of Pomerol. In fact, its direct neighbours are two luscious Pomerol performers, L'Évangile and La Conseillante. Cold-blooded people sometimes accuse Cheval Blanc of being more like a Pomerol than a St-Émilion – more lush, more exotic – well, that's why.

There's something charmingly unpretentious about Cheval Blanc. Not the wines – they're stellar and thrilling – but the place, the compact château, the small rooms. Behind this charming traditional château is a remarkable new winery (see overleaf). But here for a quiet moment, you can imagine nothing has changed for generations.

Above: The astonishing new winery, designed by well-known architect Christian de Portzamparc and finished in 2011, dwarfs the original chateau to the right and shows the amount of investment money available at the top Bordeaux properties. The owners, Bernard Arnault of LVMH and Baron Frère, wanted a building that would anticipate the future while blending into St-Émilion's historic landscape, a UNESCO World Heritage site. Located in the heart of the vineyard the 'winery under the hill' looks like a hanging garden floating over the vines.

Forty per cent of the vineyard is on the deep, dense clay that many of Pomerol's great properties enjoy. But the far north-western zone of St-Émilion is called the St-Émilion *graves* – gravel St-Émilion – and 40 per cent of Cheval Blanc is on gravel soil. Of all the other top St-Émilions only Figeac can match this gravel content. In fact, Figeac is Cheval Blanc's neighbour as well. The remaining 20 per cent of the vineyard is sand, but most of the grapes from this don't make the final blend.

The gravel is so important because 58 per cent of the vines are Cabernet Franc. This is the unsung hero in St-Émilion, where the Merlot is very much the dominant grape. But Cabernet Franc adds a certain firmness and a definite bright perfume to the wines it's part of and is generally held to be responsible for Cheval Blanc's remarkable ability to age. Merlot is more responsible for the wine's incredible, immediate sensuous appeal. But even here, Cheval Blanc is different. Whereas the current vogue in St-Émilion is to maximize the Merlot's ripeness, or frankly overripen it, the director Pierre Lurton is adamant that by picking the Merlot earlier, less ripe, he preserves Cheval Blanc's irresistible freshness and appeal. I couldn't agree more.

Above: Move over stainless steel. Cement was once dismissed as old-fashioned and ugly, but more and more winemakers now realise that it provides the most predictable and homogenous conditions for fermenting, storing and blending red wines. And these cement 'conicals' aren't that ugly, either.

Right: Pierre Lurton has managed Cheval Blanc since 1991 and has overseen the extraordinary changes at the château. Somehow he finds the time to also manage the great Sauternes property, Ch. d'Yquem.

Château Clinet

Under new ownership in the 21st century, Clinet is no longer the massive mouthful it once was but is now deep, balanced and ripe.

CHÂTEAU CLINET

Pomerol AC
❄ *Merlot, Cabernet Franc, Cabernet Sauvignon*

I first visited Clinet in 1990 with Michel Rolland. We tasted the 1989 – a wine that oozed such succulence I could barely swallow it. Michel smiled contentedly. This was going to change the way people thought about Pomerol, and by God it did.

Rolland insisted on lowering yields, harvesting very late, using 100% new oak and not fining or filtering. This was the beginning of a revolution in red wine, an expansion of the frontiers of the possible – and all through the 1990s and into the 2000s, Clinet has made one of the most gobsmacking wines in Bordeaux almost every year. Not always easy to drink, mind you, but one helluva mouthful whatever you did with it. These syrup-rich wines were rarely my favourite in a given vintage, but I always sought them out, if only to purse my wine-stained lips and shake my head in amazement. Best years: 2010, '09, '08, '07, '06, '05, '04, '03, '02, '01, '00, '99, '98, '96, '95, '90, '89, '88.

Clos L'Église

Clos L'Église is now rich and succulent, full of blackberry and blackcurrant fruit, but with enough structure for aging at least 10 years.

CLOS L'ÉGLISE

Pomerol AC
❄ *Merlot, Cabernet Franc*

A tiny 6-ha (15-acre) property on the Pomerol plateau, Clos L'Église has been transformed since its purchase by the Garcin-Cathiard family, owners of Ch. HAUT-BERGEY in Pessac-Léognan, in 1997. Investment in modern viticultural and winemaking practices has had an overnight effect making the wine rich, full and luxurious and in need of at least seven or eight years' bottle age. Not surprisingly prices have also risen stratospherically. Best years: 2010, '09, '08, '07, '06, '05, '04, '03, '02, '01, '00, '99, '98.

Clos Fourtet

Clos Fourtet could be one of the most fascinating wines in St-Émilion. Dark, concentrated, oaky but always with a highly individual flavour.

CLOS FOURTET

St-Émilion Grand Cru AC, Premier Grand Cru Classé
❄ *Merlot, Cabernet Sauvignon, Cabernet Franc*

This 20-ha (49-acre) estate has a privileged position just outside St-Émilion's handsome town walls. The extensive cellars, carved out

of the limestone rock, are worth a visit, too.

The wine has not always lived up to its Premier Grand Cru Classé status, largely because a rather murky personality often clouded their evidently exceptional terroir, but since the late 1980s there has been considerable improvement. Better selection and an increase in new oak for aging has added greater concentration, suppleness and structure. New ownership and investment since 2001 has also given added impetus. The wines are now impressive and dense, ripe and scented with herbs. Most vintages need five to ten years to show how good they can be. Best years: 2010, '09, '08, '07, '06, '05, '04, '03, '02, '01, '00, '99, '98, '96, '95, '90, '89.

Clos de L'Oratoire

This wonderfully rich, dark-fruited wine is quite different to those made at von Neipperg's other two excellent properties in St-Émilion.

CLOS DE L'ORATOIRE

St-Émilion Grand Cru AC, Grand Cru Classé
❄ *Merlot, Cabernet Franc, Cabernet Sauvignon*

Since 1991 Stephan von Neipperg has lavished the same attention to detail, and investment, on this estate as he has on his other two high-flying domaines, CANON-LA-GAFFELIÈRE and La MONDOTTE. The 10-ha (25-acre) vineyard is located on St-Émilion's northern slopes and, as at the other two properties, it has been the work undertaken in the vineyards that has boosted quality.

The Merlot-dominated wines are now deeply coloured, redolent of dark, ripe berry fruits, finely textured and structured, and are best with at least five to six years' aging. Best years: 2010, '09, '08, '07, '06, '05, '04, '03, '02, '01, '00, '99, '98, '96, '95, '90.

Clos St-Martin

*You don't often see a bottle of this – it's a tiny
vineyard – but the quality and ageability of the wine
make it well worth seeking out.*

CLOS ST-MARTIN

St-Émilion Grand Cru AC, Grand Cru Classé
※ *Merlot, Cabernet Franc, Cabernet
Sauvignon*

This pocket-sized Grand Cru Classé is
located on a top-notch, south-west-facing
limestone slope just east of the town of St-
Émilion and surrounded by the vineyards of
Premiers Grands Crus Classés ANGÉLUS,
BEAUSÉJOUR, BEAU-SÉJOUR BÉCOT and CANON.

St-Martin enjoys a great terroir but the
domaine only really started realizing its full
potential when the owners, the Reiffers
family, employed Sophie Fourcade to take
on the management in 1997. Lower yields,
better vineyard management and 100% new
oak barrels were part of the recipe. Now the
wines are modern in style with better fruit
expression and firm but fine tannins for
long aging, up to 20 years or more. The
same family also owns two other St-Émilion
properties, Grand Cru Classé Ch. Les
Grandes Murailles and the excellent value
Grand Cru Ch. Côte de Baleau. Best years:
2010, '09, '08, '07, '06, '05, '04, '03, '02, '01,
'00, '99, '98.

Château La Conseillante

*Conseillante's style is for gentle, ripe and soft wines
with a creamy texture and plum fruit, that are lovely
young but will also age well.*

CHÂTEAU LA CONSEILLANTE

Pomerol AC
※ *Merlot, Cabernet Franc*

This 12-ha (30-acre) property has some of
the best land in Pomerol, in the north-east
corner, but has never consistently managed
to reach the heights attained by its
neighbours and appellation leaders, Ch.
PÉTRUS and CHEVAL BLANC. Nonetheless, this
is sumptuous, exotic, velvety wine that
blossoms beautifully after five to six years'
aging but can age much longer. I've got
magnums of 1973 – hardly a must-have
vintage – that are still mellow and rich. As
with many of these fleshy Pomerols, its
popularity has rocketed in recent years and
scarcity has meant the price has rocketed too.
Second wine: Duo de Conseillante (from
2007).Best years: 2010, '09, '08, '07, '06, '05,
'04, '03, '02, '01, '00, '99, '98, '96, '95, '94,
'90, '89.

Château La Couspaude

*The powerful blockbuster wines of recent vintages
are totally different from the mellow, soft style I used
to like.*

CHÂTEAU LA COUSPAUDE

St-Émilion Grand Cru AC, Grand Cru Classé
※ *Merlot, Cabernet Franc, Cabernet
Sauvignon*

Having lost Grand Cru Classé status in 1986
the owners got to work and the 7-ha (17-
acre) property was reclassified in 1996. The
vineyard on the limestone plateau to the east
of the town of St-Émilion was overhauled
and oak vats introduced, and the wines are
now rich, smooth and modern, coated in
vanilla oak but still marked by their terroir.
Best years: 2010, '09, '08, '06, '05, '04, '03,
'02, '01, '00, '98, '96, '95, '94, '90, '89.

Château Croix-Beauséjour

*This is a good, gutsy wine with a certain amount of
St-Émilion texture from just outside the village of
Montagne.*

CHÂTEAU CROIX-BEAUSÉJOUR

Montagne-St-Émilion AC
※ *Merlot, Cabernet Franc, Malbec, Cabernet
Sauvignon*

The 'satellite' appellation of Montagne-St-
Émilion is a rich source of good-value St-
Émilion lookalikes, such as the wine made by
this 8-ha (20-acre) property located on clay-
limestone soils. The barrel-aged *cuvée* is
generous and fruity, kissed by a little vanilla
oak, the Clos La Croix d'Arriailh from 80-
year-old vines is richer and more intense.
Drink the wines from four to five years. Best
years: 2010, '09, '08, '05, '04, '03, '01, '00,
'99, '98.

Château Les Cruzelles

Les Cruzelles is a well-situated property close to Pomerol producing elegant, minerally wines to drink young or to age. .

CHÂTEAU LES CRUZELLES

Lalande-de-Pomerol AC
❊ *Merlot, Cabernet Franc*

Denis Durantou could see the white shutters of Les Cruzelles from his Ch. L'ÉGLISE-CLINET home in Pomerol and sourced fruit there for his Lalande-de-Pomerol brand, La Chenade. So when the property came up for sale he thought, why not? His first vintage was 2000. At present there are 8-ha (20-acres) of vines under production on gravel, clay and sandy soils. The wines are fresh and elegant and drink well from three years. Best years: 2010, '09, '08, '06, '05, '04, '03, '02, '01, '00.

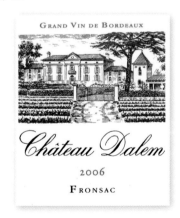

Château Dalem

Dalem from a warm vintage is almost syrupy rich but with good, black plum fruit and tannin for aging.

CHÂTEAU DALEM

Fronsac AC
❊ *Merlot, Cabernet Franc*

Michel Rullier acquired this property, with an elegant 18th-century château, in 1955. The 14-ha (35-acre) vineyard is located on the slopes above the village of Saillans. The wine, made essentially from Merlot, is a good example of how these slopes produce richer, fresher styles than most of the rest of the Fronsac appellation. A typical Dalem wine will be quite tannic when young but should have ripe, dry, black plum fruit sometimes touched by syrupy richness that really needs six or seven years to open out and become more complex. Since 2003 there's been more finesse, but luckily not too much. Best years: 2010, '09, '08, '06, '05, '04, '03, '01, '00, '99, '98, '96, '95, '90, '89.

Château de La Dauphine

With a new owner in 2000 La Dauphine's wines have been getting darker and richer, better for aging but without losing their sweet core.

CHÂTEAU DE LA DAUPHINE

Fronsac AC
❊ *Merlot, Cabernet Franc*

The 11-ha (27-acre) property, complete with handsome 18th-century château and sister vineyard Canon-de-Brem, was purchased from *négociant* Jean-Pierre Moueix by Jean Halley in 2000. There's a new state-of-the-art winemaking facility producing fresh, fragrant, soft-fruited wines that are ready from three years but will age. Canon-de-Brem fruit has now been incorporated into La Dauphine, so look for more structure from 2006. The total vineyard is now 31ha (77 acres). Best years: 2010, '09, '08, '06, '05, '04, '03, '01, '00, '98.

Château La Dominique

This is not that intense a wine but it has good glyceriny texture and attractive acid and tannin for aging.

CHÂTEAU LA DOMINIQUE

St-Émilion Grand Cru AC, Grand Cru Classé
❊ *Merlot, Cabernet Franc, Cabernet Sauvignon*

An acclaimed wine in the 19th century, La Dominique is less well known today despite its good location adjoining CHEVAL BLANC. After the industrialist Clément Fayat bought the estate in 1969 (he also owns Ch. Prieurs de la Commanderie in Pomerol and Ch. Clément-Pichon in the Haut-Médoc), substantial modernization began.

More recently, under the direction of enologist, Michel Rolland, new oak is being used to nurture ripe fruit and gives a well-structured wine, opulent in its youth, yet able to age extremely well. Even so, the wines often lacked the extra scent and finesse of true class, but a new drainage system in the vineyards has greatly improved the fruit and from 2006 *garagiste* Jean-Luc Thunevin of Ch. VALANDRAUD has been managing this and the other Fayat estates. Second wine: St-Paul de Dominique. Best years: 2010, '09, '08, '06, '05, '04, '03, '01, '00, '99, '98, '96, '95, '94, '90, '89, '88.

Château Durand-Laplagne

Durand-Laplagne is almost on the border with Castillon and this wine shares some of the Castillon appellation's typical texture and flavour.

CHÂTEAU DURAND-LAPLAGNE
Puisseguin-St-Émilion AC
❉ Merlot, Cabernet Franc, Cabernet Sauvignon

The Bessou family have owned this 14.5-ha (36-acre) property since 1850. The present incumbent, Bertrand Bessou, aims to give his clients value for money and the barrel-aged Cuvée Sélection is round, fruit driven and honest in both flavour and price. Best years: 2010, '09, '08, '05, '04, '03, '01, '00, '98.

Château L'Église-Clinet

Classic Pomerol with plenty of plum and chocolate depth but not a massive intensity, and good balance for aging.

CHÂTEAU L'ÉGLISE-CLINET
Pomerol AC
❉ Merlot, Cabernet Franc

A tiny 5.5-ha (13-acre) domaine in the heart of Pomerol, L'Église-Clinet has a very old

vineyard – the vines are on average 50 years old – one of the reasons for the depth and elegance of the wines. The other is the winemaking ability of owner, Denis Durantou.

The wine is expensive and in limited supply, but worth seeking out. It can be enjoyed young for its rich, plum and chocolate self-indulgence, though the best examples should be aged for ten years or more. Second wine: La Petite Église. Best years: 2010, '09, '08, '07, '06, '05, '04, '03, '02, '01, '00, '99, '98, '96, '95, '90, '89.

Château L'Évangile

L'Évangile produces one of the richest, most exotic Pomerols, though it usually needs 10 years' aging to display all its beauty.

CHÂTEAU L'ÉVANGILE
Pomerol AC
❉ Merlot, Cabernet Franc

A neighbour of PÉTRUS and CHEVAL BLANC, L'Évangile is a top Pomerol and has a price tag to match. The Rothschilds of Ch. LAFITE-ROTHSCHILD purchased a controlling interest in 1990 and quality improved for the rest of the decade, but things really moved up a gear when the Rothschilds took over running the estate in 1999.

The Merlot-dominated wines from this 14-ha (35-acre) estate have always been big, rich and powerful, with layers of exotic fruit and spicy complexity. However, Ch. Lafite is Pauillac's most elegant wine and the Lafite effect, along with the benefit of their winemaking control, is now beginning to be felt on L'Évangile. A floral bouquet has

joined the wine's sweet black cherry and blackcurrant fruit and the cream cheese and glycerine softness to create a spectacular Pomerol style. The wine is brilliant young, but much better after ten or more years' aging, and good vintages will age for 20. A new *cuverie* with a circular barrel cellar was inaugurated in 2004. Second wine: Blason de L'Évangile. Best years: 2010, '09, '08, '07, '06, '05, '04, '03, '02, '01, '00, '99, '98, '95, '90, '89.

Château Faizeau

The Vieilles Vignes **cuvée** *is dense, rich and round with nicely integrated tannins and is ready to drink from 5–6 years.*

CHÂTEAU FAIZEAU
Montagne-St-Émilion AC
❉ Merlot

The 10-ha (25-acre) property is under the same ownership as La Croix de Gay in Pomerol and receives the treatment of a St-Émilion Grand Cru. Consequently, Ch. Faizeau is one of the leading estates in the Montagne appellation. The vineyards are on the same high land as Ch. CALON, the highest point in the whole St-Émilion area. Best years: 2010, '09, '08, '06, '05, '04, '03, '02, '01, '00, '99, '98.

Château Faugères

This is a serious wine, dense but lush, with black plum and blackberry fruit backed up by good acid and tannin.

CHÂTEAU FAUGÈRES

St-Émilion Grand Cru AC

❧ *Merlot, Cabernet Franc, Cabernet Sauvignon*

Film director Péby Guisez and his wife Corinne put this 49-ha (121-acre) property on the map in the 1990s. With Michel Rolland pulling the winemaking strings they invested in the vineyard and cellars to produce dense, dark, powerful modern St-Émilion wines which still retained their core of juicy, sweet black fruit. Péby Faugères, a garage wine from a parcel of 8ha (20 acres) of Merlot, was introduced in 1998. Swiss industrialist Sylvio Dentz acquired the estate in 2005 and has built a new state-of-the-art cellar. Best years: 2010, '09, '08, '07, '06, '05, '04, '03, '02, '01, '00, '99, '98, '96, '95, '94.

Château Feytit-Clinet

Feytit-Clinet is now being run by the family and the wines have benefitted – they are now richer, darker and more scented.

CHÂTEAU FEYTIT-CLINET

Pomerol AC

❧ *Merlot, Cabernet Franc*

Until 2000 *négociant* Jean-Pierre Moueix managed this tiny property next to Ch.

CLINET and LATOUR-À-POMEROL. Surprisingly, the wines were fairly ordinary but since the owners, the Chasseuil family, have taken back the reins, reduced yields and invested in new oak barrels the wines have become richer and more exciting. Best years: 2010, '09, '08, '07, '06, '05, '04, '03, '01, '00, '98, '95.

Château Figeac

Young Figeac can seem dry, even a little lean, but I can promise you the wine will become wonderfully scented given time.

CHÂTEAU FIGEAC

St-Émilion Grand Cru AC, Premier Grand Cru Classé

❧ *Cabernet Sauvignon, Cabernet Franc, Merlot*

Thierry Manoncourt, the delightful though zealous owner of Ch. Figeac, died in 2010 (with 63 vintages under the belt). Whenever I visited him you had hardly finished shaking hands before he marched you into the vineyards, and pointed accusingly to the north. Half a mile away sit the small, whitewashed buildings of CHEVAL BLANC, acknowledged as St-Émilion's greatest wine. This small area, at the western end of the AC, is called *graves* St-Émilion because of the high proportion of gravel soil which gives the wine its special quality. Yet who has the most gravel? Not Cheval Blanc, but Figeac. Indeed you quickly learn that Cheval Blanc used to be part of Figeac, was only sold as 'Vin de Figeac', and derives its name (meaning 'white horse') from the fact that it was there that Figeac used to have its stables.

Well, all this is true, but Manoncourt should not have worried so much because Figeac's own wine is superb, though in a different way from Cheval Blanc. Figeac uses 35% Cabernet Sauvignon (rare for St-

Émilion) and 35% Cabernet Franc – both are grape varieties which love gravel – and only 30% of St-Émilion's main variety, Merlot. The result is wine of marvellous, minty, blackcurrant perfume, with some of the cedar and cigar-smoke spice of the great Médocs, and accompanied by a caressing gentleness of texture.

Things became a bit erratic in the late 1980s and '90s – though the '93 was very good – and it wasn't until 1996 that Figeac once again began to produce the blackcurrant-scented, finely balanced reds that make it such a star property. The wines of the 2000s have been splendid. Figeac is lovely young, but positively gorgeous with 10–20 years' aging. Second wine: La Grange Neuve de Figeac. Best years: 2010, '09, '08, '07, '06, '05, '04, '03, '02, '01, '00, '99, '98, '96, '95, '90, '89.

Château La Fleur de Boüard

This wine is rich and vibrant and sometimes even a little dense, with good earthy tannin and even a hint of cedar to come.

CHÂTEAU LA FLEUR DE BOÜARD

Lalande-de-Pomerol AC

❧ *Merlot, Cabernet Franc, Cabernet Sauvignon*

This is a star wine out of nowhere! Well, not exactly nowhere, because Hubert de Boüard de Laforest is the boss of one of St-Émilion's modern tyros, Ch. ANGÉLUS, and he applies the same rigorous winemaking techniques at this 19.5-ha (48-acre) property. The wines (first vintage 1998 and still very tasty) are rich, but not sweet, scented, dark and beautifully balanced. A special *cuvée*, Le Plus de la Fleur de Boüard, from 100% Merlot, is

even more extravagant, having been aged in new oak barrels for 33 months. Impressive young, the beauty comes with five or six years' aging. If proof were needed that Lalande-de-Pomerol could make wines as great as its more famous neighbour Pomerol, La Fleur de Boüard provides it. Best years: 2010, '09, '08, '07, '06, '05, '04, '02, '01, '00.

Château Fleur Cardinale

This often starts out a little dry and closed as do many wines from the hard St-Émilion limestone plateau – but it will be delicious in 5 years.

CHÂTEAU FLEUR CARDINALE

St-Émilion Grand Cru AC, Grand Cru Classé

Merlot, Cabernet Franc, Cabernet Sauvignon

This estate came to light in the 1980s under the talented winemaking hands of Stéphane Asséo. Owned since 20010 by Dominique Decoster, the good progress has continued and there's been additional investment in new cellars and the vineyard. The reward was promotion to Grand Cru Classé status in 2006. The 18-ha (44-acre) vineyard is to the east of St-Émilion on the plateau and slopes that overlook the village of St-Étienne-de-Lisse. The wine is dense, ripe and full-bodied, and requires five years' aging to show at its best. Best years: 2010, '09, '08, '06, '05, '04, '03, '02, '01, '00, '98, '96, '95, '90, '89.

CHÂTEAU LA FLEUR-PÉTRUS

Pomerol AC, Bordeaux, France

Merlot, Cabernet Franc

Like the better-known PÉTRUS and TROTANOY, this is owned by the dynamic Moueix family, and is among Pomerol's top dozen

properties. Unlike its stablemates, it is situated entirely on gravel soil and tends to produce tighter wines with less immediate fruit but considerable elegance and silky texture, and good potential for aging to a delightful, mouthfilling focussed maturity of blackcurrant and mint. My first taste of this wine was the '71 and I can still remember it. Among Best years: 2010, '09, '08, '06, '05, '04, '03, '02, '01, '00, '99, '98, '97, '96, '95, '94, '90, '89.

Château Fombrauge

Fombrauge is a powerful, deep and ripe wine, but still well-balanced while the Magrez-Fombrauge cuvée is denser and oakier.

CHÂTEAU FOMBRAUGE

St-Émilion Grand Cru AC

Merlot, Cabernet Franc, Cabernet Sauvignon

With nearly 60ha (148 acres) under production to the east of St-Émilion on the plateau and slopes of St-Christophe-des-Bardes this is the largest of the St-Émilion Grands Crus. The wines used to be fairly 'classic' and middle of the road but since Bernard Magrez of Ch. PAPE-CLÉMENT acquired the property in 1999 they've become meatier with a modern concentration of loganberry and raspberry fruit wrapped in a swathe of new oak – but they've still kept their welcoming St-Émilion texture. There's also a tiny production of the intense, sweet *garage* wine, Magrez Fombrauge, from a small amphitheatre of perfectly sited vines on the property. Best years: 2010, '09, '08, '06, '05, '04, '03, '02, '01, '00, '99, '95, '90, '89, '85.

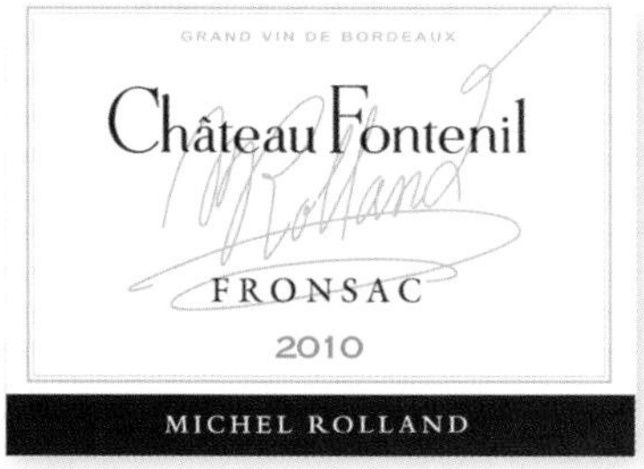

Château Fontenil

The Rollands push ripeness to the maximum at Fontenil but know just when to hold back – crucial in the increasingly warm, dry vintages of the 21st century.

CHÂTEAU FONTENIL

Fronsac AC

Merlot, Cabernet Sauvignon

Ch. Fontenil is the property of celebrated enologists Dany and Michel Rolland, owners also of Ch. LE BON PASTEUR in Pomerol, and if you want to see the genius of these two at work Fontenil is an affordable way to do so. They purchased the 9-ha (22-acre) estate in 1986 and have since applied the Rolland method to produce one of the appellation's outstanding wines, with the hallmark Rolland style of lush, seductive texture, joyous, juicy, black plum and black cherry fruit that falls just short of being overripe, and when the oak shows it is scented with mocha. These wines are lovely straight off the vat but will happily age for 10 years.

The Rolland technique includes hand harvesting at optimum ripeness, destemming the grapes, fermenting part of the crop in barrel, a long *cuvaison* of three weeks and aging in oak barrels, 50% of which are renewed yearly. Défi de Fontenil is an experimental, *garage* wine first produced in 2000. Best years: 2010, '09, '08, '06, '05, '04, '03, '02, '01, '00, '99, '98, '97, '96, '95, '90, '89, '88.

Château La Gaffelière

La Gaffelières still produces a relatively mild St-Émilion despite the attention of star consultant Stéphane Derenoncourt.

CHÂTEAU LA GAFFELIÈRE

St-Émilion Grand Cru AC, Premier Grand Cru Classé

✻ *Merlot, Cabernet Franc, Cabernet Suuvignon*

The de Malet-Roquefort family have owned this estate for over 400 years. The vineyard is located on the *côtes* and *pied-de-côtes* slopes below Ch. BELAIR and AUSONE just to the south of the town of St-Émilion. The wine is elegant rather than powerful for a Premier Grand Cru Classé, and even in the best vintages in the 1990s and 2000s only occasionally show greater concentration and harmony.

Winemaking consultant Stéphane Derenoncourt has been helping to add a little more depth and purity to the wine since 2004. Drink with at least seven or eight years' age. Second wine: Clos la Gaffelière. Best years: 2010, '09, '08, '07, '06, '05, '04, '03, '01, '00, '98, '96.

Château Garraud

Wine from Ch. Garraud will take a while to come round with the slightly grainy tannins generally needing a few years to soften and sweeten.

CHÂTEAU GARRAUD

Lalande-de-Pomerol AC

✻ *Merlot, Cabernet Franc, Cabernet Sauvignon*

The Nony family have kept this 37-ha (91-acre) estate in Néac at the forefront of the Lalande-de-Pomerol appellation for a number of years. Steady investment in the cellars and controlled yields have been the principal reasons. The wines are full-bodied and deep, but you can feel the tannins. Drink from five years onwards. Best years: 2010, '09, '08, '06, '05, '04, '03, '02, '01, '00, '99, '98, '95.

Château Le Gay

Le Gay has always been one of the most impressive yet reserved of Pomerols. Recent vintages, aided by über-guru Michel Rolland, are richer and more approachable.

CHÂTEAU LE GAY

Pomerol AC

✻ *Merlot, Cabernet Franc*

Once the property of the Robin family, along with neighbouring Ch. LAFLEUR, this 10-ha (25-acre) estate on Pomerol's central plateau was acquired by Cristal d'Arques heiress, Catherine Péré-Vergé in 2002. There's no doubt she aims to lift Le Gay to unprecedented heights as already a new cuverie has been built, further investment made in new oak barrels and in the vineyard, and super consultant Michel Rolland has been retained as enologist.

I'll be interested to see what effect this all has, because Le Gay has always been a very forthright, beetle-browed wine, not at all easy to understand or become fond of. Time, quite a lot of time, did mellow the best vintages, but first sips of the new wave Le Gay have a richness and decidedly modern allure that makes me think that Monsieur Rolland is weaving his magic spell successfully. Best years: 2010, '09, '08, '07, '06, '05, '04, '03, '01, '00, '99, '98, '95, '90, '89.

Château Gazin

Gazin's personality marries soft mulberry and black plum fruit with a pleasant fat texture, and with 3–5 years' age, always improves and deepens.

CHÂTEAU GAZIN

Pomerol AC

※ Merlot, Cabernet Sauvignon, Cabernet Franc

It was the 1964 of this wine that I loved, bottled by a brewery in Warwick, Thornley Kelsey, and available for years for very little money. It was creamy, soft; it swept over my palate like a sensuous tide of sweet black fruit. And I could afford it. But Gazin, although very famous on the British market, was pretty erratic in the 1960s, '70s and most of the '80s, despite a brilliant vineyard located in a single block of 24ha (59 acres) situated on Pomerol's eastern plateau next to Ch. PÉTRUS and L'ÉVANGILE.

In 1988 the owner, Nicolas de Bailliencourt, asked the *négociant* firm of Jean-Pierre Moueix to become involved as consultants. For a few years Gazin was brilliant, and scented with strange delights like lavender and sandalwood, but since the mid-1990s it has been more mainstream. It is still rich, ripe and unctuous with finely woven tannins, delicious young but capable of long aging. Recent vintages have been pretty good. Second wine: L'Hospitalet de Gazin. Best years: 2010, '09, '08, '07, '06, '05, '04, '03, '02, '01, '00, '99, '98, '96, '95, '90, '89.

Château La Gomerie
La Gomerie is one of the most famous garage wines – it is a spectacular mouthful if you can get hold of a bottle – or even a glass.

CHÂTEAU LA GOMERIE

St-Émilion Grand Cru AC

※ Merlot

This tiny 2.5-ha (6-acre) property at the foot of St-Émilion's western slopes has been owned by the Bécot family of Ch. BEAU-SÉJOUR-BÉCOT since 1995. The wine is a super-rich, *garage* wine – lush and opulent with plenty of new oak for up to 18 months and no filtering – and as quantities are limited the price is, needless to say, high. Best years: 2010, '09, '08, '07, '06, '05, '04, '03, '02, '01, '00, '98.

Château Gracia
This densely structured, richly fruited and utterly honest wine is, to me, the essence of Bordeaux's garage movement.

CHÂTEAU GRACIA

St-Émilion Grand Cru AC

※ Merlot, Cabernet Franc, Cabernet Sauvignon

This tiny 3-ha (7.4-acre) vineyard emerged during the *garage* revolution of the mid-1990s and, unlike a number of others, has stayed the course. The wine is made in garage-sized cellars in St-Émilion but the vines are located on the limestone-clay soils of St-Christophe-des-Bardes in the north of the appellation. Alain Vauthier of Ch. AUSONE advises, but above all the wines reflect the personality of Michel Gracia, master stonemason, horny-handed, wild-haired – and passionate advocate of healthy soils and natural winemaking.

Critics of the *garagiste* movement should meet Michel Gracia, talk to him about life,

philosophy, soil, organics, limestone and masonry – while tasting this dark, dense but ultimately rich and joyous wine that embodies the close relationship of the true *garagiste* to the soil. A sort of second wine, Les Angelots de Gracia, is produced from vines grown on sandy soils. Best years: 2010, '09, '08, '06, '05, '04, '03, '02, '01, '00.

Château Grand-Mayne
Ch. Grand-Mayne makes a big, high-octane, oaky style of wine, but it's well balanced and has an attractive, glyceriny texture.

CHÂTEAU GRAND-MAYNE

St-Émilion Grand Cru AC, Grand Cru Classé

※ Merlot, Cabernet Franc, Cabernet Sauvignon

A medium-sized estate of 21ha (52 acres), Grand-Mayne lies to the west of the town of St-Émilion, on the edge of the famous *côtes* with its limestone subsoil on which the vines do so well. It produces a firm, dark, modern-style wine, aged in oak barrels of which 80 to 100% are new each year.

As at so many other properties in the St-Émilion region, there have been significant improvements in recent years and the wine is now a powerful but beautiful beast, high in alcohol, rich in extract but keeping its Merlot softness and glycerine texture coated in the toffee-chocolate of new oak. Keep for five years or more. Second wine: Les Plantes du Mayne. Best years: 2010, '09, '08, '07, '06, '05, '04, '03, '02, '01, '00, '99, '98, '95, '89, '88.

Château Grand Ormeau

From being a bit too brawny, Grand Ormeau is now rich and round but easier to enjoy and its voluptuous texture and personality is very like a good Pomerol.

CHÂTEAU GRAND ORMEAU

Lalande-de-Pomerol AC

⁑ *Merlot, Cabernet Franc, Cabernet Sauvignon*

The creator of the famous French fizzy drink Orangina, Jean-Claude Beton owns this 14-ha (35-acre) estate to the west of the appellation now run by his daughter Françoise. The standard release is pretty rich and used to err on the side of being a bit too beefy when restraint might have made a better drink. There is a more extravagant, Merlot-dominated Cuvée Madeleine made from older vines, which, unusually for a prestige *cuvée*, is better balanced and more enjoyable to drink than the regular release. Both need four to five years' bottle aging. Best years: 2010, '09, '08, '06, '05, '04, '03, '01, '00, '99, '98.

Château Grand-Renouil

Red fruits dominate this wine and sit easily with the telltale metallic streak found in many Fronsac wines.

CHÂTEAU GRAND-RENOUIL

Canon-Fronsac AC

⁑ *Merlot*

⁑ *Sauvignon Blanc, Sémillon*

The 5.5-ha (13.6-acre) vineyard is on well-exposed, clay-limestone slopes in St-Michel-de-Fronsac, and the 100% Merlot wine is among the most ambitious in Fronsac. The grapes are hand harvested, vinified in temperature-controlled cement tanks, and aged in oak barrels of which 20% are renewed yearly. The wine has subtle, red strawberry fruit – unusual for the Fronsac appellation – but also a fairly evident metal earthly weight, and some savoury spice which all blends pretty well together. It is best drunk at five to six years old. A tiny amount of white , Blanc de Grand Renouil, the only one produced in Fronsac (but with the Bordeaux AC label), is made from barrel-fermented Sauvignon Blanc and Sémillon. Best years: 2010, '09, '08, '06, '05, '04, '03, '02, '01, '00, '99, '98, '96, '95, '94, '90, '89.

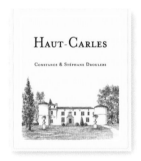

Château Haut-Carles

You look at the label and see that the wine is at over 14%, but Michel Rolland has done well and somehow the wine keeps its balance.

CHÂTEAU HAUT-CARLES

Fronsac AC

⁑ *Merlot, Cabernet Franc*

This Merlot-dominated (95%) wine is made from the best parcels of vines at Ch. de Carles in Saillans, which is itself probably Fronsac's best wine village, but exists as a separate entity. With help from consultant Michel Rolland and Alain Raynaud it has been made since 2003 in its own specially constructed, gravity-fed *cuverie*. It's a sensuous, heady, alcoholic wine of dense, ripe black fruit piled up in the glass, strapped with tannin and drizzled with soft oak vanilla. Best years: 2010, '09, '08, '07, '06, '05, '04, '03, '02, '01, '00, '99, '98.

Château La Sergue

La Sergue has all the rich plum and blackberry, earthy fruit of the regular cuvée, Haut-Chaigneau, but is oakier and deeper.

CHÂTEAU HAUT-CHAIGNEAU/ LA SERGUE

Lalande-de-Pomerol AC

⁑ *Merlot, Cabernet Sauvignon*

La Sergue is made by enology consultant Pascal Chatonnet from selected parcels of old vines on the Chabrol plateau behind Néac. The wine is produced at the family property, Ch. Haut-Chaigneau, and as Chatonnet's speciality is barrel aging it's given the full treatment of new oak barrels. The oak is always fairly strident early on but with five or six years' aging becomes better integrated into this dark, dense wine. Best years: 2010, '09, '08, '06, '05, '04, '03, '02, '01, '00, '99, '98, '96.

Château Hosanna

These clay-gravel soils cope well with extreme heat and drought as in 2003, '05 and '09 and the wine is super-rich, chocolaty, creamy, but very good.

CHÂTEAU HOSANNA

Pomerol AC

Merlot, Cabernet Franc

A fairly recent (1999) addition to the stable of Pomerol properties owned by the *négociant* firm of Jean-Pierre Moueix this 'rebaptized' wine comes from the best part of the former Ch. Certan Guiraud; less good, lower-lying parcels of vines were sold off to neighbouring properties. This parcel of clay-gravel soils sits on Pomerol's high plateau surrounded by the top châteaux of PÉTRUS, LAFLEUR and VIEUX-CHÂTEAU-CERTAN. With a pedigree like that you would expect excellence – and you get it, the wine having beautifully balanced but discreet ripe fruit, finesse and plenty of restrained power as well. It should need at least eight or nine years' bottle age. Best years: 2010, '09, '08, '07, '06, '05, '04, '03, '02, '01, '00, '99.

Château Laborderie-Mondésir

This vineyard is in the west of the appellation where the wines are usually less substantial, but this one is ripe, rich and firm.

CHÂTEAU LABORDERIE-MONDÉSIR

Lalande-de-Pomerol AC

Merlot, Cabernet Sauvignon

Laurent Rousseau is one of the region's talented young winemakers. He produces a rich, firm Lalande from this tiny vineyard on gravel soils to the west of the appellation. The Cuvée Excellence from 100% Merlot and new oak is more opulent. Drink from four to five years. Best years: 2010, '09, '08, '06, '05, '04, '03, '02, '01, '00, '99.

Château Lafleur

This is a seriously powerful red but if you give it some time and consideration you can see the brilliance that challenges Pétrus in the heart of the wine.

CHÂTEAU LAFLEUR

Pomerol AC

Merlot, Cabernet Franc

I tried to visit Lafleur once. I drove up to what I can only call something midway between between a shack, a barn or cowshed. I looked around, trod on a few chickens, called out 'Hello. Anyone at home?' – or the French equivalent – and presumed I'd come to the wrong place. But I hadn't.

This unkempt, bedraggled outhouse was Ch. Lafleur, home of one of Pomerol's greatest wines, from a tiny 4.5-ha (11-acre), gravelly, mineral-rich vineyard that old-timers say rivals its neighbour, PÉTRUS, for quality. I've only drunk it a few times but it was a helluva wine – influenced by having 50% old Cabernet Franc in the vineyard – hedonistic, rich, concentrated, and in top vintages starting out by exhibiting a massive, old-fashioned, unsubtle brute strength loaded with the fatness of oak and soaked in the sweet fruit of plums – unforgettable mouthfuls. As the wines of the '80s are now showing, this unlikely mixture does evolve into a memorable wine eventually. The price, though, is as monumental as the wine. Second wine: Pensées de Lafleur. Best years: 2010, '09, '08, '07, '06, '05, '04, '03, '02, '01, '00, '99, '98, '96, '95, '90, '89, '88.

Château Latour-à-Pomerol

Latour-à-Pomerol is famous for its glyceriny, soft core, but there's enough body and structure for the wine to age very well.

CHÂTEAU LATOUR-À-POMEROL

Pomerol AC

Merlot, Cabernet Franc

Luscious, almost juicy fruit, soft and ripe and very easy-to-drink wine has always been a hallmark of Latour-à-Pomerol, but the wines also have enough tannin to age well for ten years and more. Recent vintages, directed by Christian Moueix of Ch. PÉTRUS, show a beefier, brawnier style, but still with superripe softness of fruit. The vineyard covers 8ha (20 acres). Best years: 2010, '09, '08, '07, '06, '05, '04, '03, '02, '01, '00, '99, '98, '95, '90, '89.

Château de Lussac

New owners and a couple of good vintages couldn't immediately deliver the goods but Ch. de Lussac is now beginning to hit form.

CHÂTEAU DE LUSSAC

Lussac-St-Émilion AC

Merlot, Cabernet Franc

This beautiful property was brought back to life in 2000. The 19th-century château on the edge of the village of Lussac has been renovated, the 26-ha (64-acre) vineyard restructured and new cellars and *cuverie* built. Wines that used to be thin and weedy are now ripe, full and modern with a dash of vanilla from aging in 40–50% new oak barrels. Drink from four to five years old. Ch. Vieux Maillet in Pomerol and Franc-Mayne in St-Émilion are under the same ownership. Best years: 2010, '09, '08, '06, '05, '04, '03, '02, '01, '00.

Château Lyonnat
These are pleasant, modern, vaguely chocolaty and toffee-style wines, with that ever-present Lussac earth.

CHÂTEAU LYONNAT

Lussac-St-Émilion AC
❋ *Merlot, Cabernet Franc, Cabernet Sauvignon*

Situated to the east of the appellation on limestone soils this 48-ha (118-acre) property has had an up-and-down career – once producing wines that were dense and impenetrable, then becoming a beacon of modern winemaking in a rather backwoods appellation and now settling down into an attractive mainstream existence.

The wines are now characterized by soft, red berry fruit flavours mingled with chocolaty oak, a third of the barrels for aging being renewed yearly. Drink from three to four years. Best years: 2010, '09, '08, '05, '04, '03, '01, '00, '98.

Château Magdelaine
Situated on fabulous limestone slopes this is either lush and soft in cooler years or dense and powerful in warmer, dryer vintages.

CHÂTEAU MAGDELAINE

St-Émilion Grand Cru AC, Premier Grand Cru Classé
❋ *Merlot, Cabernet Franc*

Magdelaine is very much a wine of two personalities. In lighter years – because of its tremendously high percentage of Merlot (90%), the highest among St-Émilion's First Growths – the wine has a gushing, tender juicy fruit and is easy to drink at only four to five years old, which seems to epitomize the indulgent softness of St-Émilion wines.

However, in the grand vintages, like those of 2009, '05, '00 and 1998, Magdelaine changes gear. Those 11ha (27 acres) of Merlot-dominated vineyard sit on the steep slopes or *côtes* just south-west of the town of St-Émilion adjacent to the vineyards of Ch. Canon and Belair-Monange – a plum position for superripeness. Because the property is owned by the quality-conscious *négociant* company of Jean-Pierre Moueix in nearby Libourne, the grapes are left to hang until the last possible moment, when an army of pickers swoops in. Then the wine is fermented long and slow, and finally aged in predominantly new barrels for a year and a half. And what is the result?

These are dark, firmly structured wines, yet behind the tough exterior there is luscious fruit and oaky spice and as the tannin fades, a gentle glyceriny texture takes over. Great vintages take 15 years to mature. Second wine: Ch. St Brice. Best years: 2010, '09, '08, '06, '05, '03, '01, '00, '99, '98, '96, '95, '90, '89.

Château La Mauriane
The rich, dense ripe fruit and fine, spicy oak of this wine shows what can be done in the St-Émilion satellites with the right approach.

CHÂTEAU LA MAURIANE

Puisseguin-St-Émilion AC
❋ *Merlot, Cabernet Franc, Cabernet Sauvignon*

Pierre Taix's grandfather planted the 3.5ha (9 acres) of vines used to produce this wine so they're now a good 50 years old. The terroir is limestone-clay on a high point in Puisseguin and that comes through in the wine, which also shows a rich, dense ripeness of fruit and fine, spicy oak from aging in 80% new oak barrels. Best years: 2010, '09, '08, '06, '05, '04, '03, '02, '01, '00, '99, '98.

Château Monbousquet
Monbousquet, out on the broad plans towards the Dordogne, seems to prefer cooler vintages for preserving its lush personality.

CHÂTEAU MONBOUSQUET

St-Émilion Grand Cru AC, Grand Cru Classé
🌿 Merlot, Cabernet Franc, Cabernet Sauvignon
🌿 Sauvignon Blanc, Sauvignon Gris, Sémillon, Muscadelle

I had lunch here once. Long, long ago when it was a nice dozy château outside the town of St-Émilion that now and then made wines as soft as butter and as sweet as strawberry jam. 1970 was like that. 1982 as well. Well, things have changed a lot here since then.

Gérard Perse, the supermarket tycoon who also owns Ch. PAVIE, bought this property on the Dordogne plain in 1993 and in his inimitable, unstoppable way, has transformed it into one of St-Émilion's 'super-crus' with the help of consultancy from Michel Rolland. The reward was Grand Cru Classé status in 2006. There is actually a vein of decent gravelly soil here among the flat sands, and Perse has quickly identified these gravel grapes and put them at the core of his rich, voluptuous and very expensive wine, a blend of 60% Merlot, 30% Cabernet Franc and 10% Cabernet Sauvignon. The wines are drinkable from three to four years, but will age much longer, for 15–20 years. There is also a tiny amount of white wine which is rather good. I haven't been invited to lunch recently, but I suspect it wouldn't be half such a relaxed affair. Best years: 2010, '09, '08, '07, '06, '05, '04, '03, '02, '01, '00, '99, '98, '96, '95, '94.

La Mondotte

Always concentrated, intense, powerful when very young but beautifully proportioned, gentle not savage, and even in hot years, beautifully scented.

LA MONDOTTE

St-Émilion AC
🌿 Merlot, Cabernet Franc

La Mondotte really only exists because its owner Stephan von Neipperg was outraged when he was refused permission to merge these vineyards with his Grand Cru Classé CANON-LA-GAFFELIÈRE because La Mondotte wasn't classified. No one could complain about its soils and position, however, up on the plateau just behind TERTRE-RÔTEBOEUF and next to TROPLONG-MONDOT, with loads of limestone evident with the clay. Petty bureaucracy, he fumed, and set out to prove that the 4.5-ha (11-acre) La Mondotte could not only be better than the very good Canon-la-Gaffelière but could be one of St-Émilion's greatest wines – classified or not. His efforts have been a resounding success and La Mondotte is now a rich, exotic flavour-packed leader of the so-called *garagiste* movement of tiny but excellent properties, primarily in St-Émilion. Best years: 2010, '09, '08, '07, '06, '05, '04, '03, '02, '01, '00, '98, '97, '96.

Château Moulin Haut-Laroque

This is a very ripe style of Fronsac, yet usually manages to retain its scent and freshness.

CHÂTEAU MOULIN HAUT-LAROQUE

Fronsac AC
🌿 Merlot, Cabernet Franc, Cabernet Sauvignon, Malbec

Ch. Moulin Haut-Laroque is one of the top estates responsible for the renewed interest in the Fronsac appellation. The wine is Merlot-dominated but in ripe vintages the 65-year-old Cabernet Franc vines add extra complexity, as well as an alcoholic level that often tops 14%. One-third of the oak barrels are renewed annually and Michel Rolland is retained as consultant enologist. Give the best vintages three to five years' age. Best years: 2010, '09, '08, '06, '05, '03, '01, '00, '98, '96, '95, '90.

Château Moulin Pey-Labrie

In cool or warm years, Moulin Pey-Labrie manages to produce balanced, savoury wines capable of long aging but drinkable young.

CHÂTEAU MOULIN PEY-LABRIE

Canon-Fronsac AC
🌿 Merlot, Cabernet Sauvignon, Cabernet Franc

Since arriving from the north of France in 1988, Grégoire and Bénédicte Hubau have raised the quality of Moulin Pey-Labrie, and it is now one of the best producers in Fronsac. Each parcel of the 7-ha (17-acre) estate is vinified separately. The final blend varies but can be as much as 100% Merlot. Since 1994 the malolactic fermentation has been completed in barrel.

The wine is powerful, concentrated with a complexity of aroma and is best with at least five years' aging. The Hubaus also produce Ch. Haut-Lariveau, in the neighbouring Fronsac AC. Best years: 2010, '09, '08, '06, '05, '04, '03, '02, '01, '00, '99, '98, '96, '95, '94, '90.

Château Moulin St-Georges

You could drink this dark, ripe wine at a few years old, but its depth of fruit and inviting promise of perfume and sweetness means it really needs aging.

CHÂTEAU MOULIN ST-GEORGES

St-Émilion Grand Cru AC
🌿 Merlot, Cabernet Franc

The sloping vineyards of Ch. Moulin St-Georges stand opposite those of Ch. AUSONE, just outside the town of St-Émilion on the famous *côtes*. Both properties are owned by the Vauthier family and the wines are made by the 'maestro' Alain Vauthier.

Progress has been significant since the 1990s and the wines are without doubt now of Grand Cru Classé level. The 7-ha (17.3-acre) vineyard was replanted in 1982 and is now in good condition with more mature vines. Stainless steel tanks and temperature control were introduced in the early 1990s, and the percentage of new oak barrels for aging has steadily increased to 100%. The Merlot-dominated wines are supple, balanced and deliciously aromatic, ready for drinking at five to six years, but will age longer. Best years: 2010, '09, '08, '06, '05, '04, '03, '02, '01, '00, '99, '98, '96, '95.

Château Nénin

Nénin makes a good, rather strong style, a little earthy but there's good plum fruit there too, that bodes well for some extended bottle aging.

CHÂTEAU NÉNIN

Pomerol AC

❋ *Merlot, Cabernet Franc*

The Delon family, owners of Ch. LÉOVILLE-LAS CASES in St-Julien, bought Ch. Nénin in 1997 and have made a number of radical changes. They've added a part of what used to be Ch. Certan Guiraud, extending the vineyard to 34ha (84 acres), built spanking new cellars and introduced the detailed work practices that helped put Las Cases on a pedestal; and there's no question that from the 2000 vintage the sullen, stewy and not always entirely clean traditional style of Nénin has been banished, to be replaced by a wine still of stern countenance for a Pomerol, but of far mellower texture, richer fruit and with some cedar and mineral scent. I am certain the Delons will do everything to maximize Nénin's potential, but after such a long period of mediocrity, I don't yet know what that potential is. Second wine: Fugue de Nénin. Best years: 2010, '09, '08, '07, '06, '05, '04, '03, '02, '01, '00, '98.

Château Pavie

The wine is dense, dark and difficult to judge when young, but it has many passionate supporters around the world.

CHÂTEAU PAVIE

St-Émilion Grand Cru AC, Premier Grand Cru Classé

❋ *Merlot, Cabernet Franc, Cabernet Sauvignon*

Pavie has been the most controversial château in Bordeaux in the 2000s, partly because of the remarkable style of wine it is currently producing and partly because this style seems to divide the wine world right down the middle, with two high profile critics in particular – Robert Parker of the USA and Jancis Robinson of Europe (or the UK; they mean much the same thing in this debate) utilizing their dramatically opposed views of the wine to bite chunks out of each other. This is all very entertaining for those of us on the sidelines but it glosses over a couple of very important points.

Firstly, the astonishing transformation the owner Gérard Perse wrought on this historically great but underperforming property really did seem to 'invent' a new style of Bordeaux unlike anything we had seen before. Secondly – and very importantly – Pavie is now owned by Gérard Perse. He is absolutely at liberty to make whatever kind of wine he likes. And he likes big, rich, sensuous, dense-textured wines that cling to the side of your mouth and roll like rough velvet down your throat. So that's what he makes by dint of enormous enthusiasm, intense commitment and self-belief, and the expenditure of a shedload of money. We should spend more time praising him for the remarkable results he has achieved rather than belittling him as some kind of nouveau riche upstart who doesn't know what Pavie should taste like. Pavie doesn't have to taste of anything, except what its passionate owner wants it to taste of.

Now I don't always like it – sometimes the new Pavie is grand, magnificent, sometimes I think it is a caricature. But I would defend Perse's right to make it thus, just as I would defend Parker's or Robinson's right to their opinions, and I would ask Parker, in particular, to be more sensitive to those who disagree with him. This may seem like an awfully long discourse in the middle of a château profile, but there are many battles being fought in the new Bordeaux and one of the most important is being fought right here at Pavie, the superbly sited, steep, south-facing Premier Grand Cru just east of the town of St-Émilion. After Ch. FIGEAC, it's the second biggest St-Émilion Grand Cru (37ha/93 acres), and it used to be known for classically mellow, soft-centred wines.

But successful vintages were few and far between by the time Perse arrived in 1998 and set about creating the most dramatic, super-ripe, densely rich, ultra-oaked, shocking or thrilling interpretation of a terroir in recent memory. Detractors say the terroir has been massacred, supporters say this overpowering mouthful is the very essence of all that Perse's terroir can give. Some years I agree with the gainsayers, yet some years – 2000 is an example – despite all my years of appreciating a more traditional sort of St-Émilion, I find Pavie memorable and magnificent. Best years: 2010, '09, '08, '07, '06, '05, '04, '03, '02, '01, '00, '99, '98, '90, '89, '88.

Château Pavie-Decesse

With a small vineyard, this is almost a garage wine, and certainly its density and supercharged richness suits the garage tag.

CHÂTEAU PAVIE-DECESSE

St-Émilion Grand Cru AC, Grand Cru Classé

Merlot, Cabernet Franc

Pavie-Decesse lies on the plateau above Ch. Pavie with views over the Dordogne valley, and like Pavie, it too has succumbed to the Gérard Perse revolution. What used to be a slightly lean wine is now rich, dense and powerful, almost a mirror image of Pavie. This is because, since Perse's arrival in 1997, a year before he bought Ch. Pavie, also from Jean-Paul Valette, yields have been radically lowered, the cellars revamped and 100% new oak barrels introduced. The vineyard has also been reduced in size (6.5ha/16 acres are now legally part of Ch. Pavie) and it is now only 3.5ha (9 acres). The wine needs seven to eight years' aging. Best years: 2010, '09, '08, '07, '06, '05, '04, '03, '02, '01, '00, '99, '98, '90, '89.

Château Pavie-Macquin

In general I am a great fan of the deep, ripe black fruit and herbs style of Pavie-Macquin.

CHÂTEAU PAVIE-MACQUIN

St-Émilion Grand Cru AC, Premier Grand Cru Classé

Merlot, Cabernet Franc, Cabernet Sauvignon

This has become one of the stars of the St-Émilion Grand Cru AC since the 1990s and its success was crowned with Premier Grand Cru Classé status in 2006. Pavie-Macquin is owned by the Corre family but management and winemaking are in the capable hands of Nicolas Thienpont (of Ch. PUYGUERAUD in the Francs region) and star consultant Stéphane Derenoncourt, and the old vines, with an average age of 40 years, have been farmed more or less biodynamically since 1990. Rich, firm and reserved, the wines need seven to eight years to open up and will age longer, between 10 and 20 years.

The wine is quite different to its neighbours PAVIE and PAVIE-DECESSE and it is exciting for consumers that there are now three Pavie châteaux battling it out for supremacy every vintage. Best years: 2010, '09, '08, '07, '06, '05, '04, '03, '02, '01, '00, '99, '98, '96, '95.

Château Perron (La Fleur)

This wine, the top cuvée of Ch. Perron, captures the soft, succulent and mellow richness of the sandy soils to the west of Lalande de Pomerol.

CHÂTEAU PERRON (LA FLEUR)

Lalande-de-Pomerol AC

Merlot, Cabernet Sauvignon, Cabernet Franc

La Fleur is the prestige *cuvée* here at Ch. Perron located in the village of Lalande and run by Bernard Massonie.

It is definitely a notch up from the Ch. Perron, the regular *cuvée*. Produced from 100% Merlot grown on 5ha (12 acres) of sandy-gravel soils to the west of the appellation it gets the full modern treatment of lower yields and aging in 80 to 100% new

oak barrels. The resulting wine is succulent, fruity and fresh. The regular *cuvée* has been improving since 2000 and is now barrel-aged. Drink both wines from five years. Best years: 2010, '09, '08, '06, '05, '04, '03, '01, '00, '99, '98.

Château Petit Village

The 2000s have seen a big change in Petit Village's style – still solid and burly but packing in much more stewed black plum fruit.

CHÂTEAU PETIT VILLAGE

Pomerol AC

Merlot, Cabernet Franc, Cabernet Sauvignon

This is not the wine to get in a blind tasting because, although this property produces one of the top Pomerol wines, the style is much sterner and less sumptuous than that of its neighbours, Le PIN and La CONSEILLANTE and you're quite likely to place it in the Médoc. This may be partly because its style was first developed by two of the Médoc's top managers, Bruno Prats, at that time owner of COS D'ESTOURNEL, and Jean-Michel Cazes of LYNCH-BAGES. Petit Village has been owned by AXA-Millésimes (see PICHON-LONGUEVILLE page 157) since 1989.

However, the soil also plays a part. There was a time when half this 11-ha (27-acre) vineyard was planted with just Cabernet Sauvignon, reflecting its high gravel content, though now the plantings are 65% Merlot, 18% Cabernet Sauvignon and 17% Cabernet Franc. A new cellar and even better quality from 2006 have resulted in wines showing more luscious plum and blackberry fruit. Anything before 2000 is likely to be fairly stern and need more aging than you'd normally offer to a Pomerol. Best years: 2010, '09, '08, '07, '06, '05, '04, '03, '02, '01, '00, '99, '98, '95.

Château Pétrus

You'd drive straight past. I have. The most famous château in the world, the one producing the most sumptuous red wine, frequently the most sought after and expensive on the planet, slavered over by connoisseurs and collectors, is quite absurdly self-deprecating when it comes to bricks and mortar.

Where's the grand château, the Palladian arches, the tree-lined gravel drive, the fairytale towers and designer-chic cellars and *chais*? Where's the hype, the self-glorification, the chest-thumping 'look at me I'm the best'? Well, you won't find it at Pétrus. Pomerol and its neighbour St-Émilion are probably the centres of Bordeaux's razzle dazzle world, but Pétrus is basically a modest little farmhouse, on the corner of a nondescript street in a nondescript hamlet. And whereas other Bordeaux superstars have employed 'galactico' architects to create jaw-dropping cellars that could win prizes in design competitions, Pétrus's cellar, despite recent renovation, is still a thing of simplicity.

But the wine is not. Anything but. It's not a wine I taste very often, but my occasional experiences of it have seared themselves onto my tasting brain, and none more so than my first cautious sip. It was my first visit. And the wine we would taste was the 1982. I can remember the shock and exhilaration as if it were yesterday, I can remember the flavours and texture as though the wine still stood shimmering in the glass in front of me. And I can also remember being speechless, much to the amusement of Christian Moueix, in charge of Pétrus's distribution and brother of Jean-François Moueix who owns Pétrus.

So I thought I'd ferret out my old tasting notes on a block of yellowing notepaper. Huh! Some tasting notes. I quote – 'Amazingly…' Amazingly what? Nothing, just that. 'It hasn't even…' Even what? And it goes on like that, superlatives strung together without form, sentences unfinished. One half-sentence make a little sense: 'It's like a sweet dry syrup, an essence…' But once again the note trails away.

Well, my memory tells me that the wine was like a celestial syrup of ripest blackcurrants, blackberries, mulberries, plums and cream, overlaid with mint and tobacco, the heady scent of the kasbah and some kind of mineral power mined from the deep earth. And also the promise, in time, of the perilous, moist excitement of fresh-dug truffles. I'm sure there was more, but that's what I remember. And with the exception of one bizarre period in the 1980s – right after the '82, unbelievably, when Pétrus was forced squealing into a curious lean travesty of itself before triumphantly re-emerging with the '89 – Pétrus has proudly, exotically, scentedly, thrillingly lived up to its superstar status.

Quick guide

CLASSIFICATION
Pomerol AC

VINEYARD
11.5ha (28 acres) planted with Merlot (100%)

TYPICAL BLEND
100% Merlot

ANNUAL PRODUCTION OF THE GRAND VIN
30,000 bottles

BEST YEARS
2010, '09, '08, '07, '06, '05, '04, '03, '02, '01, '00, '99, '98, '96, '95, '90, '89, '88, '86, '85

CLASSIC OLDER VINTAGES
1982, '75, '71, '70, '67, '66, '64, '62, '61, '50, '49, '48, '47, '45, '21

SECOND WINE
None made

Château Pétrus

Pétrus has made a string of other-worldly wines since 1990, and 2000 is one of the best of these.

Just one of hundreds of tiny properties surrounded by a sea of vines? Another anonymous llittle *petit château*? Well, you could be excused for thinking so, but if you peer closely at the left side of this low farm building, you'll see the word 'Pétrus' on the wall. Pétrus. One of the world's.greatest reds, and a place of pilgrimage for any lovers of the lusher styles of Bordeaux red wines. But you'd miss it if you blinked when driving by.

It's difficult to make the connection. This half-full plastic box of Merlot grapes is set to become part of the latest vintage of Ch. Pétrus, the wine that's got me half hysterical in the photograph on the right. No wonder I'm laughing. That's about £20,000 ($32,000/€23,000) worth of wine I'm holding – an extremely rare 5-litre jeroboam of one of the greatest Pétrus vintages – the 1990. I asked if I could have a taste. First, show me your money, said the owner of the shop in Bordeaux.

If the château is no great shakes, the vineyard doesn't look too special either, except that it's one of the muddiest, most clay-clogged pieces of land my shoes have ever had the ill luck to slither through. And that's the secret. They call it the 'button', an oval of imperceptibly higher land which is virtually solid clay shot through with nuggets of iron. It's only 20ha (50 acres) in all, and Pétrus occupies 11.5ha (28 acres) of them, while various other great properties scrabble for a hectare or so each of this remarkable soil that allows the Merlot grapes to produce wine that is profound yet seductive, exotically perfumed and flirtatiously plump, yet tautened with seams of minerality that is positively metallic.

Pétrus has been making stupendous wine since the beginning of the 20th century at the very least, but I've got wine books from only 50 years ago that merely accord Pomerol a couple of paragraphs in the 'other Bordeaux wines' section. It was the gorgeously ripe 1982 vintage which

created Pomerol's modern reputation. That and the arrival on the scene of Robert Parker, the American über-critic and Pomerol devotee who lauded these lush wine styles to the skies and persuaded a willing American public to begin a love affair with Pomerol that shows no sign of dimming. Other properties have attempted to challenge Pétrus, most famously Le Pin, but they're not sitting in the heart of that button of thick blue clay. Pétrus is.

Above: The buildings at Pétrus used to be so shabby you'd drive straight by and never notice them. Well, they're still tiny, but the whole set up looks a bit more loved and cherished than before.

Right: This is the most important thing at Pétrus. Mud. And pebbles. This is the famous blue clay which produces such memorable Merlot grapes – and that's a footprint from my oldest pair of boots.

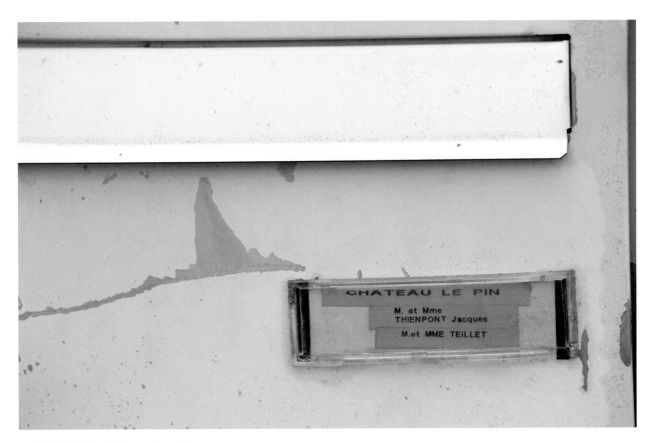

Château Le Pin

Just looking at the label of the 1990 Ch. Le Pin makes me drool. This is seriously beautiful stuff and it sold for astronomical prices.

CHÂTEAU LE PIN

Pomerol AC

Merlot

I was on a visit to Bordeaux when Jacques Thienpont asked me whether I wanted to pop into a little project I've got – we were on our way to Francs-Côtes de Bordeaux – I had no idea that I was getting a preview of what would become one of Bordeaux's most astonishing success stories.

We drove the car up to a very nondescript house, tramped through the mud round to the back where Jacques opened the garage door and in the dim light of a single bulb I saw a handful of barrels. Six? Eight? Something like that. Jacques lowered his pipette into one of them and drew out a half glassful of purple wine, so thick it seemed to stick to the edge of the glass. The flavour burst like stars across my palate and into my brain. Only Pétrus '82 had ever previously sent me reeling, with its richness, its viscosity, its arrogant sensuality. This was in the mid-1980s and Jacques was showing me his Le Pin '85.

He'd only made the first vintage in 1979, yet now it is one of the most expensive wines in the world, auction prices frequently outstripping those for Ch. Pétrus. The '82, only the fourth vintage, became so insanely popular that its price reached £3000 ($5000/€3512) a bottle. The 2009, another great classic vintage which should last for 25 years or more, was also selling for similar sums in 2011.

If you think Le Pin's letterbox is unimpressive, you should have seen the château, just a simple workman's cottage. It's been knocked down and replaced by something rather grander now but I still think of it whenever I taste the wine.

The reasons for this sensation are twofold: scarcity and style of wine. There are barely 2ha (5 acres) of gravelly, iron-rich clay vineyard, superbly located close to Ch. TROTANOY and VIEUX-CHÂTEAU-CERTAN, which produce an average 6000 bottles a year from lowly yields of some 35 hectolitres per hectare. The wine, 100% Merlot and lavishly aged in 100% new oak barrels for 12–18 months, is rich, lush and velvety with an almost Burgundian aroma of ripe cherries and raspberries and exotic spice.

Le Pin is a magical experience but you have to dig deep in the pocket for the privilege of tasting it. It is best with five to ten years' aging, though it will age comfortably for 20 years or more. Best years: 2010, '09, '08, '07, '06, '05, '04, '02, '01, '00, '99, '98, '96, '95, '94, '90, '89, '88, '86, '85.

Château Quinault L'Enclos

This rich, oaky wine is one of the pacesetters on the Right Bank and is now part of the same stable as Cheval Blanc.

CHÂTEAU QUINAULT L'ENCLOS

St-Émilion Grand Cru AC

Merlot, Cabernet Franc, Cabernet Sauvignon, Malbec

Bizarrely located behind the Libourne football stadium and hemmed in on all sides by housing, this 12-ha (30-acre) vineyard was snatched from the hands of property developers by Dr Alain Raynaud in 1997. With the experience of running the family estates, La Croix-de-Gay in Pomerol and FAIZEAU in Montagne-St-Émilion behind him, he set about resuscitating this old property with its sandy-gravel soils and 50-year-old vines. There's been no expense spared for consultants and vineyard and cellar equipment. Perhaps that's why he sold the property to Bernard Arnault and Albert Frère, owners of CHEVAL BLANC, in 2008.

The wines are modern in style with supple fruit, spicy oak aromas and freshness on the finish, and are drinkable almost immediately though they are perfectly happy with five to ten years' aging. Best years: 2010, '09, '08, '06, '05, '04, '02, '01, '00, '99, '98.

Château de La Rivière

This used to be the most famous property in Fronsac. It's less famous now but the wines are definitely better than they used to be.

CHÂTEAU DE LA RIVIÈRE

Fronsac AC

Merlot, Cabernet Sauvignon, Cabernet Franc

This large estate with its Renaissance château has been revamped since the mid-1990s and has continued to evolve under new ownership since 2003. In the 1980s the wines were fairly tough and tannic but aged well. Now they've taken on a bit of refinement and have a modern expression of the fruit. A special *cuvée*, Aria, made from 100% Merlot, was first made in 2000. There's a rosé as well. Age the reds for at least five years. Best years: 2010, '09, '08, '06, '05, '04, '03, '02, '01, '00, '99, '98, '90, '89.

Château Rocher Corbin

This is fundamentally a soft round style of wine, but it can be quite powerful for a Montagne-St-Émilion in warmer years.

CHÂTEAU ROCHER CORBIN

Montagne-St-Émilion AC

Merlot, Cabernet Franc, Cabernet Sauvignon

Consistency is what Philippe Durand offers at his 10-ha (25-acre) estate on clay-limestone slopes on the edge of the little town of Montagne. There's always that red fruit character, soft, round texture and fine tannins from a little barrel aging (25% new oak). Drink from three to five years. Best years: 2010, '09, '08, '06, '05, '04, '03, '02, '01, '00, '99, '98.

Château Rol Valentin

Rol Valentin is a classic example of the new wave wines of high quality being made from vineyards previously thought of as merely ordinary.

CHÂTEAU ROL VALENTIN

St-Émilion Grand Cru AC

Merlot, Cabernet Franc, Cabernet Sauvignon

Former footballer, Eric Prissette, got the winemaking bug while recuperating from a career-terminating injury. He purchased a tiny plot of vines on some of St-Émilion's more nondescript 'ancient sands' soils in 1994 and made his mark with a powerful, concentrated *garage* wine on its first release. He produced all the wines until 2009 when he sold the property. With time and experience and the addition of another vineyard on the clay-limestone slopes of St-Étienne-de-Lisse the Merlot-dominated wines have become more refined, though equally rich and powerful. They need at least five or six years' aging. Best years: 2010, '09, '08, '06, '05, '04, '03, '02, '01, '00, '99, '98, '96, '95.

Château La Rousselle

La Rousselle is based in one of the best parts of Fronsac overlooking the Dordogne from the steep slopes above La Rivière. The small amounts of wine are beautifully balanced.

CHÂTEAU LA ROUSSELLE
Fronsac AC
❉ *Merlot, Cabernet Franc, Cabernet Sauvignon*

In 1971 Jacques and Viviane Davau made it their lives' work to restore and work this tiny 4.6-ha (11-acre) domaine overlooking the Dordogne valley above La Rivière. Assisted by star consultant Stéphane Derenoncourt Viviane Davau now produces a beautifully balanced wine with ripe fruit, smooth tannins and freshness on the finish. Best years: 2010, '09, '08, '06, '05, '04, '03, '02, '01, '00, '99, '98.

Château St-Georges

This gentle, perfumed wine is often the best to be produced in the St-Georges-St-Émilion appellation.

CHÂTEAU ST-GEORGES
St-Georges-St-Émilion AC
❉ *Merlot, Cabernet Franc, Cabernet Sauvignon, Malbec*

This 47-ha (116-acre) estate with eye-catching 18th-century château and magnificent formal gardens accounts for nearly one-third of the tiny St-Georges-St-Émilion appellation. The wines are full-bodied, fresh and age well. They are sold by mail order or through importers. Best years: 2010, '09, '08, '05, '04, '03, '01, '00, '99, '98, '96, '95.

Château Soutard

This underrated St-Émilion Grand Cru Classé produces fine, mouthfilling reds for long aging, easily lasting 20 years in top vintages.

CHÂTEAU SOUTARD
St-Émilion Grand Cru AC, Grand Cru Classé
❉ *Merlot, Cabernet Franc*

A gorgeous 18th-century château forms the centrepiece of this fine, old estate on St-Émilion's limestone plateau. Unlike many properties that have changed their style of viticulture and winemaking in recent years, this Grand Cru Classé remained resolutely traditional until recently.

In the vineyard, there's an organic approach while in the cellars the wines take their own time to ferment and after barrel aging are bottled without filtration. However, there's now a flux of change. The property was sold to the same insurance group that owns Grand Cru Classé Ch. Larmande in 2006 and a brand new winery has been built and the vineyard overhauled. Second wine: Clos de La Tonnelle. Best years: 2010, '09, '08, '07, '06, '05, '04, '03, '01, '00, '99, '98, '96, '95, '94, '90, '89, '88, '85.

Château Taillefer

This is one of the lightest yet still succulent Pomerols from the south of the appellation, and the price is reasonable.

CHÂTEAU TAILLEFER
Pomerol AC
❉ *Merlot, Cabernet Franc*

It's not easy to recommend a 'good-value' Pomerol as prices are generally high for wines from this appellation and the lesser names are not always up to scratch.

This 12-ha (30-acre) estate, though, hits the mark. Back in 1923 this was the first wine estate bought by Antoine Moueix when he arrived in Libourne from the Corrèze, a poor department in central France, in search of a better life. He then went on to become the founder of the famous wine dynasty which now also own Ch. PÉTRUS and many other local properties.

The soils in the south of the appellation are sandy gravel so there's not the power of the wines from the big boys on the plateau further north but the estate is immaculately run by Catherine Moueix and the wines are pure, perfumed and elegant with just enough fat to let you know you're in Pomerol. The winemaking is looked after by Professor Denis Dubourdieu of Ch. REYNON and one of Bordeaux's most respected wine experts. Drinkable from six or seven years. Best years: 2010, '09, '08, '06, '05, '04, '03, '02, '01, '00, '99, '98.

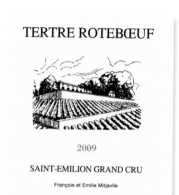

Château Tertre-Rôteboeuf

This is remarkable wine from a small but beautifully sited vineyard tumbling down the limestone slopes.

CHÂTEAU TERTRE-RÔTEBOEUF

St-Émilion Grand Cru AC

❋ *Merlot, Cabernet Franc*

François Mitjavile was way ahead of his time when he took this unheralded little 5.7-ha (14-acre) property by the scruff of the neck in the 1980s and proved that so-called lesser terroirs could produce wines to equal or indeed eclipse those of the ancient Classed Growth hierarchy of St-Émilion. St-Émilion is now flooded by these micro-crus, often called *garage* wines because their tiny volumes could be vinified in your garage – and some of the first ones were! These wines are marked by tiny yields, intense concentration of fruit and lavish use of new oak barrels.

Some examples of *garage* wines became mere parodies, but Tertre-Rôteboeuf is actually on a beautiful little amphitheatre slope of limestone easily of Premier Grand Cru quality and clearly ideally suited to top quality grape-growing. Equally important, Mitjavile is a thoughtful, sensitive and passionate wine man deeply rooted in his soil and its vines. As the dark-fruited, glycerine-rich wine washes through your mouth it bubbles with seriousness and humour, philosophy and practicality in equal parts and invigorates your mind. (See also Ch. ROC DE CAMBES, page 271.) Best years: 2010, '09, '08, '07, '06, '05, '04, 03, '02, '01, '00, '99, '98, '96, '90, '89.

The charming, philosophical François Mitjavile making a point about his delicious Tertre-Rôteboeuf which I may or may not understand. That's his tasting room, by the way, his kitchen.

Château Teyssier
*This is an oaky, kirsch-scented, modern-style
St-Émilion from sandy soils now enhanced with fruit
from better sites elsewhere.*

CHÂTEAU TEYSSIER
St-Émilion Grand Cru AC
❊ *Merlot, Cabernet Franc*

Dynamic Englishman Jonathan Maltus bought Ch. Teyssier in 1994 because it was such a pretty house. It was only when he'd settled in that a thoughtful neighbour quietly whispered that the house might be nice but that the vines were on the worst land in all of St-Émilion and nobody would want to buy the wine. Maltus' attitude was pure British bulldog. Certainly the village of Vignonet down by the Dordogne, with its pale sandy soils, is poorly regarded but Maltus bought up patches of land in much better parts of St-Émilion and blended in their grapes, so that the Vignonet plot now makes up barely a quarter of Teyssier's fruit.

The modern Teyssier is rich, scented with cherries and swathed in soft, nutty oak. It is now one of the biggest selling St-Émilion Grands Crus. But there's more to Maltus than just Teyssier. He is an inveterate *garagiste* – finding and exploiting little plots of land all over St-Emilion as micro-crus – and his wines are all sharply defined and very different. Tasting Le Carré, Les Astéries and Le Dôme next to each other shows three very exciting, completely different wines. Good *garage* wines are not homogenized; they are an accentuation of a vineyard's personality. Maltus has now exported his ideas to Australia's Barossa Valley where he makes astonishing, heart-stopping wines under names like Exile, Emigré, Expatrié, Étranger and what have you. He's doing the same in California as well. Best years: 2010, '09, '08, '07, '06, '05, '04, '03, '02, '01, '00.

Château La Tour-Figeac
*Biodynamic wines are rare in Bordeaux but in ripe,
warm years the method clearly works at La Tour-
Figeac.*

CHÂTEAU LA TOUR-FIGEAC
St-Émilion Grand Cru AC, Grand Cru Classé
❊ *Merlot, Cabernet Franc*

A biodynamically run Grand Cru Classé? It hardly seems likely but it's true. Fashionable consultant Stéphane Derenoncourt and his wife Christine put into practice what they preach at this 14.6-ha (36-acre) property owned by the Rettenmaier family. Fruit and harmony are the bywords especially as the sand and gravel soils close to Ch. FIGEAC mitigate against big, powerful wines. There's a coating of toast and vanilla, though, as the wines mature in 60% new oak barrels.

The wines don't always convince me, and they need five or six years' bottle aging, but the most successful vintages, like 1998, are an exquisite expression of lush, balanced, deeply satisfying St-Émilion. Best years: 2010, '09, '08, '07, '06, '05, '04, '02, '01, '00, '99, '98, '96, '95, '90.

Château Les Troix Croix
*The result of traditional winemaking and some aging
in new oak is a rather lovely wine, full of fragrant
fruits and smooth tannins.*

CHÂTEAU LES TROIS CROIX
Fronsac AC
❊ *Merlot, Cabernet Franc*

A rather lovely, harmonious wine with smooth tannins is produced at this 14-ha (35-acre) Fronsac property. Perhaps that's not surprising since from 1995 it's been owned by Patrick Léon, the former technical director of Ch. MOUTON-ROTHSCHILD. His son, Bertrand, looks after the winemaking and has obviously inherited the family skills. Drink th wine from four to five years. Best years: 2010, '09, '08, '06, '05, '04, '03, '02, '01, '00, '99, '98, '96.

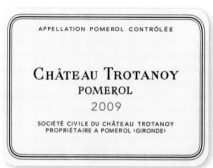

Château Troplong-Mondot

Big, rich powerful reds from good plateau vineyards next to La Mondotte, but sometimes they thud into your palette rather than caress it.

Château Trotanoy

Trotanoy is traditionally one of the richer Pomerols after Pétrus and is now back on form after a dip in the 1980s.

Château Trottevieille

This was a fine but underperforming property but since the 2000 vintage it has made a string of elegant, balanced wines in the ttrue tradition of St-Émilion.

CHÂTEAU TROPLONG-MONDOT

St-Émilion Grand Cru AC, Premier Grand Cru Classé

❦ *Merlot, Cabernet Franc, Cabernet Sauvignon*

Owned by Christine Valette and husband Xavier Pariente, Ch. Troplong-Mondot was one of a group of supposedly second-division St-Émilion Grands Crus Classés – Ch. CANON-LA-GAFFELIÈRE was another – who ripped up the rule book at the beginning of the 1990s and began making dense, intense reds quite unlike anything they'd ever done before.

Finally promoted to the rank of Premier Grand Cru Classé in 2006, Troplong-Mondot has been making solidly structured, mouthfillingly, dark unfiltered wines for more than a decade now, but I think that Canon-la-Gaffelière – and its micro-cru La MONDOTTE which is right next to Troplong-Mondot – have more beauty to them. Best years: 2010, '09, '08, '07, '06, '05, '04, '03, '02, '01, '00, '99, '98, '96, '95, '90, '89.

CHÂTEAU TROTANOY

Pomerol AC

❦ *Merlot, Cabernet Franc*

Trotanoy puts itself up as Ch. PÉTRUS' main challenger for the title 'King of Pomerol' but, in general, it has to be content with the role of crown prince. The wine is tremendous stuff, though, and back on form after a dip in the mid-1980s (due to lots of replanting in the vineyards).

Trotanoy is another example (along with Ch. Pétrus, HOSANNA, LATOUR-À-POMEROL and a gaggle of others) of the brilliant touch of the Moueix family whose *négociant* company, Jean-Pierre Moueix based in Libourne, owns this 8-ha (19-acre) property to the west of Pétrus on slightly more gravelly soil. Though the plantings of 90% Merlot and 10% Cabernet Franc do give a rich, massively impressive, Pétrus-like wine, they are also likely to have a tempering of leather and tobacco scents, and just lack the magic mingling of sweetness, spice and perfume which makes Pétrus so memorable. Best years: 2010, '09, '08, '07, '06, '05, '04, '03, '02, '01, '00, '98, '96, '95, '90, '89.

CHÂTEAU TROTTEVIEILLE

St-Émilion Grand Cru AC, Premier Grand Cru Classé

❦ *Merlot, Cabernet Franc, Cabernet Sauvignon*

The Trottevieille estate, owned by the Castéja family, occupies an isolated site on the plateau to the east of the town of St-Émilion, away from the other Premiers Grands Crus Classés. The easterly exposure of the vineyard and 50- to 60-year-old vines augured well for the quality of the wine but it was not until the mid-1980s that the property began to make much of an effort. Even then it performed under par and only started to show its real class from 2000.

Lower yields and advice from enology professor Denis Dubourdieu have worked wonders since then. The 2000s have exhibited beautifully balanced, restrained yet classic glycerine and blackcurrant flavours and eminently drinkable texture. The owners have resisted leaping into the cauldron of hyper-concentrated St-Émilion, and have instead simply returned Trottevieille to its true St-Émilion roots. The best vintages can be rich, powerful and extremely long-lived. Keep for at least five to ten years. Best years: 2010, '09, '08, '07, '05, '04, '03, '02, '01, '00, '99, '98, '95, '90, '89.

Château Valandraud

This tiny estate has only existed since 1991 yet the immensely rich and concentrated wine has already become one of Bordeaux's most famous.

CHÂTEAU VALANDRAUD

St-Émilion Grand Cru AC

❄ *Merlot, Cabernet Franc, Cabernet Sauvignon, Malbec*

This is the very heart of the *garagiste* movement, because Jean-Luc Thunevin, the ex-disc jockey and bank clerk who has brilliantly raised this tiny property from obscurity to superstardom, really did make his first vintages, starting in 1991, in a backstreet garage in St-Émilion, from grapes grown in a forlorn, forgotten 0.5-ha (1.2-acre) plot out near the municipal vegetable allotment (see page 203). The wine was good, and people quickly began to take notice of this passionate newcomer who seemed to come from nowhere. That's the *garagiste* way .

Valandraud is made from the original plot and parcels of vines on classic limestone soil in St-Étienne-de-Lisse. It is now a rich, densely structured but wonderfully hedonistic wine that drapes its flavours over your palate like velvet. Thunevin stands as spokesperson for the *garagistes* when he calls his wine 'hand-sewn'. With no money, the original *garagistes* achieved concentration, and memorable intensity in their wines, by obsessive attention to detail. There are many such wines now, especially in St-Émilion; some made not by poor men but by multimillionaires; nonetheless, the spirit of the *garage* wine resides at Valandraud. Best years: 2010, '09, '08, '07, '06, '05, '04, '03, '02, '01, '00, '99, '98, '96, '95.

Château La Vieille Cure

La Vieille Cure is one of the few Fronsac properties whose wine is seen quite widely on the export market.

CHÂTEAU LA VIEILLE CURE

Fronsac AC

❄ *Merlot, Cabernet Franc, Cabernet Sauvignon*

La Vieille Cure enjoys an excellent location at Saillans with vineyards in one block on a slope above the river Isle. Purchased in 1986 by a group of American bankers with a passion for wine, the estate has been steadily renovated since then and now produces some of the best value-for-money wines in the area. Part of the 18-ha (45-acre) vineyard has been replanted, a new cellar built, modern vinification equipment installed and aging in oak barrels introduced.

The technical management is also at a high level with Michel Rolland retained as consultant enologist and, since 1994, Jean-Noël Hervé (owner of neighbouring Ch. MOULIN HAUT-LAROQUE) engaged as overall manager. The wine is rich in extract, firm and solid rather than particularly expressive and marked with toasted oak in youth. It requires four to five years' bottle age after which it opens out very attractively. Best years: 2010, '09, '06, '05, '04, '03, '02, '01, '00, '99, '98, '96, '95.

Vieux-Château-Certan

This beautiful property is often thought of as second only to Ch. Pétrus in Pomerol and makes a much drier style of wine.

VIEUX-CHÂTEAU-CERTAN

Pomerol AC

❄ *Merlot, Cabernet Franc, Cabernet Sauvignon*

The first time I tasted this wine, the '52, it was in a blind tasting competition. No one guessed it as a Pomerol. Most of the other tasters were with me in deciding on Pauillac or St-Julien. I felt a little better when I discovered that VCC, as it is often called, is described as the most Médoc-like of all Pomerols, frequently not exhibiting any of the lush, hedonistic, loose-limbed and juicy-lipped gorgeousness that has made Pomerol the star attraction for red wine pleasure-seekers worldwide.

Traditionally it played the role of being Pomerol's number two – behind PÉTRUS, but totally different to it. Now there is a bunch of properties trying to ape Pétrus – Le PIN and TROTANOY are just two – but no one tries to ape VCC. It is owned by the Thienpont family and, although it is only just down the road from Pétrus, its soil is different, mixing sand and gravel with its clay. But most importantly it has only 60% Merlot as against Pétrus' virtually 100%. The rest of the 13.5-ha (33-acre) vineyard is 30% Cabernet Franc and 10% Cabernet Sauvignon, and it is this unusually strong presence for Pomerol of Cabernet which makes the VCC style drier, leaner, less sumptuous. The slow-maturing wine gradually builds up over 15–20 years into an exciting 'Médoc' blend of blackcurrant and cedarwood perfume just offset by the brown sugar and roasted nuts of Pomerol. Best years: 2010, '09, '08, '07, '06, '05, '04, '02, '01, '00, '99, '98, '96, '95, '90, '89, '88, '86, '85.

Vieux Château St-André

This is elegant, restrained wine from the recently retired chief winemaker in charge of Ch. Pétrus and other key Right Bank estates.

VIEUX CHÂTEAU ST-ANDRÉ

Montagne-St-Émilion AC

❋ *Merlot, Cabernet Franc*

This 6-ha (15-acre) property is owned by Jean-Claude Berrouet, recently retired winemaker/enologist for the *négociant* firm of Jean-Pierre Moueix, and is run by his son Jean-François. If you know the Moueix house style you'll know that the emphasis is placed on fruit and balance and this is exactly what you get here. The oak component is minimal, with only 15% new oak barrels each year and one-third of the wine is aged in vat. Drinkable at three to four years, the wine can age for at least 15. Best years: 2010, '09, '08, '06, '05, '04, 03, '02, '01, '00, '99, '98, '96, '95, '90.

Château Villars

These are some of Bordeaux's best value wines: they can be enjoyed at five years but will become scented and soft after another few years

CHÂTEAU VILLARS

Fronsac AC

❋ *Merlot, Cabernet Franc, Cabernet Sauvignon*

In the late 1970s Jean-Claude Gaudrie was one of the early pioneers to show that with hard graft and a little investment the Fronsac appellation, and especially the vineyards around the village of Saillans, really had something to offer. His son Thierry, the eighth generation of his family to run the estate, continues the good work, producing wines loaded with plummy fruit when young, but also showing an attractive and typical metallic edge, and with powerful tannins rounded by aging in 40% new oak barrels. Best years: 2010, '09, '08, '06, '05, '04, '03, '02, '01, '00, '99, '98.

Quick guide • Best producers

CANON-FRONSAC AC
Barrabaque, Canon-Pécresse, Cassagne Haut-Canon, La Fleur Cailleau, Gaby, Gazin, Grand-Renouil, Haut-Bellet, Haut-Mazeris, Lamarche Canon Candelaire, Mazeris, Moulin Pey-Labrie, Pavillon, Vrai Canon Bouché.

FRONSAC AC
Carolus, Dalem, La Dauphine, Fontenil, La Grave, Haut-Carles, Magondeau Beau-Site, Mayne-Vieil, Moulin Haut-Laroque, Plain-Point, La Rivière, La Rousselle, Tour du Moulin, Les Trois Croix, La Vieille Cure, Villars.

LALANDE-DE-POMEROL AC
Annereaux, Bertineau St-Vincent, La Croix-St-André, Les Cruzelles, La Fleur de Boüard, Garraud, Grand Ormeau, Haut-Chaigneau, Haut-Surget, Les Hauts Conseillants, Jean de Gué, Laborderie Mondésir, Perron (la Fleur), Sergant, Siaurac, Tournefeuille, Viaud.

LUSSAC-ST-ÉMILION AC
Barbe-Blanche, Bel-Air, Bellevue, Courlat, La Grenière, Lussac, Lyonnat, Mayne Blanc, Rochers.

MONTAGNE-ST-ÉMILION AC
Calon, Couronne, Croix-Beauséjour, Faizeau, Gachont, Laurets, Montaiguillon, Roc-de-Calon, Rocher Corbin, Roudier, Vieux-Bonneau, Vieux Château St-André.

POMEROL AC
Beauregard, Bellegrave, Bonalgue, Le Bon Pasteur, Bourgneuf-Vayron, La Cabanne, Certan-de-May, Clinet, Clos du Clocher, Clos L'Eglise, Clos René, La Conseillante, L'Eglise-Clinet, L'Evangile, Feytit-Clinet, La Fleur-Pétrus, Le Gay, Gazin, Guillot, Hosanna, Lafleur, Latour-à-Pomerol, Montviel, Moulinet, Nénin, Petit-Village, Pétrus, Le Pin, Plince, La Pointe, Sales, Taillefer, Trotanoy, Vieux-Château-Certan.

PUISSEGUIN-ST-ÉMILION AC
Bel-Air, Branda, Durand-Laplagne, Fongaban, Guibot-la Fourvieille, Haut-Bernat, Laurets, La Mauriane, Môle, Producteurs Réunis, Soleil.

ST-ÉMILION GRAND CRU AC
Angélus, L'Arrosée, Ausone, Balestard-la-Tonnelle, Barde-Haut, Beauséjour, Beau-Séjour-Bécot, Belair-Monange, Bellefont-Belcier, Bellevue, Berliquet, Canon, Canon-la-Gaffelière, Cap de Mourlin, Carteau-Côtes-Daugay, Cheval Blanc, Clos de La Cure, Clos Dubreuil, Clos Fourtet, Clos de L'Oratoire, Clos St-Martin, Clos Trimoulet, La Clotte, La Couspaude, Destieux, La Dominique, Faugères, Figeac, Fleur Cardinale, Fombrauge, Fonplégade, La Gaffelière, La Gomerie, Gracia, Grand-Mayne, Grand-Pontet, Lapelletrie, Larmande, Lavallade, Magdelaine, Mangot, Monbousquet, La Mondotte, Moulin St-Georges, Pavie, Pavie-Decesse, Pavie-Macquin, Petit Fombrauge, Pressac, Quinault L'Enclos, Rol Valentin, Soutard, Tauzinat l'Hermitage, Tertre-Rôteboeuf, Teyssier, La Tour-Figeac, Trimoulet, Troplong-Mondot, Trottevieille, Val d'Or, Valandraud, Vieux Ch. Pelletan.

ST-GEORGES-ST-ÉMILION AC
Calon, Macquin-St-Georges, St-André-Corbin, St-Georges, Tour du Pas St-Georges, Vieux-Montaiguillon.

The Côtes and Between the Rivers

Bordeaux's famous wine regions – the Médoc, the Graves, the Right Bank – are nicely self-contained, with identifiable styles of wines, a particular history and an established status. But the five Côtes – Blaye, Bourg, Castillon, Francs and the Cadillac-Côtes de Bordeaux? I'm not even sure that I should be joining all these areas up under one heading because they are all so different in their wine styles, and their present fortunes and future prospects are so mixed.

Yet the five Côtes areas have been loosely trying to market themselves as a grouping since the 1980s, albeit without much success. However, from 2009 four areas (except Bourg for the time being) decided to bind themselves up in a single new appellation called Côtes de Bordeaux – the slopes of Bordeaux – preceeded by their regional name. I'm not really convinced it's the right idea. For an umbrella marketing description, yes, but for an appellation? Blaye is different from Bourg, and Castillon and Francs are very different from the first two, while the Cadillac-Côtes de Bordeaux slopes are on another river – the Garonne – and a different geological system entirely. As for poor old Entre-Deux-Mers – the great swathe of land between the Dordogne and Garonne rivers – well, it would probably embrace any ideas that would help it sell its own vast oceans of often undistinguished wines, but, not surprisingly, the 'Côtes' haven't invited Entre-Deux-Mers to join in.

This is the point where the Garonne and Dordogne rivers join to become the Gironde estuary, which then sweeps past us towards the Atlantic to the right of the photograph. These vineyards are in the Côtes de Bourg, established by the Romans who loved the way the land slopes down to the estuary; they particularly loved the limestone plateau acting as a base to the shallow soils. The whiteness of the little track is evidence of the limestone just beneath the surface.

SPOTLIGHT ON
The Côtes
& Between the Rivers

Blaye is one of Bordeaux's oldest vineyard areas. There is even a vineyard on the citadel ramparts overlooking the broad waters of the Gironde towards the Médoc on the far side. The ferry from Lamarque docks just behind the trees.

Right, let's get started. Take a quick look at the map opposite, and then I'll get to work trying to inject some kind of sense of place into these peripheral yet substantial regions of Bordeaux.

BLAYE-CÔTES DE BORDEAUX

We'll begin at the top, in the north, with the Blaye-Côtes de Bordeaux. I wouldn't be a bit surprised if most of you said 'where on earth is Blaye?' It's not exactly a household name, is it? But it was, 2000 years ago. If you climb up the slopes behind the town and stand amongst the vines tumbling back down towards the Gironde estuary, sure you can look out across the muddy brown waters towards the currently world famous vineyards of St-Julien and Margaux just a short ferry ride away. But *you* are standing in vineyards established by the Romans, and held in high regard by the English when they ruled over South-West France up until 1453. St-Julien and Margaux were swamps when Blaye was famous. Now St-Julien and Margaux are full of superstars, and Blaye has been forgotten. Yet there's a new mood abroad in Blaye and real signs of a new generation here determined not to let the region wither away.

Quick guide • The Côtes and Between the Rivers

LOCATION
A number of appellations around the region with a sound foundation of good soils and sun-drenched slopes hold out great promise for reds, while the Entre-Deux-Mers – literally the wedge of land between the Dordogne and Garonne rivers – is one of Bordeaux's last bastions of white wine.

APPELLATIONS
The Côtes de Bourg and Blaye-Côtes de Bordeaux (where the best reds can be labelled simply Blaye AC) are directly across the Gironde from the celebrated communes of the Médoc, while the sun-drenched slopes of Francs-Côtes de Bordeaux and its

neighbour Castillon-Côtes de Bordeaux extend inland from the more famous Right Bank appellations of St-Émilion and Pomerol. These appellations are all succeeding primarily with reds but also produce a small amount of white wine.

Entre-Deux-Mers is an appellation solely for dry whites, but this region between the two rivers is also responsible for much decent red, rosé and white Bordeaux AC. It contains a small enclave of reds at Graves de Vayres, and sub-regions of supposedly higher quality at Ste-Foy, Haut-Benauge and St-Macaire, but the best red wines from between the rivers take the new Cadillac-Côtes de Bordeaux

appellation. Good dry whites are made here too but can only claim the basic Bordeaux AC.

GRAPES
For red grapes these sites are mostly Right Bank and inland with clay in the soil calling for a high proportion of Merlot. Cabernet Franc offers stolid support with some Cabernet Sauvignon (especially in Bourg) and Malbec sometimes added to the blend, too. Sauvignon Blanc is increasingly the grape of choice for white wines, but you will find plenty of Sémillon and some Muscadelle too, with dwindling quantities of Merlot Blanc, Colombard and Ugni Blanc.

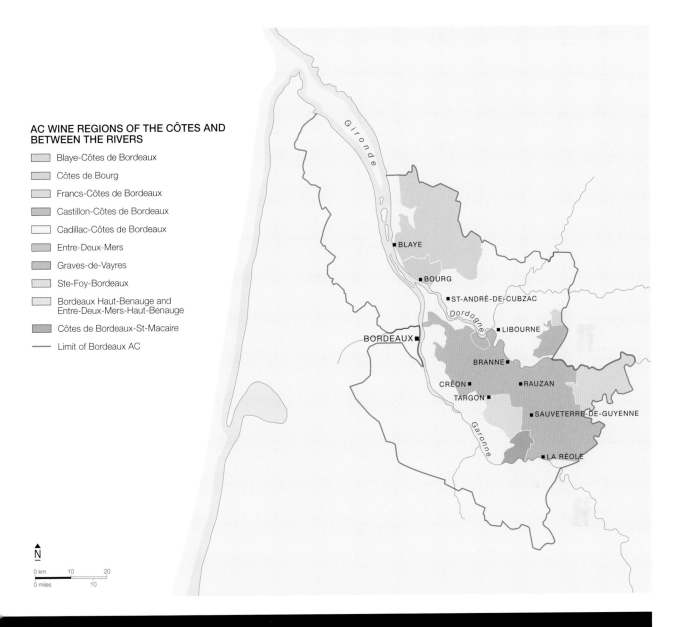

AC WINE REGIONS OF THE CÔTES AND BETWEEN THE RIVERS

- Blaye-Côtes de Bordeaux
- Côtes de Bourg
- Francs-Côtes de Bordeaux
- Castillon-Côtes de Bordeaux
- Cadillac-Côtes de Bordeaux
- Entre-Deux-Mers
- Graves-de-Vayres
- Ste-Foy-Bordeaux
- Bordeaux Haut-Benauge and Entre-Deux-Mers-Haut-Benauge
- Côtes de Bordeaux-St-Macaire
- —— Limit of Bordeaux AC

CLIMATE

Bourg and Blaye are warm but a little damp due to their exposure to the ocean. The inland Côtes have hotter summers and colder winters than elsewhere in Bordeaux, as France's continental climate starts to make its presence felt, and are among the driest vineyard sites in Bordeaux. Entre-Deux-Mers has a maritime climate, further moderated by the presence of the two rivers.

SOIL AND ASPECT

South-facing hillsides with plenty of limestone in the clay are the key to success with reds. Francs-Côtes de Bordeaux is most blessed with these, and the Cadillac-Côtes de Bordeaux rich with limestone,

while the best vineyards in Castillon are on the limestone *côtes*, whereas flatter ones have a lot of clay, making this an exciting but variable appellation. The Entre-Deux-Mers gently undulates over clay, limestone and sand and a fair amount of loam.

VINTAGE VARIATIONS

Bourg and Blaye along the Gironde need a hot, dry year to excel. The inland Côtes are more reliably good and Entre-Deux-Mers is always productive, often excessively so, although ripeness is an issue, especially for reds. A well-sited, well-run vineyard counts for more than the vintage here, as in most parts of the world.

ORGANIZATION

Modern co-operatives lead the way in Entre-Deux-Mers, while small estates, often under the same ownership as illustrious properties in neighbouring premium appellations, are the trailblazers here as well as in the Côtes.

A FEW FACTS

Vineyards in the Côtes add up to 16,100ha (39,767 acres), over a third of them in the Blaye region. The Entre-Deux-Mers region has around 32,500ha (80,300 acres) of vines, but only 1,460ha (3,606 acres) use the Entre-Deux-Mers AC – the rest is sold as Bordeaux or Bordeaux Supérieur and 78% is red.

Quick guide • Blaye and Bourg

OVERVIEW

Blaye is an excellent source for soft-textured, tasty affordable red wines to drink young or to age for three to five years. Côtes de Bourg makes a sterner, more Cabernet-influenced style, good for those who like a little bite in their wine. They usually benefit from five years' aging.

WINES TO TRY

Blaye-Côtes de Bordeaux

- Ch. Bel-Air La Royère (also Ch. Les Ricards)
- Ch. Bois-Vert, Cuvée Prestige (also white)
- Ch. Cailleteau-Bergeron (also white)
- Ch. Camille Gaucheraud
- Ch. Cap St-Martin
- Ch. Charron
- La Croix du Prieuré
- Ch. Frédignac, Prestige
- Ch. Gigault, Cuvée Viva
- Ch. Grand-Barrail, Cuvée Prestige
- Ch. Haut Bertinerie (also white)
- Ch. Haut-Colombier (also white)
- Ch. Haut-Grelot
- Ch. Haut-Terrier
- Ch. Les Jonqueyres
- Ch. Monconseil Gazin
- Ch. Mondésir-Gazin
- Ch. Montfollet
- Ch. La Rose Bellevue, Prestige
- Ch. Segonzac
- Ch. des Tourtes, Prestige

Côtes de Bourg

- Ch. du Bousquet
- Ch. Brulesécaille (also white)
- Ch. Bujan
- Clos Alphonse Dubreuil
- Ch. Le Clos du Notaire, Notaris
- Ch. Falfas, le Chevalier
- Ch. Fougas
- Ch. Guerry
- Ch. Les Graves de Viaud, Grande Cuvée
- Ch. Haut-Guiraud Péché du Roy
- Ch. de la Haute Libarde
- Ch. Haut-Macô
- Ch. Haut-Mondésir
- Ch. Labadie
- Ch. Lamblin, Cuvée Hommage
- Ch. Macay (also Original)
- Ch. Martinat
- Ch. Mercier
- Ch. Roc de Cambes
- Ch. de Rousselet
- Ch. Sauman
- Ch. Tayac
- Ch. La Tuilière, Les Armoiries

Blaye isn't just a vineyard region. In fact the 6,500ha (16,055 acres) of vines only represent about 15 per cent of the agricultural land, and quite a lot of the land is simply unsuitable for vines. If you take the coastal road north from the splendid citadel-dominated town of Blaye, you pass a lot of vines, but you also cross marshes so low and wet that you feel as though the road has been built on a sponge as the overloaded drainage channels lap at the side of the tarmac. Yet you need only a small rise of 5–10m (16–33ft) above the water meadows and vines sprout everywhere, particularly around Braud-et-St-Louis and St-Ciers-sur-Gironde – and then suddenly you pass a road sign saying 'Welcome to the Charentes'! That's the Cognac region, brandy not wine. You're not in Bordeaux any more. You can't tell the difference standing straddling the boundary in the vineyard – well, there isn't a wine difference; it's a bureaucratic one – but it's significant that there's still some white Ugni Blanc and Colombard planted up here. They're both primarily distillation grapes and are the mainstay of the Cognac vineyards, but actually, Colombard also makes very attractive, zesty white wine. And although Blaye-Côtes de Bordeaux is basically a red wine region, the big co-operative in Marcillac– the Cave des Hauts de Gironde – is one of the best producers of basic white – especially from local Sauvignon Blanc – in Bordeaux. Even so, with all that marsh about and low exposed clay hillocks providing most of the vineyard land, I'd expect myself to say: rip out the vines, the wines can't be any good. And yet they are. The whites have a round, juicy, soft quality. So do the reds, and for a world that wants easy-drinking reds, the better Merlot-dominated examples from the northern Blaye can be delightful.

There are two other major areas in Blaye with altogether higher aspirations. The first is the one the Romans found. They saw the fine limestone cliffs that front up the Gironde and snub their noses at the flat, boggy Médoc across the way; they found fertile plateaux behind the cliffs and even tumbling slopes of limestone clay perfectly oriented towards the warm west sun just south of Blaye at Plassac. They planted their vines. They built their villas – you can see some pretty good remains at Plassac if you want – and they made wines that, as far as we can tell, were pretty cool. If you visit the Plassac estate of Ch. Mondésir-Gazin you'll be standing on the slopes the Romans planted – limestone covered by a little clay and angled towards the evening sun.

In the whole area spreading inland from Blaye, limestone and clay are the most important components in the soil. This is good soil, but not all red grapes can cope with it. Cabernet finds it difficult to ripen, but Merlot loves it. There are a number of good villages on the low hills inland from Blaye, but Cars in particular, with its very pale limestone clays and rolling hills, some of them quite steep, turns up a lot of lush reds, with some of the oak-aged prestige cuvées from properties like Haut-Colombier and Bel-Air la Royère managing to be juicy but rich and powerful at the same time. There are various other good villages on these calm, relaxing, billowing slopes, like St-Martin-Lacaussade, St-Paul and Mazion, but those clay-rich slopes of Cars are, for me, the heartland of the new ripe, soft red Blaye style.

There's one more important Blaye area and it contains what is probably Blaye's most go-ahead property – the Bertinerie estate. This area is south-east of the town of Blaye, inland, based in the canton of St-Seurin and located on a big, south-west facing semi-circle of limestone. You can't see it from the surface but the contours on any decent map will show it to you. The soils on top of this are a mix of pure clay, limestone clay and sandy clays mixed in with iron sand and some patches of gravel. Sand and gravel are both warm soils – clay is cold – and so it is possible to grow the late-ripening Cabernet Sauvignon here up to a point. The soils aren't that warm (the best Médoc villages, where Cabernet Sauvignon thrives, have deep beds of warm white gravel to help the variety ripen: in Blaye we're just talking about streaks and patches of gravel in the clay). Even so, Bertinerie – especially with its top Haut-Bertinerie label – does ripen Cabernet pretty well, partly because it uses a revolutionary vine-training system called the lyre. One vine is trained to produce two canes that sweep upwards and do look like a lyre, and the increased leaf area allows you to ripen a quite big crop eight to ten days earlier than a conventionally pruned vine. This is crucial for the late-ripening Cabernet Sauvignon. Neighbouring vineyards may ripen it fully a couple of times a decade, Bertinerie's lyre vines ripen it fully virtually every year.

By the way, a word on the confusing Blaye appellations. In whites, you'll probably only see Blaye-Côtes de Bordeaux on the label. In reds, you've got both Blaye-Côtes de Bordeaux and simple Blaye. However, Blaye is the better appellation – the wine comes from vineyards planted with a greater density of vines and with a lower yield (both factors that increase ripeness and improve quality), followed by a reasonably severe tasting panel that can and does reject inferior wines.

CÔTES DE BOURG

If you look at the map again, you'll see that the Blaye area pretty much encircles Bourg, but there's a good reason for Bourg to have an entirely separate appellation. Conditions really are different, and whereas Blaye has to rely largely on the easy-ripening Merlot to create soft, attractive red wines, Bourg has a lot more of the late-ripening, sturdily-structured Cabernet Sauvignon. If conditions were the same as in Blaye, you couldn't ripen the Cabernet. So let's examine the differences. If you drive into Bourg from the north, east or south, as soon as you cross the boundary, the bland rolling hillocks become dramatic slopes with dizzying swoops of vines up and down the valley sides. The locals call it the 'Little Switzerland of the Gironde' and that pretty much says it – you won't find many more

Much of the Bordeaux region is pretty flat, but not Bourg. Vines swoop up and down in all directions, and create excellent conditions for making dry but ageworthy reds from Cabernet Sauvignon and Merlot.

Quick guide • Côtes de Bordeaux

OVERVIEW

Côtes de Bordeaux is a new (2009) grouping for dry reds from four regions – Blaye, Castillon, Francs and Cadillac; and dry whites from Blaye and Francs. The regions are generally kept separate and Côtes de Bordeaux is preceded on the label by the regional name e.g. Castillon-Côtes de Bordeaux. The region's wines can be blended together under the Cotes de Bordeaux title (about 15% in 2009). Red wines comprise 97% of the total.

White wines can be dry or sweet: dry whites can use the Cotes de Bordeaux appellation (except for in Cadillac where they have to use the Bordeaux AC label). In the Blaye area they can use the Blaye or Côtes de Blaye appellation (this latter is almost non-existent and is being phased out by 2020, but most whites merely use the Bordeaux Blanc title.

There are four sweet wine appellations along the right bank of the Garonne: Premières Côtes de Bordeaux (not allowed for red wines any more), Cadillac, Loupiac and Ste Croix du Mont (see page 275).

Confused? Join the club.

dramatic landscapes than this in Bordeaux. And with this landscape come some challenging and interesting vineyard conditions.

Let's go back to the Romans. If you thought the limestone cliffs were good in Blaye, they're better in the Côtes de Bourg. If you drive out of Bourg towards Blaye and immediately take a sharp left turn after the citadel – yup, they've got one too – you'll drop down to the banks of Dordogne. You can follow the shore for miles on a little road cut into the sliver of land between the cliffs and the shore, but the best idea of what sent the Romans weak at the knees is right by the town of Bourg. You immediately come upon the warm, protected site of Bourg's superstar, Ch. Roc de Cambes, set in an amphitheatre of limestone debris that has fallen from the plateau over millennia. The steep slope angled towards the sun gives you the chance to maximize the sweet, generous ripeness in your grapes, while the crumbled limestone allows the vine roots to go deep into the rock. Limestone gives refreshing acidity to the grape, and the genius of this soil is that it allows you to ripen your grapes way into the autumn without them becoming baked because the refreshing acidity keeps overripeness at bay. Generosity of fruit and freshness of acidity: that's the magic formula, and these tumbled terrace vineyards have it.

Drive on a little and you come to Ch. Tayac and Ch. Eyquem – both with beautiful vineyards sloping down towards the Dordogne as it joins the Garonne to form the Gironde estuary, but you'll also see they have vines actually on the plateau stretching back behind the cliffs. The subsoil on top here is solid, unbroken limestone, the vines' roots can't penetrate it so easily and the acidity from the soil isn't quite so marked, so you can't let the grapes hang lazily way into the autumn like you can on the riverside slopes. You pick the grapes earlier. The wines are still good, but they don't quite have the lush, warm body of Roc de Cambes.

It was wines from these vineyards close to the water that made Bourg famous 2000 years ago, and until the rise of the Médoc and the Graves estates in the 17th century many people were still calling Bourg Bordeaux's greatest parcel of vineyard land. They don't any longer. But as Roc de Cambes shows, the potential is there. What the region needs is more passion, belief and investment. And the riverside vineyards with their wonderful views and higher real estate values are not the only places where Bourg could shine again.

There are two other good sub-regions. First there's a high ridge running north from Bourg to the town of Berson. Take the road and twist and turn through good wine villages like Samonac and St-Trojan and you'll see fierce red soil on both sides, full of iron gravel on a

A view along the Bourg corniche near Ch. Tayac, overlooking the Gironde. These vines are sited on limestone debris and are top quality. To the right of the road is the limestone plateau, still good fpr growing vines but less special.

bedrock of limestone. These are Bourg's highest vineyards, but they're warm soils, and Cabernet Sauvignon can ripen here. If you go back to Bourg and then head north-east towards Pugnac, climbing away from the river, the soil becomes sandier and there are numerous outcrops of white gravel –not quite so high as the Bersan Ridge – and warm soils again, where Cabernet can flourish.

Côtes de Bourg is the only appellation here, and it's almost all red. Bourg wines do have more Cabernet than Blaye wines and that makes them tougher, more serious, less easy to gurgle back but full of potential for aging. They also have quite a lot of Malbec here, one of Bordeaux's forgotten red grapes. Some growers love the dark colour and juicy fruit it gives the wine. Ask another and he will say, 'Merlot gives generosity, Cabernet gives structure, Malbec is only good for filling up the vat'.

CASTILLON-CÔTES DE BORDEAUX

I've talked a lot about the limestone cliffs and the limestone plateau that have such an influence on Blaye and Bourg wines. Well, their influence is far more widespread than that, running all the way down the Dordogne to the Fronsac region which has some fairly forbidding cliffs towering over the main road into Libourne, resurfacing in St-Émilion and playing an absolutely crucial role in quality by forming what are called the St-Émilion côtes and then, without a blink of the eye, St-Émilion becomes Castillon-Côtes de Bordeaux as this limestone plateau surges eastwards towards Bergerac and out of Bordeaux altogether. Limestone is a smashing base for vineyards – especially white wine vineyards – but it is a challenging one for red wines, because vines with roots in limestone give grapes that have fairly high-acid juice. Pick these too early – or even at what might be regarded elsewhere as a normal level of ripeness – and the wines will seem lean, tart and hard. But that acid can be the key to thrilling flavours if you are brave enough and patient enough to delay your harvest, because as the sugar builds and builds in the grape, the acid keeps the juice marvellously fresh and the resulting wines are some of the most approachable and irresistible flavours in Bordeaux. The top producers in St-Émilion have known this for some time. They can get good prices for their wines and so can take the risk with delaying the harvest. But Castillon-Côtes de Bordeaux next door was traditionally regarded as little more than a Bordeaux Supérieur. Their prices were only a fraction of a leading St-Émilion. They couldn't take the risk. Not until now.

So what is Castillon? First there are two parts to Castillon-Côtes de Bordeaux – a low, flattish, rather clay-dominated area of vineyard down towards the Dordogne river near the town of Castillon itself. Wines from here have traditionally tasted a bit muddy and dull. But did they have to? Not all of them. There are reasonable streaks of gravel – a warm soil that

The château at d'Aiguilhe may be in ruins but the smart stonework on the gate portals should alert you to the fact there is another side to the property – spanking new winemaking facilities and a wine that is one of Castillon's stars.

OVERVIEW

Castillon-Côtes de Bordeaux is basically an extension eastwards of St-Émilion, and most of the best vineyards lie on the same limestone plateau as the St-Émilion côtes. This is now a star region, and some of the wines reflect it in their price, but there are still many excellent wines at affordable prices, similar to St-Émilion in style, able to be drunk young but capable of ten years' aging. Francs-Côtes de Bordeaux is a small, high but sunny corner of Bordeaux just north of Castillon-Côtes de Bordeaux. There aren't all that many properties but they're worth seeking out because they have really interesting mineral, herb and blackcurrant flavours to drink young or to age five to ten years.

WINES TO TRY
Castillon-Côtes de Bordeaux
- Dom. de l'A
- Ch. d'Aiguilhe (also second wine Seigneurs d'Aiguilhe)
- Ch. Ampélia
- Ch. de Belcier
- Ch. Blanzac
- Ch. Cap de Faugères
- Ch. Castegens, Sélection Première
- Ch. Clarière Laithwaite
- Ch. Clos l'Église
- Clos Les Lunelles
- Clos Puy Arnaud
- Ch. Côte Montpezat
- Ch. Fontbaude
- Ch. Grand Tertre
- Ch. Grand Tuillac (also Cuvée Elegance)
- Ch. Joanin-Bécot
- Ch. Manoir du Gravoux
- Ch. Montlandrie
- Ch. Moulin de Clotte, Cuvée Dominique
- Ch. Picoron
- Ch. de Pitray
- Ch. Poupille, Poupille
- Ch. Robin
- Ch. Roque le Mayne
- Ch. Ste-Colombe
- Ch. Terrason
- Ch. Valmy Dubourdieu-Lagrange
- Ch. Veyry
- Vieux Ch. Champs de Mars

will ripen your grape without leaving a muddy mark on the palate. But that's not where the action is. That's not why some of the smartest money in St-Émilion has been buying up and developing properties in Castillon. They're all after the other Castillon, the high Castillon away from the Dordogne, and the great ridge of limestone that makes the St-Émilion côtes so special, and continues right through Castillon, west to east.

To show you how attractive this Castillon soil is, let's get in the car. We've been driving east along the D245 right at the foot of the slopes of the St-Émilion côtes as they twist and turn in and out of the limestone. Through St-Laurent-des-Combes, through St-Étienne-de-Lisse, with classy-looking vineyards flowing down the slopes, and then we turn north looking for the exciting new-wave St-Émilion Ch. Faugères. It's perched on a knoll in the middle of a wide valley. Look over to the east, and you can see earthworks, new terracing, new vineyards and buildings, so we drive around to approach Faugères from that side, except now the road sign doesn't say Faugères, it says Cap de Faugères – and that's not a St-Émilion wine, it's a Castillon-Côtes de Bordeaux – but it's still pointing back to the same knoll in the middle of the valley! Without realizing, without seeing any change in the geology, we've left expensive St-Émilion and crossed into little-known Castillon-Côtes de Bordeaux. Are the conditions the same? At Faugères, basically yes, yet one side of the vineyard is St-Émilion and one is Castillon-Côtes de Bordeaux. In fact, wherever the mighty limestone ridge makes its presence felt, the conditions are pretty much the same – either slopes tumbling down the face of the ridge strewn with shattered limestone, or broader acres up on the plateau with reasonably shallow soils on a bedrock of limestone. But the thing that has caused an explosion of development here is the price of the land. Because the wine can't use the chic St-Émilion name on the label, the price of land on these limestone outcrops and plateaux is far below that of St-Émilion – that's why there was so much development going on near Faugères on the eastern side of the valley. But you can make wine just as good and the methods you use and the grape varieties you employ in St-Émilion are valid here too. I've sometimes preferred the Cap de Faugères Castillon to the admittedly excellent Faugères St-Émilion. They're both star wines. And other leading St-Émilion producers have invested heavily here and are producing beautiful scented, sensual reds. Stephan von Neipperg of Canon-la-Gaffelière with his Ch. d'Aiguilhe, Beau-Séjour Bécot with their Joanin-Bécot, Gérard Perse of Pavie with his Clos L'Église. These are joining established names like Pitray and de Belcier in making Castillon a true force to be reckoned with – affordable and deliciously rich yet balanced wines – awfully like St-Émilion, in fact. There's just one thing. Those plateau vineyards are getting a bit high, sometimes touching on 100m (330ft) above sea level – that delays ripening. And the limestone is getting a little harder, making it a bit more difficult for the vines roots to penetrate and create that acid juice. You should probably wait 10–15 days after the harvest in the western end of St-Émilion to pick your grapes. With global warming this is more and more possible and with slightly lower limestone acidity we should see more lush Castillon-Côtes de Bordeaux reds every year. The best villages to look for in the small print on the label are St-Philippe d'Aiguille, Gardegan, St-Colombe, St-Genès-de-Castillon and Le Salles-de-Castillon. Belvès de Castillon has some nice softer styles.

FRANCS-CÔTES DE BORDEAUX

If you take the D123 north from St-Philippe d'Aiguille, after a kilometre or so, you'll see Ch. Puygueraud. Turn down the little road, drive past the château and then stop at a gap in the trees. You're absolutely on the edge of the limestone ridge. The little road slithers away beneath you to the north-east, into what seems to be a broad bowl of pale limestone and clay soil, covered in vines. This is Francs-Côtes de Bordeaux, a tightly packed little appellation of 534ha (1320 acres) that snuggle right up against the département border with the Dordogne. It's an area I'd tipped for stardom as long ago as the 1980s, based on its dry climate and the presence of several high-profile families from Pomerol and St-Émilion. They're still there, controlling châteaux like Puygueraud, Laclaverie and de Francs itself – and you only have to look at some of the other proprietors' names – Limbosch Zavagli, Moro, Holzberg – to realise that inward investment continues.

This charming property is Ch. Puygueraud, the leading light in the Francs-Côtes de Bordeaux appellation and able to produce rich, scented reds year after year. The first vintage I tried was the 1985 and it was so serious, yet succulent that I aged a bottle for 15 years – and it was still serious and succulent, which shows how beautifully balanced these wines are.

Yet the star status has proved elusive. Despite the dryness of the climate, many of these vineyards are fairly high and it can be a little cold. This would be fine if the soils were warm, but those pale limestone clays are relatively deep and relatively cool, which means the vines need a fair bit of help from man and nature to ripen fully. You stand down by the little village of Francs beneath its moribund ugly co-operative and you can see escarpments on three sides, yet most of the vines are on the heavier soils below them. It may be significant that the consistently finest property – Puygueraud – is perched on the escarpment, and other important properties like Laclaverie, de Francs and Marsau are all on high ground. Yet even the less successful properties make wine with really interesting flavours – not at all like 'me-too' St-Émilions. Minerals, herbs, melted butter, savoury softness, lush blackberry fruit ripeness – these are some of the flavours that Francs wines deliver, and as global warming has an increasing impact on Bordeaux in the 21st century, and given that the climate in this little corner of vines is about the driest in Bordeaux, allowing you to let your grapes hang until they are truly impressively ripe, we may yet see Francs claim its star status.

Francs-Côtes de Bordeaux
- Ch. Charmes-Godard
- Ch. Franc-Cardinal
- Ch. de Francs
- Ch. Laclaverie
- Ch. Marsau
- Ch. Nardou
- Ch. Pelan
- Ch. La Prade
- Ch. Le Priolat
- Ch. Puygueraud
- Ch. Vieux Saule

CADILLAC-CÔTES DE BORDEAUX

Now it's time to head south, over the Dordogne river and across the vast vineyard of the Entre-Deux-Mers to Cadillac-Côtes de Bordeaux on the right bank of the Garonne river. We may be on a different river, but once again it's limestone which makes the difference here. If you take the autoroute across the Garonne from the city of Bordeaux you'll see limestone cliffs jutting out above the flat alluvial riverside land. These are the front markers of Cadillac-Côtes de Bordeaux, and they stretch a good 60km (37 miles) from Bassens, north of Bordeaux, right down to St-Macaire opposite Langon at the southern end of the Graves. If you turn off just over the river and take the D10 or the D113 south, you'll be continually looking up to the cliffs to try to take your mind off the sullen ribbon developments and occasional drab basic AC Bordeaux vineyard strung along the muddy edge of the river. I don't blame you. Until you get to Langoiran, about 18km (11 miles) down the road, all the vineyard action is on the plateau behind the cliff face. There, the quality of the vineyard will largely depend on the depth of the soil and the absence of over-fertile loam soils. Shallow soils on the limestone bedrock can produce good reds at places like Cambes and Tabanac, though I often prefer the whites made under the simple Bordeaux AC. I suggest you get off the main roads, and drift through forest and meadow and vine, and keep looking to the south and the west as some of the views across the Garonne to the Graves and Sauternes will make you catch your breath with delight.

Lovely this may be, but it wine terms this isn't the most exciting part of the Cadillac-Côtes de Bordeaux. You should cut back to the river at Langoiran and here you'll notice a sudden change. North of Langoiran the cliff faces are steep with no vines. But south of here is a flowing vinescape of broad slopes rolling down to the river. Perfectly angled to the south-west, these look like pretty serious vineyards. Way back in the Middle Ages, some of them were. Some of them are now, and many more could be. If you've read the chapter on sweet wines (see pages 274–301), you'll already have come across this southern part of Cadillac-Côtes de Bordeaux, because the sweet wine appellations of Cadillac, Loupiac and Ste-Croix-du-Mont line the bank where the slopes are particularly steep. It's a struggle earning money from sweet wine nowadays and many of the top châteaux here are making pretty good dry wines in increasing quantities. But there's an anomaly in the appellation system here that makes no sense to me. Growers in Cadillac can claim the Cadillac-Côtes de Bordeaux appellation for their dry reds, but the guys in Loupiac and Ste-Croix have to make do with plain Bordeaux. It's hardly fair. Dry whites – and there are some serious wines here – come under the basic Bordeaux AC too.

Ch. Bauduc is the beautiful property that caught the eye of Gavin Quinney when he was wandering around Bordeaux with no great intention of buying a château. He did buy it, though, and has quickly turned it into a successful concern, selling red, white and rosé to private customers and top restaurateurs like Gordon Ramsay and Rick Stein.

In effect, Cadillac-Côtes de Bordeaux is the southern face of the vast Entre-Deux-Mers, but they're very different. In particular, the soils are different, the aspect to the sun is superior, the heat in the vineyards is greater and the ambition in growing the grapes is greater too. The soil is especially important. Much of Entre-Deux-Mers is composed of rich loamy soil. That's great for beetroot, potatoes or wheat. But it's far too fertile for the vine, especially if you're trying to make good red. Cadillac-Côtes de Bordeaux, on the other hand, has very little loam. What you've got is the same basic limestone as St-Émilion, a variety of clays including the thick blue clay that makes Pomerol so famous and, as you climb to the top of the slope, really gravelly soil 1.5–2m (60–80in) deep, as stony and lean as the famous Pessac-Léognan soils over the river Garonne. And when you get past these gravels and the thick, cloddish loam kicks in, that's the end of the appellation because it's the end of your chance of making good red wine on a regular basis. It's easy to see. If you drive up from Béguey past the excellent Ch. Reynon to Ch. Carsin, you'll be looking at a mix of limestones, clays and gravels. But as the road turns away after Carsin, the soil seems to lose its lustre. That's loam. And if you look on the vineyard map you'll see you've passed out of Cadillac-Côtes de Bordeaux and into Entre-Deux-Mers.

I still think Cadillac-Côtes de Bordeaux is a work in progress, not least because when you've got shallow soils over limestone, as many of these river-leaning slopes have, you must ensure you push for extra ripeness to counteract the acidity from the limestone. A lot of the reds still have a lean edge which lower yields and better viticulture could rectify, but remember, the southern part of Cadillac-Côtes de Bordeaux makes sweet whites. These rely on warmth and humidity in the vineyard to produce noble rot. Rot of any kind is a curse for reds, so some years, despite all your best intentions, you'll have to pick your red crop before it's really ready. Even so, the leading properties are finding a juiciness in their reds that is well suited to a bit of oak aging and which bodes well for the future.

ENTRE-DEUX-MERS OR BETWEEN THE RIVERS

But what of the future for Entre-Deux-Mers? Well, first let's look at its present and its past. This area is an 80-km (50-mile) wedge of land mainly between the rivers Garonne and Dordogne (that's where the name Entre-Deux-Mers – between two seas – comes from). It starts on the border of the Gironde *département*, and heads north-west, getting narrower and narrower as the rivers converge till it peters out on a spit of land north of Bordeaux just past Bourg. There are a whole load of vines here, and while some of the vineyards are charming and some of the landscape is a sylvan delight of tiny roads dipping and twisting through the forest, orchard and meadowland, placid streams glistening in the sun

---

Quick guide • Cadillac-Côtes de Bordeaux

OVERVIEW

This is the limestone-dominated area of slopes and plateaux on the right bank of the Garonne. The wines are inclined to be a little lean, but each year more producers come on the scene determined only to harvest fully ripe grapes and make wines of body and fruit. They benefit from up to five years' aging, especially the cuvées prestiges made by many of the châteaux.

WINES TO TRY
- Ch. Bauduc
- Ch. Carignan, L'Orangerie de Carignan
- Ch. La Caussade
- Ch. Chelivette
- Clos Bourbon
- Clos Ste-Anne
- Ch. Delord
- Ch. Le Grand Housteau
- Ch. Grand-Mouëys
- Ch. Les Guyonnets, Prestige
- Ch. Lamothe de Haux, Cuvée Valentine
- Ch. Laroche, Cuvée Edouard
- Ch. Lezongars (Special Cuvée also good)
- Ch. Mont-Pérat
- Ch. Plaisance
- Ch. de Plassan
- Ch. Puy-Bardens
- Ch. La Rame, La Charmille
- Ch. Reynon
- Ch. Ste-Marie, Alios de Ste-Marie
- Ch. Suau

The Entre-Deux-Mers is a land of rolling hills, dips and turns in the road, nestling villages – this is Verdelais near St-Macaire – and always vines. However, single châteaux are not so common, since most of the grapes are processed by giant co-operatives.

● Recommended wines produced in the Entre-Deux-Mers region can be found on pages 31–32. See also Best cuvée prestige wines on page 65, and Best producers on page 273 for recommended growers using the Entre-Deux-Mers AC.

and friendly villages with tree-lined squares and the lure of prix-fixe restaurants – it isn't all like that. Most of Bordeaux's basic wine comes from here, and though there are several supposedly smarter appellations – Graves de Vayres in the north, Haut-Benauge in the middle, St-Macaire in the south and Ste-Foy in the north-east – the majority of the wine is simply declared as AC Bordeaux. To create cheap Bordeaux – and you can find it for little more than a couple of euros in some of northern Europe's discount stores, while British supermarkets also offer a version for little more than £4 ($6) – you need vast economies of scale. Whenever you get anywhere near a production centre – and that, in Entre-Deux-Mers, means a big co-operative – you enter vineyard prairie-land. As far as the eye can see, vines. No châteaux, no road signs offering tastings and visits, no trees to brighten up the view, just a high, exposed rolling prairie of vines. You might like to visit the little towns of Rauzan and Sauveterre-de-Guyenne to see what I mean. And if you think those vines are spaced a bit more widely than usual, you're right. They are.

Nowadays pretty much every bottle of wine produced in the Bordeaux region has an appellation controlée label, but it wasn't always so. As recently as the 1960s, a large part of Bordeaux production was mere table wine – vin de table – and most of this was sweetish and white. In 1967 half the production was white, sugared up to a medium sweetness, dosed with sulphur and shipped off to northern Europe where it sold for very little money and made large numbers of people miserable. But to create these oceans of cheap wine, you had to employ the lowest-cost production method. So they ripped out all the old-fashioned, close-planted vines, and replanted with perhaps only a third of the number of vines, trained high on wires, so that everything could be done by machine. You don't think of Bordeaux as an agro-industrial place, but out here it is. A large amount of the Entre-Deux-Mers soil is rich, fertile loam. Well, if you've only got a third of the number of vines, you're going to want to triple the yield of grapes per vine. With rich loam soils you can triple the yield, but you can't ripen the fruit. Loam is a cold soil, these Entre-Deux-Mers vineyards are relatively high and one of the basic rules in wine is that to ripen a crop you must restrict the yield, not triple it.

You could just about get away with this if you were making sugared-up cheap whites – you can almost always push the yield of whites much higher than reds – but during the 1970s and '80s people got tired of these sickly whites and demanded reds. Cabernet Sauvignon was the sexy grape, so they converted these high-yielding wide trellises to Cabernet. Cabernet is a late-ripener and needs restricted yields and warm soils. No one wanted this thin, raw wine, and so, in the 1990s, fashion turned towards Merlot and the vineyards were largely replanted again – with Merlot. Now Merlot ripens early and can tolerate cool soils but you still need to restrict yields if you're going to make decent red. But the great limiting factor in the Entre-Deux-Mers is the price. The top Bordeauxs get more expensive every year. But the bottom end of the red wine market gets cheaper, and now has floods of competition from every corner of the globe. People want ripeness. Chile, Australia, California, Italy, Spain – they can offer ripeness at a low price. Bordeaux can't. It's reckoned that to pay workers to prune and care for traditional narrow-planted vineyards, to get some modern winemaking equipment, to buy some new barrels – not many, but a few – you need to be earning about €6 ($7) for every bottle that leaves the cellar door. Half of these wines are being sold in retail stores, after everyone's taken a cut, for way less than that. In big vintages, like 2004, when good producers had cut off over half the fruit during the summer to allow the remainder the chance to ripen properly, members of wine co-operatives all over the Entre-Deux-Mers were turning up at the winery with vast loads of unripe grapes because at the rock bottom prices their wines were getting, they couldn't afford to employ anyone to reduce their crops.

It's not easy out there in the Entre-Deux-Mers but there are rays of light. First, all these high-yielding Merlot vines could make very good rosé. There's a surge in demand for good, dry pink at the moment. It's cheaper to produce, doesn't need deep coloured, totally ripe grapes, and Bordeaux can do this style very well. One of Bordeaux's best – and most expensive rosés – is from the Entre-Deux-Mers – Ch. de Sours. There could be many others. Second, dry whites. There's been so much replanting of whites with reds that there's actually a shortage of decent white grapes. Entre-Deux-Mers is ideally placed to produce very attractive fresh whites and several estates already do so in big volumes. Ch. Bonnet, Ch. Thieuley, Ch. Tour de Mirambeau – they are all modern, committed, large-scale producers creating lovely zippy dry whites (as well as reds).

And there's another bright spot in the Bordeaux hinterland. Although much of the soil is too fertile and unsuitable for high quality wines, all over the region there are sudden eruptions of excellent soil just waiting for someone to come and give them the Rolls Royce treatment. Appellations are often big clumsy things that say if most of the soil isn't good then the whole region must be declassified into a basic appellation like AC Bordeaux.

But tell that to Monsieur Vatelot of Ch. de Reignac on the northern borders of the Entre-Deux-Mers. He's had his soil checked. If it was in the Haut-Médoc it would be good enough for a top Classed Growth and he could earn big sums per bottle. So he treats it like a top Classed Growth. The wine tastes fantastic – and he gets big sums per bottle for it. The appellation – as if it mattered – is AC Bordeaux. Tell that to the guys at Dourthe who are producing super, ripe, rich reds at Ch. Pey la Tour near Salleboeuf, a few kilometres south of Reignac. Tell that to Gavin Quinney whose delicious, succulent wines come from Ch. Bauduc near Créon and who numbers überchefs Rick Stein and Gordon Ramsay among his satisfied customers. These, and many others, are showing that where there's a will there's a way in Entre-Deux-Mers. And where there isn't a will, they should rip out the vines and plant potatoes.

Rosé is usually sold by the bottle for not too much money in the summer following the vintage. De Sours is different. It's sold by the case – *en primeur* – before it's even in the bottle, and the price will make you sip it rather than glug it back. And another thing. That's a screwcap at the top, not a cork.

Domaine de L'A

This is a high quality, new wave red from one of Bordeaux's leading wine consultants, Stéphane Derenoncourt.

DOMAINE DE L'A

Castillon-Côtes de Bordeaux AC

❊ *Merlot, Cabernet Franc, Cabernet Sauvignon*

This is the tiny 8-ha (20-acre) property of winemaking guru Stéphane Derenoncourt and his wife Christine, who run it biodynamically. The wines are aromatic and finely textured with good fruit expression. Best years: 2010, '09, '08, '06, '05, '04, '03, '01, '00, '99.

Château d'Aiguilhe

Outstanding Merlot-based, rich, sensuous wine from the same team who make top St-Émilion, Ch. Canon-la-Gaffelière.

CHÂTEAU D'AIGUILHE

Castillon-Côtes de Bordeaux AC

❊ *Merlot, Cabernet Franc*

Owned since 1998 by Stephan von Neipperg of La MONDOTTE and Ch. CANON-LA-GAFFELIÈRE fame, this 50-ha (124-acre) property has rapidly become the leading light in Castillon. Under the new ownership the vineyard has been overhauled and a spanking new circular cellar now sits alongside the spectacular ruins of the 13th-century château. The wines have a marvellous scented yet rich black cherry and blackcurrant fruit smoothed by oak, 80% of which is new each year. Seigneurs d'Aiguilhe is the topnotch second label. Best years: 2010, '09, '08, '07, '06, '05, '04, '03, '02, '01, '00, '99.

Château Bauduc

Les Trois Hectares is Bauduc's top, barrel-fermented white and is based on Sémillon vines planted in 1947.

CHÂTEAU BAUDUC

Cadillac-Côtes de Bordeaux AC

❊ *Merlot, Cabernet Sauvignon, Cabernet Franc*

❊ *Sauvignon Blanc, Sémillon*

'It's a dangerous thing for a young man to have too much cash in his pocket.' Gavin Quinney was talking about himself, because after he'd sold his shares in a computer business for really quite a lot of money, he was wandering around France, pockets full, and he woke up one morning to find he'd bought a château. The first thing his wife knew about this sudden urge to become a château owner was when he rang and said 'I've bought Ch. Bauduc. Sell the house in London and get down here. We've got a harvest to bring in.'

Well, it may have started off chaotically, but since the first vintage in 2000 the Quinneys have made Bauduc into a very smart operation, selling direct to consumers through mail order and the internet, and gaining regular listings with such star chefs as Gordon Ramsay and Rick Stein. The wine deserves it. Red, pink and white, they are utterly drinkable, each possessing a classic, mouthwatering Bordeaux texture and easy-going fruit. Special *cuvées* Les Trois Hectares Bordeaux Blanc white and Clos des Quinze Premières Cotes de Bordeaux red are serious oak-aged styles, but remain affordable. [By the way, there's also a lovely farmhouse you can rent and Gavin offers private wine tours to châteaux all over Bordeaux.] Best years: 2010, '09, '08, '06, '05, '04, '03, '02, '01, '00.

Château Bel-Air La Royère

This is big, dense, oaky wine and rather international in style from Blaye's top winemaking village of Cars.

CHÂTEAU BEL-AIR LA ROYÈRE

Blaye-Côtes de Bordeaux AC, Blaye AC

❊ *Merlot, Malbec, Cabernet Sauvignon*

Rich, dark, smooth and spicy, this modern-style Bordeaux has led the way in reinvigorating Blaye. Charentais couple Xavier and Corinne Loriaud bought the property in 1992 but things only got exciting with the 1997 vintage. Also look out for the good value, soft, fruity Ch. Les Ricards produced from younger vines grown on sandy-gravel soils. Best years: 2010, '09, '08, '06, '05, '04, '03, '02, '01, '00, '99.

Château Bonnet

Pessac-Léognan specialist, André Lurton makes large quantities of this high-quality dry white at Ch. Bonnet.

CHÂTEAU BONNET

Entre-Deux-Mers AC

🍇 *Merlot, Cabernet Sauvignon*

🍇 *Sauvignon Blanc, Sémillon, Muscadelle*

Located at Grézillac in the north of the Entre-Deux-Mers, Ch. Bonnet is the region's pioneering estate for quality and consistency. The best wines are white, and the owner, André Lurton of La LOUVIÈRE fame, makes large volumes of good, fruity, affordable Entre-Deux-Mers as well as Bordeaux AC rosé and red. The reds can be a little lean, but the barrel-aged Merlot-Cabernet Réserve is quite serious and needs three to four years' aging. A special *cuvée*, Divinus, was launched in 2000. Best years: (Réserve) 2010. '09, '08, '06, '05, '04.

Château Brulesécaille
This full, ripe style of red is made in large quantities (80,000 bottles every year).

CHÂTEAU BRULESÉCAILLE

Côtes de Bourg AC

🍇 *Merlot, Cabernet Sauvignon, Cabernet Franc*

🍇 *Sauvignon Blanc*

This is a lovely 26-ha (64-acre) vineyard high on the limestone plateau and is just the kind of site the Romans would have planted. Mentioned in the 1868 edition of the Bordeaux 'bible' Cocks et Féret as a Cru Bourgeois of the Côtes de Bourg, this estate continues to produce well-crafted wine. The name Brulesécaille refers to the burning of the vine cuttings following pruning. The red is ripe, rich with a hint of toasted oak and can age up to five or six years. There's also quite a decent white. Best years: 2010, '09, '08, '06, '04, '03, '02, '01, '00.

Château Bujan
This earthy, dry red is typical of the Côtes de Bourg but this one has enough depth to benefit from a few years' aging.

CHÂTEAU BUJAN

Côtes de Bourg AC

🍇 *Merlot, Cabernet Sauvignon, Cabernet Franc*

A hilly, south-facing vineyard provides good growing conditions. Firm, solid with earthy red fruit and just a hint of oak, the wines from this 17-ha (42-acre) property are reliable and foursquare. Best years: 2010, '09, '08, '05, '04, '03, '01, '00.

Château Cap de Faugères
The quality of this succulent, scented red with loads of black plum fruit shows why Castillon is a region buzzing with new investment.

CHÂTEAU CAP DE FAUGÈRES

Castillon-Côtes de Bordeaux AC

🍇 *Merlot, Cabernet Franc, Cabernet Sauvignon*

Cap de Faugères is the sister property to Ch. Faugères (and *garage* wine Péby Faugères) in neighbouring St-Émilion but has its own winemaking facility. They have both benefitted from the enormous investment and commitment given by Péby and Corinne Guisez and from new owner Swiss industrialist, Sylvio Dentz, from 2005. Cap de

Faugères is a dark, fruity, full-on wine and sometimes develops cedar scent with age. Best years: 2010, '09, '08, '06, '05, '04, '03, '02, '01, '00.

Château Carignan
Prima is Ch. Carignan's big, dense, oaky prestige cuvée and it usually needs a few years of aging to soften.

CHÂTEAU CARIGNAN

Cadillac-Côtes de Bordeaux AC

🍇 *Merlot, Cabernet Sauvignon, Cabernet Franc*

Owned by Belgian Philippe Pieraerts until 2007 and now by an American wine importer, this 65-ha (160-acre) estate has made immense strides since 1998. There are three principal *cuvées*: the fruity, accessible L'Orangerie de Carignan, the ripe, modern Ch. Carignan and the rich, lavish, chocolaty Prima aged in 100% new oak barrels. The latter needs three or four years' bottle aging, but not for the first time I find myself thinking I actually prefer the lighter, more refreshing damson- and lily-scented L'Orangerie as a style. And it's much cheaper, too. Best years: 2010, '09, '08, '06, '05, '04, '03, '02, '01, '00.

Château Les Charmes-Godard

Les Charmes-Godard produces juicy, mouthwatering wines from the high, cool vineyards of the Francs plateau near St-Émilion..

CHÂTEAU LES CHARMES-GODARD

Francs-Côtes de Bordeaux AC

❋ *Merlot, Cabernet Franc*

❋ *Sémillon, Sauvignon Gris, Muscadelle*

A tiny 6-ha (15-acre) property, Les Charmes-Godard is owned by the Thienponts of Ch. PUYGUERAUD. The barrel-fermented white (a rarity in the Côtes de Francs) is rich, fat and aromatic with balancing acidity while the high percentage of Merlot in the red makes for a juicy, charming mouthful. Best years: (reds) 2010, '09, '08, '07, '06, '05, '04, '03.

Château Charron

The red premium cuvée, Les Gruppes, is a powerful, round, oak-dominated wine for drinking at over 3–5 years.

CHÂTEAU CHARRON

Blaye-Côtes de Bordeaux AC

❋ *Merlot, Cabernet Sauvignon*

❋ *Sémillon, Sauvignon Blanc*

Charron is part of a huge portfolio of properties, including Ch. de la Roulerie and de Fesles in the Loire, owned by the Germain-Saincrit family. The regular *cuvées*

are decent if unspectacular but the lush, barrel-fermented white Acacia and rich, modern, oak-dominated red Les Gruppes (in an absurdly heavy bottle) have got more to them. Best years: (reds) 2010, '09, '08, '06, '05, '04, '03.

Château Clos L'Église

This rich, ripe, powerful, modern wine is more obviously a Gérard Perse-style of wine than a typical Côtes de Castillon.

CHÂTEAU CLOS L'ÉGLISE

Castillon-Côtes de Bordeaux AC

❋ *Merlot, Cabernet Sauvignon, Cabernet Franc*

Gérard Perse of St-Émilion Premier Grand Cru Classé Ch. PAVIE also owns this 16-ha (40-acre) estate in the Côtes de Castillon. It gets the same type of treatment as Ch. Pavie and is another wine that stands out from the Castillon crowd. Best years: 2010, '09, '08, '06, '05, '04, '03, '02, '01, '00, '99.

Clos Puy Arnaud

This is a powerful style of Castillon with a tannic backbone for reasonable aging and good wedges of dark fruit.

CLOS PUY ARNAUD

Castillon-Côtes de Bordeaux AC

❋ *Merlot, Cabernet Franc, Cabernet Sauvignon*

This biodynamic estate has been in the vanguard of top Castillon properties since 2000. The wines have an elegance of fruit, balance and firm but fine tannins. Best years: 2010, '09, '08, '06, '05, '04, '03, '02, '01, '00.

Château Falfas

Ch. Falfas is one of the few properties in Bordeaux run on biodynamic principles. The wine is dense and needs a few years' aging.

CHÂTEAU FALFAS

Côtes de Bourg AC

❋ *Merlot, Cabernet Sauvignon, Cabernet Franc, Malbec*

Biodynamic estate making concentrated, structured wine that needs four to five years to soften and is best in warm years. Le Chevalier is a Cabernet Sauvignon-dominated *cuvée* from 80-year-old vines that is chunky but good. Best years: 2010, '09, '08, '06, '05, '04, '03, '02, '01, '00.

Château de Fontenille

This is an attractive green apple, coffee bean and green leaf crunchy style of white for drinking young – just what Entre-Deux-Mers should be.

CHÂTEAU DE FONTENILLE

Entre-Deux-Mers AC

❋ *Merlot, Cabernet Franc, Cabernet Sauvignon*

❋ *Sauvignon Blanc, Sémillon, Muscadelle, Sauvignon Gris*

Stéphane Defraine makes consistently good value, fresh, aromatic whites and fruity

Bordeaux reds and clairet at this 25-ha (62-acre) estate at La Sauve just east of Créon. Drink the wines young.

Château Fougas

Maldoror is the top wine from Ch. Fougas and has some almost treacly oak richness in warm years, but a most digestible creaminess in cooler years.

CHÂTEAU FOUGAS
Côtes de Bourg AC
❊ *Merlot, Cabernet Sauvignon*

Fougas Maldoror is the top wine at this 17-ha (42-acre) estate north-east of Bourg and represents 80% of the production. Modern winemaking produces a rich, almost treacly red with a hefty dose of oak. Best years: 2010, '09, '08, '07, '06, '05, '04, '03, '02, '01, '00.

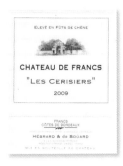

Château de Francs

The Les Cerisiers cuvée has good deep blackberry and plum fruit and a fine mineral streak and is one of the best wines in the Francs appellation.

CHÂTEAU DE FRANCS
Francs-Côtes de Bordeaux AC
❊ *Merlot, Cabernet Franc, Cabernet Sauvignon*

Hubert de Boüard of top property St-Émilion Premier Grand Cru Classé Ch. ANGÉLUS is a part owner here. The regular

cuvée is always attractive, usually nicely layered with ripe, red and black fruit and some minerality; the ripe, exotic, 100% new oak, barrel-aged Les Cerisiers is more than a notch above. Best years: 2010, '09, '08, '06, '05, '04, '03, '02, '01, '00.

Château Gigault

Cuvée Viva is a pretty rich, stewed plum style of wine, but it is balanced and it works.

CHÂTEAU GIGAULT
Blaye-Côtes de Bordeaux AC
❊ *Merlot, Cabernet Sauvignon*

Ch. Gigault has a lengthy history but the first vintage of the superior Cuvée Viva, now 75% of the production, was 1998. This is a fairly dense, fruit-accented wine, fine for drinking early on but with considerable aging potential, too. Best years: 2010, '09, '08, '07, '06, '05, '04, '03, '02, '01, '00, '99, '98.

Château Grand-Moueys

Bright, fresh, juicy clairet – Bordeaux should make more of these fun-coloured, deep rosés.

CHÂTEAU GRAND-MOUEYS
Cadillac-Côtes de Bordeaux AC
❊ *Merlot, Cabernet Sauvignon, Cabernet Franc*
❊ *Sémillon, Sauvignon Blanc, Muscadelle*

Large 90-ha (222-acre) estate producing sound, drinkable, medium-bodied reds which always used to have just a bit more focussed dark fruit than their neighbours, and still do, despite increasing competition. There is also fruity clairet and fresh, clean whites. Reds are for drinking over three to four years. Best years: 2010, '09, '08, '05, '04.

Château Haut Bertinerie

Haut-Bertinerie is a pioneering property in Blaye making serious, ageworthy though approachable wood-aged reds and whites.

CHÂTEAU HAUT BERTINERIE
Blaye-Côtes de Bordeaux AC
❊ *Merlot, Cabernet Sauvignon, Cabernet Franc*
❊ *Sauvignon Blanc, Sauvignon Gris, Muscadelle*

A pioneering estate with lyre trellising in the vineyard and new €6-million ($7,600,000) cellar complex, Haut Bertinerie leads where others in the region should follow. The fresh, fruity, easy-drinking *cuvées* of red and white are labelled Ch. Bertinerie while Ch. Haut Bertinerie is reserved for a more complex, barrel-fermented white, full of refreshing coffee bean and nectarine fruit, and a spicy, ripe, plum- and cherry-scented red. Best years: (reds) 2010, '09, '08, '07, '06, '05, '04, '03.

Château Haut-Macô

The regular cuvée is a bright dry style of wine with an attractive hint of blackcurrant at the finish.

CHÂTEAU HAUT-MACÔ
Côtes de Bourg AC

Merlot, Cabernet Sauvignon, Cabernet Franc

The Mallet brothers have made this a consistent property. There's a firm, fruity regular *cuvée* and the richer, longer-aging Cuvée Jean-Bernard, aged in 100% new oak barrels. Best years: 2010, '09, '08, '06, '05, '04, '03, '01, '00.

Château Les Jonqueyres

Packed with dark, damson, blackcurrant and blackberry fruit, this wine can be drunk young or aged for at least 5 years.

CHÂTEAU LES JONQUEYRES
Blaye-Côtes de Bordeaux, Blaye AC

Merlot, Cabernet Sauvignon, Malbec

This is an ambitious château: quantities from the 14-ha (35-acre) vineyard are limited and the wines are best reserved *en primeur* –

amazing for a Blaye wine! The wine is Merlot-dominated and always dense, ripe and bursting with dark fruit. There is also 0.5ha (1 acre) in the Côtes de Bourg AC from which owner Pascal Montaut produces the Clos Alphonse Dubreuil, a dark, super-ripe red. Best years: 2010, '09, '08, '07, '06, '05, '04, '03, '02, '01, '00.

Château Laclaverie

This is an attractive dry but scented and nicely balanced wine that benefits from aging for 4–5 years.

CHÂTEAU LACLAVERIE
Francs-Côtes de Bordeaux AC

Merlot, Cabernet Franc, Cabernet Sauvignon

This estate is owned by the Thienponts, as are Ch. PUYGUERAUD and Les CHARMES-GODARD. A greater percentage of Cabernet provides a subtle, aromatic nuance and reasonable ageability, but a little less satisfying weight than in the Puygueraud. Best years: 2010, '09, '08, '05, '04, '03, '02, '01, '00.

Château Lezongars

Lively, fruit-driven wines are the style here produced under a range of labels. The top reds are big, plummy, attractively oaky and can be drunk young or aged for 5 years or so.

CHÂTEAU LEZONGARS
Cadillac-Côtes de Bordeaux AC

Merlot, Cabernet Sauvignon, Cabernet Franc

Sauvignon Blanc, Sémillon

Ex-British owner Philip Iles shook up this property at Villenave-de-Rions when he acquired it in 1998. The Special Cuvée and L'Enclos du Château Lezongars are the top red selections (Ch. Lezongars is the regular *cuvée*) and while they're a bit 'international' in style, I don't think that that's really a criticism in the Cadillac-Côtes de Bordeaux area because it's up to each different proprietor to create a style of wine they like. None really existed before. The Ch. de Roques label is used for a further red and a crisp, 100% Sauvignon Blanc white.

At the beginning of 2012 the Iles family sold up to new Chinese owners, yet another sign of the ever increasing links between Bordeaux and the Chinese market. Best years: (reds) 2010, '09, '08, '06, '05, '04, '03.

Château Marjosse
Attractive soft red for easy drinking made by the master of Cheval Blanc.

CHÂTEAU MARJOSSE

Entre-Deux-Mers AC, Bordeaux AC

⚜ *Merlot, Cabernet Sauvignon, Cabernet Franc, Malbec*

⚜ *Sauvignon Blanc, Sémillon, Muscadelle*

This is where high flier Pierre Lurton likes to lay his head at night – after spending his days in the vinous stratosphere running both top flight Ch. d'YQUEM and CHEVAL BLANC. Luckily, Marjosse is situated about half way between the two of them, and it's a charming, relaxing place, typical of many properties in the Entre-Deux-Mers – just what Pierre needs when, in his spare moments, he makes instantly drinkable, value for money reds and whites. Drink young – and remember, this is what the guy from Cheval Blanc and Yquem has for his Sunday lunch.

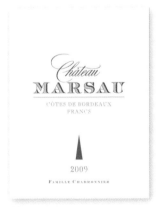

Château Marsau
This wine is a mighty 14.5% alcohol number that manages to be chocolate-rich now yet promises perfume and plummy ripeness in 5 years.

CHÂTEAU MARSAU

Francs-Côtes de Bordeaux AC

⚜ *Merlot*

This is the property of Jean-Marie Chadronnier, recently retired CEO of CVBG-Dourthe Kressmann. The wine is 100% Merlot – and it shows in a lush, glyceriny style that still keeps hold of its mineral core. Prélude is the lighter, young-vines offering. Best years: 2010, '09, '08, '07, '06, '05, '04, '03, '02, '01, '00.

Château Mercier
Mercier's grapes grow on a good gravelly ridge and the Cuvée Prestige adds oaky power to ripe, well-balanced fruit.

CHÂTEAU MERCIER

Côtes de Bourg AC

⚜ *Merlot, Cabernet Sauvignon, Cabernet Franc, Malbec*

Christophe Chety is the 13th generation to run this family-owned estate. The regular release is a very attractive, fresh and fruity red while the Cuvée Prestige is considerably more powerful and oaky. Best years: 2010, '09, '08, '05, '04, '03.

Château Mondésir-Gazin
This Blaye red is a deep, savoury wine from well-sited vineyards on limestone soil overlooking the Gironde at Plassac.

CHÂTEAU MONDÉSIR-GAZIN

Blaye-Côtes de Bordeaux AC, Blaye AC

⚜ *Merlot, Cabernet Sauvignon, Malbec*

Marc Pasquet arrived from Brittany, via a spell at Ch HAUT-MARBUZET in St-Estèphe, in 1990 and has since made Mondésir-Gazin one of Blaye's leading domaines. The wines are rich and firm, with a deep, serious, savoury ripeness to them. Ch. Mondésir is the second wine. There's also a powerful, chunky Côtes de Bourg called Haut-Mondésir. Best years: 2010, '09, '08, '07, '06, '05, '04, '03, '02, '01, '00.

Château Nardique la Gravière
These are fresh but full-bodied wines for drinking young – they are delicious and a good example of Entre-Deux-Mers.

CHÂTEAU NARDIQUE LA GRAVIÈRE

Entre-Deux-Mers AC

⚜ *Merlot, Cabernet Franc, Cabernet Sauvignon*

⚜ *Sémillon, Sauvignon Blanc, Muscadelle*

Ch. Nardique la Gravière has 20ha (50 acres) devoted to vines at St-Genès-de-Lombaud. Lively, round, fruity whites are the staple. The reds are soft and light for early drinking.

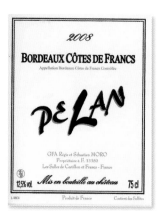

Château Pelan

This dark, full, ripe wine is slightly international in style but its fairly tannic structure means that it will age well.

CHÂTEAU PELAN

Francs-Côtes de Bordeaux AC

🌿 *Cabernet Sauvignon, Merlot*

Pelan grows an unusually high percentage of Cabernet Sauvignon (80%) for the Francs region and this gives its wine a minty, blackcurrant aroma but also a fairly tannic structure and a dark, closed but ripe style. Pelan is owned by the Moro family of VIEUX CHÂTEAU CHAMPS DE MARS in the Castillon-Côtes de Bordeaux. Best years: 2010, '09, '08, '05, '04, '03, '01, '00.

Château Plaisance

Alix is a powerful but scented red wine from the Magrez stable.

CHÂTEAU PLAISANCE

Cadillac-Côtes de Bordeaux AC

🌿 *Merlot, Cabernet Sauvignon, Cabernet Franc*
🌿 *Sémillon*

The purchase of this 28-ha (70-acre) property at Capian by Philippe Magrez, son of Ch. PAPE-CLÉMENT's Bernard Magrez, in 2005 has meant a big change in management and direction. There are now only three wines produced: two fruit-driven reds, Tradition and the more structured Alix and a barrel-fermented, pure Sémillon white (also called Alix) which needs three or four years' bottle age. Best years: (reds) 2010, '09, '08, '07, '06, '05, '04, '03.

Château Poupille

The top cuvée, Poupille, is a pretty big mouthful but the oak and richness are well-handled and it is best kept for 4–6 years.

CHÂTEAU POUPILLE

Castillon-Côtes de Bordeaux AC

🌿 *Merlot, Cabernet Franc*

Poupille is the Merlot-dominated (99%) top cuvée at this well-known Castillon property in Ste-Colombe, representing 40–60% of the production. The wine is rich and concentrated with fine oak, giving it a touch of elegance and polish. Best years: 2010, '09, '08, '07, '06, '05, '04, '03, '02, '01, '00.

Château Puy-Bardens

Puy-Bardens' Cuvée Prestige is not as dense as some other examples but nevertheless it is still well covered by oak.

CHÂTEAU PUY-BARDENS

Cadillac-Côtes de Bordeaux AC

🌿 *Merlot, Cabernet Sauvignon, Cabernet Franc*

The Cuvée Prestige is this property's reliable mainstay. The Merlot provides soft, round fruit and the Cabernet Sauvignon a minerally freshness and light but firm structure. It's best at three to five years old. Best years: 2010, '09, '08.

Château Puygueraud

Year after year this is the Francs' region top wine – scented with rich plum fruit and a slight brush of herbs.

CHÂTEAU PUYGUERAUD

Francs-Côtes de Bordeaux AC

🌿 *Merlot, Cabernet Franc, Cabernet Sauvignon, Malbec*

George Thienpont acquired Ch. Puygueraud, perched precariously on the rim of the Francs bowl, in 1946. The vineyards were in ruins and for 30 years he turned the land over to mixed farming. The vines were replanted in 1979 and the first vintage produced in 1983.

Now run by one of George's sons, Nicolas Thienpont (cousin Alexandre is responsible for VIEUX-CHÂTEAU-CERTAN), it is without doubt the leader of the pack in this small but interesting appellation. Cabernet Sauvignon and Cabernet Franc used to make up to 50% of the blend. These varieties almost always ripen here – not always easy in the cool Francs soils – and this allows the wine to slowly develop a lovely cooked plum, rich depth with the rasp of herbs and the lilt of flowers. In 2005 the Cabernet Sauvignon was ripped up and replaced with Cabernet Franc. Rich but serious, the wine can age for 10–20 years and is one of the best value fine wines in Bordeaux. A special Cuvée George with an important percentage of Malbec was introduced in 2000. Best years: 2010, '09, '08, '06, '05, '04, '03, '02, '01, '00.

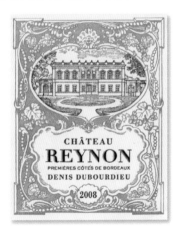

Château Reynon
Fresh, bright minerally whites made by one of Bordeaux's great white wine innovators, Professor Denis Dubourdieu.

CHÂTEAU REYNON

Cadillac-Côtes de Bordeaux AC
❀ Merlot, Cabernet Sauvignon
❀ Sauvignon Blanc, Sémillon

This leading Cadillac-Côtes de Bordeaux château is owned by the brilliant and influential enology professor, Denis Dubourdieu. It's not just the excellent wine. Try and wheedle a visit if you can because Dubourdieu is one of the most erudite and

informative guides to the vagaries of Cadillac-Côtes de Bordeaux region that you could wish to meet.

You may well have tried the tangy, refreshing, minerally dry whites already – they're well distributed and often a beacon of light on a bad wine list. The reds often need a few years to show their delicious blackcurrant and raspberry fruit and creamy texture to best advantage, but that soft, creamy texture means you can drink them as soon as they're bottled. Ch. Reynon no longer produce a sweet Cadillac wine (see page 295). Best years: (reds) 2010, '09, '08, '07, '06, '05, '04, '03.

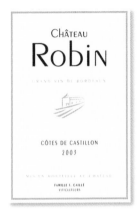

Château Robin
This is a good example of what the Côtes de Castillon can do so well – round harmonious reds that can take a few years of aging.

CHÂTEAU ROBIN

Castillon-Côtes de Bordeaux AC
❀ Merlot, Cabernet Franc, Cabernet Sauvignon

A new owner arrived at Ch. Robin in 2004 but the winemaking team remained the same and the wines (reds only) are as consistent as ever. They are round and harmonious and drinkable at four to six years. The property is sited on some of the highest land in Castillon. Best years: 2010, '09, '08, '07, '06, '05, '04, '03, '02, '01, '00.

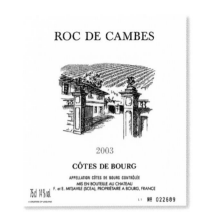

Château Roc de Cambes
Sour cherry syrup, ripe earth and lush creamy texture make this brilliant wine enjoyable now or able to take at least 10 years' aging.

CHÂTEAU ROC DE CAMBES

Côtes de Bourg AC
❀ Merlot, Cabernet Sauvignon, Cabernet Franc, Malbec

This is a wonderful property tumbling down the limestone slopes outside the town of Bourg and the land forms a natural amphitheatre with the vines catching all the heat from the sun and the Gironde estuary below. François Mitjavile, the poet-philosopher of Bourg who also runs Ch. TERTRE-RÔTEBOEUF in St-Émilion, bought this 10-ha (25-acre) jewel in 1988 and has worked ceaselessly to make it the star of the Bourg appellation.

The wines are dark and glyceriny, full of cherry sweetness and lush texture yet never quite losing the flavour of the stones where the vines grow. Domaine de Cambes from vines by the estuary is also very good. Best years: 2010, '09, '08, '07, '06, '05, '04, '03, '02, '01, '00, '99, '98.

Château Roland la Garde

The Grand Vin is quite a mighty mouthful even from cooler vintages and will benefit from at least 4 years' aging.

CHÂTEAU ROLAND LA GARDE

Blaye-Côtes de Bordeaux AC
❋ *Merlot, Cabernet Sauvignon, Malbec*

Bruno Martin has given a new lease of life to this family property in Blaye. They produce three *cuvées*: the rich, yet savoury Tradition, a barrel-aged Prestige and Grand Vin, a dark, concentrated, Pomerol-style wine aged in 100% new oak barrels that needs three or four years' bottle aging. Best years: 2010, '09, '08, '05, '04, '03, '01, '00.

Château Ste-Marie

This bright ripe white has wonderful fruit intensity and freshness and is quintessential Entre-Deux-Mers.

CHÂTEAU STE-MARIE

Entre-Deux-Mers AC
❋ *Merlot, Cabernet Sauvignon, Petit Verdot*
❋ *Sauvignon Blanc, Sémillon, Muscadelle*

Owned by the Dupuch-Mondon family since 1956, Ch. Ste-Marie is at Targon in the centre of the Entre-Deux-Mers. If all Entre-Deux-Mers was as consistently good as this example the appellation would have no problem selling its wine. Run by the Dupuch brothers, Gilles and Stéphane, Ste-Marie also produces the more complex, white barrel-

fermented Madlys, as well as an excellent Cadillac-Côtes de Bordeaux red called Alios. This is full of dark, cassis and plum fruit and floral perfume unusually matched by a salty, savoury earthiness that makes for a very interesting style. Cadillac-Côtes de Bordeaux is a bit of a work in progress for reds, but these guys are doing well. Best years: (reds) 2010, '09, '08, '07, '06, '05, '04, '03.

Château Suau

Dry but attractively balanced red from an equal blend of Merlot and Cabernet Sauvignon, tinged with a little chocolaty oak.

CHÂTEAU SUAU

Cadillac-Côtes de Bordeaux AC
❋ *Merlot, Cabernet Sauvignon, Cabernet Franc*
❋ *Sauvignon Blanc, Sémillon, Muscadelle*

Over the last 20 years Monique Bonnet has invested a lot of time, energy and money to keep Ch. Suau up to scratch. (Don't confuse this Suau based at Capian with Ch. Suau in Barsac across the Garonne.) The Cuvée Prestige is the top red and it's good stuff, ripe but dry with attractive, chocolaty oak. The Bordeaux Blanc Sec is barrel-fermented and pretty classy stuff. Best years: (reds) 2010, '09, '08, '05, '04, '03, '02, '01.

Château Tour de Mirambeau

Cuvée Passion is a stupendous white, packed with flavours of peach, nectarine and coffee bean. It could easily pass for a top Pessac-Léognan.

CHÂTEAU TOUR DE MIRAMBEAU

Entre-Deux-Mers AC
❋ *Merlot, Cabernet Sauvignon*
❋ *Sauvignon Blanc, Sémillon, Muscadelle*

The Despagne family own 300ha (740 acres) and six different properties in the Entre-Deux-Mers. The white wines have always been excellent value and have led the way in the area with their tangy fruit and clean fresh styles.

The reds have proved more difficult, and though they get better each year, they are still far outclassed by the whites. A case in point is the Cuvée Passion from the flagship estate, Tour de Mirambeau. The white is stupendous and far outstrips the red. Cadillac-Côtes de Bordeaux Ch. Mont-Pérat is a serious wine but much rounder and riper after advice from Michel Rolland. The micro-cru Girolate, from a single, densely planted plot, made with every modern technique you can think of, is powerful, turbo-charged and at last beginning to match power with very attractive fruit. When the harvest weather is suitable there's also a Noble Sémillon which is rich, pineappley and honeyed.

Château des Tourtes

This is a good example of the gentle style of red from northern Blaye – deep damson fruit and a whiff of perfume.

CHÂTEAU DES TOURTES

Blaye-Côtes de Bordeaux AC, Blaye AC
❋ *Merlot, Cabernet Sauvignon*
❋ *Sauvignon Blanc*

Ch. des Tourtes is a Blaye estate right up on the Charentais border, offering wines with a lovely soft texture and a modern emphasis on fruit. Cuvée Prestige has round, ripe, black fruit and sometimes a touch of leafy acidity while Attribut des Tourtes is richer and more intense. The barrel-fermented Sauvignon Blanc is a lovely, creamy, citrussy mouthful. Best years: (reds) 2010, '09, '08, '06, '05, '04, '03.

Château Turcaud

Drink this Entre-Deux-Mers young for its bright scented green fruit. The Turcaud reds are soft and fruity and also for early drinking.

CHÂTEAU TURCAUD
Entre-Deux-Mers AC

❊ *Merlot, Cabernet Sauvignon, Cabernet Franc*

❊ *Sauvignon Blanc, Sémillon, Muscadelle*

A reliable name in the Entre-Deux-Mers, Maurice Robert bought Turcaud in 1973 while working as estate manager for André Lurton (of Ch. BONNET). He is now ably assisted by his daughter, Isabelle, and son-in-law, Stéphane. The whites, both the classic and barrel-fermented Cuvée Majeure, are fine and aromatic, the reds soft and fruity.

Château Veyry

Exciting rich yet savoury red from the Côtes de Castillon with some good tannin allowing a few years' aging.

CHÂTEAU VEYRY
Castillon-Côtes de Bordeaux AC

❊ *Merlot*

Enologist Christian Veyry works alongside Michel Rolland but in his spare time makes this intense but polished Castillon-Côtes de Bordeaux. Production is tiny but the wine with its thrilling blackberry richness, appetizing acid and tannin balance and whiff of cedar is highly recommended if you can find a bottle. Best years: 2010, '09, '08, '06, '05, '05, '04, '03, '01, '00.

Vieux Château Champs de Mars

The regular cuvée has ripe, black plum fruit sprinkled with a peppery spice and is ready for drinking after several years' aging.

VIEUX CHÂTEAU CHAMPS DE MARS
Castillon-Côtes de Bordeaux AC

❊ *Merlot, Cabernet Franc, Cabernet Sauvignon*

Régis Moro has been one of the pillars of Castillon for some time (see also Ch. PELAN). The regular *cuvée* is round and supple while the special *cuvée* Johanna is more structured and intense. Best years: 2010, '09, '08, '06, '05, '05, '04, '03, '02, '01.

Quick guide • Best producers

BLAYE AC, BLAYE-CÔTES DE BORDEAUX AC
Bel-Air la Royère, Bois-Vert, Cailleteau-Bergeron, Cap St-Martin, Charron, Confiance, La Croix du Prieuré, Frédignac, Gigault, Grand Barrail, Les Grands Maréchaux, Haut Bertinerie, Haut-Colombier, Haut-Grelot, Haut-Sociando, Haut-Terrier, Cave des Hauts de Gironde, Les Jonqueyres, Loumède, Monconseil Gazin, Mondésir-Gazin, Montfollet, Roland la Garde, La Rose Bellevue, Segonzac, Tourtes.

CÔTES DE BOURG AC
Bousquet, Brulesécaille, Bujan, Clos Alphonse Dubreuil (see Les Jonqueyres), Le Clos du Notaire, Falfas, Fougas, Les Graves de Viaud, Haut-Guiraud, Haute Libarde, Haut-Macô, Haut-Mondésir, Labadie, Lamblin, Macay, Martinat,

Mercier, Roc de Cambes, Rousselet, Tayac, Tour de Guiet, La Tuilière.

CASTILLON-CÔTES DE BORDEAUX AC
Domaine de L'A, Aiguilhe, Belcier, Blanzac, Cap de Faugères, Castegens, Clos l'Église, Clos Puy Arnaud, Côte Montpezat, Fontbaude, Grand Tertre, Grand Tuillac, Manoir du Gravoux, Montlandrie, Moulin de Clotte, Picoron, Pitray, Poupille, Roque Le Mayne, Robin, Ste-Colombe, Terrason, Valmy Dubourdieu-Lagrange, Veyry, Vieux Château Champ de Mars.

FRANCS-CÔTES DE BORDEAUX AC
Les Charmes-Godard, Franc-Cardinal, Francs, Laclaverie, Marsau, Nardou, Pelan, La Prade, Puygueraud, Vieux Saule.

ENTRE-DEUX-MERS AC
Bonnet, Fontenille, Marjosse, Nardique la Gravière, Ste-Marie, Tour de Mirambeau, Turcaud.

CADILLAC-CÔTES DE BORDEAUX AC
Bauduc, Brethous, Carignan, La Caussade, Chelivette, Clos Bourbon, Clos Ste-Anne, Delord, Le Grand Housteau, Grand-Mouëys, Laroche, Les Guyonnets, Haux, Lamothe-de-Haux, Lezongars, Mont-Pérat, Plaisance, Plassan, Puy-Bardens, La Rame, Reynon, Ste-Marie, Le Sens, Suau.

Millésime
2004
Anonymat

Loupiac Blanc

323

Sweet White Wines

The production of fine sweet wine is an exhausting, risk-laden and extremely expensive affair, requiring nerves of steel, a huge bank balance and just the right mix of grape varieties, vineyard sites and local climatic conditions – especially local climatic conditions. When you're making dry red wines or dry white wines, nowadays a good vineyard manager and winemaker can react and respond to most weather conditions – hot or cold, wet or dry – and come up with good to excellent wines. But when you're making great sweet wine, you're much more at the mercy of the weather gods. You need a particular mixture of humidity and warmth, of foggy mornings and sunny afternoons in September and October, to encourage the formation of a rare, beneficial fungus called 'noble rot', which dramatically intensifies the sweetness in the grapes and allows you to make rich dessert wines. Most areas of the world don't have any regions where noble rot regularly develops, but Bordeaux has half a dozen localities where, to a greater or lesser extent, the vineyards and the climate get it right. Greatest of these are Barsac and Sauternes. Just north of the town of Langon, the little river Ciron sidles up from the south to join the river Garonne and creates the foggy yet warm vintage conditions that allow the grapes to rot nobly. On the Ciron's east bank lie the vineyards of Sauternes and on its west bank those of Barsac. There are other neighbouring areas who make sweeties, albeit to a less high level. Adjoining Barsac to the north is Cérons, whose speciality is a light sweet white and on the opposite bank of the Garonne are Cadillac, Loupiac and Ste-Croix-du-Mont whose speciality is also sweet white, but whose vineyards rarely produce anything of the concentration of a good Barsac or Sauternes. It's the little river Ciron that makes all the difference, and only Barsac and Sauternes have it.

I love the golden allure of these bottles, magnified by the rays of sunlight. But they're not here just to please me. These samples of sweet wines from the 2004 vintage in Loupiac are lined up for tasting by the appellation committee, who will reject any that don't make the grade.

SPOTLIGHT ON
Sweet white wines

The time to visit the Sauternes vineyards is in the autumn when the leaves of the vines turn as golden as the wine – and they may still be picking the last berries off the vines.

I think my last trip to Sauternes was the first time I hadn't got hopelessly lost. Normally I'm on the phone about an hour after the tasting was supposed to have started, bleating that I'm going round in circles and will someone please come and collect me from the middle of goodness knows where. It's one of those deeply rural parts of France where all the roads keep coming back to the same place and as the sun starts to fade to the west you begin to doubt your safety and your sanity. But on this latest trip I acquired a highly skilled local driver, patient beyond belief as I meticulously tried to piece together the patchwork of fields and streams, low hills and high stands of poplars that make up the region of Sauternes. And it all started to make sense.

Now, for anyone of a certain age, the very mention of the word Sauternes brings back bilious memories of a garish yellow liquid, sweet but heavy with sulphur, which was usually Spanish, always cheap and always filthy. Imitation may be a sincere form of flattery, but caricature is not. What this Spanish hooch was caricaturing was Sauternes sweet wine made from grapes grown in one very specific area of South-West France, just 40km (25 miles) south-east of the city of Bordeaux. And the name Sauternes had been adopted by the Spanish because when it was good, real Sauternes was the greatest sweet wine in the world. It wasn't good all

Quick guide • Sweet white wines

LOCATION
The classic sweet wine appellations of Sauternes and Barsac are in the south of the Graves region, close to the river Garonne and, importantly, its tributary the Ciron. Cérons lies immediately to the north-west, while further vineyards look on from the sunny hillsides across the Garonne in the appellations of Cadillac, Loupiac and Ste-Croix-du-Mont.

APPELLATIONS
Sauternes and Barsac are renowned for sweet wines made from grapes affected by noble rot. Cérons produces a lighter, less unctuous sweet style and wines from the côtes appellations of Cadillac, Loupiac and Ste-Croix-du-Mont range from very simple and rustic to reasonably rich and liquorous. Although these appellations are only for sweet

wines, an increasing number of vineyards in all but the best sites of Sauternes and Barsac also make dry reds and whites, often labelled Bordeaux AC.

GRAPES
Sémillon, the variety most susceptible to noble rot, is blended with much smaller amounts of Sauvignon Blanc, and sometimes a little Muscadelle, which is most useful in vintages when there is little noble rot to intensify flavours.

CLIMATE
Sauternes and Barsac are milder and wetter than Graves. The crucial factor for the growing of grapes for sweet wine is the combination of early morning autumnal mists rising off the Garonne and the Ciron rivers and plentiful sunshine later in the day – humidity and warmth being ideal conditions for promoting noble rot.

SOIL
The common theme here is clay with varying mixtures of gravel, sand and limestone. All the best Sauternes properties have considerable amounts of gravel mixed with clay whereas Barsac has shallow, sandy soil over limestone. Both Sémillon and Sauvignon Blanc vines can do well in all these conditions.

ASPECT
The landscape ranges from moderately hilly around the villages of Sauternes, Bommes and Fargues to lower, virtually flat land towards the river Garonne in the villages of Barsac and Preignac. The côtes areas across the Garonne are steeply sloped and south-facing, so the grapes see less of the morning mists and achieve their sweetness thanks more to shrivelling by the sun than to noble rot.

that often – and there were legions of drab, stale, mucky bottles with authentic Sauternes labels on as well – but when the weather conditions were right, and the human passion was evident, the wine was superb. And unique. You could only make wine of this character, majesty and lushness in a couple of thousand hectares sitting on the left bank of the river Garonne, and bisected by the tiny Ciron river. Ah, now we're starting to get to the nub of things but before we start talking about the Sauternes vineyards and grape varieties, let me make it clear that there's no such thing as Spanish Sauternes any more – the EU has long since put a stop to such cavalier labelling of wines. But there is far more of the real thing, made to a far higher standard than anyone can remember.

NOBLE ROT – PART ONE

The main grape in Sauternes is called Sémillon, which produces a waxy style of wine when ripe enough. The Sauvignon Blanc is there to add a bit of freshness and zip. And sometimes you'll find a bit of Muscadelle, largely because it can add a musky fruit depth to the wine in average years. But these grapes are grown all over Bordeaux and they make dry wine. How do you get super-sweet wine from them? You cajole and cherish and caress them with all the devotion a grape grower can muster, of course – until they go rotten on the vine. I mean it. If you want to make great Sauternes sweet wine you've got to encourage your grapes to rot. But this is a very special kind of rot, called noble rot, and one of the only places in the world it regularly appears is in Sauternes.

There are numerous sorts of rot, and virtually all of them destroy your grape and ruin your harvest. Except noble rot, which wine people have known about for so long it's even got a Latin name – *Botrytis cinerea*. This magic fungus actually intensifies the sweetness of your grapes without making them go sour. Given the right conditions – and I'll come back to those later – the spores land onto the skin of the grape and gradually weaken it so that if you have warm, humid autumn weather, the skin starts to shrivel, the water content of the grape is dramatically reduced and the sugar content and the glycerol and acidity are intensified. These grapes look horrible, and they feel sludgy and slimey – but close your eyes, ease one off the vine and pop it into your mouth. You'll never have tasted a more memorably honeyed, syrupy sweet grape. And memorable, honeyed, syrupy sweet wine is what they'll produce.

Now this explanation of how to create Sauternes was never going to be simple – and I've not finished with the tricky stuff yet. This richness of sugar might be twice the level you could achieve through natural ripening,

Above: The cold waters of the little Ciron river are the reason why Barsac and Sauternes can make such fine sweet wines.

Below: Ch. Rieussec on a misty harvest morning with the sun just breaking through. In September and October humid overnight and early morning fogs, followed by long, hot sunny afternoons and evenings are crucial for the development of noble rot.

SAUTERNES AND OTHER SWEET WHITE WINE REGIONS

TOTAL DISTANCE NORTH TO SOUTH 18KM (11MILES)

 VINEYARDS

N

● CHÂTEAUX FEATURED ON PAGES 286–297

WHERE THE VINEYARDS ARE The heart of sweet winemaking in France is the strip of land that runs along both sides of the river Ciron in the centre of the map. The Sauternes vineyards are spread over five communes, and one of these, Barsac, can call its wine either Barsac or Sauternes. The mesoclimate that creates noble rot is all important. Barsac is relatively flat, and relies upon its proximity to the Ciron and the Garonne for the noble rot conditions to develop. Preignac is also fairly flat, but its major property – Ch. Suduiraut – is on a small hillock right next to Sauternes' greatest property, Ch. d'Yquem. All the top properties in Bommes, Fargues and Sauternes itself are spread over little hillsides. They get the benefit of noble rot in the autumn and better conditions to produce ultra-ripe grapes. The result is wines of a more intense, luscious character. The map also shows Bordeaux's other sweet wine areas: Cérons and across the Garonne in Cadillac, Loupiac and Ste-Croix-du-Mont.

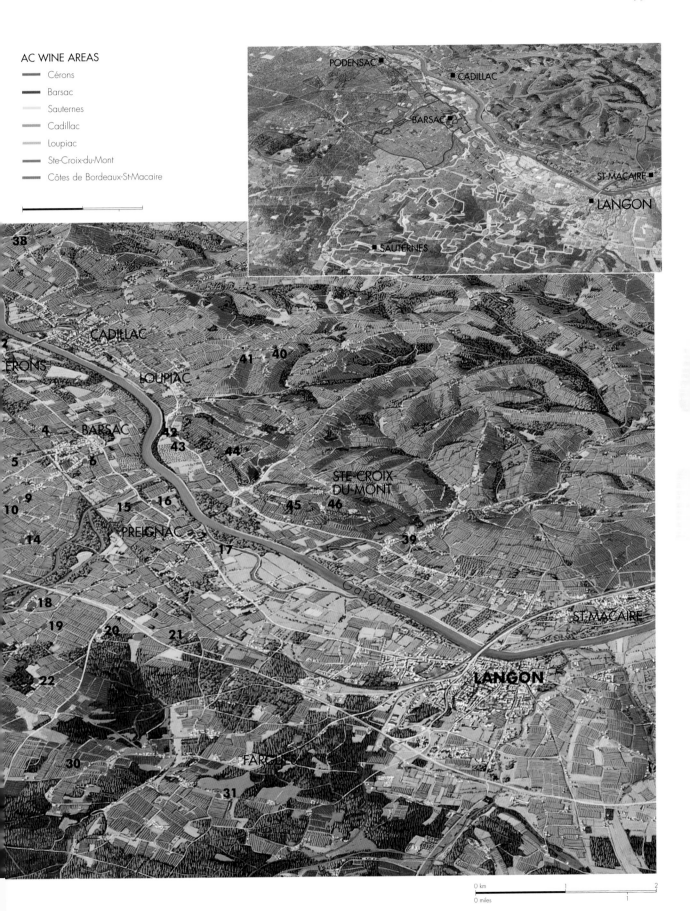

AC WINE AREAS

- ▬ Cérons
- ▬ Barsac
- ▬ Sauternes
- ▬ Cadillac
- ▬ Loupiac
- ▬ Ste-Croix-du-Mont
- ▬ Côtes de Bordeaux-St-Macaire

PODENSAC

CADILLAC

BARSAC

ST-MACAIRE

LANGON

SAUTERNES

38

CADILLAC

CÉRONS

LOUPIAC

41 40

BARSAC

4

5   6

42

43

44

9

10

14

15   16

STE CROIX
DU-MONT

45   46

PREIGNAC

17

39

18

Garonne

ST MACAIRE

19

20   21

LANGON

22

30

FARGUES

31

0 km   1   2
0 miles   1

Look at the difference in colour between the younger wine, the 2001 on the right, and the 1996 on the left. Sauternes gradually becomes darker with age and the flavour changes from bright, fruity and sweet to something much deeper, full of barleysugar, honey and marmalade. Really old Sauternes can be deep orange in colour and still taste luscious.

and it's this level of sugar in the grapes that determines the potential alcohol in the wine. Since yeasts convert sugar into alcohol, noble-rotted Sauternes grapes might have the sugar level for a potential alcohol anywhere between 20 and 25 per cent. But the yeast can't work at levels above 14 to 15 per cent alcohol, it simply suffocates in the heady alcoholic turbulence of its own frantic activities and sinks lifeless to the bottom of the vat. So all the sugar that the yeast failed to convert stays in the wine as sweetness. This is the only way to naturally produce the excessively high sugar levels which allow you to create superbly liquorous sweet wine. Without attack by the noble rot, the great sweet wines of Sauternes would not exist.

CLIMATE CHANGE

Ready for a bit more vineyard chat? Well, vineyard and climate. Sauternes can be made inside the boundaries of five small villages – Sauternes itself, Fargues, Bommes, Preignac and Barsac. Most of the wines embrace the Sauternes title, but Barsac wines can call themselves either Barsac or Sauternes. To be honest, it doesn't really matter. What does matter is one swirling stream of ice-cold water, water that has risen in a deep chilly spring and runs its short but energetic course through the thick forest of the Landes, and is never warmed by the rays of the sun until it turns away from the woodland for its last few miles and surges through the vineyards of Sauternes and out into the mighty Garonne. This sliver of a stream is called the Ciron, and it's seriously cold. By the end of summer the Garonne isn't cold, its leisurely flow has been continually warmed by the sun, and the collision of the two very different temperatures at the mouth of the Ciron

---

Classic wine styles • Sauternes & Barsac

OVERVIEW

Quite simply the greatest sweet wines in the world, these gems hail from a few treasured pockets of land in the southern Graves. Here the vineyard sites and climate strike the perfect balance to produce grapes intensified to heavenly sweetness by the presence of noble rot. The wines are expensive and risky to produce, so inevitably command a high price even before the laws of supply and demand take over for the leading properties.

TASTING NOTE

These are wines of deep, mouth-coating richness, full of flavours of pineapples, peaches, apricots, barleysugar, syrup and spice. All this is smoothed over with a gooily indulgent creamy nuttiness until a tingle of acidity freshens your mouth up for the next sip.

WHEN TO DRINK

Enjoy wines from unclassified properties somewhere between five and ten years from the vintage. The better the château, the longer the wait, and the greater the reward. Fifteen to 20 years will bring the best to their peak, and they'll stay right up there for decades to come.

BEST YEARS

2010, '09, '07, '05, '03, '02, '01, '99, '98, '97, '96, '95, '90, '89, '88, '86, '83.

AFFORDABLE WINES TO TRY

Some of these wines are from less well-known or less well-situated properties, while others are second labels of the smart châteaux. In good vintages these wines can be really tasty.

• Ch. d'Arche-Lafaurie (second wine of Ch. d'Arche)
• Ch. Bastor-Lamontagne
• Ch. Broustet

• Ch. Cantegril
• Castelnau de Suduiraut (second wine of Ch. Suduiraut)
• Ch. Fontebride (second wine of Ch. Haut-Bergeron)
• Ch. Haut-Bergeron
• Ch. Haut-Bommes (second wine of Clos Haut-Peyraguey)
• Ch. Haut-Grillon
• Ch. Haut-Mayne
• Ch. Les Justices
• Ch. Laville
• Ch. Liot
• Ch. de Myrat
• Ch. St-Amand
• Ch. St-Marc
• Ch. de Ste-Hélène (second wine of Ch. de Malle)
• Ch. Simon

For more ideas see pages 285 and 297

creates morning mists that spread back up the Ciron and across the vineyards that flank the stream. So long as the autumn is warm and the rainclouds hold off, every day dawns to reveal this blanket of cold, cottony mist that has crept up the rows of vines during the night, and by about lunchtime the sun should have blazed its way through the mist and burnt it all away. So now the vineyards are hot, but all the humidity left by the mists makes the air as clammy and stifling as a Turkish bath. I've been in the vineyards in late September, sweat breaking out on my brow as if I were in the steam room. And rot breaking out all over the bunches of grapes. This rare mixture of cold misty mornings and warm autumn sunshine makes the perfect conditions for the sugar-concentrating noble rot. There are other areas of Bordeaux, some only a few kilometres from Sauternes, that make sweet wines, but they don't get the same perfect conditions, and their wines are never as sweet.

Yuk. It's difficult to believe that these foul, furry grapes that look like a space invader from Alien will go to make up Ch. d'Yquem, Bordeaux's greatest sweet wine. But that horrible fungal growth is crucial – without it the grapes would never get sweet enough. The grapes in the bottom picture don't look quite so disgusting – just shrivelled and dried out but they've been attacked by noble rot too and will make excellent liquorous wine.

NOBLE ROT – PART TWO

I say 'perfect conditions'. Well, this would imply that noble rot breaks out on the vines all at once, that the lush richness develops evenly across the vineyard and that you just sit and wait for the perfect moment to pick. But nature's not like that. Some days the autumn sun doesn't shine, some days it may rain, some vines are young, others old, some are in a dip in the ground, others on slopes, all factors which will affect the development of noble rot. And in any case, there are three stages to this noble rot infection. The first is the 'speckled grape' phase where the grape is fully ripe and sweet but the juice isn't yet fully concentrated. Then there's the 'full rotted' stage – when the colour quickly changes to purple brown and the grape seems to collapse in on itself as it loses most of its water content. You can make really good wine from these grapes. But it gets better. If you're brave and the autumn weather stays sunny and warm even as winter looms, the grapes reach a third stage – the 'roasted' stage, shrivelled and covered in fungus. The sugar and acids concentrate into a syrup, the glycerol shoots up, and finally you've got grapes that can give the dramatic flavour of a great Sauternes. But at what cost!

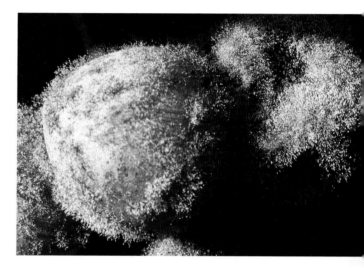

DEVOTION TO THE CAUSE

If you're determined to make memorable stuff, you're going to want as many of these 'roasted' berries as possible. There are some very favourable years when the

Picking grapes off each bunch with the right amount of noble rot requires great skill and concentration. Look how the grapes in the basket are totally shrivelled, while many still on the vine haven't yet fully rotted. This picker is in the vineyards of Ch. d'Yquem.

pendulum swing between misty mornings and bright sunny afternoons is so regular that whole bunches of grapes shrivel up and rot at the same rate. Then you can just snip off the bunches whole. Even so, the entire vineyard never gets to this level at precisely the same time and you'll have to keep an army of pickers ready to go through the vines several times with precise instructions about how to recognize fully rotten bunches. Of course, if you're less ambitious, the pickers can be less choosy and they can go through the vineyards fewer times. This means you'll probably be mixing fully rotten grapes with less affected and therefore less sweet ones. Your wine will be less profound as a result.

But you can also afford to sell it more cheaply. The very best properties are sufficiently concerned about quality that they tell their pickers that if necessary they must harvest the crop grape by shrivelled grape. They must go through the vineyards again and again looking for the single berries that are sweet and rotted enough. This is particularly relevant in less good years when the arrival of the noble rot spores in the vineyard has been erratic and the infection of the grapes very patchy. In years like this, you'll hardly ever find full bunches perfect for plucking, and you'll have to separate single good berries from loads that aren't good enough. Your pickers might have to go through the vines ten or a dozen times, painstakingly picking off the best berries. And even that might not be enough. You might taste the wine and realize that despite all the effort the quality isn't there and you can't release it under your property's label. This has happened several times at the great Ch. d'Yquem, Sauternes' leading property. In 1972 the pickers passed through the vines 11 times vainly seeking decently rotted grapes and after all that effort, none of the wine was thought good enough to be released.

So you see what I mean about cost. Sometimes these pickers have to be kept on hand – and paid – well into November. Sorties into the vines during December are not unheard of. Also,. think how little liquid those bunches of grapes are giving you. You might only get a single glass of wine per vine at a top château. If you were making top red wine you'd expect more like a bottle per vine at least. And just as with the top red wine properties you're going to have to buy dozens if not hundreds of new oak barrels in which to ferment and store the wines. The costs all add up.

A POISONED CHALICE

This should, of course, mean that these great sweet wines are sold for many times more money than equivalent top reds. But it doesn't work like that. Sauternes is a wine of fashion. Sometimes the glitterati of the world can't get enough of it. There were times in the 19th century when top Sauternes was Bordeaux's most expensive wine, and the Imperial Tsars of Russia were obsessed enough with truly rich wines to keep the price high. But more recently any attempts to create a substantial interest in Sauternes wine has fallen short. Sometimes, as with the superb 2001 vintage, interest from collectors and connoisseurs is high and the golden nectar sells quickly and well. But interest fades just as fast and even at the top properties you hear tales of owners being unable to shift a bottle of the less trumpeted vintages like 2002 or '04.

So perhaps they shouldn't bother making sweet wines. What about a dry red or white? Well, some of the properties do make dry white, rarely of exciting quality, and a couple make pretty drab reds. But let's consider. The Sauternes and Barsac appellations – for whatever they are worth – are only applicable to sweet white wines from low-yielding approved vines. So you'd have to title your wines simple 'Bordeaux'. That in itself is no longer such a problem. Every year sees more and more ambitious proprietors in less famous areas go to market with excellent red and white wines at quite steep prices that only sport the Bordeaux appellation. That quality speaks for itself is the self-evident message. But as I've been saying, the sweet wines of Sauternes and Barsac are special because of the cold misty mornings followed by hot humid afternoons. These conditions rot the grapes. And, the last thing you want if you're making dry reds or tangy, modern whites is even a hint of rot on your grapes. It doesn't work. So the producers here are stuck with the periodically poisoned chalice of making some of creation's greatest sweet wines, even in times when the world doesn't seem to want them.

CÉRONS

This cyclical disdain for fine sweet wine is painfully felt in Sauternes and Barsac, but there are other neighbouring areas who make sweeties, albeit to a less high level. One of the chief reasons that Sauternes and Barsac are so good at making noble-rotted sweet wines are those fogs spreading out from the little river Ciron. None of the other sweet wine areas border the Ciron, though they're not far away.

Cérons is directly north of Barsac, separated by the sweep of a bureaucrat's pen rather than by nature. Yet if you walk the Cérons vineyards near Barsac they do seem heavy and clayish, and as you suddenly discover a streak or two of gravel or an exposed patch of limestone, check your map and you'll realize you've strayed into Barsac, closer to the Ciron. And if you spent a week in late September in Cérons, each morning you could look across the Ciron to the clutch of low hills on the other bank, each hosting one of Sauternes' top properties, and you'd see them cloaked in fog long after your thin veil of mist has lifted in Cérons. Neither the soil nor the conditions are the same. Nor is the ambition. You're allowed to make 40 hectolitres of sweet wine per hectare in Cérons. In Sauternes you can only make 25 hectolitres, and all the good guys know that to excel you'll probably have to reduce that yield by half as much again. Fifty years ago most of Cérons made some sort of

This peaceful scene of the riverbank of the Garonne just below Cadillac. These old fishing boats do still bring in a daily catch, but it's the effect of the river and its little tributary, the Ciron, in creating autumn mists that is of more importance in the production of Bordeaux's sweet wine.

In the sweet wine areas across the Garonne from Barsac and Sauternes noble rot occurs less frequently so producers rely on their vines being planted on steep slopes to catch all the sun they can to shrivel the grapes and concentrate the sugar. These vineyards are in the Cadillac appellation and are just as likely to be used for dry white AC Bordeaux as sweet Cadillac.

sweet wine. Now just a handful of growers do, admittedly to a pleasant standard. But what Cérons has in its favour, unlike Sauternes and Barsac, is that it can label its dry red and white wines as Graves AC rather than just simple Bordeaux. Graves isn't the sexiest of appellations but, especially in stonier communes like Illats and Podensac, you can make pretty good reds and excellent dry whites. There is, by the way, another sweet appellation clustered round the Sauternes borders – Graves Supérieures – which can make pleasant semi-sweet wines, although production is on the decline.

OTHER SWEET WINE APPELLATIONS

It's a similar story on the right bank of the Garonne, although here a lot more producers have persevered with making sweet wine of some sort of quality, at least partly because they don't have a vaguely classy appellation like Graves to fall back on for their dry wines. So they had to persevere with sweet wines and there are just enough growers who near-as-dammit make wines as good as Sauternes. Even so, they are still an endangered species. There are three main appellations – Ste-Croix-du-Mont (the best), Loupiac (one or two bright spots) and Cadillac (mostly dull). There's also a Premières Côtes de Bordeaux appellation stretching up the right bank of the Garonne (now for sweet whites only, no longer for reds), but in all only about 200-ha (500-acres) of this medium sweet wine are declared. (Two other obscure appellations, Côtes de Bordeaux-St-Macaire and Ste-Foy-Bordeaux, reckon the market wants dry reds and whites, so that's mostly what they make.)

The border of Loupiac and Ste-Croix-du-Mont is almost directly opposite the mouth of the Ciron, so some of the autumn fogs that create noble rot in Sauternes and Barsac do manage to permeate these vineyards too. But whereas Barsac is almost flat and Sauternes has a series of hillocks for its best sites, at Loupiac the vineyards pull away quite steeply from the Garonne river, and at Ste-Croix-du-Mont the vines have to climb a cliff-like slope to the plateau on top. So the fog, which favours somewhere rather less vertically challenging like Sauternes or Barsac, only has an intermittent effect here. However, the best of these fairly steep vineyards can partially make up for noble rot not being all-invasive with their open, south-facing aspect. If the autumn sun shines, the power of the sun's rays can shrivel the grapes and concentrate the sugar. The flavours won't be as fascinating and beautiful as ones created by noble rot, but they're not a bad second best.

Yet in a time when even the top Sauternes wines don't find it easy to sell their wares, imagine how much more difficult it is for these country cousins. Even a seriously made Loupiac or Ste-Croix-du-Mont would be lucky to get half the price of a good Sauternes and greater effort in reducing yields, holding on for noble rot, employing pickers to make several passes through the vineyards, and the purchasing of expensive new oak barrels will only bring a reward of an extra two or three euros a bottle. So the investment in quality is rarely made, and so the chance of increasing your price is even more remote.

In Cadillac, which gets even less of the fog effect or the sun-shrivelling, I've found some decent wines, but only passingly sweet, which made me wonder when you'd drink them – perhaps as a sweetish aperitif, if those ever come back into fashion. Loupiac's general character is richer and waxier, with some good producers making generally sweet styles, especially in their prestige cuvées. Ste-Croix also has a small handful prepared to try to emulate their glittering, golden neighbours just across the Garonne in Barsac and Sauternes. But even on what are often attractive good-quality limestone soils, growers are increasingly turning to the production of dry reds and whites, and I can see why.

Quick guide • Lighter, less lush sweet wines

OVERVIEW
Sweet wine is produced throughout the Graves and between the Garonne and Dordogne rivers, although these days producers tend to prioritize making dry wines. The effects of noble rot are felt less often and less dramatically outside Sauternes and Barsac and many of these wines are made from grapes sweetened and intensified by the action of the sun alone. Like Sauternes and Barsac, these wines are based on Sémillon and Sauvignon Blanc, but are more likely to call on a little Muscadelle to add some richness and exotic spice to the blend.

TASTING NOTE
Compared with the famous sweet wines of Sauternes, these are lighter and less complex, and may be semi- rather than fully sweet. Flavours of peach and apricot are common, perhaps with a nicely honeyed sweetness. Wines from Cérons, Cadillac, Loupiac and Ste-Croix-du-Mont are less expensive alternatives to Sauternes and Barsac as they often see some noble rot and offer a degree of lusciousness and concentration.

WHEN TO DRINK
The lighter the wine, the sooner you should drink the bottles up. Freshness is important for semi-sweet bottles. Top Ste-Croix-du-Mont is the longest-lived of these wines and the best examples can develop for up to ten years from the vintage.

BEST YEARS
2010, '09, 05, '03, '02, '01, '99, '98.

SOME WINES TO TRY
Cérons
- Ch. de Cérons
- Grand Enclos du Ch. de Cérons
- Ch. Haura
- Ch. du Seuil

Cadillac
- Ch. La Bertrande
- Ch. Reynon
- Ch. Tanesse

Loupiac
- Ch. du Cros
- Ch. Dauphine-Rondillon
- Ch. Fortin
- Ch. Loupiac-Gaudiet
- Domaine du Noble
- Ch. de Ricaud
- Ch. Les Roques
- Ch. La Yotte

Ste-Croix-du-Mont
- Ch. Grand-Peyrot
- Ch. Mouras
- Ch. Loubens
- Ch. Lousteau-Vieil
- Ch. La Rame

For more ideas see page 297

Ch. Reynon used to produce a delicious Cadillac in suitable vintages. Production ceased after 2001 when Denis Dubourdieu took over from his father at Ch. Doisy-Daene and at Reynon he now concentrates on making good red and dry whites.

Château d'Arche

The d'Arche wines are Sémillon-dominated (up to 90%) and the result is a good, rich, beeswaxy style, fat and satisfying.

CHÂTEAU D'ARCHE

Sauternes AC, 2ème Cru Classé

Sémillon, Sauvignon Blanc

This estate, lying on some of the highest land in Sauternes, was revitalized after it was leased in 1981 to Pierre Perromat. Picking became essentially more selective, yields were kept low and a substantial proportion of the wine was aged in new oak.

New investors arrived in 1996 and the estate, now 40ha (99 acres) in size, has continued to progress. The result is a fat, full-flavoured Sauternes of considerable power. Good vintages can age for five to ten years. An extremely elegant bed-and-breakfast service operates from the 17th-century *chartreuse* (see page 88). Best years: 2010, '09, '07, '06, '05, '03, '02, '01, '99, '98, '97, '96, '90, '89, '88, '86, '83.

Château Bastor-Lamontagne

Year after year this large Sauternes estate produces luscious, honeyed wine typically showing fine botrytis character and ripe apricot fruit at a reasonable price.

CHÂTEAU BASTOR-LAMONTAGNE

Sauternes AC

Sémillon, Sauvignon Blanc, Muscadelle

There's no such thing as a good, cheap Sauternes. Good Sauternes is fiendishly expensive to make, the vineyard yield is low and the incidence of the sweetness-inducing noble rot erratic and unpredictable. There is one shining exception – Ch. Bastor-Lamontagne. This 56-ha (138-acre) property is on a good site in the commune of Preignac, just north of the great Ch. SUDUIRAUT. Time after time it produces luscious, honeyed wine at a price which allows you to wallow in the delights of high-class Sauternes without taking out a second mortgage (just). Second label: Les Remparts de Bastor. Best years: 2010, '09, '07, '05, '03, '02, '01, '99, '98, '97, '96, '95, '90, '89, '88, '86, '85.

Château Broustet

In the warm vintages the wine has a rich fruit and spicy oak with an intriguing peppery edge and enough balance to age further.

CHÂTEAU BROUSTET

Barsac AC, 2ème Cru Classé

Sémillon, Sauvignon Blanc, Muscadelle

This 16-ha (40-acre) estate in the centre of Barsac has greatly improved since the early 1990s. The wines tend to be fresh and of medium intensity but with tropical fruit notes and some honey. Fermented in stainless steel and partially aged in oak barrels, the wine will be delicious young or at any time up to about ten years, though wines from the best years can improve further. In 2010 the property was sold to Denis Merlaut of the family that owns CH. GRUARD-LAROSE. Best years: 2010, '09, '07, '05, '03, '02, '01, '99, '98, '97, '96, '95.

Château Caillou

I used to know Caillou because the local jazz maestro was the winemaker. It was pleasant then, it's pleasant now but the joint ain't jumpin'.

CHÂTEAU CAILLOU

Sauternes AC, 2ème Cru Classé

Sémillon, Sauvignon Blanc

The 13-ha (32-acre) family-run property is actually located in Barsac but uses the Sauternes label. The word *caillou* means pebble in French and the soil certainly has plenty of them. Older vintages are proof that this harmonious, medium-bodied wine can age successfully for many years. In top vintages (such as 1997, '99, '01 and 2003) a richer Special Cuvée is made labelled Cuvée Reine or Cuvée Prestige. Best years: 2010, '09, '07, '05, '03, '02, '01, '99, '98, '97, '96, '95, '90, '89, '88, '86, '85, '83.

Château de Cérons

When the conditions are good as in 2001 and '07, this is an attractive, elegant wine full of fresh fruit and golden syrup richness.

CHÂTEAU DE CÉRONS

Cérons AC

Sémillon, Sauvignon Blanc

The Perromat family have been *viticulteurs* in the Graves region since the 19th century and they have owned this 14-ha (35-acre) property since 1958. Winemaking follows the same principles as in Sauternes – successive *tries* through the vines to select botrytized grapes and then a long, slow fermentation and aging in barrel. With a healthy percentage of Sauvignon Blanc (35%) in the blend the wines are on the fresh, elegant side, sweet and full but never heavy. Best years: 2010, '09, '07, '05, '03, '02, '01, '99, '98, '97, '96, '95, '90.

Château de Chantegrive
A good example of gentle attractive Cérons that in the best years can be satisfyingly rich.

CHÂTEAU DE CHANTEGRIVE
Cérons AC
Sémillon, Sauvignon Blanc

This huge 94-ha (232-acre) estate is better known for its red and white Graves but in exceptional years it produces a little sweet Cérons, around 6,000 bottles per vintage. Most of the blend is Sémillon (90%) and the rest is Sauvignon Blanc. The wine has citrus and tropical fruit flavours and an appealing freshness on the finish. Best years: 2005, '01, '99, '95, '90.

Château Climens
The leading estate in Barsac, using rigorous selection to keep yields low, makes rich, elegant wines with a light, lemony acidity ensuring wonderful freshness.

CHÂTEAU CLIMENS
Barsac AC, Premier Cru Classé
Sémillon

For many years this has been Barsac's leading property. The 30-ha (75-acre) vineyard (run biodynamically since 2010) lies on the highest ground in the AC to the south-west of the village of Barsac, its vines coming to rather an abrupt end when they meet the A62 *autoroute* that runs between Bordeaux and Toulouse. This slightly higher altitude gives Climens a particularly well-drained vineyard and helps to account for its reputation as the most elegant and refined of all Barsac properties.

The wines are rich, luscious and exotic. They may not burst with the peach and pineapple fruit of some 'sweeties', but they make up for this with an exciting syrupy sweetness, a most appetizing, toasty, nutty, dry edge and a light, lemony acidity that keeps the wine fresh. They are easy to drink at five years old, but a good vintage will be much more succulent and fascinating after ten to 15 years. There's a lovely second wine called Cyprès de Climens which often has as much style as a Classed Growth itself. Best years: 2010, '09, '08, '07, '06, '05, '04, '03 '02, '01, '00, '99, '98, '97, '96, '95, '90, '89.

Clos Dady
Clos Dady is a good rich wine from a welcome, trendy new producer in Sauternes.

CLOS DADY
Sauternes AC
Sémillon, Sauvignon Blanc, Muscadelle

A passion for Sauternes led Catherine Gachet to give up her job as press attaché and take over her grandfather's vines in Preignac near Ch. BASTOR-LAMONTAGNE. A

smart move as the wines she produced were practically of Classed Growth quality, rich and honeyed but with balancing acidity and plenty of oak spice from barrel fermentation and aging. Good at five or six years but will age longer. Eli Ragimov, an Israeli based in Moscow, bought the property in 2011 and will hopefully continue the good progress. Best years: 2010, '09, '07, '05, '04, '03, '02, '01, '00, '99.

Château Clos Haut-Peyraguey
Clos Haut-Peyraguey is often rich, thick-textured and rather traditional in style, but nevertheless tasty and with good acidity.

CHÂTEAU CLOS HAUT-PEYRAGUEY
Sauternes AC, Premier Cru Classé
Sémillon, Sauvignon Blanc

Until 1978 these well-sited vineyards at the highest point of Bommes were part of Ch. LAFAURIE-PEYRAGUEY. It used to be better as an apéritif wine rather than as a rich dessert wine, but owner Jacques Pauly and now his daughter Martine have aimed for a more powerful, serious style. Barrel fermentation has given the wine greater complexity and structure, and recent vintages have been more concentrated without sacrificing finesse. Stylish whether drunk young or with ten years' age or more from a top vintage. Second wine: Ch. Haut-Bommes. Best years: 2010, '09, '07, '06, '05, '04, '03, '02, '01, '00, '99, '98, '97, '96, '95, '90, '89, '88, '86.

Clos Jean

This is usually a gentle, mellow wine, but in hot vintages can become concentrated and syrupy.

CLOS JEAN

Loupiac AC

🌿 *Sémillon, Muscadelle*

Seven generations of the Bord family have run this domaine on the high point of Loupiac overlooking the river Garonne. The wine never has the power and richness of Barsac and Sauternes across the river but it still has a gentle, apricot-flavoured concentration and lively acidity. Drink at three to four years. Best years: 2010, '09, '07, '05, '03, '02, '01, '99, '97, '96.

Château Coutet

Barsac's largest Cru Classé property makes sweet wines that are aromatic and complex with added concentration in recent vintages.

CHÂTEAU COUTET

Barsac AC, Premier Cru Classé

🌿 *Sémillon, Sauvignon Blanc, Muscadelle*

This is Barsac's largest Classed Growth property, with 38.5ha (95 acres) under vine. For over a century, until 1922, it was owned by the Lur-Saluces family of YQUEM fame.

Traditionally a close second to Barsac's

other First Growth, Ch. CLIMENS, Coutet was disappointing in the 1980s and early '90s. Luckily, vintages since 1995 have shown a return to form with wines of excellent balance and concentration. Coutet blends up to 20% Sauvignon with the Sémillon, producing a wine more delicate than powerful. Even so, the wines are aromatic and complex with notes of tropical fruits, honey and spicy oak and very suited to aging. In top years, a minuscule quantity of specially selected Cuvée Madame is produced – a wine that has few rivals when it comes to aroma and intensity and which can easily age for 15 years or more (last released vintage of this is the 1995). Best years: 2010, '09, '07, '06, '05, '03, '02, '01, '00, '99, '98, '97, '96, '95, '90, '89, '88.

Château du Cros

Ch. du Cros does get proper botrytis infection in top years and makes good peach and apple syrupy wines.

CHÂTEAU DU CROS

Loupiac AC

🌿 *Sémillon, Sauvignon Blanc, Muscadelle*

Only selected grapes from certain parcels of the 40-ha (99-acre) vineyard go into the Ch. du Cros Loupiac wine. The rest are used for the very good Bordeaux dry white and red. For the Loupiac, fermentation is in stainless steel followed by a further selection to pick the best wines for 12 months' aging in barrel. In this way there's some complexity and concentration, the wines taking on a floral aspect in youth which moves on to confit fruit with 10–15 years' bottle age. Best years: 2010, '09, '07, '05, '03, '02, '01, '99, '97, '95, '90.

Cru Barréjats

Wines like this are evidence that the Sauternes region is alive and kicking and attracting new blood and new ideas. These rich, oaky wines seem to age well.

CRU BARRÉJATS

Sauternes AC

🌿 *Sémillon, Sauvignon Blanc, Muscadelle*

Cru Barréjats is the realization of a dream of owners Doctors Mireille Daret and Philippe Andurand. From 6ha (15 acres) of vines located in Barsac, richly botrytized wines are produced under the Sauternes AC label. The first vintage was 1990. The grapes are hand picked in successive passages, or *tries*, through the vines, then pressed in an old vertical hydraulic press. The juice is fermented and the wines aged in 100% new oak barrels. Rich and aromatic, the first vintages already rank in quality with the Classed Growths and have a long aging potential. Second wine: Accabailles de Barréjats. Best years: 2010, '09, '07, '05, '04, '03, '02, '01, '00, '99, '98, '97, '96, '95, '94, '90.

Château Doisy-Daëne

Delicious, rich, balanced wine, honeyed but streaked with lemon and with round, waxy texture.

CHÂTEAU DOISY-DAËNE

Sauternes AC, 2ème Cru Classé
Sémillon, Sauvignon Blanc

Since 1989, the wines from this 17-ha (42-acre) neighbour to the great Ch. CLIMENS have been stunning. This is a consistently good Barsac estate, though it uses the Sauternes AC, and is made almost exclusively from Sémillon – rich, powerful and bursting with tropical fruit flavours.

Owner Denis Dubourdieu's recipe for success has been low yields, successive selective picking, and vinification and aging in oak barrels. The wines are beautiful to drink young, but will happily age ten years or more. In top years such as 2003 and '05 an infinitesimally small amount of super-rich Sauternes from individually picked botrytized grapes is produced under the label Extravagant. Doisy-Daëne Sec, made essentially from Sauvignon Blanc and sold under the Bordeaux AC, is a dry, perfumed, full-bodied white for early drinking. Best years: 2010, '09, '07, '05, '04, '03, '02, '01, '99, '98, '97, '96, '95, '90, '89.

Château Doisy-Dubroca

Doisy-Dubroca always keep a lemony scent and freshness, despite aging to barley sugar richness over 10–15 years.

CHÂTEAU DOISY-DUBROCA

Barsac AC, 2ème Cru Classé
Sémillon

With just over 3ha (7 1/2 acres) of vines Doisy-Dubroca is the smallest of the Sauternes Classed Growths. The production is trifling (barely 6000 bottles per vintage) but the quality is as assured as you might expect from a vineyard next to Ch. CLIMENS. The grapes are selectively picked and the wines vinified and aged in oak barrels. There's opulence but also that lively Barsac freshness on the finish, too. Best years: 2010, '09, '07, '05, '04, '03, '01, '99, '98, '97, '96, '95, '90, '89.

Château Doisy-Védrines

From the commune of Barsac, this rich, fat, intensely fruity wine is one of the most reliable Sauternes, and usually fair value, too.

CHÂTEAU DOISY-VÉDRINES

Sauternes AC, 2ème Cru Classé
Sémillon, Sauvignon Blanc

Next door to DOISY-DAËNE in the Barsac AC, this is the largest of the Doisy estates and, like its neighbour, also uses the Sauternes AC

label. Unlike most other Barsac estates, Doisy-Védrines produces a wine with more of the richness and weight of Sauternes from its very low-yielding vines. Fermented and aged in barrel, the wines are fat and powerful, marked by new oak when young, and need at least eight to ten years' bottle age to be at their best. Best years: 2010, '09, '07, '06, '05, '04, '03, '01, '99, '98, '97, '96, '95, '90, '89, '88, '86.

Château de Fargues

This small property is owned by the Lur-Saluces family and run with perfectionist zeal.

CHÂTEAU DE FARGUES

Sauternes AC
Sémillon, Sauvignon Blanc

The most remarkable thing about Ch. de Fargues is that, even though it is unclassified, it regularly sells for more than any other wine in the AC save the great Ch. d'YQUEM. It is owned by the Lur-Saluces family, owners of Yquem for over four centuries until 1999. The vineyard – 15ha (37 acres) on the edge of the Sauternes AC in the village of Fargues – is by no means ideal, and the quality of the wine is more a tribute to the commitment of the Lur-Saluces family than to the inherent quality of the estate.

The vines ripen around ten days later than at Yquem, and the selection of grapes is so strict that each vine only yields two-thirds of a glass of wine. The result is that the total annual production rarely exceeds 10,000 bottles of rich, reasonably exotic wine, very honeyed, indeed almost syrupy, with something of the taste of pineapples and peaches, and a viscous feel, like lanolin, which coats your mouth. This is fine, rich wine but there are several Classed Growths which are better, and less expensive. Best years: 2010, '09, '07, '06, '05, '04, '03, '02, '01, '99, '98, '97, '96, '95, '90, '89, '88, '86.

Château Filhot

Impressive château, impressive estate and grounds and potentially excellent vineyards, but sadly the wine rarely inspires me.

CHÂTEAU FILHOT

Sauternes AC, 2ème Cru Classé
Sémillon, Sauvignon Blanc, Muscadelle

This large 62-ha (153-acre) vineyard surrounds one of the most handsome châteaux in the region. In 1788 Thomas Jefferson, later to be the third US president, thought it the best Sauternes after YQUEM, and its reputation was maintained throughout the 19th century.

Almost alone among the Sauternes Classed Growths, Filhot has failed to invest in more than a tiny number of oak barrels. Consequently when compared to its peers, the wine can be one-dimensional and lacking in character. Some vintages have been made with insufficient care, resulting in occasional faults and some premature oxidation. Although recent vintages are not very highly priced, it does not represent good value while vintages from the mid-1990s remain variable. Moreover, the wines are difficult when young and need at least eight to ten years in bottle. Best years: 2010, '09, '07, '05, '03, '01, '99, '97, '96, '95, '90, '89, '88.

Château Gilette

The Crème de Tête wines from Ch. Gilette, with their wonderfully rich, viscous pineapple and barleysugar flavours, are remarkable oddballs but usually succeed.

CHÂTEAU GILETTE

Sauternes AC
Sémillon, Sauvignon Blanc, Muscadelle

This extraordinary wine is fermented in stainless steel, then aged for 16–20 years in concrete vats before being finally released as Crème de Tête a minimum of 15 years after the harvest. This method greatly reduces the oxygen contact and preserves the wine's lively fruit character. The wines have a deep golden colour, sumptuous bouquet of raisined fruits, orange zest, coffee and vanilla and a rich unctuousness on the palate with a never-ending finish. The volume of wine produced from the tiny 5-ha (12-acre) vineyard is minimal (an average of 5000 bottles a year). Best years: 1989, '88, '86, '85, '83, '82, '81, '79, '78, '76, '75, '71, '70, '67, '61, '59, '55, '53, '49.

Grand Enclos du Château de Cérons

This delightfully drinkable and surprisingly rich and lush sweet wine is unfortunately only made in small quantities.

GRAND ENCLOS DU CHÂTEAU DE CÉRONS

Cérons AC
Sémillon

This estate with its high, stone wall sits right in the heart of the village of Cérons. The wines had a certain reputation of old but since 2000 and its acquisition by Giorgio Cavanna, part-owner of top Chianti Classico, Castello di Ama, there's been a bit of a revolution.

Buildings have been renovated, a new *cuverie* put in place and working methods changed. Grapes are now selectively picked and the wine fermented and aged in oak barrels. The result is a rich, lush complex wine that will age. Unfortunately quantities are limited. The property also makes red and white Graves under the Grand Enclos and Ch. Lamouroux labels. Best years: 2010, '09, '07, '05, '04, '03, '02, '01.

Château Guiraud

Ch. Guiraud produces a rich, powerful, oaky and tremendously deep and impressive wine, despite containing more of the refreshing Sauvignon Blanc than any other Sauternes Premier Cru.

CHÂTEAU GUIRAUD

Sauternes AC, Premier Cru Classé
Sémillon, Sauvignon Blanc

In 1981 Guiraud was bought by a quality-obsessed Canadian, Frank Narby, who, with his son Hamilton, was bent on making great Sauternes and for over 20 years they ran a successful ship. The 1983 was exceptional, the '86 was stunningly rich right from the start and the '90, '96 and '97 even more so – and so on, until in 2006 the Narbys sold to a consortium headed by the Peugeot car family and local wine talent in the name of Domaine de CHEVALIER, Stephan von Neipperg of Ch. CANON-LA-GAFFELIÈRE, and Xavier Planty, Guiraud's winemaker and manager.

Planty ruthlessly selects only the best grapes, uses at least 50% new oak each year to ferment and age the wine, and justifiably charges a very high price. The wine needs at least ten years to reach its peak – and top years may need 15–20. Second wine: (dry) G de Ch. Guiraud. Best years: 2010, '09, '07, '06, '05, '04, '03, '02, '01, '99, '98, '97, '96, '95, '90, '89, '88.

Château Haut-Bergeron

A rich, honeyed style, from vines averaging 60 years old, perhaps lacking a little focus but nevertheless a satisfying mouthful.

CHÂTEAU HAUT-BERGERON
Sauternes AC
🌿 *Sémillon, Sauvignon Blanc, Muscadelle*

Outside the Classed Growths it's not always easy to find worthwhile Sauternes but Haut-Bergeron has maintained a good level of consistency for a number of years. The 15-ha (37-acre) vineyard is not far from that of YQUEM and the owning Lamothe family know how to selectively harvest botrytized grapes. There's less purity of flavour than in the Sauternes top growths but the wines are still rich and unctuous, the best aging remarkably well. Best years: 2010, '09, '07, '06, '04, '03, '02, '01, '99, '97, '96, '95, '90, '89, '88, '86, '83.

Château Les Justices

Less fascinating than the remarkable wine from Ch. Gilette, Les Justices is a good, full-bodied but balanced sweet wine.

CHÂTEAU LES JUSTICES
Sauternes AC
🌿 *Sémillon, Sauvignon Blanc, Muscadelle*

This 8.5-ha (21-acre) property at Preignac is under the same ownership as Ch. GILETTE. The wines, though, are made more 'classically' with fermentation and aging in barrel, and are drinkable much sooner. The citrus, tropical fruit and honeyed flavours can be appreciated at four to five years. Best years: 2010, '09, '07, '05, '03, '02, '01, '99, '97, '96.

Château Lafaurie-Peyraguey

From a property now on cracking form again, this is wonderfully balanced, beautifully rich Sauternes and usually scented with new oak to great effect.

CHÂTEAU LAFAURIE-PEYRAGUEY
Sauternes AC, Premier Cru Classé
🌿 *Sémillon, Sauvignon Blanc, Muscadelle*

It's fashionable to criticize the detrimental effect on quality following the takeover of a property by a large merchant, but the large Domaines Cordier company has always taken great care of its properties (they bought this one in 1913). In the 1980s and '90s their investment and commitment in this 36-ha (89-acre) Premier Cru in the village of Bommes made Lafaurie-Peyraguey one of the most improved Sauternes properties.

Now the good work continues under the ownership of the Groupe Suez Bank. The property has made outstanding wines in great vintages since the early 1980s (I have some delicious 1983 which is perfection now) but has also come through well in the lesser years. The wine has a deep apricot and pineapple syrup sweetness, a cream and nuts softness and a good, clear, lemony acidity which give it wonderful balance for long aging. Best years: 2010, '09, '07, '06, '05, '04, '03, '02, '01, '99, '98, '97, '96, '95, '90, '89, '88, '86, '85, '83.

Château Lamothe

Good but not thrilling wine with nice, lemon and apple acidity and fair richness.

CHÂTEAU LAMOTHE
Sauternes AC, 2ème Cru Classé
🌿 *Sémillon, Sauvignon Blanc, Muscadelle*

The original Lamothe estate was split up in the early years of the 20th century, and this Ch. Lamothe is now the smaller part with only 7ha (17 acres) of vines. The wines have steadily improved over the years since the arrival of Guy Despujols in 1989 but they still lack the purity of the top Sauternes names. In recent vintages the wines have showed more concentration, particularly the Sélection Exceptionnelle. This was first made in 1998 but it is not produced every year. A little awkward when young, the wines are better with seven or eight years' bottle age. Best years: 2010, '09, '07, '05, '04, '03, '02, '01, '99, '98, '97, '96.

Château Lamothe-Guignard

Recent vintages have displayed depth and richness, though oak is very evident when the wine is young..

CHÂTEAU LAMOTHE-GUIGNARD
Sauternes AC, 2ème Cru Classé
🌿 *Sémillon, Sauvignon Blanc, Muscadelle*

This is the larger part of the original Lamothe estate. In 1981 it was bought by the Guignard family, who set about restoring its fortunes. They built a new cellar in 1990 and the wines have since been vinified in small-volume stainless steel tanks before being aged in oak *barriques*. For a while the wines seemed overly oaky, but since 2003 the balance and richness of the wines has greatly improved. The wine is now concentrated and lively but not over-fat. Best vintages can be drunk between five and 15 years' old. Best years: 2010, '09, '07, '05, '04, '03, '02, '01, '99, '97, '96, '95, '90.

Château Loubens

The wine is not intensely sweet but has attractive barley sugar depth which start to show with a little maturity, and Loubens generally ages well.

CHÂTEAU LOUBENS

Ste-Croix-du-Mont AC

🌿 *Sémillon, Sauvignon Blanc*

A leading name in the Ste-Croix-du-Mont AC, this historic domaine dating back to the 16th century has 15ha (37 acres) of ideal south-south-west-facing vineyard located in a single parcel on the appellation's famous bed of fossilized oysters (*ostrea aquitanica*). The Ste-Croix-du-Mont wine is 100% Sémillon from vines with an average age of 45 years. The vineyards are selectively harvested with successive passes (*tries*) through the vineyard. Fermentation and aging in tank helps preserve the harmonious fruit character which is best sampled with four to five years' bottle age. Other wines are Ch. des Tours, also a Ste-Croix-du-Mont, a dry white Bordeaux called Fleuron Blanc du Ch. Loubens and a red Bordeaux, Ch. Le Grand Pré. Best years: 2010, '09, '07, '05, '04, '03, '02, '01, '99, '97, '96, '95, '90, '89.

Château de Malle

This is one-stop shopping at its finest: grand château, magnificent historic gardens, top Sauternes and good dry white and red Graves wines.

CHÂTEAU DE MALLE

Sauternes AC, 2ème Cru Classé

🌿 *Sémillon, Sauvignon Blanc, Muscadelle*

A gem of a château forms the centrepiece of this estate and is the major tourist attraction of the region. Since the premature death of the owner, the Comte de Bournazel, de Malle has been energetically run by his widow and there have been substantial improvements since the mid-1980s.

De Malle was never one of the fatter wines of Sauternes, but it used to be distinctly one-dimensional, even dull. This is no longer the case, and it now shows grace and considerable concentration of flavour. The consistency, too, has been impressive since 1988; though no wine was made in 1992 or '93 this château succeeded while a number of fancied First Growths failed in 1994 and '95 – and recently '01, '03 and '07 were particularly striking. Drink after ten years or more. Also produced are a good dry white Graves (M de Malle) and red Graves (Ch. de Cardaillan). Best years: 2010, '09, '07, '06, '05, '03, '02, '01, '99, '98, '97, '96, '95, '94, '90, '89, '88.

Ch. de Malle with its magnificent Italianate gardens is one of the finest châteaux you can visit in the whole Bordeaux region. It has remained in the same family for four centuries.

Château Manos

This is a reasonably full, waxy, honeyed style of wine which can take several years of aging.

CHÂTEAU MANOS
Cadillac AC

🌿 *Sémillon, Sauvignon Blanc, Muscadelle*

The youngest vines at this tiny 3.5-ha (9-acre) property are 60 years old and the oldest 85 years. They're mainly Sémillon but with a small amount of Sauvignon Blanc and Muscadelle vines mixed in. Needless to say there's a lovely rich, unctuous quality about the wines which are part-aged in barriques. Only 12,000 bottles are produced a year, and in exceptional vintages there is a 100% Sémillon Réserve version. Best years: 2010, '09, '07, '05, '04, '03, '01, '97, '96, '95, '90.

Château Mémoires

Drinkable young, good vintages will age to a barley sugar and orange depth.

CHÂTEAU MÉMOIRES
Cadillac AC

🌿 *Sémillon, Muscadelle, Sauvignon Blanc*

Jean-François Ménard is a bit of a 'sweety' nut. From his 7ha (17 acres) in Cadillac he

produces a regular tank-aged, fruit-driven cuvée and then in special years (2009, '05) the richer, barrel-aged Grains d'Or and then in exceptional ones (2001) a wine called L'Or ('Gold'). He used to make wine in Loupiac as well (last vintage 2005) but no longer owns the vineyard. Best years: 2010, '09, '07, '05, '03, '02, '01, '99, '98, '97, '96, '95, '94.

Château de Myrat

Good, rich, honeyed wine, a bit oaky but showing some real beeswaxy class.

CHÂTEAU DE MYRAT
Sauternes AC, 2ème Cru Classé

🌿 *Sémillon, Sauvignon Blanc, Muscadelle*

Around the charming 18th-century château of this small Barsac property lie vineyards whose production, until 1976, was mostly sold off to wholesalers. Myrat was therefore rarely sold under the estate name. This lack of commitment to the vineyards resulted in their uprooting in 1976. After the owner's death in 1988, his sons replanted the vines. The first crop was harvested in 1990 but sold as Bordeaux AC since the vines were too young to claim the Barsac AC. Having weathered the difficult vintages that followed, they produced a sound 1994 and gradually as the vines have aged the wines have got better and more concentrated – and they're still quite good value. Best years: 2010, '09, '07, '06, '05, '04, '03, '02, '01, '00, '99, '97, '96, '95.

Château Nairac

The influence of fermentation and aging in new oak casks produces a concentrated oaky but rich wine.

CHÂTEAU NAIRAC
Barsac AC, 2ème Cru Classé

🌿 *Sémillon, Sauvignon Blanc, Muscadelle*

An established star in Barsac, which produces a wine sometimes on a level with the Sauternes First Growths – not as intensely perfumed, not as exotically rich, but proudly concentrated, with a fine lanolin richness and buttery honeyed fruit. Annual production is rarely more than 15,000 bottles – sometimes less – from this 16-ha (40-acre) property. Aging in new oak casks adds spice and even a little tannin, making the wine a good candidate for aging for ten to 15 years. There's also a fresher style Esquise de Nairac. Best years: 2010, '09, '07, '06, '05, '04, '03, '02, '01, '99, '98, '97, '96.

Domaine du Noble

Attractive young, good vintages are really serious, with good waxy depth and nutty, peachy richness.

DOMAINE DU NOBLE
Loupiac AC

🌿 *Sémillon, Sauvignon Blanc*

A benchmark estate in the Loupiac AC and one of only a handful of producers there to use oak barriques for aging. Two or three different wines are produced according to the vintage, including a barrel-fermented *cuvée*. Best years: 2010, '09, '07, '05, '04, '03, '02, '01, '99, '97.

Château du Pavillon

The sweet wines here are slightly old style but they are still reasonably fat and mouthfilling.

CHÂTEAU DU PAVILLON

Ste-Croix-du-Mont AC

🌾 *Sémillon, Sauvignon Blanc, Muscadelle*

The delightful 18th-century château and vineyards overlook the Garonne and Ciron rivers. The wines are tank aged and made in a relatively light style but they are still consistently expressive. Production from the 4-ha (10-acre) vineyard is small, the wines usually released when drinkable with three or four years' bottle age. Best years: 2010, '09, '07, '05, '04, '03, '02, '01, '99, '97.

Château Rabaud-Promis

Rich opulent wines with fine balancing acidity from a large quantity, revitalized estate.

CHÂTEAU RABAUD-PROMIS

Sauternes AC, Premier Cru Classé

🌾 *Sémillon, Sauvignon Blanc, Muscadelle*

Ch. Rabaud, in the commune of Bommes, was divided into Rabaud-Promis and SIGALAS-RABAUD in 1903. The two halves were reunited between 1929 and 1952 and some excellent wines were produced in the late 1940s.

However, in the following decades this, the larger half, went into decline. Radical improvements to what had become a badly-neglected estate came in the 1980s. Now the estate once again produces rich, refined Sauternes of First Growth quality. Impressive with five years' aging, even better with ten. Best years: 2010, '09, '07, '06, '05, '03, '02, '01, '99, '98, '97, '96, '95, '90, '89, '88.

Château La Rame

Attractively rich, peach syrup and honey style with refreshing acidity that will allow it to age for a few years.

CHÂTEAU LA RAME

Ste-Croix-du-Mont AC

🌾 *Sémillon, Sauvignon Blanc*

The sweet wines from this 20-ha (49-acre) estate, particularly the Réserve du Château, are consistently among the best produced on the right bank of the Garonne. Yields are maintained at around 25–30 hectolitres per hectare and the grapes are selectively harvested.

Some of the various *cuvées* produced are aged in vat, but those selected for the Réserve du Château are aged in oak barrels for 8–24 months. Top vintages can be nearly as powerful as a Sauternes with 14% alcohol and 100gm/l residual sugar. They are accessible young but will age for ten years or more. Best years: 2010, '09, '07, '06, '05, '04, '03, '02, '01, '99, '98, '97, '96, '95, '90, '89.

Château Raymond-Lafon

Powerful, intense wine, almost brooding in its depth, and asking for a good 10 years of aging to show at its best.

CHÂTEAU RAYMOND-LAFON

Sauternes AC

🌾 *Sémillon, Sauvignon Blanc*

This unclassified estate now ranks with the best of the Sauternes Crus Classés. It was purchased in 1972 by Pierre Meslier, the former director of Ch. d'YQUEM, and is now run by his sons and daughter. The same rigorous procedures are applied as at neighbouring Yquem: only botrytized grapes are selected during successive passes (*tries*) through the vineyard and the wine is fermented and aged for three years in new oak barrels. It is consequently rich and powerful and can be aged for a considerable length of time. Second wine: Ch. Lafon-Laroze. Best years: 2010, '09, '07, '06, '05, '04, '03, '02, '01, '99, '98, '97, '96, '95, '90, '89, '88, '86, '85, '83, '80, '79, '76, '75.

Château Rayne-Vigneau

Huge investments in the 1980s have brought impressive results at this great Sauternes property .

CHÂTEAU RAYNE-VIGNEAU
Sauternes AC, Premier Cru Classé
🌿 Sémillon, Sauvignon Blanc

This large estate of 80ha (198 acres) occupies a hill studded with semi-precious stones and blessed with probably the finest soil and mesoclimate after Ch. d'YQUEM. In the 1970s and early '80s the quality did not quite match the splendour of the site, but huge investments helped improve the situation.

Since 1985 when the improvements started to show the wines have been medium-bodied, oaky and elegant, but they still lack a degree of concentration and power that would elevate them into the front rank, though the 2009 shows great improvement. They can be aged for 10–15 years. Second wine. Madame de Rayne. Best years: 2010, '09, '07, '05, '03, '02, '01, '99, '97, '96, '95, '90, '89, '88, '86, '85.

The amazingly stony soils at Ch. Rayne-Vigneau almost sparkle in the autumn sun: this isn't surprising as in places they are full of precious and semi-precious stones: agate, onyx, sapphire, cornelian, amethyst and many more.

Château Reynon

2001 was the swan song for Denis Dubourdieu's fresh delightful Cadillac. Hopefully he'll soon start making it again.

CHÂTEAU REYNON
Cadillac AC
🌿 Sauvignon Blanc, Sémillon

Ch. Reynon is Denis and Florence Dubourdieu's beautiful property at Béguey in the Cadillac-Côtes de Bordeaux appellation. Reynon produces a range of excellent reds (sold as Cadillac-Côtes de Bordeaux) and dry whites (Bordeaux Blanc) (see page 271), and used to produce an excellent Cadillac. Production of this wine ceased after the 2001 vintage when Denis Dubourdieu took over from his father, Pierre, at Ch. DOISY-DAËNE in 2000.

But I still have some of the Cadillac and it's in great condition, so I'm going to tell you a bit about it. It contains a large percentage of late-harvested Sauvignon Blanc (over 60%) as well as Sémillon and was picked by three to six passages through the vineyards (one of the clearest signs of quality sweet white wine viticulture at work) and is both fermented and aged in barriques. All this adds up to a rich fruit and vanilla concentration as well as enormous freshness, ideally for drinking between five and six years. Best years: (Cadillac) 2001, '99.

Château Rieussec

Rieussec is often one of the richest, most succulent Sauternes. Lighter years are more delicate but still excitingly sweet.

CHÂTEAU RIEUSSEC

Sauternes AC, Premier Cru Classé
Sémillon, Sauvignon Blanc, Muscadelle

Apart from the peerless Ch. d'YQUEM, Rieussec is often the richest Sauternes. The 92ha (227 acres) of vineyards lie in one block on high ground just inside the commune of Fargues and most of them border those of Yquem.

The property was bought in 1984 by the Rothschilds of Ch. LAFITE-ROTHSCHILD and no expense was spared both in the vineyard and the cellar. Many wondered for a while if they were going to try to challenge Yquem's pre-eminence. Fermentation in barrel was reintroduced from 1995, adding extra glycerol and complexity to the marvellous trio of the 1997, '96 and '95 vintages and greater intensity to wines that are already super-rich. Happily they are affordable not only to the super-rich – which is more than one can say for Yquem. There is a dry wine called 'R' which is pretty dull. Second wines: Carmes de Rieussec, Clos Labère. Best years: 2010, '09, '07, '06, '05, '04, '03, '02, '01, '99, '98, '97, '96, '95, '90, '89, '88.

Château Les Roques

This is an attractive waxy style of Loupiac and perfect as a sweet apéritif.

CHÂTEAU LES ROQUES

Loupiac AC
Sémillon, Sauvignon Blanc, Muscadelle

This 4-ha (9-acre) property is under the same ownership as Ch. du PAVILLON in next door Ste-Croix-du-Mont. There's a lighter tank-aged *cuvée* but of most interest is the richer, more complex Cuvée Frantz, fermented and aged in barrel. This is ready to drink at four to five years old but will also age longer in top vintages. Best years: 2010, '09, '07, '05, '04, '03, '02, '01, '99, '97.

Château St-Amand

Year after year this is one of the most reliable châteaux for rich, honeyed and affordable Sauternes.

CHÂTEAU ST-AMAND

Sauternes AC
Sémillon, Sauvignon Blanc, Muscadelle

This is one of the few non-Classed Growth properties that manages to produce big, rich, classic Sauternes – and which doesn't charge the earth. The 22-ha (54-acre) estate is in Preignac – right next to the little river Ciron, whose autumn mists have so much to do with the formation of the noble rot fungus on the grapes. Best years: 2010, '09, '07, '05, '03, '02, '01, '00, '99, '98, '97, '96, '90, '89.

Château Sigalas-Rabaud

One of the clutch of great Sauternes properties to revive in the 1980s. The quality and the finesse of the wine is now a delight.

CHÂTEAU SIGALAS-RABAUD

Sauternes AC, Premier Cru Classé
Sémillon, Sauvignon Blanc

When Ch. Rabaud was divided in 1903, 14-ha (35-acre) Sigalas became the smaller of the two estates (the other is RABAUD-PROMIS). Thanks to its soils and selective picking, the wine displays good richness with balancing elegance and freshness. The owner, Comte Emmanuel de Lambert des Granges, steers clear of excessive oakiness and seeks a wine that can be enjoyed young. The team at Ch. Lafaurie-Peyraguey now makes the wines.

The excellent trio of vintages, 1988 to '90, and a rich but marvellously refined '95 have been surpassed by a string of incredible years including '96, '97, '98, '99, '01, '03, '07 and '09. Cellar for 10–15 years, though it may be drunk after five. Second wine: Lieutenant-de-Sigalas. Best years: 2010, '09, '07, '05, '04, '03, '02, '01, '00, '99, '98, '97, '96, '95, '90, '89, '88, '86, '85, '83, '79, '75.

Château Suau

Attractively beeswaxy, lanolin-rich wine on the up, and about time too, after a long dull period when I've longed for more richness of fruit.

CHÂTEAU SUAU

Barsac AC, 2ème Cru Classé
🌿 *Sémillon, Sauvignon Blanc, Muscadelle*

At last an effort is being made to get this 8-ha (20-acre) property back up to its proper Classed Growth performance. The ownership is the same as at Ch. d' ARCHAMBEAU in the Graves so there's a good chance of success. One to watch. Best years: 2010, '09, '07, '06, '05, '04, '03, '02.

Château Suduiraut

Following the arrival of new owners, AXA-Millésimes, in 1992, the wines have been back on top form.

CHÂTEAU SUDUIRAUT

Sauternes AC, Premier Cru Classé
🌿 *Sémillon, Sauvignon Blanc*

Suduiraut has often been described as a close runner-up to Sauternes' clear leader d'YQUEM, because the wine has a viscous ripeness that coats your mouth as if the whole were wrapped in melted butter and cream. Add to this a delicious fruit, like pineapples and peaches soaked in syrup, and you can get some idea of the expansive lusciousness of which Suduiraut is capable.

After a long period in the 1970s and '80s when, despite many excellent vintages, Suduiraut didn't shine, the property was bought by insurance giant AXA-Millésimes in 1992 and by the end of the decade it was back snapping at Yquem's heels. The 90-ha (222-acre) estate produces anything from 30,000–120,000 bottles a year. Second wine: Castelnau de Suduiraut. Best years: 2010, '09, '07, '06, '05, '04, '03, '02, '01, '99, '98, '97, '96, '95, '90, '89, '86, '82.

Château La Tour Blanche

Thanks to dynamic direction and a generous investment in new oak, this wine now has the rich unctuousness of great Sauternes.

CHÂTEAU LA TOUR BLANCHE

Sauternes AC, Premier Cru Classé
🌿 *Sémillon, Sauvignon Blanc, Muscadelle*

In the 1855 classification of Bordeaux wines La Tour Blanche was put top of the First Growths just behind YQUEM but until the mid-1980s it rarely justified this status. Now, thanks to a major rethink in the vineyards and the winery and a generous investment in new oak barrels for fermentation and aging, the wines are again among the best in the AC, rich and unctuous with a generous but elegant underpinning of oak. The 34-ha (84-acre) estate, owned by the French Ministry of Agriculture, is planted with 83% Sémillon, 12% Sauvignon Blanc and barely more than a handful of Muscadelle vines to add a little exotic fruitiness to the blend. Second wine: Les Charmilles de la Tour Blanche. Best years: 2010, '09, '07, '06, '05, '04, '03, '02, '01, '99, '98, '97, '96, '95, '90, '89, '88, '86.

Quick guide • Best producers

BARSAC AC
Cantegril, Climens, Coutet, Doisy-Dubroca, Haut-Grillon, Liot, Nairac, Piada, Simon, Suau.

CADILLAC AC
La Bertrande, Juge, Manos, Mémoires.

CÉRONS AC
Cérons, Chantegrive, Grand Enclos du Château de Cérons, Haura, Seuil.

GRAVES SUPÉRIEURES AC
Clos St-Georges, Léhoul.

LOUPIAC AC
Clos Jean, Cros, Dauphine-Rondillon, Fortin, Loupiac-Gaudiet, Noble, Ricaud, Les Roques, La Yotte.

STE-CROIX-DU-MONT AC
Crabitan-Bellevue, Grand-Peyrot, Loubens, Lousteau-Vieil, Mailles, Mont, Pavillon, La Rame.

SAUTERNES AC
Arche, Bastor-Lamontagne, Brousset, Caillou, Clos Dady, Clos Haut-Peyraguey, Cru Barréjats, Doisy-Daëne, Doisy-Védrines, Fargues, Gilette, Guiraud, Haut-Bergeron, Haut-Mayne, Les Justices, Lafaurie-Peyraguey, Lamothe, Lamothe-Guignard, Laville, Malle, Myrat, Rabaud-Promis, Raymond-Lafon, Rayne-Vigneau, Rieussec, Sigalas-Rabaud, St-Amand, Suduiraut, La Tour-Blanche, Yquem.

Château d'Yquem

In 1855, while they were busy classifying the red wines of the Médoc, the wine brokers also classified the sweet white wines of Sauternes and Barsac. They created nine First Growths, and they created one 'Superior First Growth'. One wine that they deemed better than all the other wines in Bordeaux. That wine was Yquem.

The First Growths proudly display their classification on their labels. But the label of the Superior First Growth simply states Château d'Yquem, Sauternes, and the vintage. During the 19th and 20th centuries the label didn't even mention Sauternes, preferring to replace it with the name of the family who had owned it since 1785 – Lur-Saluces. It's as though Yquem were saying, 'But of course we're the best, everybody knows that. It'd be rather crass to put it on our label, don't you think?' Talk about being sure of yourself.

They just might be right. Yquem is the undisputed star in the sweet white wine firmament, and however much passion and commitment you put in to making great red wine, it'll never match what is required in terms of skill and investment, sacrifice and risk to produce the supreme sweet white. And Yquem's vineyard is in exactly the right place, perched on top of the highest hill in the area, with land flowing downhill in all directions. The estate is 189ha (467 acres) but unlike neighbouring First Growths which have vines carpeting their slopes, 64ha (158 acres) of Yquem is fallow, either through crop rotation or because Yquem doesn't think it's good enough land. And of the 125ha (308 acres) planted, less than 100ha (247 acres) are used for the *grand vin*. So straight away, you're sacrificing almost half your production potential.

In fact Yquem sacrifices a lot more than that. While a red wine property might produce a bottle of wine per vine, and neighbouring Sauternes properties might produce two or three glasses per vine, Yquem's proud boast is that it only produces one single glass per vine, and in difficult years it can be even less. The vines are very severely pruned to reduce the potential crop, but that's just the start of it. The incredible richness of Sauternes wine is created by the formation of the noble rot fungus on the grapes, which concentrates the sugary juice. Because this requires very particular climatic conditions in late summer that don't always occur, involving early morning fog, followed by bright sunshine and warm long evenings, some years loads of this noble rot appears on the grapes, sometimes hardly any. So Yquem employs a team of about 150 pickers who stay on call from September until the harvest is over, and this could be early December. And they pick the grapes, berry by berry, only choosing the ones totally infected by the noble rot fungus.

Quick guide

CLASSIFICATION
Sauternes AC, Premier Cru Supérieur

VINEYARD
103ha (255 acres) planted with Sémillon (80%), Sauvignon Blanc (20%)

TYPICAL BLEND
80% Sémillon, 20% Sauvignon Blanc

ANNUAL PRODUCTION OF THE GRAND VIN
120,000 bottles on average, but ranges from zero in the worst vintages to a maximum of 130,000

BEST YEARS
2010, '09, '08, '07, 06, '05, '04, '03, '02, '01, '00, '99, '98, '97, '96, '95, '94, '90, '89, '88, '86, '83, '81

CLASSIC OLDER VINTAGES
1979, '76, '75, '71, '70, '67, '62, '59, '45, '37, '29, '28, '21

DRY WHITE WINE
Ygrec

Ch. d'Yquem
For sheer richness, for exotic flavours of vanilla, pineapple, peaches and coconut, cocooned in honey and cream, you can't beat Yquem in a top vintage such as 2001.

Above: Ch. d'Yquem is an old medieval fortress and so sits on the highest ground in the area.

Left: Sludgy, slimey grapes, 100% infected by noble rot. To achieve this you often have to pick the harvest grape by grape.

Below: For centuries until 1999 the Lur-Saluces family trod these flagstones at the entrance to the château.

Right: Yquem confounded the idea prevalent in Bordeaux that you had to be middle-aged and male to get a top job at a château when they appointed the 31-year-old Sandrine Garbay as cellarmaster in 1998.

Ch. d'Yquem is now owned by the LVMH luxury goods group, but from 1785–1999 it was owned by the Lur-Saluces family. You can still see their coat of arms on stonework around the property, and there's no suggestion it will be replaced by the Louis Vuitton logo any time soon.

So they have to go through the vines again and again, searching for the perfectly rotted grapes. In 1964 the pickers went through 13 times – and after all that, they decided the grapes still weren't good enough and they released no wine – not a bottle – that year. Find me another property that would be prepared to make such a sacrifice. After that the wine is fermented then aged for anywhere between two and a half and three years in new French barrels – losing another 20 per cent through evaporation – and then all the barrels are evaluated and only the best chosen for the Yquem label. Up to a quarter are regularly declassified. The rainy 1978 vintage saw 85 per cent of the wine declassified. And, as in 1964, no Yquem was made at all in 1972, '74 or '92. In a good year, they might make up to 130,000 bottles.

I have to admit I very rarely get to taste it, but for sheer richness, for exotic flavours, cocooned in honey and cream, so viscous and lush your mouth feels coated with succulence for an eternity after swallowing the wine, you can't beat Yquem. And that's just the young wine. Yquem will age for a decade, a generation, a century sometimes, and I have a vivid memory of a deep dark brown liquid barely glinting with gold that displayed a shocking, thrilling richness of orange chocolate, butterscotch, barleysugar and caramel as I rolled it endlessly around my mouth, unwilling to swallow it for fear of letting go the experience. That was the 1865. I had a glass of it, once.

Yquem keeps a wonderful youthful yet sensuous golden quality for a very long time. This trio are all well into their third decade, and yet have hardly reached the hue of heather honey. But wait. The change will come. These magnums on the right are a trio from 1967 – a wonderful vintage and the best in Sauternes since 1959, now deepened to the colour of barley sugar and Baltic amber. But even as the colour seems to indicate decay, the wine is actually continuing to ripen and transform, holding onto the brash richness of youth and adding unimaginable layers of experience, emotion and inspiration.

A Bordeaux lover's paradise. These are the Millésima cellars in Bordeaux, probably the largest hoard of great Bordeaux in the world. The cellars hold over 2 million bottles. Here, we have unimaginable numbers of cases of top wines, including Cantenac-Brown, Beychevelle and Talbot, with Palmer being unloaded from the pallet.

This vintage chart gives overall quality ratings for the most recent vintages in the key regions of Bordeaux. Scores are out of 10. The maturity assessments are for the better wines. Bottles from minor châteaux will usually reach maturity and then go past their peak rather sooner. See page 307 for a guide to older vintages of top wines.

Vintage guide

Bordeaux is renowned as producer of wines for long aging, but that doesn't mean you have to stuff every bottle under your stairs for 20 years. That kind of cellaring is only for the very top wines from the Médoc and the top sweet whites from Sauternes and Barsac. And even with those châteaux, modern winemaking means wines are approachable earlier – whether they have the same longevity remains to be seen, but I would expect them to last. Basic to good Cru Bourgeois-level wines need two to five years and the better ones of these will last a decade, maybe 15 years. Graves wines seem to gallop to a good drinking age far faster, maybe in five years even for a top wine, yet they have the same long aging potential as Médocs of the same quality. Right Bank wines are based on Merlot and are on a shorter trajectory than Left Bank wines. So basic St-Émilion is ready as soon as it hits the shops and even the very good Grand Cru Classé St-Émilions generally drink well at between five and ten years. In any case, you shouldn't be bound by other people's ideas of when a wine is ready. The cedarwood, cigarbox, lead pencil shavings qualities of a mature Pauillac are not the be-all and end-all of red Bordeaux. Consider how you like your wines – you may prefer fresh young fruit to the evolved aromas of mature wine.

VINTAGE VARIATION

Bordeaux is a marginal climate. What does that mean? Well, a cold snap in spring can drastically reduce the number of bunches that develop on each vine so vintages do vary a lot in terms of quantity. But Merlot flowers before Cabernet, so perhaps only one variety will be affected. That has a knock-on effect in terms of what the winemakers will have available for making up their blends. As for quality, rain at vintage time poses the

Vintage chart	10	09	08	07	06	05	04	03	02	01	00	99	98
Margaux	9◑	9◑	7◑	7●	8◑	9◑	8●	7●	7●	7●	9●	7●	7●
St.-Julien, Pauillac, St-Estèphe	9◑	10◑	8◑	7◑	8◑	10◑	8●	9◑	8●	8◑	10◑	7●	7●
Graves/Pessac-Léognan (red)	9◑	9◑	7◑	7●	7◑	9◑	8●	6●	6●	7●	9●	7●	8●
Graves/Pessac-Léognan (white)	9◑	8●	8●	9●	9●	9●	8●	6●	8●	8●	8●	7●	9●
St-Émilion, Pomerol and other Right Bank reds	9◑	9◑	8◑	7●	8◑	9◑	8●	7◑	7●	8●	9●	7●	9●
Sauternes	8◑	10◑	6●	9●	6●	9●	6●	9●	7●	10●	6●	8●	7◑

KEY: ◑ Not ready   ● Just ready   ● At peak   ◐ Past best

greatest threat, causing problems of rot and dilution. The early 1990s were dogged by September rains but the vintages of the new millennium so far have been blessed by fine autumns that have brought extra ripeness. Many in Bordeaux believe this is a sign of global warming at work, and will be the normal pattern for years to come – and I'm inclined to accept their judgement. Even if the rains do return, modern vineyard practices have done a lot to smooth out the bumps so there are very few genuine disasters these days. Of course, while a perfect harvesting season is a blessing, a wet, cold or gloomy summer will still tell its tale in the end, compromising the nuances of flavour, the depth and complexity that emerge as the wine matures.

VINTAGE ASSESSMENTS

One of the favourite debates among Bordeaux lovers is whether the latest vintage is a Right Bank or a Left Bank year. Which grapes fared best, the Médoc Cabernet or the Right Bank Merlot? In truth they've both been doing well recently, and with more Merlot being planted everywhere, the geographic schism is less evident than in the old days. On the next three pages are some notes on past vintages. They mostly relate to the better Médoc and Right Bank reds. There is less to say about reds from the Graves and Pessac-Léognan, and from the Côtes. In Pessac-Léognan, vintages are akin to those from the Médoc but rather more reliable. Among whites, it's only really Sauternes that comes under scrutiny, as by no means all years bring the right conditions for making luscious sweet wines.

Top: Only my friend, fine wine expert Michael Broadbent would have the slightest idea what these wines tasted like. Perhaps I'd best just gaze at them and imagine the pleasure without risking disappointment. 1848, now there's a vintage – it was the Year of Revolutions in Europe, but an outstanding vintage for red Bordeaux. Above: Change generally occurred in Bordeaux at a glacial rate until the 1990s, when a new breed of quality-conscious entrepreneurs turned the old order upside down. In particular they started producing wines of startling depth and concentration from small plots of land no one had ever heard of. The prices were outrageous, but there was an immediate clamorous, well-heeled queue for these cult wines. La Mondotte, made by Stephan von Neipperg of Ch. Canon-la-Gaffeliere, is one of these cult wines that deserves all the hooplah.

RED WINE VINTAGES 2010–1982

2010
A cool, rainy patch in May and early June caused difficult flowering resulting in lower yields, particularly for the Merlot. Thereafter warm, dry weather provided excellent ripening conditions. Warm days and cool nights allowed producers to harvest fine grapes at will. Like 2009 the alcohol levels are high but there's good acidity, firmer tannins, and wonderfully focussed dark fruit.

2009
A cold winter, damp spring, hot dry summer and rain when it was needed in September provided ideal ripening conditions. The wines show brilliant fruit and exuberance but there's easily enough concentration and tannins for them to age. The only problem was a May hail storm which hit certain producers on the Right Bank and Entre-Deux-Mers. Prices for the top wines bordered on the ballistic.

2008
As in 2007, the summer was cold and wet: poor fruit set and mildew were compounded by hail and frost in Graves, Pessac-Léognan, Entre-Deux-Mers and the St-Émilion satellites, resulting in tiny yields. An Indian summer saved the day, with some growers still picking in early November. Quality varies, but wines are a little more concentrated and structured than in 2007.

2007
One of the warmest Aprils on record, then a miserable summer: mildew was a constant threat. Some growers picked really late, holding off until the end of October to get that last degree of ripeness. Extremely varied wines – it's all down to the producer and *terroir*.

2006
Rain and rot in September made for a difficult and frenetic harvest. The wines have improved enormously in bottle, with Pomerol and St-Émilion putting a and the Haut-Médoc becoming darker and deeper. Stylistically a bit like 2004 with perhaps more weight and less beauty.

2005
It may seem premature to be touting a 'vintage of the century', but 2005 had it all: perfect weather conditions brought ripeness, power, balance and – crucially – freshness. Long-lasting wines and top quality at all price levels. The prices for the leading wines are stratospheric.

2004
A potentially abundant year and late harvest. Wines of balance and depth which look better, more ageworthy and morer classic every time I taste them. Prices are rising but many Médoc and Graves wines remain good value.

2003
Heatwave and drought made for wines with bags of fruit and colour and hefty alcohol levels. In the Médoc there is little consistency even within the communes, so choose with care. St-Estèphe and Médoc AC wines were most successful as their cool, water-retaining clay soils and slightly cooler climate proved an advantage for once. The heat was too much for some of the Right Bank Merlot – wines with a high proportion of Cabernet Franc were more successful.

2002
A difficult year in which Cabernet Sauvignon fared best – the Left Bank communes are the wines to look for. Merlot on the Right Bank suffered in the cold spring weather, and wines vary from modest to good.

2001
This is a very good vintage that was initially underrated, balancing the classical and modern faces of Bordeaux. The wines are loaded with beguiling sweet-fruited flavours, fresh and medium-bodied, enjoyable now but sure to last.

2000
A rollercoaster year concluded with an exceptionally fine harvest period, enabling Bordeaux to tout its millennium vintage with justifiable swagger. Across the region the wines are concentrated, fruit-rich and balanced. Their muscular bravado is a striking contrast with 2001's come-hither charms.

1999
September rains took the shine off this vintage. Well-made but rather dull wines in the Médoc. Better, riper wines on the Right Bank.

1998
A Right Bank year with magnificent wines from Pomerol and St-Émilion – though not across the board, so choose with care. Only the top properties in the Médoc and Graves managed something worth tracking down.

1997
Unseasonal weather throughout the year resulted in uneven ripening. The wines were light and only the leading châteaux have stayed the course.

1996
Best vintage of the meteorologically challenged 1990s (barring 1990 itself), but predominantly a Left Bank year. Some great wines in the Médoc, which have really hit their stride with 15 years' aging. Right Bank wines are more varied, but soft and enjoyable at best – most need drinking up.

1995
Rain spoilt what might have been an absolute humdinger of a vintage in the Médoc. Growers with the courage to wait out the autumn storms made their best wines since 1990: go for leading estates in Pauillac and St-Julien, and also Pessac-Léognan. The top Right Bank estates were the stars of the vintage and there are plenty of lovely luscious reds to be had from here despite the rain.

1994–91
All badly affected by rain. Frost also decimated '91 and there are few fine wines from the tiny cup. '94 is spoilt by unrelenting hard tannins, even in maturity.

1990
The last in the string of fabulous years that started in the early 1980s. These are heady, rich, ripe wines (yes, I'm talking about the Médoc here) and First Growths and Super-Seconds will live on into the 2020s – but drink the rest now. The hot weather was almost too much of a good thing on the Right Bank, but the top-flight wines are still showing their class.

1989
Another miraculously hot year with soft, ripe, consistently good wines. Most top Médocs are ready now, but will last. Right Bank wines are rich, concentrated and long-lived too.

1988
Médoc wines are tougher and more tannic than in '89 or '90 and are maturing slowly to the subtle, cedary, tobaccoey essence of Bordeaux. The top wines are now near their peak but will run and run. I sometimes wonder, was this the last great vintage in the classic image of Bordeaux, before modern vineyard and winemaking techniques combined with the long dry summers of the early 2000s to create the riper, richer, more alcoholic wines that are the standard now?

1987
A light and enjoyable vintage now finished.

1986
A Left Bank year. The wines started out with monumental tannin levels but the best have a fresh acidity that has preserved the fruit until the tannins have at last softened. These top wines will drink well for another decade, even longer in some cases, but the rest should be drunk up.

1985
Mostly light and enjoyable wines from this high-cropping year, but the best wines are still superb. Right Bank Merlot was supreme. Drink them now.

1982
Rich, supple wines and the best are still superb. Robert Parker raved about the wines and Bordeaux entered a new boom period. The first of the great 1980s vintages and considered to be a milestone for modern red Bordeaux.

MATURITY CHARTS

2005 St-Émilion Premier Grand Cru Classé
and top Pomerol

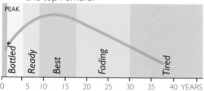

2005 Médoc Super-Second Cru Classé

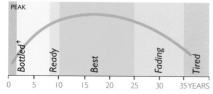

It makes my eyes water, my heart race and my brain dizzy to see this glistening array of Pétrus '61 ready for auction by Christie's. 1961 is arguably the finest red Bordeaux vintage of the 20th century. Pétrus is one of Bordeaux's superstars and frequently its most expensive wine. The last time I looked, these bottles were worth about £7000 (US$13,763/€9286) each. And I didn't even mention the taste. I bet it's brilliant. Predicatably, I don't own a bottle.

The label is as simple as ever, but 2003 is a wine from
the new era at Ch. d'Yquem, after over 200 years of
control by the Lur-Saluces family. However, quality has,
if anything, reached new heights. 2003 was a hot
torrid vintage – not a typically balanced Sauternes year
– but Yquem's golden nectar is regal, intense and
delicious. Yquem's supreme quality is reflected in its
price – at least 4 to 5 times as expensive as its nearest
rival – usually the excellent Ch. Climens.

Sauternes vintages 2010–1985

2010
Less consistent than 2009 but some great wines.

2009
Fabulous wines – a truly great vintage.

2007
Indian summer saved the day. Some superb wines.

2006
Mediocre year but selectively good at top estates. Tiny production.

2005
This was a winner for sweet whites as well as for reds. Unctuous, rich and expensive.

2004
Good, not memorable wines.

2003
A bumper crop with good aging potential – richer wines than in 2001.

2002
A small but successful vintage. Plenty of noble rot.

2001
Really classic year just starting to be ready, but top wines will age for decades yet. Excellent, very powerful and concentrated wines.

2000
While red wine makers celebrated the return of sunny harvest weather after the trying 1990s, heavy rain arrived in October to spoil the sweet wine crop.

1999–98
Small amounts of good quality wine.

1997
The best year since 1990. All drinking well now.

1996
An inconsistent year, so choose with care.

1995
Small quantities with good sweetness but not much noble rot complexity.

1994-1991
Three wet harvests, with some pleasant sweet wines, but not 'real' Sauternes.

1990
The last and best of Sauternes' hat trick of fine vintages. This is still the benchmark, only perhaps equalled by 2001 and 2009 in the last 15 years and top wines are only just ready.

1989
Top wines are very good indeed. Otherwise inconsistent.

1988
Noble rot developed slowly but surely, giving consistently fine results.

1987
Not a good year. Rain stopped play.

1986
A great vintage with noble rot shrivelling up everything in sight.

1985
Most properties picked too soon, before the noble rot really got going. Drink up.

MATURITY CHART
2007 Sauternes Premier Cru Classé

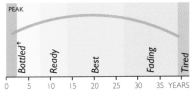

Dry white Bordeaux

Throughout this book I've taken every opportunity to enthuse about the dry white wines from Pessac-Léognan and I've begged and cajoled you to try them. Well, this looks like my last chance before the index. Just look at the maturity chart below and straight away you'll see one of the things that is so special about them.

They start out full of nectarine fruit, nettle and coffee bean tang and custard cream richness, so, unlike top Bordeaux reds, they are delicious literally from the moment the wines are released. But then they soar to a higher peak as the texture and mineral complexity take over – and they last and last like few other dry whites in the world. And they're less than half the price of equivalent white Burgundies.

Finally convinced? Then buy the 2010, '09, '08 '07 and '05. 2007 and '08 were cooler years but with astonishing aromas. 2009 was very lush, and 2010 overly focussed and bright. Older wines going back ten to 15 years will be good to excellent.

MATURITY CHART
2007 Pessac-Léognan Cru Classé

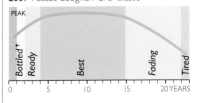

Older vintages

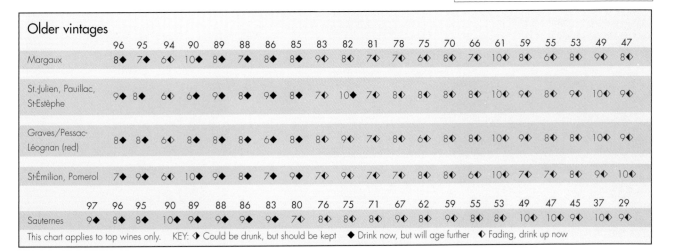

	96	95	94	90	89	88	86	85	83	82	81	78	75	70	66	61	59	55	53	49	47
Margaux	8◆	7◆	6◇	10◆	8◆	7◆	8◆	8◆	9◇	8◇	7◇	7◇	6◇	8◇	7◇	10◇	8◇	6◇	8◇	9◇	8◇
St.-Julien, Pauillac, St-Estèphe	9◆	8◆	6◇	6◆	9◆	8◆	9◆	8◆	7◇	10◆	7◇	8◇	8◇	8◇	8◇	10◇	9◇	8◇	9◇	10◇	9◇
Graves/Pessac-Léognan (red)	8◆	8◆	6◇	8◆	8◆	8◆	6◆	8◆	8◇	9◇	7◇	8◇	6◇	8◇	8◇	10◇	9◇	8◇	8◇	10◇	9◇
St-Émilion, Pomerol	7◆	9◆	6◇	10◆	9◆	8◆	7◆	9◆	7◇	9◇	7◇	7◇	8◇	8◇	10◇	7◇	7◇	8◇	9◇	10◇	

	97	96	95	90	89	88	86	83	80	76	75	71	67	62	59	55	53	49	47	45	37	29
Sauternes	9◆	8◆	8◆	10◆	9◆	9◆	9◆	9◆	7◇	8◇	8◇	8◇	9◇	8◇	9◆	8◇	8◇	10◇	10◇	9◇	10◇	9◇

This chart applies to top wines only. KEY: ◇ Could be drunk, but should be kept   ◆ Drink now, but will age further   ◇ Fading, drink up now

Bordeaux address book

Bordeaux is a huge wine region – 60 appellations, more than 250 Classed Growth wines, 8,700 growers and 800 million bottles produced a year. After you've read this book the next best way to make sense of it all is to pay a visit. You can pack a lot in even on a short weekend and planning ahead via the internet will help you make the most of your time there.

Making the most of a visit to Bordeaux

GENERAL INFORMATION

- **Maison du Tourisme de la Gironde**
  21 cours de l'Intendance, 33000 Bordeaux.
  Tel 05 56 52 61 40
  www.tourisme-gironde.fr
  tourisme@gironde.com
  Excellent website. Ask for the booklet, Gironde Trips to the Bordeaux Vineyards, packed with ideas for holidays, châteaux to visit, where to eat and stay, wine festivals and local markets.
- **Comité Régional de Tourisme de l'Aquitaine**
  Cité Mondial, 23 parvis des Chartrons, 33074 Bordeaux. Tel 05 56 01 70 00
  www.tourisme-aquitaine.info
  tourisme@crt.cr-aquitaine.fr
  Practical information on visiting Aquitaine, including the stupendous Atlantic coastline and the rural hinterland beyond the department of the Gironde.
- **Maison des Bordeaux et Bordeaux Supérieur/Planète Bordeaux**
  RN 89 (sortie 5), Beychac et Caillau.
  Tel 05 57 97 19 20/05 57 97 38 11
  www.maisondesbordeaux.com
  contact@maisondesbordeaux.com
  15km out of the city of Bordeaux on the road to Libourne. Taste and select from 1001 generic Bordeaux wines. Planète Bordeaux is an educational, interactive presentation of wine from the vine to glass.
  - **Les 'Best of' du Tourisme Viti-Vinicole**
    www.greatwinecapitals.com/bestof
    bordeaux@greatwinecapitals.com
    Prize-winning wine destinations in the Bordeaux region.
- **Le Weekend des Grands Amateurs**
  Union des Grands Crus de Bordeaux, 10 cours du XXX Juillet, 33075 Bordeaux.
  Tel 05 56 51 91 91 www.ugcb.net
  amateurs@ugcb.net ugc@ugcb.net
  A chance over a May weekend to taste over 100 top wines from the prestigious Union des Grands Crus de Bordeaux.
- **The Bordeaux Wine Experience**
  Ch. Coulon Laurensac, 1 chemin de Meydieu,

33360 Latresne. Tel 05 56 20 64 12
www.BXWINEX.com info@BXWINEX.com
Individual wine and food tours in the Bordeaux region. Small groups. Based in a lovely 18th-century château.

MÉDOC

- **Maison du Vin de Margaux**
  Place de la Trémoille, 33460 Margaux.
  Tel 05 57 88 70 82
  www.medoc-bordeaux.com
  syndicat.margaux@wanadoo.fr

Daniel Cathiard, owner of Ch. Smith-Haut-Lafitte, has found a neat way of carrying sample bottles around his neighbourhood.

- **Syndicat Viticole Médoc et Haut-Médoc and Listrac**
  18 quai Jean Fleuret, 33250 Pauillac.
  Tel 05 56 59 02 92
  www.bordeaux-medoc.com
  contact@medoc-haut-medoc-listrac.org
- **Maison du Vin et du Tourisme de Moulis-en-Médoc**
  Place du Grand Poujeaux, 33480 Moulis.
  Tel 05 56 58 32 74 www.moulis.com
  chateau@moulis.com
- **Maison du Tourisme et du Vin de Pauillac**
  SC de Lynch Bages - BP 120, 33250 Pauillac.
  Tel 05 56 73 24 21
  www.pauillac.com mv-se@wanadoo.fr

- **Maison du Vin de St-Estèphe**
  Place de l'Église, 33180 St-Estèphe.
  Tel 05 56 59 30 59 www.saint-estephe.com
  mv-se@wanadoo.fr
- **Syndicat Viticole de St-Julien**
  Mairie, 1 place de l'Hôtel de Ville, 33250 St-Julien. Tel 05 56 59 08 11
  www.saint-julien.com
  odgsaint-julien33@orange.fr

THE GRAVES AND PESSAC-LÉOGNAN

- **Maison des Vins de Graves**
  61 cours du Maréchal Foch, 33720 Podensac.
  Tel 05 56 27 09 25 www.vins-graves.com
  contact@vins-graves.com
- **Syndicat Viticole de Pessac-Leognan**
  1 cours de XXX Juillet, 33300 Bordeaux.
  Tel 05 56 00 21 90 www.vins-graves.com
  contact@pessac-leognan.com

RIGHT BANK

- **Office de Tourisme de Libourne**
  40 place Abel Surchamp, 33500 Libourne.
  Tel: 05 57 51 15 04
  www.libourne-tourisme.com
- **Office de Tourisme de St-Émilion**
  Place des Créneaux, 33330 St-Émilion.
  Tel: 05 57 55 28 28
  www.saint-emilion-tourisme.com
- **Maison du Vin de Saint-Émilion**
  Rue Guadet - BP 15, 33330 Saint-Émilion.
  Tel 05 57 55 50 50 www.vins-saint-emilion.com
  info@vins-saint-emilion.com
- **Maison des Vins de l'Union des Satellites de St-Émilion**
  Place de l'Église, 33570 Montagne-St-Émilion.
  Tel 05 57 74 60 13
  www.montagnesaintemilion.com
  contact@montagnesaintemilion.com
- **Maison des Vins du Fronsac et Canon-Fronsac**
  Rue du Tertre, 33126 Fronsac.
  Tel 05 57 51 80 51
  fronsac@wanadoo.fr
- **Maison du Vin de Pomerol**
  8 rue Tropchaud, 33500 Pomerol.
  Tel 05 57 25 06 88 www.vins-pomerol.fr
  syndicat@vins-pomerol.fr

Making the most of a visit to Bordeaux

- **Maison des Vins de Lalande-de-Pomerol**
  21 rue du 8 mai, 33500 Lalande de Pomerol.
  Tel 05 57 25 21 60 www.lalande-pomerol.com
  lalande-pomerol@orange.fr

CÔTES AND ENTRE-DEUX-MERS

- **Union des Cotes de Bordeaux**
  1 Cours du XXX Julliet, 33000 Bordeaux.
  Tel 05 56 00 21 99
  www.bordeaux-cotes.com
- **Maison du Vin de Blaye**
  11 cours Vauban, 33390 Blaye.
  Tel 05 57 42 91 19
  www.aoc-blaye.com
  info@aoc-blaye.com
- **Le Bac de Blaye**
  Maison du Tourisme de la Gironde - 21 Cours de l'Intendance - 33000 Bordeaux.
  Tel 05 57 42 04 49 for timetable
  www.tourisme-gironde.fr
  Ferry across the Gironde between Lamarque (Left Bank) and Blaye (Right Bank)
- **Maison du Vin des Côtes de Bourg**
  1 place de l'Éperon, 33710 Bourg-sur-Gironde.
  Tel 05 57 94 80 20
  www.cotes-de-bourg.com
  info@cotes-de-bourg.com
- **Office de Tourisme de Bourg**
  Hôtel de la Jurade, Place de la Libération, 33710 Bourg. Tel 05 57 68 31 76
  www.bourg-en-gironde.fr ot@bourg-en-gironde.fr
- **Office de Tourisme de Blaye**
  2 allées Marines, 33390 Blaye.
  Tel 05 57 42 12 09
  www.tourisme-blaye.com
- **Maison du Vin des Castillon-Côtes de Bordeaux**
  6 allée de la République, 33350 Castillon-la-Bataille. Tel 05 57 40 00 88
  www.cotes-de-castillon.com
  svcc@nerim.net
- **Syndicat Viticole des Francs-Côtes de Bordeaux**
  33570 St-Cibard. Tel 05 57 40 66 58.
  www.cotesdefrancs.com
  cotesdefrancs@wanadoo.fr
- **Maison des Vins des Cadillac-Côtes de Bordeaux**
  La Closière, 33410 Cadillac.
  Tel 05 57 98 19 20
  www.premierescotesdebordeaux.com
  infos@premierescotesdebordeaux.com
- **Maison des Vins de l'Entre-Deux-Mers**
  4 rue de l'Abbaye, 33670 La Sauve Majeure.
  Tel 05 57 34 32 12
  www.vins-entre-deux-mers.com
  contact@vins-entre-deux-mers.com
- **Office de Tourisme de l'Entre-Deux-Mers**
  4 rue Issartier, 33580 Monségur.
  Tel 05 56 61 82 73 www.entredeuxmers.com
  info@entredeuxmers.com

SWEET WHITES

- **Syndicat Viticole de Sauternes-Barsac**
  13, Place de la Mairie, 33210 Sauternes.
  Tel 05 56 76 60 37
  odg@sauternes-barsac.com
- **Maison du Sauternes**
  14 place de la Mairie, 33210 Sauternes.
  Tel 05 56 76 69 83
  www.maisondusauternes.com
- **Liquoreux de Bordeaux**
  Condrine 33720. Tel 05 56 27 02 43
  www.vins-loupiac.com odgliquoreux@gmail.com

There is more to the Bordeaux region than just vineyards: these are the stunning cloisters in St-Émilion.

Glossary

AC/AOC (APPELLATION D'ORIGINE CONTRÔLÉE)
The top category of French wines, defined by regulations covering vineyard yields, grape varieties, geographical boundaries, alcohol content and production method. Guarantees origin and style of a wine, but not its quality.

ACID/ACIDITY Naturally present in grapes and essential to wine, providing balance and stability and giving the refreshing tang in white wines and the appetizing grip in reds.
AGING An alternative term for maturation.

ALCOHOLIC CONTENT The alcoholic strength of wine, expressed as a percentage of the total volume of the wine. Typically in the range of 11–15% and on an upward trend in Bordeaux since the 1990s.

ALCOHOLIC FERMENTATION The process whereby yeasts, natural or added, convert the grape sugars into alcohol (Ethyl alcohol, or Ethanol) and carbon dioxide.

APPELLATION See AC.

AROMATIC In Bordeaux, this usually describes a young wine full of fruity or floral scents.

ASSEMBLAGE See Blending.

AUSTERE A wine with marked levels of tannin and acidity. Médoc red wines are typically austere when young and need to be aged for several years before drinking.

BAKED In very hot vintages wines can take on a baked quality, making the fruit flavours tasted cooked and jammy rather than fresh and pure – particularly Merlot-based Right Bank wines.

BALANCE The relationship between acidity, tannin, fruit and alcohol. When they are in harmony, with no single element dominant, the wine is balanced.

BARREL AGING Time spent maturing in wood, usually oak, during which wine takes on flavours from the wood, tannins are softened and the colour stabilized.

BARREL FERMENTATION Oak barrels may be used for fermentation instead of stainless steel to give a rich, oaky flavour to white wines.

BARRIQUE The *barrique bordelaise* is the traditional Bordeaux oak barrel of 225 litres (50 gallons) capacity.

BIODYNAMIC VITICULTURE This approach works with the movement of the planets and cosmic forces to achieve health and balance in the soil and in the vine. Vines are treated with infusions of mineral, animal and plant materials, applied in homeopathic quantities.

BLENDING (*assemblage*) The art of mixing together wines of different grape varieties or from different vineyards (even different parcels within one vineyard) to balance out flavours, body, colour, tannin, etc. It's a particularly well-honed skill in Bordeaux.

BÂTONNAGE See Lees stirring.

BODY/WEIGHT Describes the different impressions of weight and size wines give in the mouth. This is what is referred to as full-, medium- and light-bodied.

BOTRYTIS See Noble rot.

BOUQUET The smell of a wine, often applied to a mature wine.

BOURGEOIS Denoting a wine of lower than Classed Growth status. Applies particularly to estates in the Médoc and Haut-Médoc, which have an official Cru Bourgeois classification.

BUDBREAK/BUDBURST Period when the first shoots emerge from the vine buds in spring. Marks the end of the vine's dormant period during the winter.

CANOPY MANAGEMENT Adjustments to alter the exposure of a vine's fruit and leaves to the sun, to improve quality, increase yield and help to control disease. Simple measures include leaf trimming, early fruit culling and general pruning.

CÉPAGE French for a grape variety.

CHAI Outbuildings and cellars where the wine is made and stored before bottling.

CHAPTALIZATION Legal addition of sugar during fermentation to raise a wine's alcoholic strength, necessary in cool climates where lack of sun produces insufficient natural sugar in the grape. This used to be the norm in Bordeaux but top estates now pursue higher levels of natural ripening so are unlikely to need to chaptalize their wines.

CHARTREUSE A monastery building established by the Carthusian order. Some examples in Bordeaux are now wine châteaux.

CHÂTEAU French for castle, widely used in Bordeaux to describe any wine estate, no matter how big or small.

CHÂTEAU BOTTLING Any estate with pretensions to quality will bottle the wine on the premises rather than sell it in bulk to a merchant. The label and/or cork will feature the words mis en bouteille au château. The process was introduced by Baron Philippe de Rothschild at Ch. Mouton-Rothschild in 1924.

CHEWY A wine with a lot of tannin and strong flavour, but which is not aggressive.

CLARET English term for red Bordeaux wines, from the French clairet, which was traditionally used to describe a lighter style of red Bordeaux.

CLARIFICATION Term covering any winemaking process (such as filtering or fining) that involves the removal of solid matter either from the must or the wine.

CLONE Propagating vines by taking cuttings produces clones of the original plant. Vine nurseries enable growers to order specific clones to suit conditions in their vineyards.Through this clonal selection it is possible to control yield, flavour and general quality.

CLOS French for a walled vineyard – as in Burgundy's famous Clos de Vougeot – also commonly incorporated into the names of wine estates (e.g. Clos L'Église), regardless of whether they are walled or not.

COLD FERMENTATION Long, slow fermentation at low temperature to extract maximum freshness from the grapes. The introduction of cold fermentation in Bordeaux revolutionized white winemaking.

COMMUNE A French village and its surrounding area or parish.

COMPLEX A wine that has layer upon layer of flavours.

CONCENTRATION The intensity and focus of flavour in a wine.

CO-OPERATIVE In a co-operative cellar, or cave co-opérative, growers who are members bring their grapes for vinification and bottling under a collective label. In terms of quantity, the French wine industry is dominated by co-ops, but in Bordeaux they account for only around 25% of production. They often use less workaday titles, such as Caves des Vignerons, Producteurs Réunis, Union des Producteurs or Cellier des Vignerons.

CORKED/CORKY Wine fault derived from a cork which has become contaminated, usually with Trichloroanisole or TCA. The mouldy, stale smell is unmistakable. Nothing to do with pieces of cork in the wine.

CÔTE/CÔTES French word for a slope or hillside, which is where many, but not all, of the country's best vineyards are found, as in the limestone *côtes* of St-Émilion. In Bordeaux 'the Côtes' refers to the five appellations of Cadillac-Côtes de Bordeaux, Côtes de Bourg, Castillon-Côtes de Bordeaux, Francs-Côtes de Bordeaux, Blaye-Côtes de Bordeaux.

COURTIER A broker of Bordeaux wines who would traditionally act as a go-between for wine merchants and wine producers, helping source stocks and facilitating price negotiations.

CRU French for growth, meaning a specific plot of land or particular estate. In Bordeaux there are various hierarchical levels of Cru, referring to estates rather than their vineyards.

CRU BOURGEOIS French term for wines from the Médoc that are ranked immediately below the Crus Classés. Now less of a classification and more of a yearly certificate. Many are excellent value for money.

CRU CLASSÉ The Classed Growths are the aristocracy of Bordeaux, ennobled by the Classifications of 1855 (for the Médoc, Barsac and Sauternes), 1955, 1969, 1986, 1996 and 2006 (for St-Émilion) and 1947, 1953 and 1959 (for Graves). Curiously, Pomerol has never been classified. The modern classifications are more reliable than the 1855 version, which was based solely on the price of the wines at the time of the Great Exhibition in Paris, but in terms of prestige the 1855 Classification remains the most important. With the exception of a single alteration in 1973, when Ch. Mouton-Rothschild was elevated to First Growth status, the list has not changed since 1855. It certainly needs revising.

CRYO-EXTRACTION A process for concentrating grape must by lowering the temperature of the grapes to below freezing before pressing them. First adopted in Sauternes in the 1980s.

CUVÉE French for the contents of a single vat or tank, but usually indicates a wine blended from either different grape varieties or the best barrels of wine. The *cuvier* or *cuverie* is the fermenting room or vathouse.

CUVÉE PRESTIGE Most often used by producers on the Right Bank and in the Côtes ACs to denote a special bottling with lower yields and some oak aging in a percentage of new barrels. Usually made in limited quantities and hence, often sold at a higher price.

DÉPARTEMENT A French administrative region, similar to a county. The Bordeaux region lies within the Gironde department.

DOMAINE Another term for a wine estate.

DRIED OUT A wine that has gone past its mature peak and is fading. It will seem very dry and acidic with thin aromas and flavours.

EARTHY A smell and taste of damp earth – appealing in some red wines, especially those from the Graves.

EN PRIMEUR Sale of the young wine within a few months of the harvest. In Bordeaux has come to mean the sale of the latest wine as futures in the spring and early summer after the vintage before it is bottled.

ENOLOGIST Wine scientist or technician who play increasingly an important role at the blending stage. The role of consultant enologist has become an increasingly high profile one. Michel Rolland is the most famous one in Bordeaux.

EXTRACTION Refers to the extraction of colour, tannins and flavour from the juice, pulp, seeds and skins of grapes during and after fermentation. Methods of extraction include regulating the temperature, methods of submerging the solid matter in the juice (*remontage* and/or *pigeage*) and post-fermentation maceration. Wines that have been highly extracted tend to be black in colour, full-bodied and tannic. Over-extraction leads to imbalance and loss of drinkability.

FAT A wine that is full-bodied and unctuous.

FILTERING Removal of yeasts, solids and any impurities from a wine before bottling.

FINING Method of clarifying wine by adding a coagulant (e.g. egg whites, isinglass, bentonite) to remove soluble particles such as proteins and excessive tannins. Fining is a well established method in Bordeaux. Those that don't fine are either in the 'Robert Parker no fining or filtering school' as it strips the wine or because they consider that with long aging/racking in barrel the wine is sufficiently clear. Some fine, but don't filter and vice versa (depending on the year as well) – it's a technical decision with equal argument for and against.

FIRST GROWTH Refers to the Premiers Crus or top wines in most Bordeaux classifications. As a general term it refers to the top five wines in the 1855 classification (Lafite, Latour, Margaux, Haut-Brion and Mouton) and the top wines in the Sauternes classification.

FLYING WINEMAKER Term coined in the late 1980s to describe enologists, many Australian-trained, brought in to improve the quality of wines in many underperforming wine regions, mainly in Europe and South America. Things have now changed and probably the most famous flying winemaker is consultant-to-the-stars Michel Rolland, Bordeaux born and bred yet in great demand right around the globe.

FRESH A young wine with lively fruit flavours and good acidity.

GARAGISTE French term coined recently to describe a Bordeaux winemaker who makes minuscule amounts of wine from a single plot of land, originally literally in a garage, which are then sold for high prices.

GARAGE WINE Wine made by a *garagiste*.

GRAND CRU French for 'great growth', but without the word classé does not necessarily mean anything.

GRAND CRU CLASSÉ French for 'classed great growth', a term used in the classification of St-Émilion.

GRAND VIN The top blend which will be bottled under the château name.

GRAVES French for 'gravel'.

GREEN HARVEST (*vendange verte*). Removal of excess bunches of grapes to reduce the harvest.

GROWTH See Cru.

HECTARE (hl) 1 hectare = 10,000 square metres; or 2.471 acres.

HECTOLITRE (hl) 1 hectolitre = 100 litres; 22 imperial gallons or 133 standard 75-cl wine bottles.

JALLE A drainage ditch. Without the network of *jalles* installed by Dutch engineers in the 17th century, the Médoc would be a marsh with no vineyards.

LAYING DOWN The storing of wine which will improve with age.

LEAF PLUCKING In late summer growers may remove excess foliage that may be shading the grapes.

LEES Sediment – dead yeast cells, grape pips (seeds), pulp and tartrates – thrown by wine during fermentation and left behind after racking. Some wines are left on the fine lees for as long as possible for additional flavour.

LEES STIRRING (*bâtonnage*) A traditional Burgundian practice of stirring the lees of fine white wines which have been fermented in barrel to get a richer, creamier, more exciting flavour, now increasingly practised elsewhere, and occasionally used for red wines. It's a regular practice among Bordeaux's best white wine producers, less common for reds although some winemakers like Stéphane Derenoncourt apply the technique regularly.

LEFT BANK Informal term for the vineyards of the Médoc, on the left bank of the Gironde estuary. Also describes the red wines made here and in Pessac-Léognan.

LENGTH This is the flavour that persists in the mouth after swallowing or tasting. A flavour that continues or even improves for some time after the wine is gone is a mark of quality.

LIQUOREUX French term for very rich, botrytized wines.

MACERATION An important winemaking process for red wines whereby colour, flavour and/or tannin are extracted from grape skins before during or, most commonly, after fermentation. The period lasts from a few days to several weeks. A short, cold pre-fermentation maceration at 8–12°C is also occasionally used to extract colour and fruit flavour.

MALOLACTIC FERMENTATION Secondary fermentation whereby harsh malic acid is converted into mild lactic acid and carbon dioxide. Normal in red wines but often prevented in whites to preserve a fresh, fruity taste. Malolactic fermentation in barrique has been increasingly adopted by top Bordeaux estates as the wood integrates favourably and the wines taste better early on, particularly at the en primeur tastings. In the long term malolactic in barrel or stainless steel tank offers the same results.

MATURATION Positive term for the beneficial aging of wine.

MATURE Red Bordeaux is considered mature when the tannins have softened sufficiently for the wine to be enjoyable to drink, and the flavours have evolved from straightforward fruit flavours to add complex aromas such as the cigarbox and lead pencils of top Pauillac. See also Dried out.

MESOCLIMATE The climate of a specific geographical area, be it a vineyard or simply a hillside or valley.

MICRO-CRU A wine made from a selected very small plot of land, usually very ripe and concentrated with plenty of new oak aging. Garage wines fit the bill, as do some *cuvées prestiges. Micro-vin* and *micro-cuvée* are alternative terms.

MICRO-OXYGENATION (*microbullage*) The process entails a very gentle bubbling through of oxygen over an extended period of time. It is used at the beginning of alcoholic fermentation to encourage yeast action; during maceration it helps soften tannins, making wines accessible earlier; during barrel aging it's a replacement for racking and is often applied when the winemaker wants to keep the wine on the lees.

MILLÉSIME French for 'vintage'.

MUST The mixture of grape juice, skins, pips and pulp produced after crushing (but prior to completion of fermentation), which will eventually become wine.

MUST WEIGHT An indicator of the sugar content of juice – and therefore the ripeness of grapes.

NÉGOCIANT French term for a merchant who buys and sells wine. A *négociant-éléveur* is a merchant who buys, makes, ages and sells wine.

NOBLE ROT (*Botrytis cinerea*) Fungus which, when it attacks ripe white grapes, shrivels the fruit and intensifies their sugar while adding a distinctive flavour. A vital factor in creating many of the world's finest sweet wines, such as Sauternes.

OAK The wood used almost exclusively to make barrels for fermenting and aging fine wines. It adds tannin, and flavours such as vanilla to the wines. The newer the wood the greater its impact. French oak is often preferred for aging fine wine as its flavours are more subtle. Oak from the state-run forests in the centre of France like Allier and more specifically Tronçais is considered the best. American oak is also used (not generally by the top estates), as is Hungarian and Russian. Oak barrels are often used for fermentation, being almost mandatory for top white Bordeaux wines as well as Sauternes. Those white wines fermented as well as aged in new oak have a much greater lifespan.

OXIDATION Over-exposure of wine to air, causing loss of fruit and flavour. Slight oxidation, such as occurs through the wood of a barrel or during racking, is part of the aging process and, in wines of sufficient structure, enhances flavour and complexity.

PALUS The alluvial land closest to the Gironde estuary and unsuitable for fine wine production.

PHENOLICS Chemical compounds found in the pips, stalks, skins, juice and pulp of grapes, especially in red ones. Also known as polyphenols, they include tannins, colour-giving anthocyanins and flavour compounds.

PHYLLOXERA The vine aphid *Phylloxera vastatrix* attacks vine roots. It devastated European and consequently other vineyards around the world in the late 1800s soon after it arrived from America. Since then, the vulnerable *Vitis vinifera* has generally been grafted on to vinously inferior, but phylloxera-resistant, American rootstocks.

POWERFUL A wine with plenty of everything including alcohol – a hallmark of modern rather than classical Bordeaux wines.

PREMIER CRU CLASSÉ First Classed Growth; the top quality classification in parts of Bordeaux, and especially when referring to the 1855 classification.

PRIMEUR French term for a young wine, sometimes released for sale within a few weeks of the harvest but in Bordeaux during the following spring. See En primeur.

PRUNING Method of trimming the vine which takes place mainly in the winter months. It is also the primary means of controlling yields.

RACKING Gradual clarification of a quality wine; the wine is transferred from one barrel or container to another, leaving the lees behind. Racking also produces aeration necessary for the aging process, softens tannins and helps develop further flavours.

RÉSERVE French for what is, in theory at least, a winemaker's finest wine. The word has no legal definition in France.

RIGHT BANK Informal name for the vineyards of St-Émilion, Pomerol and their neighbouring appellations on the right bank of the river Dordogne around the town of Libourne. Also used to describe the wines made here.

RIPE A wine made from well-ripened grapes has good fruit flavour. Unripe wines can taste green and stalky.

ROOTSTOCK The root of the vine onto which the fruiting branches are grafted. As a result of the outbreak of phylloxera in Bordeaux in the late 19th century most rootstocks are from phylloxera-resistant American vines.

'SECOND' WINES A second selection from a designated vineyard, usually lighter and quicker-maturing than the main wine. Some châteaux in Bordeaux also make a 'Third' wine.

SEDIMENT Usually refers to residue thrown by a wine, particularly red, as it ages in bottle.

STRUCTURE 'Plenty of structure' refers to a wine with a well-developed backbone of acid and tannin but enough fruit to stand up to it. Classic Bordeaux is always 'structured' for aging.

SULPHUR Commonly used during winemaking as a disinfectant for equipment; with fresh grapes and wine as an antioxidant; and added as sulphur dioxide to the must to arrest or delay fermentation.

SUPÉRIEUR French for a wine with a slightly higher alcohol content than the basic AC, as in Bordeaux Supérieur AC.

SUPER-SECOND A term used by the Bordeaux wine trade to recognize the Second Growth châteaux making wine far above the rest of their class and often as good as those of the First Growth.

TANNIN Harsh, bitter, mouth-puckering element in red wine, derived from grape skins and stems, and from oak barrels. Tannins soften with age and are essential for long-term development in red wines.

TEMPERATURE CONTROL Of crucial importance during winemaking as it influences extraction and flavour. In Bordeaux fresh, fruity, dry whites, as well as rosé and clairet, are fermented at lower temperatures (15–20°C) while for reds the alcoholic fermentation is maintained at around 28–30°C to extract colour and tannin without loss of fruit flavour.

TERROIR A French term used to denote the combination of soil, climate and exposure to the sun – that is, the natural physical environment of the vine. It is the basis of the French *appellation contrôlée* system.

TOASTY A flavour like buttered toast that results from maturing a wine in oak barrels.

TRIAGE The process of eliminating the bruised, unripe and rotten grapes from healthy fruit. Now practised by all quality conscious châteaux, both in the vineyard and then again on arrival at the *chai*. Also refers to the precise picking of botrytized grapes in Sauternes.

VARIETAL Wine made from, and named after, a single or dominant grape variety. Bordeaux is known for its blended wines so the term is rarely used in the region even though there are some wines made from a single variety.

VENDANGE French for 'harvest'.

VIEILLES VIGNES French term for a wine made from vines at least 20 years old. Should have greater concentration than wine from younger vines.

VIGNERON French term for winegrower.

VIN DE GARAGE See Garage wine.

VINIFICATION The process of turning grapes into wine.

VINTAGE The year's grape harvest, also used to describe wines of a single year.

VITICULTURE Vine-growing and vineyard management.

VITIS VINIFERA Vine species, native to Europe and Central Asia, from which almost all the world's quality wine is made.

WEIGHT See Body.

WINEMAKER The person responsible for controlling the vinification process.

YIELD Perhaps the most important factor in determining the quality of the wine. The yield is the amount of fruit, and ultimately wine, produced from a vineyard. Measured in hectolitres per hectare (hl/ha) in France. Generally ranges from 45hl/ha for St-Émilion grand cru to 60hl/ha for Bordeaux AC wines. The legal maximum for Sauternes is 25hl/ha. Yields may vary from year to year, and depend on climatic conditions, fruit set, grape variety, age and density of the vines, and viticultural practices. The classic European appellation system is based on the premise that low yield equals high quality, but balance of the vineyard is the real key. Only in top vineyards with naturally low vigour is it feasible to dramatically reduce yield yet keep the vine in balance.

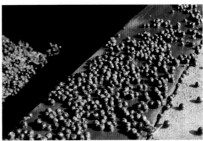

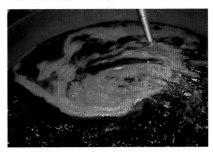

Index

Acknowledgments

Oz Clarke would like to thank the many organizations, proprietors and individuals in Bordeaux who have helped him get to know the region over the last 30 years; and, in particular, those who have given extra help in preparation for writing this book.

The CIVB (Comité Interprofessionnel des Vins de Bordeaux) and the local syndicats who organized the various tastings for this book. Also John Avery MW, Badie (V Protopopov), Éric Bantegnies, Anthony Barton, Bill Blatch, Catherine de Boechat, Olivier de Butler, Daniel and Florence Cathiard, members of the Cercle de la Rive Droite, Jean-Marie Chadronnier, Christophe Château, Edward Cox, Olivier Dauga, Stéphane Donze, Denis Dubourdieu, Fabrice Dubourdieu, Emmanuelle Garcia, Antoine Gimbert, Didier Gontier, Rosamund Hitchcock of R & R Teamwork, Russell Hone, Janice Joly, Pauline Léonard, Jean Lissague, Daniel Llose, André and Jacques Lurton, Jonathan Maltus, Jean-René Matignon, Charles Metcalfe, François Mitjavile, Stephan von Neipperg, members of Bordeaux Oxygène, Dr Michael Plumley, Freddy Price, Gavin Quinney, Alain Raynaud, Mark Savage, Christian Seely, Jean-Luc and Muriel Thunevin, Marc de Tienda, Alice Tourbier and Alain Vauthier.

Photo Credits

Château d'Arche 88

Yann Arthus-Bertrand/Altitude 94–95

Château Ausone 40 (below), 210, 211 (above), 212, 213 (above)

Château Bouscaut 176

Stephen Browett 81 (below)

Cephas Picture Library 58; (Mick Rock) 1, 12, 16–17. 20, 21, 22, 24, 25, 40 (above), 44, 46 (above), 46 (below), 48, 50, 52, 75, 79, 100 (above), 121, 135 (above), 139, 143, 145 (both), 149, 150, 154, 170, 181, 192–193, 195, 203 (above), 250–251, 276, 277 (below), 281 (below), 282, 284, 292, 295, 299 (all), 300 (above), 301 (both), 303 (above); Nigel Blythe 10, 34, 42, 104, 115, 125, 133, 141, 183 (above), 207, 214, 252, 257, 259; Karine Bossavey 281 (above); Andy Christodolo 72; Herbert Lehmann 74, 219; Clay McLachlan 209; Ian Shaw 30 (below), 47, 53, 198, 213 (below), 300 (below); Stephen Wolfenden 19, 109 (below), 135 (below), 151 (above), 167, 218, 277 (above)

Château Cheval Blanc/www.deepix.com 220, 221, 222, 223

Domaine de Chevalier 173, 178

Christie's Images Ltd 68 (below), 80, 305

CIVB, Bordeaux 105; François Ducasse 23, 313 (second and third from top); S Klein 313 (bottom); Philippe Roy 35, 199, 309, 313 (top and fourth from top)

Côtes de Bourg 255

Jeffrey M Davies 81 (above)

Decanter Magazine 70

Denis Dubourdieu 283

Château La Fleur de Boüard 206

Getty (Tim Graham) 89

Château Haut–Brion 8, 182, 183 (below), 184, 185 (both)

Château d'Issan 127

Château Lafite 43, 129, 130, 131 (both)

Château Latour 3 (inset), 92–3, 136 (both), 137

André Lurton 60, 77 (below), 166

J & F Lurton 77 (above)

Bernard Magrez 162

Château Malartic-Lagravière 174

Jonathan Maltus 202 (below)

Château Margaux 49

Château Maucaillou 147

Millésima 302

Château La Mission Haut-Brion 188

J-P Moueix 216, 239, 240 (left), 241 (above)

Château Mouton-Rothschild 151 (below), 152 (both), 153

Château Pichon-Longueville 9

Château Pichon-Longueville-Comtesse de Lalande 28 (below), 76, 111

Janet Price 15, 41 (above), 54 (both), 97, 112

Gavin Quinney 260

Michel Rolland 71

Scope (Michel Guillard) 144

Château Smith-Haut-Lafitte 171

Sotheby's 68 (above)

Château de Sours 263

Marc de Tienda 4, 26, 27, 30 (above), 31, 32, 41 (centre), 51, 55, 56–57, 61, 63, 82, 84, 86, 91, 100 (below), 109 (above), 113, 172, 175, 200, 202 (above), 205, 240 (right), 241 (below), 242, 274–275, 280, 285

Adrian Webster 2–3, 6 (above), 13, 28 (above), 66, 73, 87, 90, 96, 102, 164–165, 194, 203 (below), 211 (below), 245, 256, 262, 308, 320

Château d'Yquem: 67 (both), 306; J P Bost 41 (below), 59